African-American Athletes

AFRICAN–AMERICAN ATHLETES

Nathan Aaseng

☑®
Facts On File, Inc.

Facts On File, Inc.
132 West 31st Street
New York NY 10001

Library of Congress Cataloging-in-Publication Data

Aaseng, Nathan.
   African-American athletes / Nathan Aaseng.
     p.   cm.—(A to Z of African Americans)
Includes bibliographical references and index.
   ISBN 0-8160-4805-3
1. African American athletes—Biography—Dictionaries. I. Title. II. Series.
GV697.A1 A196 2003
796'.092'2—dc21   2002005989

Facts On File books are available at special discounts when purchased in bulk quantities for businesses, associations, institutions, or sales promotions. Please call our Special Sales Department in New York at (212) 967-8800 or (800) 322-8755.

You can find Facts On File on the World Wide Web at http://www.factsonfile.com

Text design by Joan M. Toro

Cover design by Nora Wertz

Printed in the United States of America

VB FOF 10 9 8 7 6 5 4 3 2

This book is printed on acid-free paper.

CONTENTS

LIST OF ENTRIES

INTRODUCTION

Before World War II, popular sports in the United States were almost exclusively the domain of white athletes. Since then, the field has changed so dramatically that today fans express no surprise at viewing a pro basketball game in which all the players on the court at one time are African American. At the start of the 21st century, Jason Sehorn of the New York Giants gained some notoriety as the only white cornerback starting in the National Football League (NFL).

Although the change from whites-only to black dominance was relatively swift in the context of history, it did not come painlessly or without remarkable perseverance of individual athletes. Nor is the history of sports an unbroken legacy of progress in race relations. In fact, sports took several steps backward in the early 20th century before opening its doors to all comers.

There were, in fact, black champions in the United States in the 19th century. Most of the successful jockeys of that era were black, and as early as 1890 boxer George Dixon claimed the world championship in the bantamweight division. Two years later, a Harvard University lineman, John Henry Lewis, won All-American recognition on the football field.

Yet even at that time, the drive to exclude African Americans from sport was gearing up. Major league baseball was one of the first to slam the door on blacks. In 1867 the National Association of Baseball Players voted to exclude black players from membership. That did not prevent the occasional temporary presence of a black ball player. Moses "Fleetwood" Walker played a full season for the Toledo Blue Hens of the American Association in 1884, and he was joined by his brother, Welday, for a few games. But under pressure from racists such as Hall of Famer Cap Anson, who in 1887 refused to play against African-American pitcher George Stovey, baseball executives began enforcing an unwritten rule that banned black players. Although major league baseball was not welcoming to members of any minority, blacks were singled out for exclusion. In the 1910s, the New York Giants manager, John McGraw, tried to "pass off" talented black ball players as dark-skinned American Indians, who were allowed in the major league ranks. Vigilant opponents, however, quickly detected McGraw's scheme and put an end to it before any black athlete appeared in major league uniform.

In the meantime, although boxing's lower weight divisions had open competition and crowned black champions, the prestigious heavyweight division did not. White champions such as John L. Sullivan openly declared they would never stoop to entering the ring with a black man. Jack Johnson finally managed to get a championship bout in 1908, in which he defeated Tommy Burns for the title, but his controversial career triggered a backlash that kept blacks out of the title picture for the next quarter-century.

Pro football initially included African Americans during its formative years of the 1920s. But once the NFL became established, owners adopted baseball's unwritten ban, beginning in 1933.

Like most sports played on the collegiate level, basketball offered opportunities for a select group of blacks to play with whites. But on the professional level, segregation was the rule. It was not a matter of white owners' holding that blacks were not talented enough to play; evidence to the contrary was overwhelming. The New York Rens, a black barnstorming team named after the Renaissance Ballroom, in which they played their few home games, was widely regarded as the best team in the nation in the 1930s. From 1932 to 1936, the team won 473 games and lost only 49. Their success cleared the way for another black barnstorming team, the Harlem Globetrotters.

During the early part of the 20th century, track and field provided the only real competitive sports opportunities for blacks. They were welcomed in track primarily for two reasons: Track was an individual sport rather than a team sport and so athletes of different races were not forced to become teammates except in a broad sense, and it remained an amateur sport that offered no real economic benefits either to the athletes or to the sponsors. As a result, the U.S. Olympic teams have always been racially integrated since George Poage took a bronze medal in the 1904 Olympics in the 400-meter hurdles.

The barrier began cracking again in boxing in the late 1930s with the admission of Joe Louis into the top heavyweight boxing circles. Pro sports began opening up in 1946, on two fronts. In baseball, Brooklyn Dodger general manager Branch Rickey ignored the unwritten ban by signing Jackie Robinson to a minor league contract. In the same year, football's Cleveland Rams moved to Los Angeles, where, as a condition of leasing the Los Angeles Coliseum, they had to sign the former University of California at Los Angeles (UCLA) All-American Kenny Washington. At the same time, the Cleveland Browns of the fledgling All-American Football Conference signed two players, Bill Willis and Marion Motley, who helped them create a dynasty.

Jackie Robinson then integrated major league baseball when he moved up to the Brooklyn Dodgers in 1947 and won Rookie of the Year honors. Pro basketball opened up to African Americans shortly thereafter. In 1950, the Boston Celtics made Chuck Cooper of Duquesne University the first black player drafted, and the New York Knicks signed Nat Sweetwater Clifton to a contract. Earl Lloyd of the Washington Capitals, however, actually got into a game before either of those pioneers.

By the end of the 1950s, most U.S. sports were fully integrated. The exceptions were college sports in the South and the elite sports of the upper class: tennis and golf. When an all-black starting lineup from Texas Western won the National Collegiate Athletic Association (NCAA) basketball championship in 1963, that event spelled the end for college discrimination in sports. By the end of the decade, virtually all schools were actively recruiting black athletes. The last stronghold of segregation in pro sports was the pro golf tour, which finally rescinded its "Caucasians only" requirement in the early 1960s.

In some ways, selecting entrants was easier for this book than for books about people in other areas of endeavor because accomplishments in sports are easily quantified and measured. Individual and team awards and volumes of elaborate record keeping provide documentation of the success of most modern athletes. The athletes chosen in this book have produced championships and outstanding statistics that are widely recognized as surpassing the achievements of average participants in their field. Weight is also given to those who have been evaluated by peers and awarded exceptional recognition for their efforts. In addition, athletes who have achieved celebrity status in connection with their sport and, conversely, athletes who are not well known but who were pioneers in sport and who established the way for those who followed are recognized.

Nonetheless, the wealth of African-American talent in sports has forced some difficult decisions. The limitations of space required that only a fraction of those who have achieved fame be included. In some cases, the difference between an athlete included and one excluded was almost indistinguishable and strictly a matter of judgment. Some active athletes who may well merit inclusion in the book by the time their careers are over were omitted because their present list of accomplishments does not measure up. In addition, an effort has been made to provide balance by including athletes across a wide spectrum of sports, as well as athletes in various positions within the sports.

Examples of athletes whose omission might be questioned include basketball players Dennis Rodman and Kevin Garnett; football players Donovan McNabb, Warren Sapp, Randy Moss, Michael Strahan, and Ray Lewis; and baseball players Dwight Gooden and Judy Johnson. Rodman and Sapp were passed over because, although both have talent, their considerable fame arose more from their antics off the court and playing field. Garnett, a player of unlimited potential, is still growing into a basketball superstar. McNabb is a similar case, who may well be on his way to being one of the great quarterbacks of all time but does not yet have superstar credentials. Lewis and Strahan are also on track to gain inclusion. Randy Moss, who may have more ability than anyone else who has played the game, is saddled with a lot of questions concerning his ability to harness that talent. Gooden was a spectacular pitcher for a brief time, but his career fizzled rather dramatically. And although Johnson is often cited as a star of the Negro Leagues, many contemporaries place him in a pack of similarly talented players, not all of whom could be included.

Finally, the question of which players deserved longer entries has created considerable pondering. The final criterion for inclusion in the longest entries was not raw ability but impact on the sport and on society. Thus, although experts may regard Sugar Ray Robinson as a better boxer than Muhammad Ali, Ali's far greater impact on his sport, as a worldwide celebrity, and as a symbol of the turbulent 1960s merits a longer treatment. Special consideration is also due to pioneers in their sport such as Joe Louis, Jackie Robinson, Jesse Owens, and Wilma Rudolph. On the other hand, whereas many people consider Bo Jackson the greatest athlete of the 20th century, injuries prevented him from making an impact commensurate with that ability.

Aaron, Hank

(Henry Louis Aaron)
(1934–) *baseball outfielder*

For most of his career, Hank Aaron was, as New York Yankee legend Mickey Mantle described him, "the most underrated player in baseball." A model of quiet consistency, Aaron began to attract national attention only when he drew within striking distance of some of baseball's most hallowed batting records in the late 1960s. After a turbulent chase after Babe Ruth's career home run record, Aaron emerged as the most prolific power hitter in baseball history, and he finally received his due acclaim as one of the most remarkable players of all time.

Henry Louis Aaron was born on February 5, 1934, in Mobile, Alabama, one of five children of Herbert and Estella Aaron. The family lived one block from the Carver Recreation Center, which gave Henry ample opportunity to take part in sports such as football and baseball.

One day his father took him to watch a Brooklyn Dodgers exhibition game featuring major league baseball's first African-American star, JACKIE ROBINSON. Awed by Robinson's performance, Aaron made up his mind to follow his example. Because segregated Central High School in Mobile, which Aaron attended, had no baseball team, however, Aaron was left to develop his skills

at pickup games, in local leagues, and in solo practice hitting bottle caps with a broomstick.

Although Aaron showed a flair for the game, his parents considered sports a low priority. At first he had to decline an invitation to play shortstop for the local Black Bears baseball team because the team violated his mother's religious convictions by playing on Sunday. Estella Aaron finally relented, and Hank began to attract the attention of pro scouts. This time it was his father who stood in the way of his son's desire to drop out of high school and play ball. After toiling all his life at low wages as a boilermaker's assistant in a shipyard, frequently skipping meals in order to save money, Herbert Aaron was adamant that his children have a better life, and he believed that education was the key to achieving that. "It's worth more to me that you get yourself an education than it is for me to eat, and you aren't going to drop out of school 'til you're through," he told his son.

In 1952, however, Aaron's play in an exhibition game between the Black Bears and the touring Indianapolis Clowns of the Negro Leagues impressed the Clowns' owners. When they offered Aaron $200 to play, his parents decided they could no longer stand in his way. Three weeks before he was to graduate from high school, 17-year-old Aaron boarded a train for Indianapolis, carrying little more than two dollars in his pocket and two sandwiches his mother had packed.

Hank Aaron reigns as major league baseball's career home run leader, with 755. *(National Baseball Hall of Fame Library Cooperstown, N.Y.)*

a promotion to Milwaukee's top farm club in Jacksonville in 1953. There Aaron endured the typical taunts of fans and the humiliation of being excluded from hotels where his white teammates stayed even as he was winning the league's Most Valuable Player Award.

Since the Braves had a shortage of good outfielders at the time, they sent Aaron to Puerto Rico in the winter of 1953–54 to learn how to play the outfield. The following spring he reported to the Braves' spring training camp hoping for a spot on the major league roster. When veteran player Bobby Thomson broke an ankle in an exhibition game, Aaron found himself pressed into service as Milwaukee's starting right fielder. He put up respectable numbers, batting .280 with 13 home runs until a broken bone suffered sliding into third base ended his season.

In 1955, Aaron demonstrated the strong wrists and steady eye that made him one of baseball's most consistent hitters. His wrist strength allowed him to wait until the last split-second before starting his swing and helped him generate amazing bat speed. His sophomore season showed a marked improvement to a .314 average, and his 106 runs batted in (RBI) proved his ability to hit in the clutch.

The following year, he improved and led the National League with a .328 average. Aaron never considered himself a home run hitter in the same class with free-swinging sluggers such as his teammate Eddie Matthews, and so he was satisfied with his 26 home runs that year. In 1957, however, he surprised everyone by belting 44 home runs and driving in 132 runs to lead the National League in both categories, while finishing third in batting average at .322. The soft-spoken Aaron also proved his worth as a team player by filling the Braves' need for a center fielder, even though it was not his best defensive position. Aaron's efforts earned him the National League's Most Valuable Player Award for the season.

With Aaron playing at such a high level, the Braves challenged for the National League pen-

The homesick Aaron had difficulty mixing with the veteran Clowns. Many of his social problems were eased, however, when he met Barbara Lucas while the Clowns were touring Jacksonville. The two married a year later, by which time, Aaron had left the Negro Leagues. That happened when the Clowns owner, Syd Pollock, advised the Milwaukee Braves to take a look at his new shortstop. After the Braves' scouts sent back a glowing report, Milwaukee bought Aaron's contract from Pollock on June 12, 1952.

The Braves assigned Aaron to their minor league team in Eau Claire, Wisconsin, where he batted .336 and became Rookie of the Year of the Northern League. That achievement earned him

nant in a furious race that lasted well into September. It was his dramatic home run in the 11th inning of a game against the Saint Louis Cardinals that clinched the pennant for the Braves. Even the normally reserved Aaron could not restrain his glee. He told reporters, "It's a great thrill just to win the pennant. But for me to get the hit myself—am I excited? I'm excited for the first time in my life." Aaron capped off his dream season by batting .393 and hitting three home runs as the Milwaukee Braves defeated the New York Yankees for their first World Series title. The Braves captured a second National League pennant in 1958, but they lost to the Yankees in a return match in the World Series. Soon thereafter, the team fell on lean times and Aaron never again had the opportunity to play in baseball's fall classic, although he did play in more than a dozen All-Star games.

During the next decade, Hammerin' Hank occasionally emerged as a league leader in the National League offensive statistics. In 1959, he won his second league batting title, with a career-best .355. The following year he topped the league with 126 RBIs. In 1963, Aaron again led the league in RBIs, with 130, and tied WILLIE MCCOVEY for the home run title, with 44. Yet even when he showed a late-career power surge with two more home run titles in 1966 (44) and 1967 (37), no one considered him a slugger on a level with Babe Ruth.

When the 34-year-old Aaron slipped to .287 and 29 home runs in 1968, it appeared that his solid but unspectacular career was winding down. Aaron himself wondered whether he had more than a year or two left in him. But he rebounded to another 44-homer year in 1969 as the Braves, now playing in Atlanta, won a divisional title. A year later, the publicity-shy Aaron gained headlines by becoming the first major league player to collect 500 home runs and 3,000 hits in a career.

When the apparently ageless Aaron continued to swat home runs in droves, the national media finally began paying attention to him. After Aaron hit a career-high 47 round-trips in 1971 to surpass 600 for his career, some even suggested that Aaron had a chance to break Babe Ruth's long-standing mark of 714 career home runs. At first, Aaron enjoyed the belated attention. However, the closer he drew to Ruth's mark, the uglier the fans' reaction became. By 1972, as Aaron drew within 50 of Ruth's record, those offended that a black man would break one of baseball's most cherished records bombarded him with hate mail and death threats so venomous that police had to escort him to and from the ballpark.

"All that hatred left a scar on me," Aaron said later. "I was just a man doing something that God had given me the power to do, and I was living like an outcast in my own country. . . . It should have been the most enjoyable time in my life, and instead it was hell." Eventually, the bigotry steeled Aaron's resolve and made him more intent on breaking the record.

Defying the effects of age, the 40-year-old Aaron ended the 1973 season one short of Ruth's mark. He wasted no time in tying the record, with a home run in the opening game of 1974. Then, amid a circus of national attention, Aaron blasted his way into the record books on April 8, with a fourth-inning home run off Al Downing.

At the end of the season, Aaron was traded to the Milwaukee Brewers and ended his major league career in the city in which it began. He slugged his 755th and final home run on July 20, 1976, and retired at the end of the year—his 23rd season. Since then, he has served as a senior vice president in the Atlanta Braves organization.

As the major league's reigning career home run and RBI leader, and the owner of 17 National League batting records and a reputation for excellent fielding, Aaron has a legitimate claim to being one of the best to play the game.

Further Reading

Aaron, Hank, with Furman Bisher. *Aaron.* New York: Crowell, 1974.

Aaron, Hank, with Dick Schaap. *Home Run: My Life in Pictures.* New York: Total Sports, 1999.

Aaron, Hank, and Lonnie Wheeler. *I Had a Hammer: The Hank Aaron Story.* New York: HarperCollins, 1991.

Baldwin, Stan, and Jerry Jenkins. *Bad Henry.* Reading, Pa.: Chilton Book Company, 1974.

Candee, Marjorie Dent, ed. *Current Biography.* New York: H. W. Wilson, 1958.

Money, Don, with Herb Anaston. *The Man Who Made Milwaukee Famous.* Milwaukee: Agape, 1976.

"Home Run King," *Ebony,* April 1999, pp. 132–33.

Tolan, Sandy. *Me and Hank: A Boy and His Hero, 25 Years Later.* New York: Free Press, 2000.

Abdul-Jabbar, Kareem

(Ferdinand Lewis Alcindor, Jr., Lew Alcindor)
(1947–   ) *basketball center*

Although Kareem Abdul-Jabbar set numerous National Basketball Association (NBA) records for scoring and longevity, statistics do not begin to do justice to his contribution to the sport. He perfected and performed his unique sky hook, a shot of such fluid grace that it led MAGIC JOHNSON to call Abdul-Jabbar "the most beautiful athlete in sports."

Abdul-Jabbar was born Lewis Ferdinand Alcindor, Jr., on April 16, 1947, in the Harlem section of New York City. His was a musical rather than an athletic family; his father studied at the prestigious Juilliard School of Music to be an orchestra conductor, but, unable to find career opportunities, he became a transit policeman. Lewis, Jr., an only child, grew up with the same love of music in a cosmopolitan neighborhood that included immigrants from many countries.

Lew Alcindor's first interest in sports was baseball. An enthusiastic fan of the Brooklyn Dodgers, Alcindor dreamed of playing for them. He also played basketball, sneaking into the P.S. 52 elementary school gym before the big kids arrived during the summer after first grade to see whether he could loft the ball as high as the rim.

In fourth grade, he had his first experience playing on a basketball team.

Alcindor enjoyed some success on the baseball diamond, and he even pitched a no-hitter. But as he began growing to unusual height in junior high, he shifted his focus to basketball. Alcindor reached six feet, five inches, as a seventh-grader at Saint Jude's Elementary School, where he was one of only two blacks enrolled. Alcindor also began testing his skills against other top city players at Carmansville Playground, where the basketball was so competitive that the players dubbed it "The Battlegrounds." There he found inspiration in the acrobatic moves of a tall player named CONNIE HAWKINS, who was the class of the competition.

As a result of his size and his success at harnessing those long limbs to his advantage, Alcindor began dominating competition on his level. As a freshman at the Catholic all-boy Power Memorial High School, he earned a spot in the starting lineup. By his sophomore year, he was playing at a level that no opponent could match. During his final three years at Power Memorial, Alcindor's team lost only one game. Alcindor, who had grown to a sinewy seven feet, two inches, was a unanimous choice as a prep All-American, and he became the most highly recruited high school athlete of his era.

Attracted to the calm competence of legendary coach John Wooden, Alcindor chose to attend the University of California at Los Angeles (UCLA). There he quickly served notice that UCLA's opponents were in for a bleak several years. At that time National Collegiate Athletic Association (NCAA) rules prohibited freshmen from competing on the varsity level. Although the Bruins were the defending national champions and the preseason favorite to repeat, the freshman team, led by Alcindor's 31 points, easily defeated them in an exhibition game.

Once his sophomore year began and Alcindor moved up to varsity, the Bruins were virtually invincible. In his first varsity game, he amassed 56 points. The Bruins cruised to a 30–0 record and a national championship. So dominant was the star center that in 1967 the NCAA passed a rule making the dunking of a basketball illegal, in the hope of neutralizing the advantage of extremely tall players. Alcindor, however, proved that his game involved more than stuffing basketballs through the netting. He developed a sweeping, unblockable hook shot that eventually was dubbed the "sky hook." UCLA went on to win national championships in the next two seasons as well. In all three NCAA tournaments, Alcindor earned the Most Valuable Player Award. During Alcindor's three varsity seasons, UCLA posted an 88–2 mark.

Far from a one-dimensional jock, Alcindor spent his college years exploring philosophical and religious issues. During high school Alcindor had experienced the Jim Crow system on a bus ride to the South to visit relatives. He had begun to resent the superior attitudes and status of whites in the United States, and the riots in the black community in the summer of 1964 awakened rage within him. He became fascinated with black history, particularly the history of the great African kingdoms, which led him to pursue a major in history at UCLA. His reading of *The Autobiography of Malcolm X* and its message of black pride and universal brotherhood moved him to convert from Catholicism to Islam in 1968. That same year Alcindor risked the wrath of the American public by refusing to play for the U.S. Olympic team in protest of the nation's treatment of African Americans.

When Alcindor completed college in 1969, he stood so far above his peers, figuratively as well as literally, that it was a forgone conclusion that he would be selected first in the college draft. Since the draft order is determined by a team's record, with the worst choosing first, that meant he would start his career with a terrible team. That team turned out to be the fledgling Milwaukee Bucks. In their only year of existence, 1968–69, the Bucks had struggled to a 27–55 record.

Seldom has a single player made such a dramatic difference in the fortunes of a team.

All-time NBA scoring leader Kareem Abdul-Jabbar demonstrates his patented sky hook. *(Basketball Hall of Fame)*

Alcindor's imposing presence near the basket gave instant respectability to the Bucks. NBA opponents found that not only could Alcindor score with his devastating hook, but he could rebound and defend against the stronger, heavier giants of the league. Milwaukee finished the season at 56–26, and Alcindor, who finished second in scoring to Los Angeles's Jerry West, easily won the Rookie of the Year Award.

The following season, the Bucks found help for Alcindor by obtaining veteran guard OSCAR ROBERTSON. A Hall of Fame performer who was nearing the end of his career, Robertson provided the leadership and backcourt expertise to complement Alcindor's dominating inside play. Alcindor poured in a league-leading 31.7 points per game as Milwaukee fashioned a 66–16 mark, the best in the NBA. The Bucks went on to thrash the Baltimore Bullets four games to zero in the NBA finals to claim the league title in just their third season of existence. Alcindor easily claimed the Most Valuable Player (MVP) Award for both the season and the championship series.

At the end of that season, he went public with his conversion to Islam and began using his Muslim name, Kareem Abdul-Jabbar, which means "noble and generous servant of the all-powerful Allah." However, Abdul-Jabbar rejected the more inflammatory antiwhite theories of the Black Muslims. "Emotionally, spiritually, I could not afford to be a racist," he says.

Abdul-Jabbar continued to shine in Milwaukee during the next few seasons. He won the NBA scoring title in 1971–72 with a career-high 34.8 points a game and claimed his second consecutive MVP Award. Two years later, he captured his third MVP Award. Meanwhile, the Bucks won three more consecutive divisional titles, posting records of 63–13, 60–22, and 59–23, but they could not re-create their postseason success.

In 1974–75, Abdul-Jabbar suffered his sixth corneal abrasion. Concerned about losing his sight, he began wearing the protective goggles that would be another of his trademarks. He also suffered through the first losing season of his career. Feeling out of place in the small-market midwestern city and at odds with the coach, Abdul-Jabbar asked to be traded. The Bucks accommodated him by dealing him to the Los Angeles Lakers for four top draft choices.

The trade energized Abdul-Jabbar, who won the league's Most Valuable Player Award in his first two seasons with Los Angeles. Although his scoring had declined from spectacular to consistent, he led the NBA in rebounding both seasons and won the first two of four shot-blocking titles.

It was not until the end of the 1970s, however, that the Lakers fielded a team capable of supporting Abdul-Jabbar. The arrival of MAGIC JOHNSON in 1979 sparked a run of championships and near-championships that lasted the rest of Abdul-Jabbar's career. Los Angeles won NBA titles in 1980, 1982, 1985, 1987, and 1988. The most satisfying of these for Abdul-Jabbar occurred in 1985. After a 34-point loss to archrival Boston in game one of the championship, in which the big center scored only 12 points and three rebounds, reporters openly speculated that Abdul-Jabbar was at the end of the line. He responded by scoring 30 points and grabbing 17 rebounds in a game two victory. The Lakers went on to win the championship, and Abdul-Jabbar won the series' MVP Award.

A resourceful and dedicated athlete, Abdul-Jabbar was the first in the NBA to practice alternative methods of conditioning such as yoga and tai chi. His fitness allowed him to play far longer than most NBA players; for the last five years of his career, he was the oldest player in the league. This longevity allowed him to amass 38,387 points, the most in NBA history. At the same time that he was setting offensive records, he earned a berth on the NBA All-Defensive Team 10 times, including a string of eight awards from 1974 to 1981. In view of these feats and Abdul-Jabbar's graceful, consistent effort, such authorities as BILL RUSSELL and JULIUS ERVING have declared him to be the greatest to play this game.

Further Reading

Abdul-Jabbar, Kareem, and Peter Knobler. *Giant Steps.* New York: Bantam Books, 1983.

Abdul-Jabbar, Kareem, with Mignon McCarthy. *Kareem.* New York: Warner Books, 1990.

Abdul-Jabbar, Kareem, with Stephen Singular. *A Season on the Reservation*. New York: Morrow & Company, 2000.

Black, S. "I Don't Have Any Hangups About Who I Was," *Sport*, June 1980, pp. 23–26.

Ali, Laila

(1977–) *boxer*

"My dad never had this much attention on him when he was first fighting," noted boxing novice Laila Ali. Given that her father is MUHAMMAD ALI, one of the most widely known athletes in the world, the pressure under which she has learned her craft has been suffocating. In her brief career, Ali has weathered the storm and gained recognition for women's boxing, a sport that has been struggling for legitimacy.

Laila Ali was born on December 30, 1977, the younger of two daughters born to Muhammad Ali and his third wife, Veronica. Her parents divorced when Laila was small. She grew up with her mother in Malibu, California, and had little contact with her famous father. Noted for having Muhammad's brashness, but little of his playful humor, Laila had an attitude that got her into occasional fistfights as a child. At 16, she was arrested for shoplifting, and another undisclosed offense landed her a three-month stay in juvenile detention.

Ali eventually settled down and graduated from Santa Monica Community College. She operated a beauty salon until 1999, when she grew enamored of the idea of trying out her famous bloodlines in the fledgling sport of women's boxing. Both Muhammad Ali and Veronica Ali expressed discomfort with her choice, and her father warned her pointedly of the sport's brutality. Nonetheless, when Laila Ali stuck to her decision, her parents supported her.

With no amateur experience, she stepped into the ring for the first time against April Fowler on October 8, 1999, in front of 3,000 spectators and a pack of reporters in Verona, New York. Ali scored a knockout in 31 seconds of the first round, an accomplishment that was tarnished by her opponent's obvious lack of athletic skill.

Ali then breezed through two more fights with outclassed opponents before hooking up with Crystal Arcand on March 3, 2000. Despite Arcand's 5–0 record as an amateur, she failed to last past the first round. "I've never experienced a woman with the amount of power she has," said Arcand after the fight.

The five-foot-10-inch, 166-pound Ali won four more fights before facing a formidable foe, Kendra Lenhart, on October 20. The two battled furiously for six rounds, and Ali won a decision based on her more polished boxing skills.

Ali boasted a 9–0 record going into the match that made even the previous media clamor seem subdued by comparison. Her opponent for the June 8, 2001, match was Jacqui Frazier-Lyde, daughter of Muhammad Ali's bitter rival, JOE FRAZIER. Ali and Frazier had fought three punishing fights in their time, and resentments between them had simmered all those years. Frazier-Lyde, also undefeated going into the fight, took on Muhammad Ali's role of outspoken fight promoter and billed this as an intergenerational grudge match. Ali, on the other hand, said little.

To the surprise of many observers, the fight proved to be inspired and compelling. Frazier-Lyde came out punching aggressively, as had been her father's style, while Ali displayed superior boxing skills. Ali built up a large lead in the middle rounds only to have Frazier-Lyde mount a furious comeback in the final round. Ali withstood the barrage and earned both the decision and newfound respect for her sport.

According to the Women's Boxing Page website, "Those nay-sayers who hoped it would be a laugher that would embarrass women out of the pro ring didn't get their wish. It was a fight. And there were no losers."

Further Reading

Henderson, Ashyia N. *Contemporary Black Biography*. Vol. 27. Detroit: Gale Research, 2001.

"Women's Boxing Page." Available online. URL: http://www.geocities.com. Downloaded November 8, 2001.

Ali, Muhammad
(Cassius Marcellus Clay, Jr., Cassius X)
(1942–) *boxer*

Muhammad Ali's considerable skills as a boxer earned him the world heavyweight championship, a title that he lost and regained twice. But it was the force of his personality and his unwavering personal convictions that made him a lightning rod of the turbulent 1960s and elevated him to the status of the most recognized, controversial, and admired athlete in the world.

Ali was given the name Cassius Marcellus Clay, Jr., at his birth on January 14, 1942, in Louisville, Kentucky. He took after his mother, a devout Baptist woman, rather than his father, a frustrated artist who made a respectable living as a sign painter. Young Cassius was polite, disciplined, religious, and interested in both school and sports.

As a 12-year-old, Clay was upset when his bike was stolen. The crying youngster reported the crime to Officer Joe Martin, vowing to whip the person who had done it. Martin suggested he first stop in at the boxing gym where Martin was a coach. Clay did, and he soon developed an obsession for the sport. He trained incessantly and was nearly incapable of walking without shadow-boxing at the same time. In July 1958, he cemented his reputation in Louisville by defeating Charley Baker, the city's most feared boxer.

During his amateur career, Clay won 100 of 108 fights. Although ranked as one of the top fighters in the nation, he was reluctant to try out for the 1960 U.S. Olympic team because the games were to be held in Rome, and Clay had an intense fear of flying. After much persuading, Clay did compete, won a spot on the team, and flew to Rome, wearing a parachute for the duration of the flight. At the Olympics, Clay's youthful exuberance and sparkling performances made him a favorite of fellow athletes and the media. He fought his way into the finals of the light-heavyweight division (179-pound weight limit), in which he defeated three-time European champion Zbigniew Pietrzykowski. At the same time, he earned accolades in the U.S. press for telling a race-baiting Soviet reporter, "America is the greatest country in the world." On returning home, Clay was so proud of his gold medal that he wore it at all times, even while sleeping.

One day, however, he and a friend were refused service at a fast-food restaurant in Louisville. Clay displayed the medal he had won in the service of his country, but the owner growled, "I don't give a damn who he is! I done told you, we don't serve no n _ _ _ _ _ _!" White racist gang members then moved in and ordered Clay to hand over his medal. Clay and his friend raced off on their motor bikes, only to be pursued by the gang members. Two of them caught up with Clay at a bridge on the Indiana border, whereupon Clay and his friend beat them severely. Disgusted and disillusioned, Clay ripped off his medal and threw it into the Ohio River. At that point, he felt a new inner strength that would carry him through the coming difficult years.

Clay turned pro after the Olympics and began to capture national attention with his skill and playfulness. Before each fight he made a prediction in poetic form, such as "Old Archie Moore will fall in four," and frequently he was able to end the fight in the predicted round. His eagerness to talk about himself in a unique and quotable fashion ("Float like a butterfly, sting like a bee") earned him the nickname "The Louisville Lip."

After a series of knockout victories, Clay signed on to fight the heavyweight champion, Sonny Liston, in February 1964. Liston was an intimidating puncher who had destroyed his last three opponents, including the respected ex-champion Floyd Patterson, in the first round. The underdog challenger, however, stole the spotlight with a series of actions, some sincere and others totally for show. First, he stunned the public by declaring his conversion to the Black Muslim religion. For a popular sports figure to embrace what was largely viewed as a radical and subversive group was unheard of at that time. Clay ignored advisers who told him his career would be ruined unless he renounced the Black Muslims.

He then put on a bewildering prefight display. At the weigh-in, he appeared to lose control of himself. His wide-eyed screaming convinced many reporters that he was so terrified of Liston that he was near a nervous breakdown. But insiders who met with him an hour later found him calm and confident; his hysterics appeared to have been an act to throw Liston off balance.

During the fight, Clay displayed a heretical style of boxing. Instead of crouching and shielding his head with his hands, he hopped and danced the "Ali Shuffle." He held his hands near his hips, daring Liston to swing at his unprotected face. Then, with astounding quickness for a man six feet, three inches, and 210 pounds, Clay landed flurries of hard punches. Liston was so badly beaten that he could not answer the bell for the seventh round. Shockingly, Clay was now the champion.

He immediately offended the public by renouncing his slave name of Clay and calling himself Cassius X. Shortly thereafter, he took on a new name, Muhammad Ali. This action was considered so radical that most of the media refused to call him by his new name. Ali's publicity-generating acts in which he declared himself the "greatest" and "prettiest" boxer of all time did nothing to soothe the public's discomfort. Only after many months did the media realize that Ali's discipleship in the Black Muslims was neither a publicity stunt nor defiance of the white world but an expression of Ali's inner sense of discipline and spirituality.

In the 1970s, boxer Muhammad Ali was the most famous athlete in the world. *(Library of Congress, Prints & Photographs Division, NYWT&S Collection [LC-USZ62-115435])*

During his championship reign of the 1960s, Ali was virtually unhittable, much less beatable. He dispatched of Sonny Liston with a first-round knockout punch in their rematch and thoroughly battered Floyd Patterson. One of the defeated contenders, Zora Foley, marveled, "He could write the book on boxing."

Ali's reign was cut short at its peak, however, by more controversy. Declaring himself a conscientious objector who "ain't got nothing against the Viet Cong," Ali refused to report as ordered by his Selective Service draft board. Although he could have ridden out the Vietnam War giving exhibition matches as JOE LOUIS and

SUGAR RAY ROBINSON had during World War II, Ali refused the special treatment. He paid dearly for standing on his principles. Under pressure from government authorities, boxing commissions refused to license fights for Ali. The champ was forced to go abroad to fight foreigners in 1967. But when Ali was indicted for draft evasion, he was banned from leaving the country and stripped of his title. Black activist Harry Edwards commented, "The thing about Ali that was so amazing was that he was willing to pay the price to walk away from all of the riches, all of the fame, all of the fortune, all of the prestige because of his commitment to his own personal dignity and integrity." Eventually, on June 28, 1971, the U.S. Supreme Court overturned Ali's conviction.

During Ali's three-and-a-half-year exile from the ring, JOE FRAZIER assumed the championship. While Ali's appeal was in the final stages, he was allowed to return to the ring against Frazier. Ali's prefight banter crossed the line into ridicule of Frazier, who went after Ali with a vengeance on March 8, 1971. After 14 rounds of even combat from which neither retreated, Frazier knocked down Ali in the 15th round and earned a narrow decision.

Whereas many expected the defeat to demoralize him, Ali shrugged it off, saying, "I have to show my people we know how to lose, and still come back again." Before a rematch could be arranged, however, Frazier lost his crown to an overpowering GEORGE FOREMAN, who then signed to fight Ali in Kinshasa, Zaire. A huge underdog, Ali solidified his fame with his clever "rope-a-dope strategy." For seven rounds, he let Foreman pound away at him while he dodged and smothered the punches. Foreman, who was not accustomed to opponents' lasting more than a couple rounds, wore himself out, at which time Ali came to life and knocked him out to reclaim his title.

On January 28, 1974, Ali battled Joe Frazier for a second time. Ali was closer to his top form this time and won a decision. The bitter opponents' third battle, the "Thrilla in Manila," was one so savage in its fury that many experts have called the October 1, 1975, bout the greatest heavyweight fight of all time. Ali started with a withering onslaught over the first five rounds that Frazier barely managed to survive. Frazier countered with a midfight assault of which Ali would later say, "I felt close to death. I wanted to quit in the 10th." He recovered to win a technical knockout in the 14th round.

By the late 1970s, Ali's skill had faded so that he could not afford to be careless even against lesser opponents. In 1978, he lost his championship to Leon Spinks but reclaimed the title for a third time with a convincing win over Spinks later in the year. He retired at the end of that year only to make an ill-advised return to the ring that ended with his permanent retirement in 1981.

Typically of boxing champions, Ali's personal life has been unstable, including a string of four marriages. (His daughter LAILA ALI has gone on to become a boxer.) Furthermore, the ravages of a long career appear to have taken a permanent physical toll on his health, as has Parkinson's disease. Yet years after his retirement, the man who appeared on the cover of *Sports Illustrated* 35 times continues to have hordes of admirers in virtually every locality on Earth.

Further Reading

Ali, Muhammad, with Richard Durham. *The Greatest: My Own Story.* New York: Random House, 1975.

Early, Gerald, ed. *The Muhammad Ali Reader.* Hopewell, N.J.: Ecco Press, 1998.

Hauser, Thomas. *Muhammad Ali: His Life and Times.* New York: Simon & Schuster, 1991.

Miller, Davis. *The Tao of Muhammad Ali.* New York: Warner Books, 1996.

Myers, Walter Dean. *The Greatest: Muhammad Ali.* New York: Scholastic Press, 2001.

Pacheco, Ferdie. *Muhammad Ali: A View from the Corner.* New York: Birch Lane Press, 1992.

Remnick, David. *King of the World: Muhammad Ali and the Rise of an American Hero*. New York: Random House, 1998.

Sheed, Wilfrid. *Muhammad Ali: A Portrait in Words and Photographs*. New York: Crowell, 1975.

Allen, Marcus Lemarr
(1960–) *football running back*

Versatile and indestructible, with a knack for finding the end zone, Marcus Allen enjoyed a stellar career as a National Football League (NFL) running back. As impressive as his career statistics appear, they would have been even gaudier had not a feud with his team owner limited his playing time at the prime of his career.

Marcus Lemarr Allen was born on March 26, 1960, in San Diego, California. Sports were important to the Allen family but not as important as education and discipline. When Marcus Allen showed outstanding potential as a defensive back at San Diego's Lincoln High School, his dad informed the coach, "If Marcus's grades ever fall below a B, I'm pulling him off the team."

Unlike many young athletes, Allen went out of his way to avoid the glamour positions. During his junior year, he refused his coach's request to move to quarterback and relented only after his stubbornness got him kicked off the team. Although unpolished as a passer, he ran the ball well at quarterback. When he piled up 317 yards of offense in the California state championship game, he became a prime target of college recruiters.

Allen chose the University of Southern California, where he proved his unselfishness by spending two years as a blocking back for tailback, Charles White. After helping White win the Heisman Trophy as college's top player, Allen had his turn to shine at tailback, beginning with his junior year. Allen surpassed White's performance, setting 15 National Collegiate Athletic Association (NCAA) records and earning the Heisman himself in 1981.

Despite Allen's performance, some pro scouts questioned whether he had the speed and power to be a star. Nine teams passed on him in the 1982 college draft before the Los Angeles Raiders claimed him. The six-foot, two-inch, 210-pound Allen made the doubters took foolish by scoring a league-leading 14 rushing touchdowns in his rookie season. Although his sophomore season was less spectacular, Allen made his most lasting mark in the pros when the Raiders advanced to the Super Bowl. Facing the favored Washington Redskins, whose defense had ranked number one in the league against the run during the year, Allen ripped off large chunks of yardage. In the third quarter, with Los Angeles holding a 28–9 lead, Allen started toward the left side of the line only to find himself trapped by several defenders. Showing a nimbleness that belied his size, Allen reversed his field and left defenders sprawling in his wake as he raced to a 74-yard touchdown run, the longest run in Super Bowl history. For the game, Allen averaged nearly a first down every time he carried the ball and racked up a Super Bowl record of 191 yards to earn the game's Most Valuable Player Award.

Allen continued to shine in 1984 by again leading the league in touchdowns with 18. He followed this with his best overall season, in which he proved his durability by rushing 378 times for a league-leading 1,756 yards and catching 67 passes. Over the next few years, however, Allen's relationship with the Raiders' owner, Al Davis, soured. Despite Allen's All-Pro efforts, the newcomer BO JACKSON became the Raiders' featured back. By 1989, despite being in prime condition, Allen spent most of his time on the bench. In four seasons from 1989 to 1992, he carried the ball a total of 378 times, as many as he had carried it in a single season in 1985.

Finally, in 1993, he escaped to the Kansas City Chiefs; at an age when most NFL running backs are retired, he became the Chiefs' top running back and again led the league in rushing touchdowns. Allen played five years for the Chiefs and particularly relished his success against his former team. He finished his career as the NFL's career leader in rushing touchdowns with 123, and his 12,243 career rushing yards ranks seventh in pro football history.

Further Reading

Allen, Marcus, and Carlton Stowers. *Marcus.* New York: St. Martin's Press, 1997.

Lieber, Jill. "On Top of the Heap, as Always," *Sports Illustrated,* September 1, 1986, pp. 28–30.

Moritz, Charles, ed. *Current Biography, 1986.* New York: H. W. Wilson Co., 1986.

Archibald, Nate
(Nathaniel Archibald, Tiny Archibald)
(1948–   ) *basketball guard*

Nate Archibald was one of the smallest men in the National Basketball Association (NBA), yet he managed the unprecedented feat of leading the league in both scoring and assists in the same year.

Born on September 2, 1948, in the South Bronx, New York, Nathaniel Archibald was nicknamed "Tiny" by his father. As a child, he was obsessed with the dream of playing pro basketball. He played every day in local gyms until janitors kicked him out, continued shooting at bent-rim hoops outside until dark, and then dribbled his ball home. "It's just as though he was in a cave and all that was in the cave was a basketball and a hoop," said his mother.

While Nate was in high school, he nearly allowed his dream to be derailed, however, after his father left the family. The four boys and three girls had to share a two-bedroom house with their mother, and they had no income. Archibald lost what little interest he had in schoolwork, failing so many courses that he lost his eligibility for high school basketball. He decided to quit school but was finally dissuaded by a high school coach who convinced the teenager that he was throwing his life away.

Archibald improved his grades enough to regain his eligibility for his final year. His play earned him a scholarship at Texas Western University, where he learned to blend his individual skills into a team concept. Not only did he run the team's offense, but he led the conference in scoring. In the 1970 draft of college players, Bob Cousy, a Hall of Fame NBA player who served as general manager of the Cincinnati Royals, selected him in the second round although he had never seen him play. When Cousy met Archibald for the first time, he feared he had made a mistake. Tiny, a skinny six-foot, one-inch guard, looked young enough to be in high school.

But Archibald refused to be intimidated by the NBA giants and quickly stepped in to claim the Royals starting position at point guard. By his second year, he was voted to the All-Star team, and in 1972–73, he put on a display of leadership such as the league had never seen before. Not only did he lead the league in scoring, but he also ranked first in assists, which measure how well a player sets up teammates for scores. *The Sporting News* named him its NBA Player of the Year.

Meanwhile, two of Archibald's brothers began falling into the trap of drugs in their rough Bronx neighborhood. Archibald moved them to Kansas City, where the Royals had relocated, and made a point of returning to his old neighborhood each year to set up clinics and leagues to help kids stay out of trouble.

After he led Kansas City to the playoffs in 1974–75, Archibald's career declined. A series of injuries hampered his play, and he bounced around from one bad team to another, showing only shades of his former brilliance. He finally ended up on the talented Boston Celtics, however, in the early 1980s. Playing with a winner recharged Archibald, who not only made the All-Star team but was voted the All-Star Game Most Valuable Player (MVP) in 1981. That year, Archibald's three-point play won game five of a tough play-off series with Philadelphia, and he clinched game six of that series with two free throws. The Celtics went on to defeat Houston in the finals to give Archibald his first and only NBA championship.

After retiring, Archibald maintained his interest in the disadvantaged, working with homeless people in New York City and as a school drug counselor. He was voted into the NBA Hall of Fame in 1991.

Further Reading

Littlefield, Bill. *Champions*. Boston: Little, Brown, 1993.

O'Connor, R. "Return of the Man They Call Tiny," *Sport*, May 1980, pp. 56–8.

Armstrong, Henry
(Henry Jackson, Melody Jackson)
(1912–1988) *boxer*

Although overshadowed by his contemporary, JOE LOUIS, Henry Armstrong was widely regarded as Louis's equal as a boxer. He dominated the lower weight classes during the late 1930s, and he remains the only man to hold world championships in three weight classes simultaneously.

He was given the name Henry Jackson at his birth on December 12, 1912, in rural Mississippi. Henry was the youngest of 11 children born to a black tenant farmer and his Cherokee wife. When he was four, failure of their cotton crop left the family destitute. Henry's mother took him and seven of his siblings to Saint Louis in search of a better life. But within two years, she was dead of tuberculosis.

Henry grew up under the loose supervision of siblings, and he eventually left school to work as a construction laborer. One day, however, he read about a boxer who made $75,000 in a half-hour championship fight. Having acquitted himself well in school fights in the past, he became intrigued by the possibility of earning such un-imagined wealth. Under the guidance of ex-

Henry Armstrong may have fought and won more pro boxing matches than anyone in the sport's history. *(Library of Congress, Prints & Photographs Division, Carl Van Vechten Collection [LC-USZ62-114433])*

boxer Harry Armstrong, he traveled around the Midwest, looking for fights. During his brief career as an amateur, he established himself as the top featherweight (126-pound limit) in the Saint Louis area.

Jackson then made his pro debut, fighting under the name Armstrong suggested, Melody Jackson. Having had virtually no income since he started boxing, however, Jackson had been sub-sisting on nothing but bread and water. His pitiful diet left him so weak that he lost three of his four pro fights.

Jackson decided to travel to California to restart his career. On the advice of his managers, he reentered the amateur ranks, using the name Henry Armstrong to obscure his brief fling as a pro. Frequently riding boxcars for transportation, he fought as much as three and four times a week, with spectacular results. In 1931, he won 85 consecutive fights and established himself as a strong contender for a spot on the 1932 Olympic team. In trying to make the weight limit, though, he again went on a starvation diet that cost him much of his strength, and he failed to make the team.

Armstrong then turned professional, which at that time put him at the mercy of gamblers and other shady characters. He was often cheated in decisions and on occasion took a dive when he was ordered to lose. Nevertheless, "Hurricane Hank," as he became known because of his furious style of attack, gradually established himself as the best fighter in his weight class. After losing two fixed fights to California's top featherweight, Baby Arimendi, Armstrong battered Arimendi to claim the California title.

On October 29, 1937, the 24-year-old Armstrong got the chance to fight for a world title when he faced Petey Sarron. Having grown beyond the featherweight limit, he took a chance by dieting down to reach the 126-pound limit for the fight, but he retained enough strength to knock out Sarron in the sixth round.

This success triggered an unprecedented 10-month rampage. On May 31, 1938, Armstrong challenged Barney Ross for the world welterweight title (147-pound limit). Although Ross outweighed him by nearly 10 pounds, Armstrong had a relentless attack that soon wore down the older champion, and he won a clear decision in 15 rounds. With this fight, Armstrong achieved at least a measure of the dreams of his youth, pocketing a title share of $40,000.

Less than three months later, Armstrong took aim at the lightweight title held by Lou Ambers. This contest on August 17, 1938, turned out to be one of the fiercest battles in the history of the weight division. Armstrong passed out shortly after the fight and remembered nothing about it except that it was "the bloodiest fight I ever had

in my life." Nonetheless, he won a split decision in the 15-round contest. This gave him world championships in three weight classes at once, a feat that will never be repeated since boxing authorities now prohibit simultaneous holding of titles in different weight classes. Armstrong made a valiant attempt at a fourth weight class championship in March 1940, when he fought the much larger Ceferino Garcia to a draw in their middleweight (160-pound limit) fight.

Armstrong's reign in boxing's lighter weights did not last long. The strain of reducing to featherweight class took such a toll on him that he resigned the title in 1938 without ever defending it. Ambers reclaimed his lightweight title a year after losing it with a decision over Armstrong. Armstrong successfully defended his welterweight title six times before losing a 15-round decision to Fritzie Zivic on October 4, 1940.

During his career, Armstrong probably fought as many fights as any boxer in existence, an estimated 300. At his peak in the mid-1930s, he was fighting every week. He seldom made any effort to avoid contact in the ring, and the pounding he took soon wore him down. Yet he did not retire until 1945, largely because of a free-spending life-style that forced him to continue to earn income. At that time, he drifted, broke and discouraged, until revived by a renewed interest in spirituality. In 1949, Armstrong enrolled in theology school, and he was ordained as a Baptist minister in 1951. An inspiring figure to many African-American boys in the 1930s, he continued to work with youth in Saint Louis until his death in 1988.

Further Reading

Armstrong, Henry. *Gloves, Glory, and God.* Westwood, N.J.: Fleming H. Revell, 1956.

Ashe, Arthur, Jr. *A Hard Road to Glory: A History of the African-American Athletes, 1919–45.* New York: Warner Books, 1988.

Mullan, Henry. *The Ultimate Encyclopedia of Boxing.* London: Carlton Books, 1996.

Ashe, Arthur
(Arthur Robert Ashe, Jr.)
(1943–1993) *tennis player*

At a time when the male stars of tennis were conspicuous for their bad manners and temper tantrums, Arthur Ashe provided a striking contrast. The first African American to rise to the top ranks of professional tennis won as much admiration for his dignity and thoughtful compassion as for his hard-won triumphs on the court.

Arthur Robert Ashe, Jr., was born on July 10, 1943, to Arthur, Sr., and Mattie Ashe of Richmond, Virginia. When Arthur was four, the family moved to a house in the middle of Brook Field Park, where his father was park supervisor. The 19-acre blacks-only complex included four tennis courts. Arthur grew fond of tennis and often practiced hitting a ball against a backboard when no playmates could be found.

Ashe suffered tragedy at the age of six when his mother died, leaving Arthur living alone with his father, who sometimes had to work 14-hour days. Arthur himself was small and often sickly during his early years. Along with his love of tennis, he enjoyed quiet activities such as reading and was an excellent student.

A frequent visitor to the Brook Field courts was Ronald Chairy, the best African-American tennis player in Richmond. Chairy taught Ashe what he knew and often played with the boy for hours. Young Ashe began entering tennis tournaments at the age of eight and occasionally won even against older opponents.

His success caught the attention of Dr. Robert W. Johnson, a black physician who had become an avid tennis fan and had set up a program to help promising young blacks develop their skills in the game. At the age of 10, Ashe began spending summers at Johnson's home, 95 miles west of Richmond, as part of Johnson's development team. Like all of Ashe's subsequent mentors, Johnson demanded impeccable manners on the court and they quickly became second nature to the young boy. Facing tougher opposition than he had previously encountered, the slightly built Ashe realized that he did not have the power to overwhelm opponents, and he learned to compensate with extraordinary accuracy.

Ashe's eight years in Johnson's program were crucial because of the limited opportunities available to young black tennis players. Even after Ashe won the 1955 12 & under singles championship of the American Tennis Association, the United States Lawn Tennis Association (USLTA), which was the major tennis governing body in the nation, refused to allow him to take part in their meets.

Meanwhile, at school, Ashe grew tired of being teased about playing tennis, which his peers derided as a "sissy" sport. He switched his focus to baseball during his sophomore year and made the varsity team as a pitcher at Maggie Walker High School. The school principal, however, was aware of Ashe's tennis reputation and persuaded him to drop baseball for fear of damaging his arm.

Going into his senior year, Ashe showed such promise at tennis that an admirer named Richard Hudlin recommended him to Harry Burrus, athletic director at Washington University in Saint Louis. Hudlin was concerned because the indoor courts in Richmond were open only to whites, so Ashe could not work on his game in the winter. Burrus arranged for Ashe to play year-round in Saint Louis while living with Hudlin and attending Sumner High School.

By this time, the USLTA had opened its competition to blacks, and in November 1960, Ashe advanced to the finals of the association's national junior indoor championship. He faced Frank Froehling, who was two years older. In a grueling four-and-a-half hour battle, Ashe prevailed, 6–1, 16–14, 9–11, 3–6, 6–1.

While honing his tennis skills, Ashe concentrated hard on his studies and wound up as valedictorian of his class. His combined excellence on the court and in the classroom earned him a scholarship to the University of California at Los Angeles (UCLA), regarded as one of the top ten-

Wimbledon champion Arthur Ashe volleys a backhand at the net. *(Allsport/Getty Images)*

nis schools in the nation. There, Coach Arthur Morgan helped Ashe develop the steely concentration that helped him to become an international competitor. It was also at UCLA that Ashe met Pancho Gonzales, a boyhood hero who had inspired Ashe by overcoming the obstacle of minority status to achieve tennis fame.

When Ashe could not afford to travel to England's Wimbledon tournament, the most prestigious amateur tennis event of the time, a local tennis club member offered to pay his expenses. Ashe won two matches at Wimbledon in 1963 before losing to the eventual champion, Chuck McKinley. That year he became the first African American to win a spot on the United States Davis Cup team.

Ashe improved steadily, climbing to the sixth spot in rankings of U.S. amateurs and third among collegians in 1964. The following year was his breakthrough season as he won the National Collegiate Athletic Association (NCAA) singles title and advanced to the finals of the U.S. Open. His hometown of Richmond, where he had once been banned from white tournaments, proclaimed February 4, 1966, "Arthur Ashe Day," in recognition of his success.

Typically, Ashe did not let his tennis career consume his life. He graduated on schedule from UCLA with a degree in business and then entered the army to fulfill his two-year Reserve Officers Training Corps (ROTC) commitment. Ashe was assigned to a position as tennis instructor. On leaving the army in 1968, he discovered that the tennis world had changed dramatically. The International Tennis Federation had opened up prestigious tournaments, such as Wimbledon and the U.S. Open, to professionals as well as amateurs. Ashe was thrilled to be able to take part in these events while earning money as a professional. That year, he not only helped the United States capture the Davis Cup but also won the U.S. Open with a 4–6, 6–3, 8–10, 6–0, 6–4 triumph over Robert Lutz and then reached the semifinals at Wimbledon. This string of successes made him the top-ranked tennis player in the United States.

Tennis fans also appreciated Ashe's deportment both on and off the court. One Midwest sports editor wrote, "Not only does Ashe excel in what he does, he excels in how he does it." Ashe never forgot his own humble beginnings and the racial barriers he had to overcome. Whenever he saw black youngsters with tennis racquets, he stopped to encourage them and hit a few balls with them. While traveling in Cameroon, he spotted a promising black 11-year-old named Yannick Noah. On Ashe's recommendation, the French made accommodations for Noah, who developed into an international star.

Ashe was drawn into international politics in 1969 when South Africa refused to grant him a visa to play in a tennis tournament because of his race. Ashe responded by asking tennis authorities to ban South Africa from the competition until they agreed to change their policies. Ashe's arguments carried enough weight that South Africa was barred from Davis Cup competition in 1970. After Ashe spurned South Africa's offer to travel as an "honorary white," the government gave in and ended its tennis discrimination. His

firm, dignified stance earned him the respect of tennis players, who made him president of the Association of Tennis Players.

Ashe earned several Grand Slam championships, including the 1970 Australian Open singles title and doubles titles in the 1971 French Open (with Marty Reissen) and the 1977 Australian Open (with Tony Roche). But his proudest moment occurred in the 1975 Wimbledon tournament. Despite battling a heel injury, he defeated Sweden's Bjorn Borg in four sets and then outlasted Australia's Roche in five sets to reach the finals. There he faced Jimmy Connors, the volatile young American star whose boorish behavior often rankled Ashe. After having lost all three previous matches to Connors, Ashe used a slow, conservative game to thrash his impetuous rival with a score of 6–1, 6–1, 5–7, 6–4. With nine other victories that year, the slim, bespectacled, six-foot-one-inch, 155-pounder held the number-one spot in world rankings.

On July 30, 1979, Ashe's career was suddenly cut short by a heart attack that led to quadruple-bypass heart surgery. On recovering, he continued to serve as captain of the Davis Cup team and began devoting himself to social causes. Ashe vigorously defended Proposition 42, which set academic standards for college athletes; was arrested protesting South African apartheid; and researched and wrote *A Hard Road to Glory*, a history of African Americans in sport.

In 1988 a severe bacterial infection led to brain surgery that uncovered a stunning tragedy. Ashe had contracted acquired immunodeficiency syndrome (AIDS) through a contaminated blood transfusion, traced to his heart surgery in 1983. He remained active and upbeat until his death of AIDS-related pneumonia on February 6, 1993, leaving behind his wife, Jeanne Marie, and a young daughter. So respected was Ashe that his body lay in state in the Virginia governor's mansion prior to his funeral. His fellow tennis star Martina Navratilova summed up his influence by calling him "an extraordinary human being who transcended his sport, his race, religion, and nation and in his own way helped to change the world."

Further Reading

Ashe, Arthur, Jr. *A Hard Road to Glory: A History of the African-American Athlete, 1919–45*. New York: Warner Books, 1988.

Ashe, Arthur, Jr., with Frank Deford. *Arthur Ashe: Portrait in Motion*. Boston: Houghton Mifflin, 1975.

Ashe, Arthur, Jr., and Arnold Rampersad. *Days of Grace: A Memoir*. New York: Knopf, 1993.

Towle, Mike, ed. *I Remember Arthur Ashe: Memories of a True Tennis Pioneer and Champion of Social Causes by the People Who Knew Him*. Nashville, Tenn.: Cumberland House, 2001.

Ashford, Evelyn
(1957–   ) *track-and-field sprinter*

Evelyn Ashford could have packed it in after the crushing disappointment of the U.S. Olympic boycott in 1980 spoiled four years of intense training. Instead, she persevered to claim four gold medals at an age long past prime for most sprinters.

Ashford was born on April 15, 1957, in Shreveport, Louisiana, to Samuel and Vietta Ashford. Samuel's chosen career in the U.S. Air Force made for a nomadic existence as he was transferred from post to post. Not until Evelyn's teen years did the family finally settle in Roseville, California, near Sacramento. A high school math teacher who was impressed by Evelyn's speed arranged for her to race the fastest boys in the class. When Ashford beat them all, the school's track coach invited her to join the boy's track team, because there was no team at the school for girls. Ashford won most of her races and was named cocaptain of the team in her senior year.

In 1975, the University of California at Los Angeles (UCLA) offered her one of the first women's athletic scholarships in the school's his-

tory to run track. By the end of her freshman year, she was running so fast that she qualified for the Olympics in the 100-meter dash, in which she finished a respectable fifth. Ashford kept working at her sport and earned national titles in the 200 meters in 1977 and the 100 meters in 1978. At that time, she left school so that she could train full time in preparation for the 1980 Moscow Olympics. The extra time paid off as she blazed to a U.S. record time of 21.83 at 200 meters that year. Ashford appeared to reach her peak just before the Olympics when she beat the East German record holders in both the 100 and 200 meters at the World Cup competition.

Her moment of glory, however, was torn from her when President Jimmy Carter ordered the U.S. team to boycott the Olympics to protest the Soviet Union's invasion of Afghanistan. Although deeply disappointed, Ashford committed herself to another four years of training for the next Olympics. As those games approached, however, more disappointment struck when Ashford injured her hamstring at the 1983 world championships. Nursing along the injury, she managed to set a world record with a 10.79 clocking in the 100 meters and qualified for the U.S. team in both the 100 and the 200 meters, but she withdrew from the 200 meters for fear of reinjuring the leg.

At the 1984 Los Angeles Games, the Soviets and their allies boycotted in retaliation for 1980, depriving Ashford of her main rivals. This took some of the thrill out of Ashford's long-awaited gold medal victories in the 100 meters and the 4 × 100 relay. But later that summer, she faced, for the first time, East German star Marlies Gohr at a meet in Zurich, Switzerland. Ashford exploded out of the starting blocks and surged to a convincing victory in a world-record time of 10.76.

When Ashford became pregnant and quit training, her career appeared to be over. But she returned to the track after a 17-month layoff to finish second to FLORENCE GRIFFITH JOYNER in the 100 meters in the 1988 Olympics. She followed this up with a breathtaking come-from-behind anchor leg to capture the gold medal in the 4 × 100 relay. She returned to win a fourth career gold in the 4 × 100 relay in 1992 at the age of 35, long past the age when most sprinters hang up their spikes.

Further Reading

Connolly, Pat. *Coaching Evelyn: A Fast, Faster, Fastest Woman in the World.* New York: HarperCollins, 1991.

Woolum, Janet. *Outstanding Women Athletes.* Phoenix, Ariz.: Oryx Press, 1998.

Banks, Ernie
(Ernest Banks)
(1931–) *baseball shortstop, first baseman*

Ernie Banks stands as the symbol of one of baseball's most beloved, yet snakebitten franchises, the Chicago Cubs. In 19 seasons with the Cubs, the Hall of Fame shortstop–first baseman played on such poor teams that he never had the opportunity to swing a bat in postseason play. Yet he never let the frustration cloud his legendary sunny disposition. The most lasting memory of Banks is of his smile and his trademark comment, "It's a great day for a ball game. Let's play two."

Ernest Banks was born in Dallas, Texas, on January 31, 1931. As a youngster, he shied away from sports so much that his father had to bribe him to get him to play catch. But he grew into one of Dallas's most skilled all-around athletes, and in high school he starred in football, basketball, and track as well as baseball.

At the age of 17, Banks signed with a Texas barnstorming baseball team, the Amarillo Colts, for $15 a game. His talent soon landed him on the roster of the Kansas City Monarchs of the Negro National League. But after one season at Kansas City, Banks was called into the army. By the time he returned to Kansas City two years later, baseball's color barrier had been shattered and several clubs that had previously hired whites only were

on the lookout for promising young black players. Banks soon rose to the top of the Chicago Cubs' list of prospects.

The Monarchs' owner, protective of his young shortstop, refused to sell Banks's contract unless the youngster was allowed to skip the minor leagues. Convinced that Banks was ready for the big time, the Cubs agreed and signed him near the end of the 1953 season. On September 17, 1953, the Cubs' first African-American ball player broke into the lineup as the starting shortstop.

Most baseball observers figured the Cubs had gotten themselves a slick-fielding shortstop to stabilize their infield defense. Nobody predicted that the skinny, six-foot-one-inch, 150-pound youngster would be able to hit with power. In that era, shortstops were generally "good-field, no-hit" athletes, and so the 19 home runs that Banks hit in his first full season appeared to be something of a bonus.

Unbeknown to them, Banks had barely touched the surface of his power. Despite his slight build, he was blessed with powerful wrists. These, combined with the light model bat he began using in 1955, produced a whiplike swing. Not only did it generate great power, but it allowed Banks to wait until the last instant before committing to swing. Marveled one rival, "Banks hits the ball right out of the catcher's mitt." In 1955, Banks cranked out 44 home runs, a major

20

league record for shortstops. Proving he could hit in clutch situations, he also hit a National League record five grand slams. At the same time, he led the league's shortstops in fielding percentage.

After injuries limited his effectiveness in 1956, Banks rebounded to blast 43 home runs in 1957. National League pitchers quickly learned that Banks's pleasant demeanor masked a fierce competitiveness. That season four pitchers knocked down Banks with fastballs aimed at his chin. On each occasion, Banks dusted himself off and hit the next pitch out of the park.

The barrage of long balls continued the following year as he collected a league-leading 47, topped the league with 129 runs batted in (RBIs), and achieved a career-high batting average of .313. Such an offensive display was so impressive that Banks was the first member of a losing team ever to win the National League's Most Valuable Player Award. The onslaught continued in 1959 as Banks hit 45 home runs, one short of Eddie Matthews's league-leading total, and amassed 143 RBIs, the most by a major league shortstop in more than 20 years. After a subpar fielding season in 1958, Banks worked hard on his defense in 1959 and made only 12 errors while playing all 162 games. Again, Banks was judged the National League's Most Valuable Player, the first to win the award in consecutive years.

In 1960 Banks added 41 more home runs, which meant that between 1956 and 1960, the slender shortstop hit more home runs than any other player in the game, including the Hall of Fame sluggers HANK AARON, WILLIE MAYS, and Mickey Mantle. As another mark of his versatility, Banks won his first Gold Glove that year as the National League's best fielding shortstop. Throughout this period of dominance, however, the Cubs seldom enjoyed a winning season, much less challenged for a pennant. One rival manager, evaluating Banks's supporting cast, commented, "Without Banks, the Cubs would finish in Albuquerque."

In 1961 knee injuries began taking their toll on the formerly durable shortstop. Banks man-

Ernie Banks, affectionately known as "Mr. Cub." *(National Baseball Hall of Fame Library, Cooperstown, N.Y.)*

aged only 29 home runs and lost a step or two in the field. In 1962, the Cubs, worried that Banks could no longer cover the shortstop position, moved him to first base, a position that requires less range. Banks responded with another stellar season, collecting 37 homers and 104 RBIs.

As his production began to drop off in subsequent years, the Cubs kept bringing in young prospects to replace him. The old veteran, however, hung on to his job and joined Billy Williams and Ron Santo in a potent Cubs offense through the rest of the 1960s. The 1969 season was his last productive one, as the 38-year-old pounded out 23 home runs, drove in 106 runs, and led National League first basemen in fielding. On May 12, 1970, Banks reached a hallowed milestone by hitting his 500th home run, and he retired the following year.

The man known as Mr. Cub finished his career with 512 home runs, which landed him 13th on baseball's all-time list. A nine-time All-Star, he was inducted into baseball's Hall of Fame in 1977 and was the first Chicago Cub to have his jersey number retired.

Further Reading

Honig, Donald. *The Chicago Cubs*. New York: Prentice-Hall, 1991.

Moritz, Charles, ed. *Current Biography*. New York: H. W. Wilson, 1959.

"Slugging Shortstop," *Time*, September 8, 1958, p. 36.

Barkley, Charles Wade

(1963–   ) *basketball forward*

With his unusual football tackle's build and uncensored comments on any subject, Charles Barkley became a lightning rod for attention on National Basketball Association (NBA) courts. The controversy he created sometimes overshadowed his talent as an extraordinary basketball player.

Charles Wade Barkley was born in rural Leeds, Alabama, on February 20, 1963, to Frank Barkley and Charcey Glenn. His parents separated when he was a baby, and his mother, stepfather, and grandmother raised him. From a young age, Barkley was obsessed with playing in the NBA, despite the fact that he was short and stocky. When he failed to make his ninth-grade team, he worked relentlessly on his shooting and spent hours jumping over a chain-link fence to increase his jumping ability. At a chunky five feet, 10 inches, he won a spot as a reserve during his junior year of high school. A growth spurt that shot him up to six feet, four inches, helped him crack into the starting lineup as a senior. Although he averaged 19 points and 17 rebounds, no four-year college was interested in him until he outplayed the

state's premier player, six-foot, nine-inch Bobby Lee Hurt, in a state semifinal game. That earned him a scholarship from Auburn University.

At Auburn, Barkley gained a reputation as a difficult player to coach. Despite his outstanding play, few people took him seriously. The six-foot, five-inch, 250-pound center was dubbed "The Round Mound of Rebound." "I led the conference in rebounding for three years but nobody knew it," he remembers. "I was just a fat guy who could play basketball well."

During his junior year, though, Barkley was named Southeast Conference Player of the Year, and he earned an invitation to the U.S. Olympic trials in 1984. But there the independent, outspoken Barkley ran afoul of disciplinarian coach Bob Knight and was cut from the team. Rather than return for his senior year of college, Barkley made himself available for the NBA draft and was the fifth player selected.

The rookie proved to a solid player for the Philadelphia 76ers. He was so strong that he could muscle past taller players and outfight them for rebounds, and yet he had startling quickness and leaping ability for a man his size. He posted a respectable 14.0 scoring average his first year to go with 8.6 rebounds.

Barkley improved each season in Philadelphia, until, by his third year, he was a genuine star. That year he scored 23.0 points and a career-high 14.6 rebounds per game. The following season, 1986–87, he took on an even greater share of the scoring load to average 28.3 points, along with 11.9 rebounds. The 76ers, however, gave him little support. Barkley, who was never shy about expressing himself, took the team to task in the press for lack of effort. He spoke his mind on many topics, gaining special notice for his emphatic declaration that athletes had no obligation to be role models—that was a parent's job. MICHAEL JORDAN would later say of Barkley, "Charles never holds his tongue. He says things you want to say but you don't have the courage to say."

In 1992, Barkley's frustration with the 76ers finally ended when he was traded to the Phoenix Suns. Barkley enjoyed his finest overall season in Phoenix in 1992–93, finishing fifth in the NBA scoring and sixth in rebounding and winning the league's Most Valuable Player (MVP) Award. In the play-offs, he showed his competitive fire by scoring 44 points and grabbing 24 rebounds in the conference final against Seattle to qualify for the championship series, which they lost to Jordan's Bulls.

Barkley's continued quest for an NBA title carried him to a 56-point play-off game against Golden State in 1994 and then to a last unsuccessful effort with HAKEEM ABDUL OLAJUWON and Scottie Pippen in Houston. Back injuries forced him to retire in 2000, at which time his colorful comments made him a prized recruit in the broadcasting world.

Further Reading

Barkley, Charles. *Sir Charles: The Wit and Wisdom of Charles Barkley.* New York: Time Warner, 1994.

Barkley, Charles, and Roy S. Johnson. *Outrageous!* New York: Avon, 1992.

Elgin Baylor averaged 27.4 points per game during his 12-year NBA career. *(Basketball Hall of Fame)*

Baylor, Elgin Gay
(1934–   ) *basketball forward*

Modern basketball began with Elgin Baylor. It was he who introduced the concepts of hang time, body control, and creative finishing of drives that would be picked up and refined by JULIUS ERVING a decade later and adopted by an entire generation of protégés.

Elgin Gay Baylor was born on September 16, 1934, in Washington, D.C. As a child he had no interest in basketball; in fact, he never saw a game in his life until, at the age of 13, he tagged along with older brothers to a pickup game at a local park. Baylor caught on to the sport so quickly that he made the All-City high school team as a freshman at Phelps Vocational High School.

Such success meant little to Baylor, however. At that time, pro basketball was loosely organized and had little national following, and player salaries were minimal. As a result, Baylor saw no future in the game. He disliked school, and realizing that his family could never afford to send him to college, he dropped out to work at a furniture store. Fortunately for his career, his mother persuaded him to return to school at Springarn High School, where he discovered that basketball could lead to an entirely unimagined future for him. After he was the first African American selected to a high school All-American team, he found that several colleges were willing to pay his way through school.

Baylor accepted a scholarship from the College of Idaho. The transition to the school was difficult, however, and even though he averaged 31 points and 21 rebounds for Idaho in 1954, he transferred to the University of Seattle the following year. National Collegiate Athletic Association (NCAA) rules required that a transfer sit out a year before being eligible for competition, and so Baylor did not return to the hard court until 1956. He then led Seattle to a 22–3 mark, again by averaging more than 30 points and 20 rebounds per game. In 1957–58, despite standing only six feet, five inches, he set an NCAA record for rebounds in a season, with a 23.5 average, and led his team all the way to the finals of the NCAA tournament, in which they lost to Kentucky. Seattle coach John Castellan noted, "He has the grace of a gymnast and the accuracy of an adding machine."

Baylor had a year of college eligibility left and intended to use it until the Minneapolis Lakers approached him. Because of his age, he was eligible for the pro draft, and the Lakers were in desperate need of a star. The team had finished the 1957–58 season with their worst record in team history and were teetering on the verge of bankruptcy. They made Baylor the number-one selection of the draft and talked him into leaving school early to play for them.

Team officials credit Baylor with saving the Lakers from financial collapse. In his rookie season, he averaged 24.9 points (fourth best in the National Basketball Association [NBA]) and 15.8 rebounds (third in the league) and led the team back into the playoffs. Fans were eager to see the rookie sensation, who not only was voted NBA Rookie of the Year, but added All-Star Most Valuable Player (MVP) and All-Pro Awards to his trophy case.

When the season ended, Baylor had to fulfill an obligation to spend several months in army reserve training in San Antonio, Texas. Rather than have his star miss training camp early that fall, the Lakers owner moved the entire team training camp to San Antonio so that Baylor could take part. Baylor rewarded the team's con-

sideration with an astonishing performance that season, beginning with 52 points in the season opener. A few weeks later, he scored 64 points against the Boston Celtics ace defender Tom Sanders, breaking a 10-year-old NBA scoring mark. Celtic All-Star guard Bob Cousy commented, "Elgin was the first guy who literally couldn't be stopped."

In one of a series of unfortunate timings for Baylor, he launched this unprecedented scoring outburst at about the time that WILT CHAMBERLAIN entered the league. The seven-foot Chamberlain smashed all NBA records for scoring in his rookie season of 1960–61, leaving Baylor's remarkable achievements largely unheralded.

In Baylor's third pro season, West Virginia guard Jerry West joined the Lakers to give the team a powerful one-two scoring punch. That year Baylor enjoyed his finest season, one that may never be equaled by any NBA forward. He poured in an average of 34.8 points per game and averaged 19.8 rebounds. Again, though, neither statistic led the NBA as Chamberlain averaged an unthinkable 50 points per game. Baylor's bad luck with individual awards paled in comparison to the agonies over his team's play. Led by Baylor and West, the Lakers challenged for the title every year but always fell short. Determined to taste a championship, Baylor put on some incredible offensive displays, including an NBA play-off record 71 points in game five of the 1962 championship against Boston. But again, it was his misfortune to play at a time when the Celtics were in their prime. Baylor's Lakers advanced to the championship series seven times in 11 years and lost every time, usually by razor-thin margins.

Baylor battled several severe knee injuries before retiring in 1972. Although, thanks to Chamberlain, Baylor never won a single season scoring title, he finished his career as the third-best scorer in NBA history, with 23,149 points for a 27.4 average. Statistics, however, indicate only part of the story. With his strength, explosiveness, and quickness, he may have been the greatest rebounder for his size in NBA history, and he had an unmatched ability to follow a missed shot with a rebound and a put back. Baylor's athletic instincts and leaping ability allowed him to pioneer the art of adjusting in midair to avoid defenders. In the words of his teammate Jerry West, "Elgin had that wonderful, magical instinct for making plays and doing things you just had to watch."

Further Reading

Bernstein, Ross. *Fifty Years, Fifty Heroes.* Hopkins, Minn.: Self-published, 1997.

Henderson, Edwin B. *The Black Athlete: Emergence and Arrival.* New York: Publishers Company, 1968.

"Young Pro," *Time,* January 19, 1959, p. 75.

Beamon, Bob

(Robert Beamon)

(1946–　) *track-and-field long jumper*

For one brief moment in his career, Bob Beamon achieved the ultimate goal of all top athletes—perfection. In the words of the veteran sports journalist Dick Schaap, his long jump in the 1968 Olympics was "quite possibly, the greatest individual athletic achievement in the history of mankind."

Beamon was born on August 29, 1946, in the South Jamaica section of Queens, New York, under the bleakest of circumstances. He was born out of wedlock to a mother who was so ill with tuberculosis that she never touched him and died before he reached his first birthday and he never knew his father's name. His stepfather, James Beamon, claimed Bob and Bob's grandmother took over his upbringing.

Beamon fell in with a rough crowd in their tough ghetto neighborhood. By the age of 13, he was shoplifting and selling drugs. Finally, his behavior landed him in a special high school for severe discipline problems. "I was desperate for attention," he recalls.

Bob Beamon executes his "perfect jump" at the 1968 Olympics in Mexico City. *(Tony Duffy/Getty Images)*

Fortunately, he attracted the attention he craved through athletics. Competing in a police athletic league, Beamon uncorked an astounding 24-foot long jump as a 16-year-old. The praise he received for this encouraged him to envision some new goals for his life, which he set out to achieve by transferring to the academically challenging Jamaica High School. There his leaping ability served him well in both basketball, in which he excelled as a shot blocker, and track, in which by 1965 he ranked number two among U.S. high school long jumpers and number three among triple jumpers.

After graduation, Beamon attended North Carolina A & T University on a track scholarship. Although he disliked his entire experience at the school, he improved his long jump personal best to 25 feet, 7 inches, during his first year. In January 1967, Beamon transferred to the University of Texas–El Paso (UTEP), where he regularly topped 26 feet in meets, and he challenged RALPH HAROLD BOSTON as the nation's top jumper. That year Beamon won the Amateur Athletic Union (AAU) national indoor championship with a new U.S. indoor record of 26 feet, 11 inches. Comfortable in climate-controlled conditions, he went on to break the world indoor mark twice in 1968, with a best effort of 27 feet, 2 ¾ inches. Beamon also won the national collegiate indoor title in the triple jump. His career at UTEP, however, was cut short when he was dismissed from the team for refusal to compete against Brigham Young University in a protest of that school's racial policies.

His departure from team competition did not hurt him a bit. Beamon continued to dominate jumping competitions in the United States, winning 20 of the 21 meets he entered that year. When he made the 1968 U.S. Olympic team and headed for the Mexico City Games, he was regarded as a slight favorite over a tough field of veteran performers, including Boston and the defending gold medalist, Lynn Davies of Great Britain. Both Davies and Boston, however, were more technically sound jumpers, and that competence gave them an advantage in high-pressure situations. Unlike most jumpers, Beamon did not even use runway markers to gauge his approach to the takeoff board. Most of his training involved simply increasing his sprinting speed.

Beamon's less disciplined approach nearly ruined his Olympic competition. In the preliminaries, he fouled by more than a foot on his first jump and by several inches on his second. That left him with just one more qualifying leap; if he fouled, he was out. His teammate Boston settled his nerves by suggesting he aim for a takeoff point a full foot behind the takeoff board. Beamon did and qualified easily.

The finals were held on October 18 under overcast skies under constant threat of rain. Beamon, the fourth jumper of 17 finalists, took off down the runway, thinking of nothing more than getting a legal jump in to start the competition. This time the lanky, six-foot, three-inch Beamon hit the takeoff board perfectly. He climbed into the air, soared for a seemingly impossible length of time, and stretched his legs over the sand pit.

Immediately, Beamon knew he had hit an excellent jump, but he had no inkling of what he had just accomplished. As his competitors looked on with ashen faces, the optical measuring device fell off the end of the rail. Beamon had landed beyond the limit that it could measure. A tape measure had to be scrounged to record Beamon's distance, which totaled 8.9 meters.

Not familiar with metric distances, Beamon still did not know why fans and competitors were agog. Finally, he learned that he had leaped 29 feet, 2 inches. He had not merely topped the previous record of 27 feet, 4 ¼ inches; he had absolutely destroyed it. In the 33 years since JESSE OWENS's record jump, long jumpers had improved the world record a total of 8 ½ inches. In a single leap, Beamon had advanced the world record another 21 ¾ inches. When Beamon was finally able to comprehend the distance he had jumped, his legs buckled and he sank to the ground in shock. His competitors suffered similar symptoms, knowing that Beamon had abruptly ended the competition before they had ever jumped. On his first attempt, Lynn Davies barely reached 21 feet, a distance that would not win many high school meets.

Having reached perfection, however, Beamon had no place to go but down. Although he won a few subsequent meets, he never came within two feet of his world record. He retired after an embarrassing 21st-place finish in the 1970 nationals, and he made a brief, unsuccessful comeback on the short-lived pro track circuit in the mid-1970s. For a time, the crushing disappointment of falling from the peak of sport to oblivion seriously affected his personality and finances. But he eventually came to grips with the situation and began to work in business and social service projects.

Further Reading

Nelson, Cordner. *Track's Greatest Champions*. Los Altos, Calif.: Tafnews Press, 1986.

Page, James A. *Black Olympic Medalists*. Englewood, Colo.: Libraries Unlimited, 1991.

Schaap, Dick. *The Perfect Jump*. New York: Bantam, 1976.

Bell, Cool Papa
(James Bell)
(1903–1991) *baseball outfielder*

Although it is impossible to compare old-time ball players with their modern counterparts, those who saw James "Cool Papa" Bell play insist that he was the fastest man ever to run the base paths.

James Bell was born on May 15, 1903, in Starkville, Mississippi, where his father scratched out a meager living as a farmer. Discouraged by the bleak educational and employment opportunities in Starkville, his mother, a mixed-blood Oklahoma Indian, sent 17-year-old James to live with his four older brothers in Saint Louis. There James earned a living in a packing plant while attending high school.

In what little spare time he had, he played sandlot baseball with his brothers on a team called the Compton Cubs. Bell moved on to a semipro team in East Saint Louis and then signed with the Saint Louis Stars, a professional black ball club, in 1922. Initially, Bell was noted primarily for his pitching ability. At 5 feet, 11 inches, and a rail-thin 137 pounds, Bell could not overpower batters with his fastball, but he developed a clever assortment of breaking pitches, including a knuckleball.

While pitching for the Stars, Bell was given the nickname by which he was known all his career. Some say his manager began calling him "Cool" after seeing how calmly the 19-year-old rookie struck out the legendary OSCAR CHARLESTON in their first meeting. Others say that happened after Bell fell asleep in the dugout before he was supposed to pitch. Either way, Cool Bell did not have the right ring to it, and so players lengthened it to Cool Papa Bell.

In 1923 or 1924, an arm injury put an end to his pitching career. Bell switched to centerfield, where he could put his phenomenal speed to good use. So confident was Bell in his ability to cover the outfield that he played very shallow, even occasionally covering second base on pickoff attempts.

At the plate, Bell worked hard to change himself from a right-handed hitter to a switch hitter to take advantage of the left-handed batter's box's being closer to first base. His speed on the base paths gave rise to astounding stories. Among the documented cases is an instance in an exhibition game against an all-star team of major leaguers in which he scored from first base on a sacrifice bunt; in another case he scored from second base on a sacrifice fly. According to his contemporary Judy Johnson, fielders moved in whenever Bell was at bat because "You couldn't play your regular position or you'd never throw him out." The sight of a ground ball off Bell's bat sent opponents into a panic. His teammate Jimmie Crutchfield noted, "If he hit one back to the pitcher, everyone yelled, 'Hurry!'"

Like most of the barnstorming stars of the Negro Leagues, Cool Papa Bell played for many teams. Along with 24 seasons of summer ball, he played 21 years in winter leagues in Mexico, Cuba, and California. Records show that he batted .437 in a Mexican league one year, posted a lifetime mark of .341, and had a .391 average in exhibitions against major league teams. But spotty record keeping on many teams casts a shadow over Bell's accomplishments. It remains difficult to verify the claim that he stole 175 games in a season.

Bell was known as a gentlemanly player, popular with fans and his fellow athletes. After finishing his playing career in the 1940s, he served as a part-time scout for the Saint Louis Browns until 1954. He later worked as a custodian and night security officer at the Saint Louis City Hall until 1970, and he then enjoyed a long retirement until his death on March 7, 1991.

Further Reading

Chadwick, Bruce. *When the Game Was Black and White.* New York: Abbeville, 1992.

Clark, Dick, and Lerry Lester, eds. *The Negro League Book.* Cleveland, Ohio: Society for American Baseball Research, 1994.

Pepe, Phil. *Talkin Baseball.* New York: Ballantine, 1998.

Peterson, Robert. *Only the Ball Was White.* New York: Gramercy, 1970.

Riley, James. *The Biographical Encyclopedia of the Negro Baseball Leagues.* New York: Carroll & Graf, 1994.

Bonds, Barry Lamar
(1964–   ) *baseball outfielder*

Few modern baseball players have generated such a combination of admiration and animosity as Barry Bonds. Long regarded as a supreme baseball talent, Bonds boosted his stature with a stunning, late-career home run onslaught that carried him past the top sluggers of all time.

Barry Lamar Bonds was born on July 24, 1964, in Riverside, California, and grew up surrounded by San Francisco Giants baseball stars. His father, Bobby Bonds, played for the Giants during most of his 14-year career, during which he hit 332 home runs and stole 462 bases. His godfather was the legendary Giants' center fielder WILLIE MAYS. Yet while he was growing up, Barry felt closest to his grandfather, and ever since his grandfather's death during his college years, Barry has worn a cross on a chain in memory of him.

Bobby Bonds declares that his son was such a natural ball player that he developed a perfect swing at the age of two. With such talent being shaped by the guidance of his father and Mays, Barry quickly rose far above his peers in the sport. After he batted .467 in his senior year at San Mateo High School in 1982, he was drafted by the Giants. Barry, however, opted to attend Arizona State University instead. There he won All-Conference honors as a freshman, sophomore, and junior, and he collected seven consecutive hits in the National Collegiate Athletic Association (NCAA) World Series tournament.

In 1985, the Pittsburgh Pirates made him their first selection in the draft of amateur players. After brief minor league stops at North Carolina and Hawaii, Bonds was called up to the majors on May 30, 1986. He started out slowly, batting only .223 with 16 home runs as a leadoff batter his rookie season. In his sophomore year, he showed flashes of the power and speed that reminded fans of his father, with 25 home runs and 32 stolen bases. But after a similar respectable season in 1988, Bonds slumped to .248 with 19 home runs in 1989. Going into his fifth major league season, he had done little to justify the expectations held of him.

It was in 1990 that he blossomed into a star. Moved to the number-three spot in the batting order, he batted .301 with 33 home runs and 114 runs batted in to lead the Pirates to their divisional title. Combined with his 52 stolen bases, and his exceptional range and strong throwing arm as a left fielder, Bonds proved himself to be the National League's Most Valuable Player that season. Bonds also won a Gold Glove as the top defensive player at his position, making Bobby and Barry the first father-son combination to win such an award.

Bonds began 1991 in a slump but broke out of it with a torrid summer hitting binge to finish at .292 with 34 home runs. By 1992 the fans finally began to recognize what most of his peers already had—that Bonds was the best all-around player in the league. He was voted a starter in the All-Star game that season and went on to post a .311 mark with 34 home runs and 39 stolen bases, statistics

Barry Bonds stunned baseball fans with a late-career power surge that gave him a record 73 home runs in 2001. *(Harry How/Getty Images)*

that again earned him the National League Most Valuable Player Award. Unfortunately, Bonds was unable to produce similar results in the play-offs against the Atlanta Braves' strong pitching staff and the Pirates did not get to the World Series.

Bonds left Pittsburgh in 1993 and signed with San Francisco as a free agent. He immediately provided the Giants with a huge return on their investment in him by enjoying perhaps the finest season of his career. Bonds batted a career-high .336 that season and popped 40 home runs in winning his third Most Valuable Player Award in four seasons.

Reaction to Bonds among both teammates and fans, however, was mixed. He played with such supreme confidence that his former teammate Eric Anthony said of him, "It's like he rolls out of bed, looks at himself in the mirror and knows he's the best." Nor was Bonds willing to share his knowledge of the game or his secret five-hour-a-day workout program with others for fear that opponents would use that knowledge against him. Some teammates and fans took exception to what they saw as his arrogance, a perception that was aggravated by Bonds's quiet nature and unwillingness to spend time talking to the press or hanging around teammates. Other players responded that Bonds, although not always likable, was a consummate professional who gave his best every day without complaint, regardless of injuries.

For most of his career, Bonds was viewed as a fine all-around player and not recognized as a power hitter in the class of record-breaking sluggers Mark McGwire and Sammy Sosa. It was not until 1997 that he won his first National League home run title, with 46. When he then slumped to 34, 25, and 33 home runs in the following seasons, it seemed that Bonds's days as a home run king had ended. His greatest achievement appeared to be that of becoming the first major league player to hit 400 home runs and steal 400 bases in a career.

In 2001, however, Bonds began crushing home runs at an unheard-of pace. By midseason he was on pace to break McGwire's single-season mark. Timid pitchers tried to avoid serving up homers to Bonds by keeping the ball well away from the plate. As a result Bonds easily set a major league record with 178 bases on balls. With a week to go in the season, he crushed his 70th home run of the year to tie McGwire's record. In the very next game, on October 5, he smashed one of his typical line drive home runs into the bleachers to break the mark. Bonds then added number 72 later in the game. He finished the season with 73 to set the current major league mark. In 2002 he topped the 600 mark and surprised experts by winning his first batting title. Bonds won his third consecutive National League Most Valuable Player award in 2003. The following year he topped 700 career home runs, placing him third on the all-time list and within striking distance of Hank Aaron's record. But injuries in 2005 and a growing controversy over alleged steroid use threatened to derail his quest to become the game's most prolific home run hitter.

Further Reading

"Another Side of Barry Bonds," *Ebony*, September 1997, pp. 141–42.

Keown, Tim. "That 70s Show," ESPN, October 15, 2001, pp. 52–54.

Perlman, Jeff. "Appreciate Bonds," *Sports Illustrated*, June 5, 2000, pp. 48–53.

Schwartz, A. "Going Deep," *The New York Times Magazine*, July 15, 2000, p. 17.

Boston, Ralph Harold
(1939–   ) *track-and-field long jumper*

In contrast to BOB BEAMON's explosive flash of brilliance, Ralph Boston was the model of consistency in the long jump. Unfailingly, he recorded leaps in the 26- to 27-foot range throughout nearly a decade of pressure-packed international competition, winning three Olympic medals and six straight national Amateur Athletic Union (AAU) titles.

Ralph Harold Boston was born on May 9, 1939, in the southern Mississippi town of Laurel, the youngest of 10 children. A quiet youth, Boston had to be persuaded to go out for track in high school by a coach who had enjoyed success working with his older brothers. Ralph was surprised to discover that he could do well in whatever event he tried. In one meet, he took first place in eight different events, including sprints, hurdles, pole vault, high jump, long jump, and javelin. Meanwhile, his performance in football attracted the interest of college scouts. Believing that his skills were better suited to track and field, however, Boston accepted a scholarship to compete in that sport at Tennessee State University while working toward a degree in biochemistry.

As a college athlete, Boston continued to display his versatility. In one meet, he won the triple jump, long jump, high jump, and two hurdle races. Later, he captured the conference championship in the javelin and the pole vault. But instead of competing in the ultimate test of all-around track and field prowess, the decathlon, Boston narrowed his focus to his best event, the long jump. After failing to make the U.S. team that competed in the 1959 world championships, he worked diligently at perfecting his long jump technique.

The effort paid off in 1960 when, two weeks before the Olympics, Boston broke JESSE OWENS's 25-year-old world mark with a leap of 26 feet, 11 1/4 inches. At the Rome Olympics, the favored Boston struggled in the early stages of competition. After five rounds he trailed his teammate Bo Roberson's personal best effort of 26 feet, 4 ¼ inches, and Igor Ter-Ovanesyan's mark of 25 feet, 11 inches. On his final attempt, Boston uncorked a jump of 26 feet, 7 ¾ inches, which not only earned the gold medal but surpassed Owens's Olympic record.

Boston went on to capture six consecutive AAU outdoor championships from 1961 to 1966. He remained a fierce Olympic competitor. Running into a cold wind on a wet track in Tokyo at the 1964 Olympics, he came within an inch and a half of defending his Olympic title, taking the silver behind Great Britain's Lynn Davies. Four years later, he completed his collection of Olympic medals by taking the bronze at Mexico City, with the best jump of his Olympic career, 26 feet, 9 ¼ inches. During his career, he broke the world long jump record seven times, capped by a lifetime best of 27 feet, 4 ¾ inches, in 1965.

Boston retired from competition in 1969. Widely respected for his knowledge of sport and his open, generous nature, he served for a time as an expert commentator on network television and was voted into the U.S. Olympic Hall of Fame in 1985.

Further Reading

Nelson, Cordner. *Track's Greatest Champions*. Los Altos, Calif.: Tafnews Press, 1986.

Great Athletes of the Twentieth Century. Vol. 1. Pasadena, Calif.: Salem Press, 1994.

Page, James A. *Black Olympic Medalists*. Englewood, Colo.: Libraries Unlimited, 1991.

Brisco-Hooks, Valerie
(Valerie Ann Brisco)
(1960–   ) *track-and-field sprinter*

Early in Valerie Brisco's high school track career, her coach gave her a copy of WILMA GOLDEAN RUDOLPH's autobiography to read for inspiration. Nine years later, Brisco matched Rudolph's medal collection by taking three golds in the 1984 Olympics.

Valerie Ann Brisco was born on July 6, 1960, in Greenwood, Mississippi. Shortly thereafter, the family moved to Los Angeles. Valerie tried hard to tag along with her older brother, Robert, as he jogged in training for high school track. In 1974, Robert was killed by a stray bullet while working out on the track at Locke High School. Valerie, who had followed him into track, dedicated her career to her brother.

She excelled as a short sprinter at Locke High School, where her performances earned her a scholarship to California State University at Northridge. There she came under the tutelage of famed sprint coach Bob Kersee. Brisco made steady improvement, running both in college and for the Los Angeles Mercurettes Track Club. In 1979 she managed a third-place finish in the 200 meters at the AAU indoor championships. The following year she reeled off a time of 22.53 in the same event and placed second to the reigning U.S. sprint queen, EVELYN ASHFORD.

She gradually lost interest in track after marrying a fellow Cal-Northridge student, Alvin Hooks, who later played wide receiver for the Philadelphia Eagles, in 1979. Eventually, Brisco-Hooks retired from the sport in 1981 in order to start a family. However, after giving birth to a son in 1982, she yielded to the encouragement of Kersee and her family members and gave the sport another try, despite the fact that she was now 40 pounds overweight. Brisco-Hooks had second thoughts about the effort almost immediately when Kersee, a relentless taskmaster, ordered early morning practices that the late-rising Brisco-Hooks detested. At one point, he pushed so hard that Brisco-Hooks called off the comeback, but the two patched up their differences and she resumed training.

Brisco-Hooks was surprised to discover that she seemed to be stronger after giving birth than she had been before. She moved up to run the 400 meters, which she called a "frightening event," as well as the 200, and began running world-class times in both events. She surprised even herself by becoming the first U.S. woman to run the 400 in under 50 seconds and made the U.S. Olympic team in both events.

The 1984 Olympics were marred by the absence of the boycotting Eastern European countries, traditionally strong in women's track. Brisco-Hooks took advantage of the void to sprint to victory and Olympic records in both of her events. In the 200, she overcame a poor start to finish far ahead of FLORENCE GRIFFITH JOYNER in an Olympic record 21.84. She notched an Olympic record when she staved off her teammate Chandra Cheeseborough to win the 400 in 48.83, and she earned a share of a third record and gold medal in the 4×400 relay. It was Brisco-Hooks's singular moment in the sun; later she competed in the 1988 Olympics and added a relay silver medal to her collection.

Further Reading

Cort, M. "Catch a Rising Star," *Women's Sport*, November 1984, pp. 46–48.
Page, James A. *Black Olympian Medalists*. Englewood, Colo.: Libraries Unlimited, 1991.

Brock, Lou
(Louis Clark Brock)
(1939–   ) *baseball outfielder*

Baseball fans regarded Saint Louis's 1964 trade of 18-game winner Ernie Broglio for the Chicago Cubs inept center fielder Lou Brock as one of the most one-sided deals of all time. They were right that the deal was one-sided, but as it turned out, Saint Louis got the bargain.

Louis Clark Brock was born on June 18, 1939, in El Dorado, Arkansas. When he was small, his father walked away from the family, prompting his mother to move to Monroe, Louisiana, to be near relatives. Brock knew nothing about baseball until the fourth grade, when a teacher punished him for throwing a spitball by sending him to the library to research biographies of ball players.

Brock became enamored of the idea of a baseball career, although he did not begin playing the game until the summer before high school.

Brock started out as a pitcher at Union High School. Originally a left-handed batter, he developed himself into a switch-hitting outfielder. He did not play well enough to attract any scholarship or pro offers, but he did well enough in class to earn an academic scholarship from Southern University in Louisiana. Lax study habits caused him to lose his scholarship his freshman year, and Brock desperately tried to make up for it by getting a baseball scholarship. Through hard work, he boosted his freshman batting average of .186 to a sizzling .542.

That achievement caught the attention of the Chicago Cubs, who signed him to a minor league contract in 1961. With a glaring need for outfielders, the Cubs rushed him to the majors by the end of the season. Brock batted .263 and demonstrated speed in the outfield and on the base paths. But the following year his average dipped to .258, and he made costly mistakes as a fielder. When the 1964 season started out even worse, the Cubs lost patience with him and, on June 15, traded him for Broglio, a proven starting pitcher.

While Broglio developed arm trouble and lost his effectiveness, Brock blossomed in his new surroundings. He batted .348 during the remainder of the season, then clouted a home run in Saint Louis's World Series win over the New York Yankees.

Brock flashed his stealing potential in 1966 by swiping 74 bases to break the six-year reign of MAURY WILLS as baseball's steals leader. It was the first of four consecutive stolen base titles for the Cardinals' center fielder. His base stealing rattled pitchers so badly that he became the prime focus of opposing pitchers. When the Cardinals advanced to the World Series in 1967, Dick Williams, manager of the opposing Boston Red Sox, said, "Our job is to keep that darned Brock from getting to first." The idea was good; the execution, poor. In game one of the series, Brock reached base five times, on four hits and a walk; stole a base; and scored both Cardinals runs in a 2–1 victory. Brock led both teams with 12 hits, tied a World Series record by stealing seven bases in seven attempts, and scored eight of his team's 25 runs to help Saint Louis to victory. Brock delivered a repeat performance in the 1968 World Series, but this time his 13 hits and seven stolen bases were not enough to overcome the Detroit Tigers.

In 1969, Brock led the club in batting average with a .298 mark. The following year he hit .304, and then he topped that in 1971 with a career-high .313, leading the league in runs scored with 126 and in stolen bases with 64.

In 1974, the 34-year-old veteran shocked baseball experts by swiping bases at a record rate. By July, he already had 56 steals in 64 attempts, more than he had had in the entire previous season. With his .294 batting average and ability to draw walks, he received many opportunities and he made maximal use of them. He shattered Maury Wills's record of 104 steals by his pilfering of 118 bases, which remains the National League record.

Brock retired in 1979 with a record 938 career steals. A popular and sportsmanlike player, Brock won many awards for charitable contributions, many of them involving the Lou Brock Boys Club he established in Saint Louis.

Further Reading

Brock, Lou. *Stealing Is My Game.* New York: Prentice-Hall, 1976.

Carmichael, John P. *My Greatest Day in Baseball.* New York: Grosset & Dunlap, 1968.

Moritz, Charles, ed. *Current Biography, 1975.* New York: H. W. Wilson, 1975.

Porter, David C., ed. *Biographical Dictionary of American Sports.* Westport, Conn.: Greenwood Press, 2000.

Brown, Earlene Dennis

(1935–1983) *track-and-field shot putter*

Earlene Brown is arguably the most unheralded U.S. athlete of all time, largely because she competed in an event that has been considered distinctly nonfeminine. More than a quarter-century after her retirement, however, she remains by far the best thrower in U.S. track and field history.

Earlene Dennis was born in Latexo, Texas, on July 11, 1935, and moved with her family to Los Angeles shortly thereafter. Her natural athletic ability found an outlet and encouragement in the Los Angeles Police Athletic League. She played catcher for one of the region's top female softball teams and regularly won running and throwing events in track and field. Eventually, her size and strength steered her into the throwing events.

Earlene was already married, taking the last name of Brown, when she joined the Amateur Athletic Union (AAU) for the first time in 1956. The 20-year-old newcomer made an immediate splash by earning a spot on the U.S. Olympic team. Her friendly personality made her a crowd favorite among the fans at the Olympic Games in Melbourne, Australia. When notified that she had broken the Victorian state record in a pre-Olympic warmup meet, she quickly apologized, "I'm sorry, honey; if I'd known I was going to do that I wouldn't have thrown it so far." In the Olympics, she was one of four women who stood head and shoulders above the other competitors, but her throw fell two feet short of a medal. Her discus throw of 168 feet, 5 ½ inches, however, set a new U.S. record, as did her sixth-place shot put of 49 feet, 7 ½ inches.

Throughout her career, Brown had obligations as a mother and a provider for her family that took precedence over her track-and-field career, and she never was able to train full time. Nonetheless, she won the national AAU shot put title eight times, including seven years in a row from 1956 to 1961, and captured three national discus titles.

Her finest year as a competitor was 1960, when she set U.S. records in both the discus (176 feet, 10 inches) and the shot put (54 feet, 9 inches). Her proudest moment also occurred that year, when, in the Rome Olympics, she uncorked a throw of 53 feet, 10 ½ inches, to beat out Valerie Sloper of New Zealand for the bronze medal by an inch. Hers remains the only medal ever won by a U.S. woman in the shot put.

Brown continued throwing and winning national titles until 1964. That year she made her third Olympic team and finished off her international career with a 12th-place finish in the shot.

In an event in which sheer bulk and power are enormous assets and male competitors are routinely described as "whales," sports writers of the late 1950s and early 1960s were almost embarrassed to focus on women competitors. As a result, Brown's accomplishments received virtually no publicity. But Jesse Robinson, a veteran reporter at many Olympics, has remarked, "My great woman athlete is Miss Earlene Brown. . . . No one has been as strong and dominant as Earlene Brown over the series of Olympic Games."

Further Reading

Oglesby, Carole, et al., eds. *Encyclopedia of Women and Sport.* Phoenix: Oryx Press, 1998.

Page, James A. *Black Olympian Medalists.* Englewood, Colo.: Libraries Unlimited, 1991.

Brown, Jim
(James Nathaniel Brown)
(1936–) *football running back*

Nearly 40 years after he walked away from pro football, Jim Brown maintains legendary status among sports buffs as one of the toughest men in the world. His fierce self-assurance combined with his prodigious all-around athletic skill made Brown the standard by which all other pro running backs have been measured.

James Nathaniel Brown was born on February 17, 1936, on Saint Simons Island, off the Georgia coast. He never knew his father, Swinton Brown, an ex-boxer who moved away a few weeks after his birth. Unable to support her son, Teresa Brown also left the island in search of a better living, leaving Jim to be raised by his great-grandmother. Despite growing up without parents, Brown remembers his childhood as carefree and fun.

When Brown was eight, he was put on a train to rejoin his mother, who was working as a domestic in Great Neck, New York. That ride took him into a largely white neighborhood and some of the best schools in the state. Although Brown briefly formed a gang called the Gaylords, he soon began playing so many sports that he had little time for anything but school and competition. He began playing on the varsity football team at age 14 and earned 13 varsity letters at Manhasset High School in baseball, basketball, football, lacrosse, and track. As a bruising power forward in basketball, Brown once scored 53 points in a game. He threw two no-hitters in baseball and turned down an offer to sign a contract with the New York Yankees. He gained All-State recognition in football as a linebacker and running back who averaged nearly 15 yards per carry.

Such all-around ability attracted many scholarships, particularly in football, but Brown chose to attend Syracuse University, which did not award him a scholarship. Unknown to Brown, who thought he was on scholarship, a friend of his had arranged financing for the first year on the promise from a coach that Brown could earn a scholarship with his play.

Brown had never experienced racial problems at Manhasset High, but at Syracuse, according to Brown, "I ran chin first into overt racism. Someone had changed all the rules, forgotten to tell me." Brown was assigned to a dormitory and a food service apart from the white players, which upset him to the point that he wanted to leave school. His family, however, persuaded him to stick it out.

Before his sophomore year, the Syracuse coaches wanted to move Brown from running back to end, a position in which he would have a better chance of playing. Demonstrating the unwavering independence that became a trademark, Brown declined and began his sophomore year as the team's fifth-string running back. Early

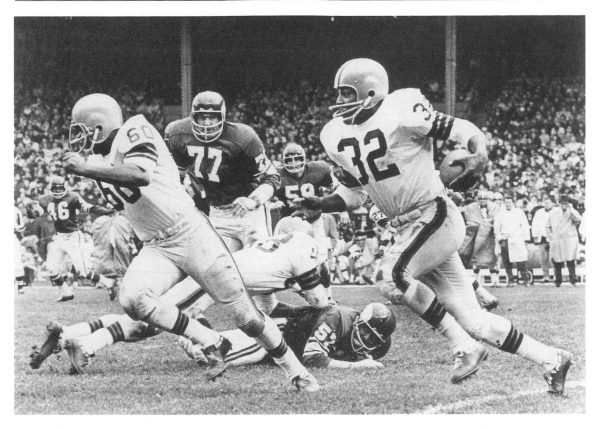

Jim Brown accelerates behind his blockers against the Minnesota Vikings. *(Henry Barr/Diamond Images)*

season injuries to other runners gave Brown a chance to play, and he made the most of it. In the sixth game, he raced through the Cornell defense on a 54-yard touchdown run that ended all debate. From then on, Brown was the star running back in the Syracuse attack. Brown achieved All-American status and led Syracuse to a prestigious Cotton Bowl berth during his senior season.

Meanwhile, he continued his all-around athletic endeavors, winning a total of 10 athletic letters in four sports. In his senior year he led the Syracuse lacrosse team to an undefeated season and became the only person ever to win All-American status in both football and lacrosse. He also played basketball and, as a sophomore, finished fifth in the decathlon in a national track-

and-field competition despite limited training. He was given a shot at making the U.S. Olympic team in 1956 but turned it down because he knew the training would conflict with football, which was providing his scholarship. Brown also rejected a lucrative offer in professional boxing.

The name Brown dominated Cleveland football in 1957 when Coach Paul Brown of the Browns selected Jim Brown in the first round of the college draft. Once described by the basketball legend BILL RUSSELL as the most competitive man he ever met, Jim Brown showed his perfectionism in rating his rookie season "not outstanding." In reality, he broke the National Football League (NFL) single-game rushing record with 237 yards against Los Angeles, led the NFL in rushing with 942 yards, and helped the Browns win the divisional title.

Superbly chiseled at six feet, two inches, 230 pounds, with a 32-inch waist, Brown could blast through tackles in the middle of the line and run over defensive backs racing up to support against the run. Rather than attempt to avoid hits, he preferred to initiate contact and use his strength and size to punish defenders physically. Opponents learned to beware of what Brown dubbed "The Blow," a forearm shot that left defenders gasping for breath. Yet Brown also had the speed to outrun defenders on end sweeps and to break long runs for touchdowns. His desire to win was so fierce that he wore little padding, accepting the extra bruises that resulted rather than carry the extra weight that might slow him down. The combination of these attributes made him nearly unstoppable even though opposing defenses began designing their defenses specifically to stop him. A discouraged Washington Redskin defender commented, "The best way to tackle Jim Brown is to hold on and wait for help."

Coach Brown was not shy about using his new star. "When you've got a big gun, why not fire it as often as possible?" was his philosophy. In 1958 Brown showed that he could handle the work load. He carried the ball 257 times for 1,527 yards, which shattered the previous rushing yardage mark by nearly 400 yards and also set a new record for rushing touchdowns with 17. The ultimate team player, Brown in 1959 took on the dangerous kick return duty, normally reserved for more expendable reserve players, while again leading the league in rushing. The 1960 and 1961 seasons were more of the same, as Brown added a fourth and a fifth consecutive rushing title.

Behind this record of success, however, frustrations were beginning to appear. At the end of the 1961 season, he was openly critical of Cleveland for trading a complementary offensive threat, Bobby Mitchell. Under Paul Brown, the Cleveland offense had become stagnant and predictable. The Browns seldom sent Brown on his patented end sweeps. Although he admired his coach in many ways, the star back chafed at being used solely as a battering ram that plowed into the masses of defenders positioned to stop him. He began to speak of retirement.

Matters hit bottom in 1962 when the Browns suffered through a mediocre season and Brown did not come close to leading the league in rushing. But the running back received new life in 1963 when Coach Brown was released and Blanton Collier took over. Collier installed a more wide-open style of offense that allowed Brown to use all of his abilities, and he responded with his best season. Carrying the ball 291 times, he smashed his own rushing record by more than 300 yards, rolling up 1,863 yards at an eye-popping 6.4 yards per carry.

The following season was even more successful in that it satisfied Brown's quest for a championship. Brown again led the league with 1,446 yards rushing, but Cleveland had other weapons to complement him. In the championship game, the Browns flattened the favored Baltimore Colts and star quarterback John Unitas, 27–0.

In 1965, Brown again captured the league rushing title with a total of 1,544 yards. By this time, he had launched a successful career as a motion picture actor. He signaled that he was contemplating retirement, and as the training camp opened, he remained on the set of a movie production. The Browns owner Art Modell then made the mistake of announcing that he was fining Brown $100 a day until he showed up in camp. "Art should have known intimidation does not work with me," Brown has observed. The affront ended Brown's quandary about whether to return to football. While he was still the reigning Most Valuable Player (MVP) in the National Football League, he called it quits on his own terms and never looked back.

When his film career faded, Brown devoted much of his time to social work and community projects, although his image took a hit when he was sentenced to six months in jail in 2000 for domestic abuse. He remained bluntly outspoken on all topics, particularly on the spoiled and mercenary nature of modern athletes. When Franco Harris, whom Brown criticized for running out of bounds to avoid being hit, threatened Brown's career rushing record in the early 1980s, Brown threatened to return to the game. "If he was going to represent football history," said Brown, "I felt he should not set a bad standard."

Although Brown never intended to make a comeback, his point was made. The standard and the legacy that he left were as solid as they come. In nine years of heavy-duty action as football's marked man, Brown never missed a down because of injury. And although modern runners have surpassed his career rushing mark of 12,312 yards and his single-season total of 1,863, they have required many more games and carries in which to do it. For most of his career, Brown played 12-game seasons as opposed to the current 16. No runner has come close to matching Brown's record of eight rushing titles in nine seasons nor his lifetime rushing average of 5.22 yards per carry.

Further Reading

Brown, Jim, with Myron Cope. *Off My Chest*. New York: Doubleday, 1964.

Brown, Jim, with Steve Delsohn. *Out of Bounds*. New York: Zebra Books, 1989.

Toback, James. *Jim: The Author's Self-Centered Memoir on the Great Jim Brown*. Garden City, N.Y.: Doubleday, 1971.

Yeager, Don. "Prisoner of Conscience," *Sports Illustrated*, April 15, 2002, pp. 54–57.

Brown, Roosevelt, Jr.

(1932–) *football offensive tackle*

Roosevelt Brown entered the National Football League as an obscure tackle whom the scouts had never seen play, even on film. He left it the consummate offensive tackle who anchored the New York Giants offensive line for more than a decade.

Brown was born on October 20, 1932, in Charlottesville, Virginia. His father, Roosevelt Sr., was dead set against Brown's playing football in school, having lost a brother to a freak injury in the sport. Dutifully, Roosevelt respected his father's wishes by playing trombone in the band instead. But the elder Brown's job with the Southern Railroad took him away from home for long stretches of time. During one of these absences, football coaches persuaded Roosevelt to play. By the time his father discovered what he was doing, Roosevelt had established himself as an injury-free and capable player, good enough to attract a scholarship offer from Morgan State University.

Brown's combination of size, speed, and agility made him a multisport star at Morgan State. He lettered in baseball, was captain of the wrestling team, and excelled as a football lineman. Despite this evidence of his athletic gifts, pro football teams, who largely ignored black college players, knew nothing about him. The New York Giants selected him in the 27th round of the 1953 draft of college players only because they had run out of prospects and spotted his name in the *Pittsburgh Courier*'s selection of a Black All-America team.

The Giants found him to be an extremely raw talent who needed to be shown such basic techniques as the three-point stance. In his first training camp, the Giants matched him against their most physical lineman, Arnie Weinmeister. According to one observer, "Weinmeister almost killed him. Roosevelt kept going after him even when he couldn't see straight anymore."

Brown learned quickly and almost immediately earned a starting job as an offensive tackle. At six feet, three inches, 255 pounds, with a 29-inch waist, Brown did not have exceptional size for an offensive lineman. "I used more smarts than anything else," he recalls, "because I didn't have the strength of [JIM] PARKER. I let my guy think himself out of the play." Brown also used his quickness and became one of the first tackles to pull out and block on end sweeps.

With Brown leading the running game and protecting high-profile quarterbacks such as Y. A. Tittle, the Giants frequently contended for the championship. During his 13 seasons with New York, the Giants won six conference titles and one National Football League (NFL) championship. Brown first became a fixture as an All-Pro in 1956, when he was named the NFL Lineman of the Year. The Associated Press voted him All-Pro every season from 1953 to 1963. Brown also showed such inspired leadership that the Giants elected him the team's first African-American captain.

After his retirement after the 1965 season, Brown stayed with the Giants as an assistant coach and later a scout. In 1975, he was the second offensive lineman voted into pro football's Hall of Fame.

Further Reading

Allen, George. *Pro Football's 100 Greatest Players*. Indianapolis, Ind.: Bobbs-Merrill, 1982.

Henderson, Edwin B. *The Black Athlete: Emergence and Arrival*. New York: Publishers Company, 1968.

Bryant, Kobe

(1978–   ) *basketball guard*

In a league that has been desperately searching for a successor to MICHAEL JORDAN as a main attraction, Kobe Bryant has often been cited as the best hope. The youngest player ever to start in an All-Star game, Bryant has combined with SHAQUILLE RASHAUN O'NEAL to make the Lakers the dominant team at the dawn of the 21st century.

Kobe was born on August 23, 1978, in Philadelphia, the son of Joe and Pam Bryant. Joe "Jellybean" Bryant played for eight years in the National Basketball Association (NBA), primar-

ily with Philadelphia. He had a miniature basketball court set up in their home for Kobe when the boy was three. When Kobe was five, the family moved to Italy, where the elder Bryant was able to continue his basketball career. According to Joe Bryant, "Living in Italy was the key" to Kobe's fast-developing maturity and sense of responsibility.

Eight years later, Joe Bryant accepted an offer to return to Philadelphia as an assistant coach at LaSalle University. Kobe again had to make a major adjustment, this time to a school that was 90 percent white and where the other blacks had little in common with him. Bryant made his major adjustment on the basketball court, where he became a starter as a freshman at Lower Merion High School, in Ardmore. In four years at the school, Bryant became the all-time leading scorer in Pennsylvania high school basketball history, led his team to the 1996 state title, and was named the 1996 *USA Today* High School Player of the Year.

As a fine student and star athlete, Bryant was recruited by hundreds of universities, but he stunned basketball experts by announcing at a press conference that he would forgo college and declare himself eligible for the pro draft. The Los Angeles Lakers took a look at him and, according to the general manager, Jerry West, "He was the most skilled player we've ever worked out." The Lakers arranged a trade with the Charlotte Hornets, who selected him as the 13th pick of the first round and then traded him to the Lakers for a center, Vlade Divac.

As the youngest player ever drafted by the NBA to that point, Bryant needed a period of adjustment. He spent most of the 1996–97 season as a reserve and averaged only 7.6 points a game, but he demonstrated his promise by winning the NBA Slam Dunk competition at midseason. The following year he emerged as a starter, showing so much poise and flair that he became the youngest person ever voted to be a starter in the league's All-Star game.

Bryant frequently clashed with the star center, Shaquille O'Neal, as each sought to emerge as the Lakers' leader. The arrival of Coach Phil Jackson in 1999 helped the two form a more cohesive relationship, which resulted in the Lakers' winning NBA titles in 2000, 2001, and 2002. Bryant, who finished fourth in the league in scoring in 2000, dominated several playoff games, including back-to-back scoring efforts of 48 and 45 points against Sacramento and San Antonio.

Indicted for rape, Bryant spent much of the 2003–2004 season engulfed in legal woes and a bitter feud with O'Neal. The Lakers' failure to win the title that year led to Coach Jackson's resignation and the trade of O'Neal to Miami, effectively ending their brief dynasty.

It was Bryant's success in making the leap from high school to the pros that accelerated the trend of top high school talents' opting to skip college and go directly to the NBA.

Further Reading

Lazenby, Roland. *Mad Game: The NBA Education of Kobe Bryant.* New York: McGraw-Hill, 1999.

Phelps, Shirelle. *Contemporary Black Biography.* Vol. 15. Detroit, Mich.: Gale Research, 1997.

Taylor, Phil. "Boy II Man," *Sports Illustrated,* April 24, 2000, pp. 43–45.

C

Calhoun, Lee Quency
(1933–1989) *track-and-field hurdler*

Although many great athletes have competed in the 110-meter high hurdles in the Olympics, Lee Calhoun is the only man who successfully defended his Olympic title in this event.

Lee Quency Calhoun was born on February 23, 1933, in rural Laurel, Mississippi, and raised on a farm. At the age of nine, he moved with his family to Gary, Indiana. He never thought of himself as a top athlete, even though he could outrun and outjump most boys his age. At Roosevelt High School, he declined to participate in track and field, believing that the coaches favored other athletes and would not accept him on the team. Instead, he spent his hours after school working. It was not until his junior year that a coach persuaded him join the team as a high jumper.

By his own admission, Calhoun was an unmotivated athlete. During his senior year, his coaches discovered that he had outstanding ability as a hurdler, yet Calhoun balked at running that event because it meant doing extra workouts. Pressured into hurdling, he qualified for the state meet in that event as well as the high jump. At state, the miserable weather bothered him so much that he failed to clear a single height in the high jump. He then hit the first five barriers in the hurdles finals but still managed to finished fifth.

That show of resilience impressed Dr. Leroy Walker, track coach at North Carolina Central University, who was the only person to offer him a track scholarship. Calhoun accepted and won the conference hurdles championship his first two years of school. In 1953, he joined the army and was stationed in Korea, where he organized an army track team that beat the Japanese national squad. Returning to college in 1955, he became the nation's number-two hurdler, second only to Jack Davis.

At the U.S. Olympic trials in 1956, Calhoun surprised experts by finishing in a tie with Davis. In the Olympic finals in Melbourne, Australia, he outleaned Davis at the tape to claim the gold medal. Running with more confidence, he won all major national meets in the remainder of 1956 and 1957. But in 1958, Calhoun lost his amateur standing for a year because he and his new wife appeared and won gifts on a television show. Although dumbfounded by the ruling, he continued to train during his year of suspension while attending graduate school.

By the time Calhoun resumed competition in 1959, a new hurdler appeared to leave him in the dust. In 1959, Hayes Jones beat Calhoun in every race they ran together, and he ranked as a heavy favorite to win the gold in the 1960 Olympics. But again, the Olympics tapped a hidden reserve of speed and determination in Calhoun. He beat

Jones in the Olympic trials and then, just before the Olympics in Rome, tied the world record by clocking 13.2 seconds. The Olympic finals were a virtual repeat of the 1956 race. Again, Calhoun ran neck and neck with his main rivals, teammates Jones and Willie May, all the way to the finish and then lunged just enough to gain a photo finish victory.

The 1960 Olympic games were his last as a competitor. He went on to coach college track at Grambling University, Yale University, and Western Illinois University. In 1976 he was an assistant coach of the U.S. Olympic team. Calhoun died on June 22, 1989, and the following year he was elected to the U.S. Olympic Hall of Fame.

Further Reading

Carlson, Lewis H., and John J. Fogerty. *Tales of Gold.* Chicago: Contemporary Books, 1987.

Page, James A. *Black Olympian Medalists.* Englewood, Colo.: Libraries Unlimited, 1991.

Campanella, Roy

(1921–1993) *baseball catcher*

Roy Campanella followed closely on the heels of JACKIE ROBINSON into major league baseball. Widely regarded as the National League's best catcher of the 1950s, he helped make the Brooklyn Dodgers perennial title contenders.

Campanella was born on November 19, 1921, in Homestead, Pennsylvania, to an Italian immigrant produce seller father and an African-American mother. When Roy was young, the family moved to North Philadelphia, where he developed into a baseball star at Simon Gratz High School. During his junior year, he filled in as catcher for a Negro League team one weekend. A coach at a rival school successfully campaigned to ban Campanella from high school ball, arguing that those games made him a "professional."

A disheartened Campanella dropped out of school and began catching with the all-black Baltimore Elites. Over the next nine seasons, Campanella played an exhausting schedule. He handled the demanding chores behind the plate for the Elites in the spring and summer and then moved on to Cuba, Puerto Rico, and Venezuela in the late fall, playing well over 200 games per year and, in one iron-man performance, catching two doubleheaders in one day.

In 1945, Branch Rickey tried to entice him to join the Brooklyn Brown Dodgers, as part of his plan to integrate major league baseball. Campanella turned down the offer but signed with the Dodgers in 1946, shortly after Robinson broke the color barrier. After spending more than two seasons in the minors, more to acclimate the baseball world to the growing black presence than as training for the already polished catcher, Campanella joined the Brooklyn club in June 1948. For the remainder of the season and into the following year, he shared catching duties with Bruce Edwards. In mid-1949, however, he began hitting so well that he took over the job permanently. He finished the season with a respectable .287 average and 22 home runs. In addition, he proved to be a deft handler of pitches and, despite his compact build, showed quickness and agility as a catcher.

Campanella continued his improvement in 1950. On August 30, he smacked three home runs in one game, and he finished the year with 31 round-trips. In 1951, the five-foot, nine-inch, 190-pound catcher pounded National League pitching for a .325 average, 33 home runs, and 108 runs batted in. Those numbers, combined with his defensive skill, earned him the league's Most Valuable Player (MVP) Award. After slumping slightly in 1952, Campanella returned to form in 1953 with a .312 average, as well as a career-high 41 homers and 142 runs batted in (both major league records for catchers), to claim a second MVP Award.

In the years that followed, Campanella battled painful and debilitating injuries, particularly a chipped bone on the heel of his hand. Sometimes the injuries got the best of him, as in 1954, when he hit only .207, and 1956, when he batted .219. But in between those disappointing seasons he was able to fight through the pain to hit .318 with 32 home runs to win his third MVP Award in five seasons.

His career ended abruptly on January 28, 1958, when his car skidded on an icy road and the resulting accident left him paralyzed. Campanella, who died in 1993, is remembered as one of the main cogs in a Dodger powerhouse team that won five National League pennants in eight years.

Further Reading

Chadwick, Bruce. *When the Game Was Black and White.* New York: Abbeville, 1992.

Fimrite, Ron. "Triumph of the Spirit," *Sports Illustrated,* September 14, 1990, pp. 94–100.

Peterson, Robert. *Only the Ball Was White.* New York: Gramercy, 1970.

Riley, James. *The Biographical Encyclopedia of the Negro Baseball Leagues.* New York: Carroll & Graf, 1994.

Campbell, Earl Christian

(1955–   ) *football running back*

One of the most punishing runners ever to play pro football, Earl Campbell overwhelmed National Football League (NFL) opponents at the start of his career as the centerpiece of the Houston Oilers' offense.

Earl Christian Campbell was born on March 25, 1955, in Tyler, Texas. The family had little money to begin with, and the situation grew even more desperate when his father, B. C. Campbell, died of a heart attack when Earl was 11. His mother, Ann, held the family of 11 children together with her unyielding will and the income from growing roses and working at domestic jobs.

Earl had no opportunity to play any organized sports until high school. Even then, Earl—the only one of the Campbell kids to give their mother trouble—frequently skipped classes as well as football practice. Not until his senior year, when he began playing running back in addition to linebacker, did he settle down and work at the sport. The effort paid off when he led Tyler High School to the state title, gained more than 2,000 yards rushing, and earned a statewide reputation as "The Tyler Rose."

Campbell then accepted a football scholarship to attend the University of Texas. He started as a freshman, grinding out 728 tough yards as fullback in the Longhorns' wishbone offense. He improved to 1,118 yards the following season before struggling through injuries his junior year. In 1977, a new coach installed a running offense designed to take advantage of Campbell's size and speed. Campbell responded with 1,744 yards rushing and 114 points, both of which led the nation, as he ran Texas to an undefeated regular season. His performance earned him the Heisman Trophy that year as the top college player in the land.

The Houston Oilers thought enough of Campbell to trade their tight end Jimmie Giles and three draft choices to Tampa Bay for the right to draft him. As had Texas, the Oilers built their offense around the burly 5-foot, 11-inch, 234-pound power back. In 1978, he gained 1,450 yards to become the first rookie since JIM BROWN to win the NFL rushing title. The highlight of the year was a four-touchdown performance on *Monday Night Football* against Miami. Brown was suitably impressed by the newcomer, commenting, "Earl was frightening. He'd come running through about two inches off the ground with those gargantuan thighs and that Mount Rushmore head."

Campbell repeated as rushing leader in 1979 with 1,697 yards and also led the league with 19 touchdowns. He reached the zenith of his career the following year when he gained more than 200 yards in four different games and easily captured his third straight rushing title with a career-best 1,934 yards.

The Oilers' inability to get past the powerful Pittsburgh Steelers in the playoffs, however, led to a change of coaches, and the new regime deemphasized Campbell's central role in the offense. Furthermore, as Campbell's ex-coach, Bum Phillips, observed, "He's got no regard for his body or anyone else's." The countless high-speed collisions took their toll, and, after Campbell reached 10th place on the NFL's all-time rushing list after just four seasons, his effectiveness diminished steadily. Campbell was traded to New Orleans in 1984 and retired after the 1985 season. He was voted into pro football's Hall of Fame in 1991.

Further Reading

Harrington, Denis J. *The Pro Football Hall of Fame.* Jefferson, N.C.: McFarland, 1991.

Moritz, Charles, ed. *Current Biography, 1983.* New York: H. W. Wilson, 1983.

Newman, B. "Roots of Greatness," *Sports Illustrated,* September 3, 1979, pp. 20–21.

Campbell, Milt

(Milton Gray Campbell)
(1934–   ) *track-and-field decathlete*

Milt Campbell was the first African-American star in the decathlon, the 10-event track-and-field competition that measures all-around athletic skill.

He was born Milton Gray Campbell on December 9, 1934, in Plainfield, New Jersey, where he gained a national reputation as an all-around athlete. As a high school football player, he scored 140 points in nine games, and he set a pool record for the 40-yard freestyle in swimming. He was unbeatable in sprints and hurdles, and on one occasion, filling in for his school's heavyweight wrestler, he scored a first-round pin over the eventual state champion.

In 1952, Campbell's track coach came across a newspaper article comparing the performance of the defending Olympic decathlon champion Bob Matthias with that of the legendary Jim Thorpe. He was convinced that Campbell could do better than either. Thanks to a generous gift of $1,500 raised by community members, Campbell traveled to the West Coast to compete in the United States Olympic decathlon trials that spring. Despite virtually no experience in events such as the pole vault, discus, javelin, and 1,500-meter run, the 18-year-old Campbell stunned veteran observers by finishing second to qualify for the team. At the Helsinki Olympics that year, the decathlon neophyte pulled an ever larger upset, overcoming a shoulder injury suffered in the pole vault to finish second to Matthias and capture the silver medal.

Campbell appeared to have limitless potential in the event until he fell victim to a series of injuries, including bursitis in his elbow that prevented him from competing in 1954 and a severe muscle pull that limited his training and competition the following year. As the 1956 Olympics approached, Campbell, who was attending Indiana University after a stint in the navy, decided to concentrate his efforts on the 110-meter high hurdles. Meanwhile, a new U.S. decathlon sensation, RAFER LEWIS JOHNSON, appeared on the scene and dominated the competition.

Campbell, however, finished fourth at the U.S. team trials in the hurdles and failed to make the team in that event. "I was stunned," he said, "but then God seemed to reach into my heart and tell me he didn't want me to compete in the hurdles, but in the decathlon."

Campbell qualified for the team in the decathlon but appeared to be far behind Johnson going into the 1956 Melbourne Olympics. In the first day of the two-day competition, however, Campbell roared off to a solid lead over an injury-hobbled Johnson, with superlative efforts in the long jump, shot put, and 400-meter run. After blazing over the hurdles in a world-class time of 14.0 seconds and hurling the discus nearly 15 feet past his mark at Helsinki, Campbell was well on the way to a world record. A bad pole vault performance left him short of the new mark, but he did top Matthias's Olympic record in beating Johnson for the gold medal.

Campbell was drafted by the Cleveland Browns football team the following year but failed to make the team. Before retiring from active competition, however, he proved his skill as a hurdler by posting a world record time of 13.4 in the 110-meter high hurdles. Since then he has been involved in an inner city school, community center, and motivational company.

Further Reading

Henderson, Edwin B. *The Black Athlete: Emergence and Arrival.* New York: Publishers Company, 1968.

Nelson, Cordner. *Track's Greatest Champions.* Los Altos, Calif.: Tafnews Press, 1986.

Williams, Charlie. "The Williams Eye View." Available online. URL: www.blackathlete.com/trackf/527.htm. Downloaded January 18, 2002.

Carew, Rod
(Rodney Cline Carew)
(1945–) *baseball infielder*

Rod Carew wielded a bat with such precision that it resembled a wand in the hands of a master magician. Far and away the best hitter of his era, he won seven batting titles during his career, often by some of the largest margins in baseball history.

He was born Rodney Cline Carew on October 1, 1945, on a moving train in the Canal Zone of Panama. Fortunately for Olga Carew, a physician, Rodney Cline, was on board, as well as Margaret Allen, a nurse from New York City. In thanks for their help delivering her son, Olga named her son Rodney Cline Carew and asked Allen to be his godmother.

Rod enjoyed playing many sports, including soccer, volleyball, and basketball, but his favorite was baseball. He listened on radio to major league games from the United States and frequently held his own batting practice, using a broomstick as a bat and wad of taped rags as a ball. He became so proficient at the game that as a 13-year-old, he played on teams with high school boys.

Margaret Allen kept in touch with the Carews and urged them to move to New York to improve their lives. In 1962, Olga followed her advice and moved her family, including 16-year-old Rod, to Harlem, where she found work in a factory. Rod had difficulty adjusting to his new life; he spoke little English and found little in common with schoolmates. Instead of playing sports, he had to work afternoons at a grocery store to make money for the family.

Carew, however, found out about a tryout for the Cavaliers, a local sandlot baseball team that played near Yankee Stadium. Not only did he make the team, but he played so well that he attracted the attention of a Minnesota Twins talent scout. When the Twins were in town for a series with the Yankees, the scout arranged for Carew to audition for them at Yankee Stadium. After a few minutes of watching Carew spray pitched balls around the stadium, the Twins manager, Sam Mele, shouted, "Get that kid out of here before somebody else sees him!" Minnesota signed Carew to a contract shortly thereafter.

Carew spent two and a half years in the minor leagues before the Twins called him up for the 1967 season. Moody and overly sensitive, the rookie had trouble fitting in on a veteran Twins ball club that was only a year removed from a World Series appearance. Nonetheless, he won a starting job at second base and batted .292, which earned him American League Rookie of the Year honors. Carew fell victim to a mild sophomore slump the following season. But in 1969, he righted himself both in his relations with teammates and as a student of batting. He raised his average to .332, best in the American League. This was the first of 15 consecutive seasons in which he would surpass the prestigious .300 mark. Most remarkable, though, was his audacious performance as a base runner. Few major league players have ever stolen home base even once in their career. Carew tied a major league record by stealing home seven times that season, succeeding on all seven attempts. On May 18, he pulled off the rare feat of stealing second, third, and home in the same inning.

Carew was well on his way to defending his batting title in 1970 with a .366 average after 51 games, when an injury shelved him for the duration of the season. Eventually, in the mid-1970s, the Twins switched him to first base, a less demanding position, to protect him from further injuries.

In 1972, American League batters suffered an off year, which allowed Carew to take his second batting crown with a modest .318 mark. Strictly a slap hitter, he was the first person to win a batting title without hitting a home run. During the next three seasons, Carew retained his title with authority, as he strung together consecutive seasons of .350, .364, and .359, all comfortably ahead of his nearest rivals. He came within an eyelash of adding a fifth straight crown in 1976 when he lost out to George Brett on the final day of the season.

Carew reached the peak of his batting artistry in 1977. For most of the season he flirted with a .400 batting average, a mark widely thought to be unreachable in the modern era. Although he fell just short of immortality, he posted a whopping .388 average with 239 hits, the most by a major league player in half a century. Carew's average was 50 points ahead of that of his nearest rival, the National League champion Dave Parker, the second largest margin in baseball history. Despite playing for a mediocre team, Carew led the league with 128 runs. Showing that he had expanded his repertoire to more than singles, he led the league in triples and also slammed 14 home runs. With his 69 bases on balls added in, Carew reached base nearly half the times he was at bat.

Baseball analysts cited Carew's deft bat control and keen batting eye as the keys to his success. Hailed as baseball's top bunter, he often wowed spectators by dropping bunts precisely onto handkerchiefs placed on the infield. With strong wrists for a man of medium build, he could wait until the last possible instant to judge the location and speed of a pitch before swinging, and

Rod Carew, the American League's best pure hitter of the late 20th century, compiled a lifetime batting average of .328. *(National Baseball Hall of Fame Library, Cooperstown, N.Y.)*

he seldom chased a pitch out of the strike zone. No one was better than Carew at studying pitchers; he often adjusted his batting stance to match the style of the pitcher facing him.

Carew's glory days in Minnesota were marred in the late 1970s by careless racial remarks uttered by the team owner Calvin Griffith and by death threats prompted by Carew's marriage to Marilyn Levy, a white Jewish woman. After the 1978 season, Carew forced a trade to the California Angels, who could afford to pay him more than the small-market Twins.

After years of playing for losing teams in Minnesota, Carew led the Angels to their first divisional title while capturing his seventh American League batting title. After finishing his career with a sparkling .328 lifetime average, he remained in baseball as a widely respected batting coach. Carew, who was named to 18 consecutive All-Star teams, was inducted into the Baseball Hall of Fame in 1991.

Further Reading

Carew, Rod, with Ira Berkow. *Carew.* New York: Simon & Schuster, 1979.

Fimrite, R. "Hitters of Singular Skills," *Sports Illustrated,* July 1, 1974, pp. 14–17.

Moritz, Charles, ed. *Current Biography, 1978.* New York: H. W. Wilson, 1978.

Carter, Cris

(Cristopher Carter)
(1965–   ) *football wide receiver*

Cris Carter rode a turbulent career in which he went from drug addict to perennial All-Pro football player. Known for his spectacular one-handed catches, Carter ranks second only to JERRY LEE RICE in career passes and touchdown passes caught.

Carter was born on November 25, 1965, in Troy, Ohio. His was an athletic family; his older brother, Butch, went on to enjoy a respectable career in the National Basketball Association (NBA). Cris displayed similar athleticism as he scored more than 1,600 points in his high school basketball career at Middletown High School, in addition to being an All-American football player. Heavily recruited by major universities, he chose to stay close to home by attending Ohio State University. As a college freshman, he drew national attention by gaining 172 yards on pass receptions in the Rose Bowl. Carter finished his career as Ohio State's all-time leader in pass receptions.

The Philadelphia Eagles drafted him in the fourth round of a special supplementary draft in 1987. In addition to his laserlike focus, exceptional eye-hand coordination, and superior athletic skills,

the six-foot three-inch, 210-pound Carter had the size and strength to break tackles and drag defenders into the end zone. Yet after three solid seasons in Philadelphia, including a 1989 campaign in which he finished third in the National Football League (NFL) with 11 touchdown catches, the Eagles abruptly released him. Although the Philadelphia coaches kept the matter confidential, the move was precipitated by Carter's failing three drug tests. Carter now admits that he had a serious substance abuse problem.

During his battle with addiction, Carter developed a deep Christian faith that helped stabilize his life. When the Minnesota Vikings decided to take a chance on him in 1990, he was well on the way toward recovery. Carter enjoyed several respectable but unspectacular seasons in Minnesota, leading the club in receptions in 1991 and 1992. Fueled by a passionate drive to be the best, he asked the Vikings running back Roger Craig, a former teammate of the peerless wide receiver Jerry Rice, how Rice went about his craft. Craig informed him of Rice's grueling off-season preparation. Carter, who had never worked out much before, dedicated himself to an off-season regimen of up to six hours per day of workouts.

The effort paid off as Carter transformed himself from a good receiver to an All-Pro. In 1993, he caught 86 passes for 1,071 yards. The following year he broke Sterling Sharpe's record of 112 pass receptions in a season, snaring 122 passes for a team record 1,286 yards. Continuing his assault on the record books, Carter matched his pass reception total of 122 in 1995, producing the highest two-year total in NFL history. At the same time, he displayed a penchant for making the crucial catches, grabbing 17 touchdown passes to shatter the club record of 11 that had stood for 34 years. In addition to catching more passes and touchdown passes than any rival from 1994 to 2001, Carter established himself as the Vikings' team leader. He was given credit for mentoring volatile young star Randy Moss, and he earned the NFL Man of the Year Award for community service in 1999. Brian Billick, coach of the Super Bowl champion Baltimore Ravens, paid tribute to Carter's competitiveness: "On Sundays, I'll take Cris over any player at any position." Carter retired after the 2001 season but came out of retirement to play five games with the Miami Dolphins in 2002.

Further Reading

Bernstein, Ross. *Fifty Years, Fifty Heroes.* Hopkins, Minn.: Self-published, 1997.

Chadiha, Jeff. "Time Trial," *Sports Illustrated,* July 3, 2000, pp. 60–63.

Phelps, Shirelle. *Contemporary Black Biography.* Vol. 21. Detroit, Mich.: Gale Research, 1999.

Carter, Vince

(Vincent Lamar Carter, Jr.)
(1977–) *basketball forward*

Vince Carter has emerged as the National Basketball Association's (NBA's) most creative and exciting slam dunker and the man the other NBA stars love to watch.

Carter was born January 26, 1977, in Daytona Beach, Florida, to Michele and Vince Carter, Sr. His childhood was marred by his parents' bitter divorce, and from the age of seven he was raised almost exclusively by his mother. She eventually married a school band leader, and Carter, who was so naturally athletic that he could dribble a basketball as a two-year-old, began to concentrate more on music than on sports. He played saxophone, wrote songs for the marching band at Mainland High School in Daytona Beach, and was offered a scholarship to Bethune-Cookman College as a drum major. But Carter was also the school's quarterback and star basketball player, and he opted instead to play basketball at the University of North Carolina (UNC).

Carter showed only intermittent signs of brilliance at North Carolina while sacrificing personal statistics in favor of a balanced team concept.

His final year, the six-foot, seven-inch forward posted modest averages of 15.6 points and five rebounds. Like the famous Tarheel alumnus MICHAEL JORDAN, he bolted college for the pros after his junior year.

On draft day, Carter was upstaged by his teammate Antawn Jamison, who had also overshadowed him at UNC. The Golden State Warriors selected Carter in the 11th choice of the 1998 draft and then swapped him plus cash to the Toronto Raptors, who had chosen Jamison with their fourth pick. Carter made an immediate impact on his new team, averaging a solid 18.3 points. But what really turned heads were his explosive slam dunks. Carter, who began dunking in the seventh grade and has never lost a slam dunk competition, put on a spectacular show to win the slam dunk exhibition at the All-Star Game that season. Before long, teammates and opponents made a point of catching the latest Carter windmill slam on the television sports highlights each night.

By the 1999–2000 season, sports publications were raving about Carter, whom they dubbed Air Canada and the successor to Jordan. Carter lifted his scoring average to 25.7 that year and received the second highest number of All-Star votes in NBA history. Despite his furious slams, he remained a dedicated team player who quietly performed whatever role was required of him. Stung when Jordan publicly criticized his defense, he focused on making himself a complete player.

Carter's improvement was evident at the 2000 Olympics in Sydney, Australia. Playing with such uncharacteristic intensity that he embarrassed even his friends with his posturing, he nonetheless carried an otherwise uninspired U.S. team to the gold medal. In 2000–01, he boosted his scoring average to 27.6, leading the Raptors into the play-offs. On the eve of the deciding seventh game against Philadelphia, he ran headfirst into controversy. Fulfilling a promise to his mother, he had completed his college courses in the off-seasons. Ignoring the criticism of sports commentators, he flew to North Carolina for his graduation ceremony and then returned to Philadelphia in time for the game. Although he played well, his buzzer-beating shot glanced off the rim, sending Toronto to defeat and generating a huge debate on societal priorities.

Further Reading

Farber, Michael. "Raptor Rapture," *Sports Illustrated,* April 19, 1999, pp. 54–55.

Price, S. L. "Semi Tough," *Sports Illustrated,* January 29, 2001, pp. 66–76.

Chamberlain, Wilt

(Wilton Norman Chamberlain, "Wilt the Stilt," "The Big Dipper")
(1936–1999) *basketball center*

An imposing seven-footer with a powerful build, Wilt Chamberlain demonstrated that a person of incredible size could be fast and athletic. In terms of raw physical gifts, Chamberlain towered over contemporary athletes to the point of making a shambles of all previous basketball scoring records.

Wilton Norman Chamberlain was born on August 21, 1936, in Philadelphia, Pennsylvania. His parents, William and Olivia Chamberlain, provided a stable upbringing in West Philadelphia for their nine children, working as a porter for Curtis Publishing and as a domestic, respectively.

Wilt began playing basketball at Shoemaker Junior High School and the Haddington Recreation Center. Like many boys in his neighborhood, he dreamed of someday joining the Harlem Globetrotters, an all-black barnstorming team that provided the only opportunity for African-American players in the era of the segregated National Basketball Association (NBA). Already an outstanding athlete, he took off on a frightening growth spurt that further enhanced his chance of success in sports. Although neither parent stood over five feet, nine inches, Wilt grew four inches the summer of his 14th year and kept climbing.

By the time he entered Overbrook High School, he was nearly 6 feet, 11 inches.

Chamberlain made his size work for him, scoring more than 2,000 points in three seasons, including one 90-point game. Far from the stereotypical gawky giant, he was fast and well-coordinated in addition to being strong. He was a champion shot putter at Overbrook, and he excelled at the 440-yard dash and high jump as well.

Of the more than 200 schools that offered him scholarships, Chamberlain chose the University of Kansas in 1955, planning to major in accounting. In his first college game as a sophomore (National Collegiate Athletic Association [NCAA] rules barred freshmen from playing varsity) he scored 52 points. That season he led his team to the finals of the NCAA tournament, in which Kansas lost by a point to North Carolina. Frustrated by the triple-teaming tactics of opponents during his junior year, which he felt were stifling his development as a player, he left school in 1958 to join his boyhood heroes, the Globetrotters.

After one season touring with the team, he returned to his hometown to play for the Philadelphia Warriors of the NBA. The rookie's impact on the league was unprecedented. Despite playing for a mediocre team, Chamberlain could score virtually at will. He led the league in scoring with an average of 37.6 points per game, more than 8 points better than the previous NBA record, and he easily topped the league in rebounds as well. Brash and outspoken from the beginning, Chamberlain charged that referees were turning a blind eye to the battering he was taking from opponents. In March 1960, he announced that he was quitting the NBA for fear that if he continued to suffer abuse he would have to fight back and he was afraid he would hurt someone.

"The Big Dipper," as he liked to be called, changed his mind over the summer and rejoined Philadelphia. In an overtime loss to Boston on November 24, 1960, he set a record that has never been challenged—55 rebounds in a game, which he accomplished playing against the legendary center BILL RUSSELL. Asked how he felt about facing Chamberlain, Russell replied, "He's four or five inches taller. He's 40 or 50 pounds heavier. His vertical leap is at least as good as mine. He can go up and down the floor as well as I can. And he's smart. The real problem with this is that I have to show up."

So dominant was Chamberlain that NBA officials tinkered with the rules to limit the damage he could do. The three-second lane was widened from 12 to 16 feet to keep him farther away from the basket. Chamberlain's patented technique of leaping up and guiding a teammate's shot into the hoop was outlawed as "offensive goal-tending," and tip-ins of balls rolling on the rim were disallowed as well.

The changes had no effect whatsoever on Chamberlain's dominance. Relying on his graceful fadeaway jump shot, he made a farce of existing NBA scoring records in 1961–62. The crowning achievement occurred on March 2, 1962, in a game against the New York Knicks, at Hershey, Pennsylvania. In a wild 169–147 romp, Chamberlain poured in 36 baskets in 63 attempts, and he sank 28 of 32 free throws to total 100 points. Few NBA players have ever scored as much as 50 points in a game; Chamberlain finished the season with an *average* of 50.4, a mark that has never been challenged. Nearly as impressive was his durability. Chamberlain stayed on the court virtually the entire season without rest, never fouling out, to average an NBA record 48.5 minutes per game.

Before the 1963 season, Chamberlain moved with the Warriors to San Francisco, where he continued to overwhelm opposing centers. In 1965, he returned to Philadelphia via a trade to play with the 76ers, and he ran his string of consecutive NBA scoring titles to seven. Yet Chamberlain felt the sting of criticism that he achieved individual glory but could not lead his team to a championship. He was constantly compared to Boston's Russell, whose Celtics won 11 NBA titles in his 13 seasons. Much of Russell's comparative success was due to his superior supporting cast; nonethe-

Wilt Chamberlain established records for National Basketball Association (NBA) scoring and rebounding that have never been approached. *(Library of Congress, Prints & Photographs Division, NYWT&S Collection [LC-USZ62-115428])*

less Chamberlain's relative lack of leadership skills prevented the success and recognition proportionate to his talent. Throughout his later career, Chamberlain appeared obsessed with this criticism. He intentionally reduced his role on offense to concentrate on rebounding, defense, and passing and as a result won no more scoring titles. His efforts at teamwork paid off somewhat. In 1967, his Philadelphia 76ers won 45 of their first 49 games and went on to dethrone the Celtics for the championship, and in 1972, Chamberlain's Los Angeles Lakers notched a league record 33 straight wins in rolling to their NBA title.

He retired from basketball in 1974, but he kept his phenomenal physical gifts on display by starring in a pro volleyball league that he helped organize and in action motion pictures such as *Conan the Barbarian*. During his NBA career, Chamberlain set 72 records, led the NBA in rebounding 11 times, posted the four highest single-season scoring marks in history, and won four NBA Most Valuable Player Awards. He died of a heart attack on October 12, 1999.

Further Reading

Chamberlain, Wilt. *A View from Above*. New York: Villard Books, 1991.

Chamberlain, Wilt, with Bill Libby. *Goliath: The Wilt Chamberlain Story*. New York: Dodd, Mead, 1977.

Chamberlain, Wilt, and David Shaw. *Wilt: Just Like Any Other 7-Foot Black Millionaire Who Lives Next Door*. New York: Macmillan, 1973.

Charleston, Oscar McKinley

(1896–1954) *baseball outfielder*

Oscar Charleston played baseball in such obscurity that even baseball fans who were aware of the Negro Leagues knew little or nothing about him. But many of those who saw him play agree with the Hall of Fame umpire Jocko Conlon, who once called Charleston "the great Negro player of that time."

Oscar McKinley Charleston was born in Indianapolis, Indiana, on October 14, 1896, the seventh of 11 children of a construction worker and his wife. Charleston grew up with baseball from the earliest days of Negro League competition, serving as batboy for the Indianapolis ABCs. At the age of 15, he left home and joined the army. While stationed in the Philippines, he found an outlet for his exceptional athletic ability by running track and playing as the only black baseball player in the Manila League.

After returning home in 1915, he signed up to pitch and play outfield for the local ABCs. In many ways, Charleston resembled a young pitcher-slugger just beginning his major league career— Babe Ruth. As did Ruth, the six-foot, 190-pound

Oscar Charleston was widely regarded as the finest all-around player of his era in the Negro Leagues. *(National Baseball Hall of Fame Library, Cooperstown, N.Y.)*

Charleston batted left-handed and generated tremendous power from a barrel chest that balanced precariously over his spindly legs. And as Ruth had, he quickly became a larger-than-life figure through his colorful style, tendency to show off, and rowdy, fearless disposition. He had barely begun playing for Indianapolis when he was arrested for assaulting an umpire and causing a riot at the ballpark. That ornery, combative streak stayed with him through most of his career. Charleston was more than willing to mix it up with all comers, both off the field and on. He once ripped the hood off a Florida member of the Ku Klux Klan, and he brawled with Cuban soldiers while playing winter ball in that country. Despite such incidents, however, contemporaries found him pleasant and good-natured most of the time. He was particularly protective of young players and was idolized by youths wherever he went.

On the field, he displayed a rare combination of speed, power, and grace. Charleston could hit for a high average, he could smash the long ball, and he could run, as he showed when leading the league during a 60-game season in 1921 in batting average (.434), home runs (15), doubles (14), triples (11), and stolen bases. At the same time, he ranked as one of the premier defensive center fielders of his time, and he had a powerful throwing arm, a deft touch as a bunter, and a knack for coming through in crucial situations.

As many Negro League stars did, Charleston migrated from team to team, depending on who could pay him. He played on 14 different teams, including the Pittsburgh Crawfords of 1935, widely considered the best of the Negro League teams. Throughout his career, he averaged .357 and clouted 151 home runs in documented games. Few players can match Charleston's longevity, as he continued to play until 1941 as a player-manager. He remained active in baseball as a manager until 1950, and he helped Branch Rickey scout black ball players in preparation for his integration of the Brooklyn Dodgers. He succumbed to a heart attack on October 6, 1954.

Further Reading

Chadwick, Bruce. *When the Game Was Black and White.* New York: Abbeville, 1992.

Clark, Dick, and Lerry Lester, eds. *The Negro League Book.* Cleveland, Ohio: Society for American Baseball Research, 1994.

Pepe, Phil. *Talkin Baseball.* New York: Ballantine, 1998.

Peterson, Robert. *Only the Ball Was White.* New York: Gramercy, 1970.

Riley, James. *The Biographical Encyclopedia of the Negro Baseball Leagues.* New York: Carroll & Graf, 1994.

Coachman, Alice
(1923–) *track-and-field jumper and sprinter*

"I've always believed that I could do whatever I set my mind to," Alice Coachman has said. That attitude led her to an unprecedented reign as the nation's top female track-and-field athlete in the 1940s. Coachman captured 25 national titles and held an iron grip on the Amateur Athletic Union (AAU) high jump, winning the event 12 consecutive years.

Coachman was born on November 11, 1923, in Albany, Georgia, to Fred and Evelyn Coachman. While attending the Monroe Street Elementary School, she discovered that "I was good at three things: running, jumping, and fighting." Her propensity for rough play worried her parents, but a fifth-grade teacher recognized her athletic potential and encouraged her to develop it. With no facilities available to her, she practiced running on dirt roads, and by the time she reached Madison High School, she was competing at the national level. In 1939, at the age of 16, she won her first national AAU high jump crown with a jump of five feet, two inches.

Her success attracted the attention of the Tuskegee Institute, a prestigious black high school, which accepted her in 1940. While continuing her amazing streak of national high jump titles, Coachman starred as an all-conference guard for Tuskegee's basketball team, which won three straight conference championships. She also proved her sprinting ability by winning the 1943 AAU national title in the 50-yard dash.

During her six years at Tuskegee, the Olympics had been shut down by the ravages of World War II, thus denying her a proper forum in which to display her skills. Although she often questioned the value of working so hard for so little tangible gain, she kept competing in track and field while pursuing her education and a career. After graduating with a degree in dressmaking from Tuskegee in 1946, she enrolled at Albany State College to study economics.

In 1948, Coachman captured her 12th consecutive AAU national high jump title. Age and injuries had taken a toll by that time, and Coachman felt ready to retire. U.S. track officials, however, begged her to participate in the Olympic Games, which had just resumed that year, and Coachman decided she could not let her country down.

When she arrived in London, Coachman was stunned to see how famous she was: pictures of her seemed to be everywhere. In the high jump finals, she lived up to her advance billing, fighting off back and hip injuries to capture first place with a jump of 5 feet, 6 ⅛ inches. Her gold medal was the first won by an African-American woman and the only one claimed by the U.S. women's team that year.

Coachman was rewarded with an endorsement contract from a soft drink company. Although it did not make her rich, it gave her another distinction—the first African-American woman ever paid to endorse a product. Coachman completed her college degree in 1949 and traded in her track shoes for a career teaching physical education.

Further Reading

Ashe, Arthur., Jr. *A Hard Road to Glory: A History of the African-American Athlete, 1919–45.* New York: Warner Books, 1988.

Smith, Jessie Carney, ed. *Notable Black American Women*, Book II. Detroit: Gale Research, 1996.

Cooper, Cynthia
(1963–   ) *basketball player*

Virtually unknown in the United States after more than a decade of playing in European leagues, Cynthia Cooper leapfrogged over her younger and more famous counterparts to emerge as the star of the fledgling Women's National Basketball Association (WNBA).

Cooper was born on April 14, 1963, in Chicago, Illinois, to a single mother, Mary Cobbs, and spent her childhood in a tough neighborhood in the Watts section of Los Angeles. In junior high, she appeared to find her niche as an exceptional track athlete. While walking through a gymnasium, however, she happened to see a girls' high school basketball game. One of the players raced downcourt, avoided a defender by dribbling behind her back, and laid the ball in the basket. Cooper was so taken with her graceful athleticism that she began paying more attention to the sport.

Her junior high had no girls' basketball team, however, so it was not until high school that she was able to participate. By that time Cooper was well established in other sports. She won the city championship in the 300-meter hurdles and also played volleyball, softball, and tennis. Yet she focused on learning basketball, and her crash apprenticeship in the game yielded remarkable results. After averaging 8 points a game in her junior year, Cooper exploded for 45 points per game as a senior.

Suddenly the target of college recruiters, she chose to stay in the neighborhood and attend the University of Southern California (USC). Cooper cracked into the starting lineup as a freshman but was overshadowed during her college career by more famous teammates such as CHERYL DEANNE MILLER and Pam and Paula McGee. During her sophomore and junior seasons (1982–83 and 1983–84), Cooper played a supporting role, averaging fewer than 10 points per game as the powerful USC team won the National Collegiate Athletic Association (NCAA) championship.

Her world temporarily collapsed in 1984 when her brother was stabbed to death and she quit school. Cooper's coach talked her into returning the following year, and she averaged 17.2 points and made All-Conference as USC made it to the finals of the NCAA tournament.

Despite her team's success, Cooper felt limited by the supporting roles she was asked to assume. She wanted to try pro basketball and discover her true potential. Since the only money to be made in women's basketball was overseas, she signed on with a Spanish team and immediately made an impact by winning the Most Valuable Player Award in her league's All-Star Game.

Unlike many U.S. players, Cooper enjoyed her European experience. She played for Segovia, Spain, from 1987 to 1994; Alcoma, Sicily, from 1994 to 1996; and Parma, Spain, from 1996 to 1997. During her 11 years in Europe, she led the league in scoring eight times. She also took time out to play for the United States in Olympic competition. In 1988, her 14.2 scoring average ranked third on the gold-medal-winning team. But four years later, she contributed little to the U.S. team as a seldom-used reserve, and she did not participate in the 1996 Games.

As a result of her long absence from the American basketball scene, few U.S. fans knew anything about her as the WNBA prepared for its inaugural season in 1998. The WNBA organizers knew enough about Cooper to include her among the top 16 players whom they evenly dispersed among the league's teams. But even they expected Cooper to play second fiddle to SHERYL SWOOPES on their assigned team, the Houston Comets.

Swoopes, however, became pregnant and retreated to the sidelines. Meanwhile, Cooper made the most of her long-awaited chance to play in front of U.S. audiences. Showing confidence and aggressive offensive moves honed in years of demanding European play, the 5-foot, 10-inch, guard was virtually unstoppable. If opponents tried to stop her ferocious drives to the basket, she pulled up and shot baskets from behind the three-point line. Fouling her was not an option because she made nearly 87 percent of her free throws. At the age of 34, Cooper led the league in scoring with a 22.2 average that included a league record 44-point outburst against Phoenix.

Cooper not only carried the major scoring load for Houston, but also ran the offense and guarded the opposition's top backcourt player. She finished sixth in the Women's National Basketball Association (WNBA) in steals and fifth in assists and easily claimed the league's Most Valuable Player (MVP) Award. She capped off her sensational season by scoring 25 points and earning MVP honors in Houston's win over the New York Liberty in the championship. "I'm living a dream," she said after the victory. "I never thought I would ever play basketball at the level I am playing at. Don't wake me up."

The dream continued as Cooper led the league in scoring the next three seasons as well and repeated as the league's Most Valuable Player in 1998. Houston continued its stranglehold on the league's championship. In 1998, despite storming through the season with a 27–3 record, Houston was on the verge of elimination in the play-offs when Cooper led a furious comeback that carried the Comets to its second title. Houston then successfully defended its championship in 1999 and 2000. In each contest, Cooper won the MVP Award, drawing comparisons with her National Basketball Association (NBA) counterpart, MICHAEL JORDAN. After retiring in 2000, she went on to coach the Detroit Shock of the WNBA.

Cooper was recognized for her off-court contributions to society as well. Such activities as serving as legal guardian for eight children prompted Ms. magazine to name her one of the Women of the Year in 1998 "for being a champion on and off the court."

Further Reading

Howard, J. "Comets Tale," *Sports Illustrated*, August 25, 1997, pp. 34–35.

Howerton, D. "Cynthia Cooper," *Sport*, January 1999, p. 43.

Schick, Elizabeth A., ed. *Current Biography, 1998.* New York: H. W. Wilson, 1998.

D

Davis, Ernie
(Ernest Davis)
(1939–1963) *football running back*

Ernie Davis never played a single down in the National Football League (NFL). Yet he was inducted into the Hall of Fame as a running back—a tribute to both his unfulfilled potential and his inspirational character.

Davis was born on December 14, 1939, in New Salem, Pennsylvania. In the first of the tragedies that were Ernie's lot in life, his father was killed in an accident before Ernie was born. When he was 14 months old, his mother left him with her parents who raised him in the west Pennsylvania coal town of West Union while she sought employment. Davis grew up with the dream of emulating Pennsylvania coal country heroes such as Johnny Lujack and Stan Musial who made good in pro sports.

At the age of 12, Davis was reunited with his mother when they moved to Elmira, New York. Ernie became a four-sport wonder at Elmira Free Academy High School, earning 11 letters. Basketball appeared to be his best sport. Davis was the leading scorer on a team that won 52 consecutive games over his final two seasons. However, football was his first love, and so he turned down a basketball scholarship for a chance to play at Syracuse University, the school where JIM BROWN, a fellow

African American who happened to be the greatest runner in football, had just paved the way.

While at Syracuse, Davis broke most of Brown's school records. In his sophomore year, Davis provided the team's main offensive threat as the team was undefeated during the 1959 regular season. He then scored 16 points as Syracuse beat Texas 23–14 in the Cotton Bowl to finish the year as the top-rated team in the nation. Davis finished his career with 35 touchdowns and an average of 6.6 yards per carry. He capped his senior year by becoming the first black athlete to win the Heisman Trophy, awarded to the top college player.

Life seemed almost too good to be true when Davis learned that the Cleveland Browns had selected him as the first overall choice in the 1962 draft. That would unite him with Jim Brown in what promised to be the finest backfield duo in NFL history. But in July 1962, just as the Browns were beginning training camp, Davis fell ill and was diagnosed with leukemia.

Widely admired for his positive demeanor and the seriousness with which he took on the responsibility of a role model for younger children, Davis battled the disease for nearly a year before he succumbed on May 18, 1963. He remained such an inspiration to those around him that his junior high school was renamed after him; the Browns retired his uniform number, 45; and in 1987 he was voted into the NFL Hall of Fame.

Further Reading

Gallagher, Robert. *Ernie Davis: The Elmira Express.* Silver Spring, Md.: Bartleby Press, 1999.

Great Athletes of the Twentieth Century. Vol. 4. Pasadena, Calif.: Salem Press, 1994.

Davis, John
(John Henry Davis, Jr.)
(1921–1984) *weightlifter*

Although his exploits were barely mentioned in the U.S. press, John Davis achieved international fame as a weightlifter who reigned unchallenged for 15 years as the world's strongest man.

John Henry Davis, Jr., was born on January 12, 1921, in Smithtown, New York. Small and thin as a child, he became obsessed with the concept of strength. Working alone at various exercises, he built himself up until he could perform amazing feats. As a young teen, accepting a dare, he lifted a 125-pound brick over his head. An amateur weightlifter who happened to see this was so astounded that he befriended the youngster and gave him access to his weightlifting room in his home. Before long, Davis was lifting far more than his weight.

Davis used his strength to excel at other sports in high school, particularly football and the throwing events in track and field. But he remained fascinated with weightlifting and, supported by generous financial backers, began entering competitions. At the age of 17 he made the U.S. weightlifting team as an alternate to the 1938 world championships in Vienna, Austria. When a U.S. light heavyweight competitor dropped out because of an injury, Davis went on a crash diet to lose 13 pounds to get down to the 181-pound weight limit. Despite being weak from the diet, he won the championship.

Davis remained undefeated in weightlifting competition for 15 years. The five-foot, nine-inch, Davis retained his light heavyweight title until 1941, when he moved up to heavyweight and won

that title. After his career was interrupted by four years of World War II military service, Davis returned to competition in 1945 and picked up where he had left off. He easily captured the heavyweight gold medal at the 1948 Olympics by a 27.5-pound margin over a fellow American, Norbert Schemansky.

Two years later, he faced the most serious challenge of his career in the form of a massive Russian named Jakov Kutsenko. Kutsenko arrived at the world championships that year amid rumors that he could lift a total of 1,019 pounds, far more than any human had ever lifted before. At the competition, Davis proved himself a true sportsman and champion. On one crucial snatch of 325 pounds, he disqualified himself for brushing the floor with his knee, although none of the judges saw it. He then proceeded to lift the weight to take a commanding lead over Kutsenko. Davis ended with a winning total of 1,019 pounds, exactly the incredible figure that the Russian had been rumored to be capable of lifting. Davis then dispatched his opponents with relative ease at the 1952 Olympics in Melbourne, capturing his second gold medal. So dominant was Davis in Olympic competition that no one ever topped him in any of the three weightlifting events, the snatch, press, or clean and jerk. He retired the following year, the owner of seven world and 11 national championships.

Although he was known throughout the world and received such popular nicknames as "Hercules Noir" among the French, Davis was one of the least appreciated athletes of his time. Virtually no one in the United States knew of him, and he toiled for a living for years as a mechanic's helper in a Brooklyn garage before taking a job with the New York Department of Corrections. He died in 1984.

Further Reading

Greenspan, Bud. "Strongest Man in the World," *Look,* April 1952, pp. 23–24.

Page, James A. *Black Olympian Medalists.* Englewood, Colo.: Libraries Unlimited, 1991.

Dawes, Dominique
(1976–) *gymnast*

For decades the U.S. gymnastics teams were frustrated in their efforts to win an Olympic gold medal. But with Dominique Dawes as a major contributor, the United States pulled off a dramatic victory in 1996 and finally claimed the prize.

Dominique Dawes was born on November 20, 1976, in Silver Spring, Maryland. Looking for a way to channel their daughter's boundless energy, Don and Loretta Dawes enrolled her in ballet and then, when Dominique was six, placed her in the Marva Tots and Teens Gym in Wheaton, Maryland. For Dominique, gymnastics was nothing special—"just another activity," as she puts it. But under the guidance of the coach, Kelli Hill, she began to excel. When she entered her first competition as a 10-year-old, she won every event.

Dawes first became serious about gymnastics at age 12, when she developed her own personal philosophy, which she distilled to "D-3": Determination, Dedication, Dynamics. Dawes wrote these words on her bathroom mirror as a daily reminder of what she needed to do to achieve her goals.

Until 1991, Dawes lived at home and led a fairly normal life. But when she began training for the 1992 Olympics, the intensity of her training schedule created problems. When the burden of waking up at 4:30 A.M. to drive to practice before school proved too taxing, she moved in with Coach Hill. Not only was she separated from family, but the tenth-grader had to switch to a new school in the middle of the school year. When she made the U.S. team, Dawes then had to leave school before the end of the year.

At the age of 15, Dawes competed in the Olympic Games in Barcelona. Although she did not qualify for the finals in any individual event, she helped the United States claim third place in the team competition. Learning from the experience, Dawes rose quickly to the top of the gymnastics world. In 1993, the graceful 5-foot, 2 ½-inch gymnast took fourth place in the all-around competition at the world championships, and she was runner-up in both the balance beam and the parallel bars. The following season, she won the vault and the balance beam at the U.S. Nationals and took second in the floor exercise. Capping a spectacular year, she was prom queen at Aithersburgh High School and graduated with honors.

Her stock continued to soar in 1995 when she became the first gymnast in 25 years to win all five events at the U.S. Nationals. But then she suffered a stress fracture of the foot, followed by a stress fracture of the wrist. The injuries set her back, but she recovered in time to make the U.S. Olympic team in 1996.

At the Olympics in Atlanta, the United States was locked in a tight competition with Russia in the team competition. Dawes contributed one of the highest scores in the parallel bars, followed by an even more outstanding floor exercise routine. Performing a blind landing in the vault, she achieved a score of 9.762, which was just enough to nudge the United States ahead of Russia to win the gold. Dawes went on to claim an individual medal as well, placing third in the floor exercise.

Further Reading
Brownlee, S. "And Her Last Name Is Not Moceanu," *U.S. News & World Report*, June 10, 1996, pp. 67–68.
Kleinbaum, Nancy H. *The Magnificent Seven.* New York: Bantam Books, 1996.

Devers, Gail
(1966–) *track-and-field sprinter, hurdler*

Gail Devers overcame a severe and potentially crippling illness to become the fastest female combination sprinter-hurdler in track history.

Devers was born on November 19, 1966, in Seattle, Washington. She grew up in San Diego, where her mother, Alabe, worked as a teacher's aide and her father, Larry, served as an associate Baptist minister. Her competitive instincts were aroused when her older brother beat her in a back-yard race and then gloated unmercifully. Gail practiced running alone, built up her speed, and then challenged him to a rematch, which she won.

Devers began running track at National City Sweetwater High School in California, initially as a middle-distance runner. During her junior year, she focused on sprints, hurdles, and long jumping. As a senior she won the state championship in both the 100-meter dash and the 100-meter hurdles, and she placed third in the long jump. That performance earned her a scholarship to the University of California at Los Angeles (UCLA), where she trained under the famed track coach Bob Kersee.

Devers made steady progress in college. In 1987, she won the 100-meter dash at the Pan American Games. The following year, in tuning up for the Olympics, she won the National Collegiate Athletic Association (NCAA) 100-meter hurdles in a U.S. record time of 12.61. Although she easily qualified for the Olympics, she developed an alarming and mysterious ailment just before the Games. Her muscles ached, she suffered severe headaches, and she tired easily. Devers finished last in her semifinal heat at the Seoul Olympics.

Over the next two years, her problems grew worse. Devers became weaker, fainted often, had trouble breathing, suffered shaking fits, and sometimes even lost her sight. Finally, she was diagnosed as having Graves' disease, a condition of the thyroid gland. The drugs used to treat the disease were on the banned list for Olympic performers, and so she opted for radiation treatment. This caused her feet to bleed and swell so badly that in March 1991 she was on the verge of having both feet amputated. A change to yet another form of treatment proved effective, however, and in April of that year she was able to resume training. The ordeal had left her so weak that at first she could barely walk one lap of a track, but within a month, she was back to nearly full-speed workouts.

Devers made such astounding progress that, later that summer, she competed at the world championships and finished second in the hurdles. "Six months ago I had no idea I would be here," she told reporters. "It was just a matter of believing in myself."

In 1992, Devers completed her comeback by qualifying for the Barcelona Olympics in both the 100 meters, which she won, and the 100-meter hurdles. The following year, she won both events at the world championship, the first woman in 45 years to accomplish the feat. *Track & Field News* named her U.S. Female Athlete of the Year. After missing most of 1994 as a result of an automobile accident, Devers came back to set a world record of 12.68 in the hurdles in 1995, and she defended her gold medal victory in the 100 meters at the 1996 Olympics. She capped her improbable career in those games with her third career gold medal, which she earned in the 4 × 100 relay event. Since then she has actively promoted Gland Central, a foundation involved with thyroid diseases.

Further Reading

Bigelow, Barbara Carlisle. *Contemporary Black Biography.* Vol. 7. Detroit, Mich.: Gale Research, 1994.

Lessa, Christina. *Stories of Triumph: Women Who Won in Sport and Life.* New York: Universe, 1998.

Woolum, Janet. *Outstanding Women Athletes.* Phoenix, Ariz.: Oryx Press, 1998.

Dickerson, Eric Demetric
(1960–   ) *football running back*

Eric Dickerson is one of the most paradoxical football stars. JIM BROWN called him "the most skilled running back in football," at about the same time that the sports commentator Pete Axthelm described him as "one of the most overrated players in the history of the game." Many regarded him as lazy at the same time that others asserted he was the hardest worker they had ever known. In any case, Dickerson reached 10,000 rushing yards faster than any other player in National Football League (NFL) history.

He was born Eric Demetric Dickerson on September 2, 1960, in Sealy, Texas, and grew up in a bizarre family situation. He knew his father, Richard Seales, a sprinter and running back for Prairie View A & M, only by reputation. It was not until he reached the age of 15 that he discovered that the person he thought was his mother was in fact his great-aunt and that his "sister," Helen, was his biological mother.

Dickerson inherited his father's speed and athletic ability. He scored four touchdowns in his first football game in junior high. During his senior year at Sealy High School, he carried his team to a 15–0 record and a state title, gaining 296 yards and scoring four touchdowns in the championship game. He also won state championships in track with sizzling times of 10.3 seconds in the 100-meter dash and 20.9 in the 200.

Widely recruited by colleges, he chose to stay close to home and to attend Southern Methodist University. There Dickerson teamed up with another fine runner, Craig James, to form a backfield known as "The Pony Express." Although sharing running duties with James, Dickerson managed to gain 4,450 yards and score 48 touchdowns in his career, and he broke the career conference rushing marks of EARL CHRISTIAN CAMPBELL. The Los Angeles Rams made him second selection of the 1983 draft, behind John Elway.

It was Dickerson's exceptionally graceful running style that led to charges about his being lazy. He ran so effortlessly, carrying himself straight up rather than crouched or leaning, that coaches at first thought he was running half-speed. Only on closer observation did they notice that he was running faster than anyone else. The Rams quickly discovered that they had a back who, at six feet, three inches, 220 pounds, combined the explosive speed of O. J. SIMPSON with the powerful burst of Jim Brown. His offensive linemen found him a joy to block for. His teammate David Hill once said, "He hits the line quick and that's the best thing that can happen for an offensive lineman."

Wearing his trademark goggle-glasses because of his poor vision, Dickerson proved to be extremely difficult to stop from the first snap of his pro career. He carried the ball 390 times for 1,808 yards in 1983, best in the NFL and by far the most production ever from a rookie, and scored 18 touchdowns. The following season he picked up right where he had left off. Ripping off 100-yard games at will, Dickerson racked up 1,792 yards with two games left in the season, which put him within range of Simpson's single-season mark of 2,003 yards. Dickerson put an early end to the suspense in the record chase by shredding the Houston Oilers for more than 200 yards in game 15. On his final carry of the game, he gained nine yards on an end sweep to break a record. He added 98 more yards against San Francisco to set the current standard of 2,105 yards. Dickerson also set a record that year for the most 100-yard games in a season with 12.

Dickerson failed, for the first time, to win the NFL rushing title in 1985, but he did manage to set a play-off record by gaining 248 yards in a 20–0 postseason win over the Dallas Cowboys. He reclaimed his rushing title the following season, carrying the ball an NFL record 404 times for 1,821 yards. Thanks to a torturous workout regimen, Dickerson could handle that work load and remain fresh enough at the end of the game to accelerate past tiring defenses and earn the moniker "Mr. Fourth Quarter."

Despite being universally recognized as the best runner in the league, Dickerson discovered in 1986 that he was not among NFL's top 10 backs in salary. Miffed that the Rams refused to rectify the situation, he forced a trade to the Indianapolis Colts early in the season. As an indication of Dickerson's value, the Colts gave up eight players in exchange for him.

The bitter squabble stained Dickerson in the public's eyes as a greedy, overpaid whiner. Fans expressed their displeasure by throwing wads of Monopoly money at him at football games. Dickerson's refusal to run certain plays that he feared would subject him to a greater risk of injury further tarnished his image. Harassed by fans and the media, Dickerson began to lose his love for the game.

Nonetheless, he continued to perform at a high level. With the Colts, Dickerson provided a ground game that had been sorely lacking and led the team to its first playoff berth in 10 years. In 1988, his first full season with Indianapolis, Dickerson claimed his fourth rushing title in six seasons by gaining 1,655 yards. He enjoyed one last productive season in 1989, gaining 1,311 yards to become the first NFL runner to gain 1,000 or more yards in seven consecutive seasons. It turned out to be his last 1,000-yard season, as he fell into a gradual decline that was due to injuries, a poor offensive line, and deteriorating skills and enthusiasm. In 1992, he returned to the Rams for one last season before retiring.

Dickerson finished his career with 13,259 yards, third most in NFL history (he has since been passed by EMMITT SMITH). His career yards-per-carry average of 4.6 is one of the best in recent years. Dickerson went on to become a sideline reporter at pro games for network television. He was inducted into the NFL Hall of Fame in 1999.

Further Reading

Dickerson, Eric, with Richard Graham Welsh. *Eric Dickerson's Secrets of Power.* New York: Warner Books, 1989.

King, Peter. "Why Is This Man Running?" *Sports Illustrated,* August 12, 1991, pp. 12–17.

Reilly, Rick. "Dog Days," *Sports Illustrated,* December 4, 1989, pp. 58–60.

Dillard, Harrison

(William Harrison Dillard)
(1923–   ) *track-and-field hurdler, sprinter*

Harrison Dillard is best known for turning shocking disappointment into triumph in the 1948 Olympics. The finest hurdler of his time, Dillard

scored an upset victory in the 100-meter dash after failing to qualify for the games in his best event.

He was born William Harrison Dillard on July 8, 1923, in Cleveland, Ohio. His exceptionally lean build earned him the nickname "Bones" at the age of eight or nine, a name that stuck with him through life. Other children frequently made fun of his appearance, a fact that he credits with creating his fiercely competitive spirit.

According to Dillard, "At that time black history wasn't taught in the North, so we naturally took our heroes from sports." His choice as a role model was Cleveland native JESSE OWENS. At the age of 13, Dillard met Owens at a parade honoring the track star for his 1936 Olympics triumph. From then on, he did his best to emulate the legend. He even arranged to enroll at East Technical High School, where Owens had attended school. At East Tech, Dillard developed into a fine sprinter and an even better hurdler, winning the Ohio State High School Championship in both the high and low hurdles during his senior year.

Dillard enrolled at Baldwin-Wallace College in Berea, Ohio, but his plans were interrupted by World War II when he was called into the army reserve. In 1943, Dillard took advantage of a three-day pass to compete for Baldwin-Wallace and give the school its first Ohio Conference Championship in track. He spent 1944 on active duty in Italy and did not compete again until 1945, when he ran for the army in interservice competition, winning accolades from General George Patton as the best athlete he had ever seen. The following year, he returned to school and, through 1948, competed in four to six events in each of Baldwin-Wallace's meets. He seldom lost. From May 31, 1947, to June 26, 1948, Dillard won 82 consecutive races, primarily in the hurdles. The streak came to end when he tired while attempting to run four races in little more than an hour.

Dillard entered the U.S. Olympic trials in 1948 as the heavy favorite in the 110-meter high hurdles. But in the finals, he hit the first hurdle, stumbled, lost his stride and his rhythm, hit two more hurdles, and failed to finish the race. At the time it seemed small consolation that he had qualified for the Olympics in the 100-meter dash with an unimpressive third-place finish. At the London Olympics, however, he stunned his favored U.S. teammate Barney Ewell by squeaking out a 12-inch victory over Ewell in one of the closest finishes in Olympic history.

Four years later in Helsinki, Dillard redeemed himself in his best event by edging Jack Davis in the hurdle finals. Added to the gold medals he won as a member of the 4 × 100 relay teams in both 1948 and 1952, it gave Dillard a total of four golds, equaling the total of his idol, Owens. Dillard went on to a successful career as chief of business development for the Cleveland School Board.

Further Reading

Carlson, Lewis H., and John J. Fogerty. *Tales of Gold.* Chicago: Contemporary Books, 1987.

Nelson, Cordner. *Track's Greatest Champions.* Los Altos, Calif.: Tafnews Press, 1986.

Doby, Larry
(Lawrence Eugene Doby, Larry Walker)
(1924–2003) *baseball infielder, outfielder*

Whereas the name of JACKIE ROBINSON is universally known, few fans remember the first African-American to break baseball's color barrier in the American League. Ironically, Larry Doby, who enjoyed a fine career, came equally close to being the first black man to manage in the major league baseball.

He was born Lawrence Eugene Doby on December 13, 1924, in Camden, South Carolina. His father, a semipro baseball player from whom Larry inherited his athletic ability and love of sports, died when Larry was eight. Doby went on to a multisport career at East Side High School, in Paterson, New Jersey, where he was the only black player on the football team.

Doby began playing professionally with the Newark Eagles in 1942 at the age of 17, using the name Larry Walker at first to protect his amateur status in case he competed in college. Except for the interruption of a brief stint in the U.S. Navy in 1944–45, he continued to play for the Eagles until the summer of 1947. During his years with Newark, he developed a reputation as a slick-fielding second baseman, speedy runner, and left-handed power hitter. Some pitchers regarded Doby as one of the premier fastball hitters in the Negro Leagues.

As black ball players everywhere did, he watched anxiously as Jackie Robinson broke major league baseball's color barrier in 1947. In midseason, Doby was batting .414 for Newark when Bill Veeck of the Cleveland Indians followed the Brooklyn Dodgers' lead and signed him to a contract, thus integrating the American League. Doby began playing for the Indians on July 5. By all accounts, it was a difficult time for him. Teammates at Newark described him as a sensitive, yet outgoing man who enjoyed joking and laughing in the clubhouse. This kind of relationship was denied him with the Indians. Although Doby kept a lid on his temper in the face of open hostility from opponents and fans, many suspect the abuse took an emotional toll.

While he did not have the impact of Robinson, Doby nonetheless performed well for Cleveland. Shifted to the outfield for his first full season in 1948, he helped the Indians win their first American League pennant in 28 years by batting .310. He then hit .318 in the Indians' victory over Milwaukee, thus becoming the first black man to win a World Series.

The six-foot, 175-pound slugger enjoyed several fine seasons in the early 1950s. In 1950, he batted a career-high .326. Two years later, he finally displayed the power he had shown in the Negro Leagues by belting a league-high 32 home runs. In 1954, Doby was the main power source for a Cleveland team that won an American League record 111 games. Doby captured his second league home run title that season with 32, and he also claimed the league's runs-batted-in (RBI) championship with 126. The Indians, however, suffered a shocking four-game defeat to the New York Giants in the World Series.

Doby played 13 seasons in the major leagues, during which he clouted 283 home runs. After spending a decade away from the game, he returned as a coach. In 1978, he took over the helm of the Chicago White Sox, following FRANK ROBINSON as the first of major league baseball's black managers. He later worked in the commissioner's office in New York. Doby died on June 18, 2003.

Further Reading

Chadwick, Bruce. *When the Game Was Black and White.* New York: Abbeville, 1992.

Clark, Dick, and Lerry Lester, eds. *The Negro League Book.* Cleveland, Ohio: Society for American Baseball Research, 1994.

Riley, James. *The Biographical Encyclopedia of the Negro Baseball Leagues.* New York: Carroll & Graf, 1994.

Dorsett, Tony

(Anthony Drew Dorsett)
(1954–) *football running back*

Tony Dorsett was the smallest running back to crack into the ranks of pro football rushing leaders. His speed and acceleration made him a key component of the Dallas Cowboys offense in the 1970s.

He was born Anthony Drew Dorsett on April 7, 1954, in Aliquippa, Pennsylvania, near Pittsburgh, the last of a series of athletic sons born to Wes and Myrtle Dorsett. Although Dorsett has described himself as a mama's boy, he was also a product of the blue-collar steel mills environment and its emphasis on football. Anthony, as he preferred to be called, joined a midget football program, in the footsteps of his brothers, Melvin, Ernie, Tyrone, and Keith, all of whom were speedy running backs. Weighing in at a little

more than 150 pounds when he entered Hopewell High School, Tony did not relish contact. But he turned out to be the fastest Dorsett of them all, able to elude tacklers with ease. Tony scored 43 touchdowns at Hopewell, including 23 during his senior year.

Although he was heavily recruited, he opted to stay close to home at the University of Pittsburgh, a school that had suffered hard times in recent years, culminating in a 1–10 record in 1972. Dorsett's arrival on campus in 1973 made an immediate impact. He gained more than a thousand yards as a freshman and made several All-America teams. At the urging of the school's athletic department, he began using the name Tony so that his initials would be the catchy and symbolic *T. D.*

During his junior year, Dorsett drew national attention by gaining 303 yards against the vaunted Notre Dame defense, the most ever allowed by the Irish in their storied history. During his college career, Dorsett set 13 National Collegiate Athletic Association (NCAA) records and became the first player ever to gain more than 1,000 yards in each of his four seasons and to gain 6,000 career yards rushing. He capped his amateur days by leading Pittsburgh to the national championship in 1976 and winning the Heisman Trophy as the nation's top college player.

Unlike most superstar players who are drafted early by losing teams, Dorsett landed with the powerful Dallas Cowboys, who traded four draft choices for the right to select him. As an Easterner with a tendency to show off, he faced a period of cultural adjustment among the veteran coaches and players in Dallas. The Cowboys saw, however, that he was a hard worker with a unique gift of acceleration. The assistant coach, Dan Reeves, noted that Dorsett was so fast that "he was getting open without using fakes." In 1977, Dorsett became the first Cowboys rookie to gain more than 1,000 yards rushing. He provided the ground attack to complement Roger Staubach's passing, a combination that led Dallas to the Super Bowl.

Shrugging off concern about his durability as a 180-pounder among giants, Dorsett gained more than 1,000 yards in eight of his first nine seasons. Ironically, the only year he won the National Football League (NFL) rushing title was the year he fell short of 1,000, during the strike-shortened 1982 season. His best year was 1981, when he gained 1,646 yards. The highlight of his career occurred against the Minnesota Vikings in 1983, when he broke through the line of scrimmage on a 99-yard touchdown run, the longest in NFL history. Dorsett finished his 11-year career with a 1988 season in Denver, where he passed JIM BROWN to take second place in NFL career rushing yards behind WALTER JERRY PAYTON with a total of 12,739 yards. After that, he retired.

Further Reading

Dorsett, Tony, and Harvey Freeman. *Running Tough.* New York: Dell, 1989.

Marshall, J., "Tony D Comes to Big D," *Sports Illustrated,* September 19, 1977, pp. 38–43.

Moritz, Charles, ed. *Current Biography, 1980.* New York: H. W. Wilson, 1980.

Drexler, Clyde Austin

(1962–   ) *basketball guard*

As have many skilled players of his time, Clyde Drexler performed in the shadow of MICHAEL JORDAN. During his 15-season National Basketball Association (NBA) career, Clyde "The Glide" played with exceptional grace and was one of the rare pro players who excel in every phase of the game.

Clyde Austin Drexler was born on June 22, 1962, in New Orleans, Louisiana, and moved to Houston at the age of four. His mother, Eunice, and his stepfather, Manuel Scott, were such firm believers in education that they nearly cost Drexler his basketball career. Concerned with his studies, Drexler declined to go out for basketball in high school until his junior year, when the Sterling High

School coach persuaded him and his mother that he could handle both sports and school.

The late-starting Drexler improved rapidly but still attracted only mild interest from college programs. The University of Houston was one of only three schools that offered him a scholarship and he took it. At college, he worked passionately to improve his game. "I never felt I was a very good player," he explains. "I was in the gym . . . at 2 A.M., practicing."

Part of his inferiority complex was the result of Houston's incredible roster of athletes, including the future NBA great HAKEEM ABDUL OLAJUWON. They so entertained crowds with their high-flying, rim-rattling dunks that the national media dubbed them "Phi Slamma Jamma." Houston made the National Collegiate Athletic Association (NCAA) Final Four two of Drexler's three years with the team. After his junior year, he noted that the Houston Rockets had two early draft choices and declared for the draft, hoping to be claimed by his home team. To his disappointment, Houston passed on him and he was selected instead by Portland.

Drexler's early years with the Trailblazers were a painful growing experience. Accustomed to the loose discipline of Houston, Drexler often played out of control and balked at taking orders. But he soon learned to harness his quickness and incredible leaping skills for the good of the team. Drexler became the leader of a Portland team that challenged for the title every year. He enjoyed his best individual seasons in 1987–88 and 1988–89 when he averaged 27.0 and 27.2 points, respectively. But his value lay in his ability to do whatever was required to win. Drexler developed a deadly outside shot to go with his athletic drives, and he became an adept passer, a fine rebounder, and an excellent defender.

Twice Drexler led the Trailblazers to the brink of an NBA championship—in the 1990 finals, when they lost to Detroit, and in the 1992 finals, when Jordan's Chicago Bulls edged them four games to two. His quest for a title and for a return to his hometown were both fulfilled when midway through the 1994–95 season he was traded to Houston, where he rejoined his old friend Olajuwon. Drexler poured in 41 points in a crucial playoff match with Utah to help the Rockets advance to the championship, in which they dispatched SHAQUILLE RASHAUN O'NEAL and the Orlando Magic in four straight games. After a 1997–98 season in which he continued to average 18.4 points, Drexler retired to take on the head coaching duties at the University of Houston.

Further Reading

Bigelow, Barbara Carlisle. *Contemporary Black Biography.* Vol. 4. Detroit, Mich.: Gale Research, 1993.

Graham, Judith, ed. *Current Biography.* New York: H. W. Wilson, 1996.

Hersch, H. "Clyde the Glide in Overdrive," *Sports Illustrated,* June 11, 1990, pp. 22–23.

Duncan, Tim
(Timothy Theodore Duncan)
(1976–   ) *basketball center/forward*

Tim Duncan has quietly made himself one of the National Basketball Association's (NBA's) most complete big men. He has teamed with DAVID MAURICE ROBINSON to give the San Antonio Spurs basketball's most formidable frontline duo.

He was born Timothy Theodore Duncan on April 25, 1976, in Saint Croix, Virgin Islands. His father, William, was employed as a mason and hotel employee and his mother, Ione, worked as a midwife. The Duncan children were accomplished swimmers. Tim's sister Tricia competed for the Virgin Islands in the 1988 Olympic Games, and many regarded Tim as having even more potential. At the age of 13, he was easily the top swimmer on the island in the 400 freestyle.

But in 1989, Hurricane Hugo ripped through the island and destroyed the swimming complex. For a time, Duncan's only training option was the ocean, and he had a fear of sharks. At about that

time, his brother-in-law urged him to try basketball. "I remember thinking that after the basketball season ended I'd go back to swimming, but the basketball season never ended," Duncan remembers. Then, when his mother died of breast cancer in 1990, Duncan lost interest in swimming altogether.

Duncan's focus on basketball increased when he grew nearly a foot during his years at Saint Dunstan's Episcopal High School. Although there were only four basketball courts on the island and he had little competition, Duncan progressed steadily. Nonetheless, the Virgin Islands' reputation for basketball was so poor that only four colleges offered him scholarships. He chose Wake Forest and entered college in 1993.

At first Duncan found the pace of play so overwhelming that, in his first game as a freshman, he did not even attempt a shot. But he adapted well enough to set a school record for blocked shots that year. His offensive play improved so rapidly that he led Wake Forest to two Atlantic Coast Conference (ACC) championships, defeating perennial powerhouses North Carolina and Duke. Duncan resisted offers to leave school to join the pros and finished his career at Wake Forest with a spectacular senior year in which he averaged 20.8 points despite being triple-teamed and led the nation in rebounding with a 14.7 average.

The San Antonio Spurs, although well stocked at the post position with David Robinson, selected Duncan with the first choice in the 1997 draft. Both Robinson and Duncan proved to be intelligent, unselfish players who worked well in tandem. Once Robinson discovered Duncan's offensive abilities, he relinquished his role as the Spurs' go-to option in favor of the rookie.

Duncan responded by averaging 21.1 points and nearly 12 rebounds per game, easily winning the NBA Rookie of the Year Award in 1997. It was Duncan and not Robinson who spearheaded the Spurs' impressive championship season in 1999, and he was voted the Most Valuable Player of the finals. In 2002 Duncan and Robinson became the only players ever to be named to the All-NBA and All-Defensive teams in their first three years of professional play. Duncan was named the NBA's Most Valuable Player in both 2001–2002 and 2002–2003. He capped the latter season by leading the Spurs to their second NBA championship. Praised for his poise, versatility, and solid, calm demeanor, Duncan is considered one of the most complete players in the league. The Milwaukee coach, George Karl, calls him "a quiet assassin who is skilled in all aspects of the game."

Further Reading

Crothers, T. "Demon Deacon," *Sports Illustrated*, February 17, 1997, pp. 28–31.

Phelps, Shirelle. *Contemporary Black Biography*. Vol. 20. Detroit, Mich.: Gale Research, 1999.

Thompson, Clifford, ed. *Current Biography*. New York: H. W. Wilson, 1999.

E

Edwards, Teresa
(1964–) *basketball player*

Teresa Edwards went from being the "kid" on the 1984 U.S. Olympic basketball team to being the "old lady" on the 1996 team. During her unprecedented 13-year Olympic career, she earned gold medals on three different teams and tirelessly promoted the growing sport of women's basketball.

Edwards was born on July 19, 1964, in Cairo, Georgia, the daughter of 16-year-old Mildred Edwards. Although her father, Leroy Copeland, contributed what he could, Mildred had to leave high school and work in the vegetable fields to make ends meet.

Teresa loved sports, especially basketball, and spent hours shooting baskets through an old bike rim nailed to a tree. When her mother, a traditionalist who did not believe sports were for girls, told her not to try out for her middle school team, Teresa disobeyed her and earned a spot on the team. Edwards went on to become a high school All-American and earned a scholarship from the University of Georgia, the first in her family to attend college.

The 5-foot, 11-inch, point guard led her team to Southeastern Conference titles in three of her four seasons at Georgia, as well as trips to the Final Four in 1983 and 1985. She finished her college career as the school's all-time leader in steals and assists. Her coach, Andy Landers, described her as "the greatest competitor ever to lace up a pair of shoes."

It was as an Olympian that Edwards left her greatest mark. She was a surprise addition to the 1984 U.S. team. As the youngest player in the group, she saw limited playing time and scored only 15 points in six games during the team's gold medal run at the Los Angeles Olympics. Four years later, however, she took on a major role as the floor general of the 1988 team. Showing remarkable poise, at the Olympic Games in Seoul, Korea, she led the team in field goal percentage, assists, and steals, and she ranked second in scoring to lead the United States to a second straight gold medal.

Because U.S. women's basketball was nonexistent after the college level, Edwards had to market her talents abroad between Olympic contests. She spent nine years in Europe and Japan, earning as much as $250,000 in a season. Her best year was 1991, when she scored 31.8 points a game for Mitsubishi Electric Corporation to lead the league in scoring.

The 1992 Olympics was a disappointment as the United States slumped to a third-place finish. Edwards, however, continued her fine level of play by leading the team in assists and finishing third in scoring.

Many observers thought Edwards's declining skills would prevent her from making the 1996

U.S. Olympic team. But, as Landers said, "Show her something she can't do and she'll throw it in your face by proving you wrong." Edwards not only made the team but started all eight games and led the gold medal winners in assists, including an Olympic record 15 against Australia.

The three-time USA Basketball Female Athlete of the Year went on, as a star and player-coach in the pioneer American Basketball League, to help build women's professional basketball in the United States. The *Sports Illustrated* writer Alexander Wolff summed up her impact on the game: "The growth of the game over the past dozen years is best reflected in the career of Edwards."

Further Reading

Corbett, Sara. *Venus to the Hoop.* New York: Doubleday, 1997.

Woolum, Janet. *Outstanding Women Athletes.* Phoenix, Ariz.: Oryx Press, 1998.

Elder, Lee
(Robert Lee Elder)
(1934–   ) *golfer*

In a sport in which racial discrimination has limited African-American access, Lee Elder blazed his own trail. He was the first consistent black money winner on the professional golf tour.

Robert Lee Elder was born on July 14, 1934, in Dallas, Texas. He suffered double tragedy in childhood as his father, Charles, was killed in World War II combat and his mother died shortly thereafter. Twelve-year-old Elder was sent to Los Angeles to live with a sister.

Elder had been fascinated with golf ever since the age of seven or eight when he saw some men playing a round. In Los Angeles, he worked as a caddy, occasionally skipping school to earn money. At night, he would sneak onto the course to play until he was chased off. It was not until he was 16 that Elder was able to play a full round of 18 holes. Eventually, he dropped out of Manual

Arts High School and took whatever jobs he could to get on a golf course. While working in pro shops and locker rooms, he learned from watching the clients play. After a while he developed his own style of play and made side money as a hustler, winning bets, for instance, by playing on his knees.

Elder's break occurred when he was playing a match with JOE LOUIS, an avid amateur golfer. His play impressed Louis's personal instructor, Ted Rhodes, who took Elder under his wing and arranged for Elder to accompany him to golf tournaments. "Whatever success I have attained I owe to him," Elder later said.

After three years under Rhodes's tutelage, Elder was drafted into the army. There he had the good fortune of working under a commander who loved golf and recognized talent when he saw it. He put Elder on special duty so that he could work on his golf game and thus win service championships for his post.

After being discharged in 1961, Elder joined the United Golf Association (UGA), a black pro golfing tour. He won the UGA championship five times and once put together a string of 21 wins in 23 matches. But with winners' purses of $500, he barely scraped together a living.

In 1967, at the age of 32, Elder finally was admitted to the Professional Golfers' Association (PGA). He started slowly, with a tie for third his best finish that season. The next year, he tied Jack Nicklaus for first at the American Golf Classic, but he lost the play-off and finished 40th on the tour in earnings. He improved steadily, finishing in the top five in four tournaments in 1973, and he finally entered the winners' circle at the Monsanto Open in 1974.

After slumping in 1975, he rededicated himself to his craft and enjoyed his best season in 1976. That year he won the Houston Open and finished in the top 10 in four other tournaments. Three years later, he ranked 13th on the PGA tour in earnings and became the first African American invited to join the U.S. Ryder Cup team.

In 1984, at the age of 50, he joined the senior tour, in which he put together a string of victories. Elder suffered a heart attack in 1987 but recovered completely and won the Machado Classic in 1988. He earned more than $1 million on the senior tour, which increased his total career earnings to more than $2 million.

Further Reading

Bigelow, Barbara Carlisle. *Contemporary Black Biography*. Vol. 6. Detroit, Mich.: Gale Research, 1994.

Henderson, Edwin B. *The Black Athlete: Emergence and Arrival*. New York: Publishers Company, 1968.

Moritz, Charles, ed. *Current Biography, 1976*. New York: H. W. Wilson, 1976.

Erving, Julius
(Julius Winfield Erving III, Dr. J)
(1950–   ) *basketball forward*

Julius Erving changed the game of basketball by transforming the slam dunk into an artistic form of self-expression. Universally admired for his creativity, grace, and class, Dr. J opened the door for an entire generation of players eager to strut their stuff above the rim.

He was born Julius Winfield Erving III on February 22, 1950, at Hempstead, Long Island, New York. His father abandoned the family when Julius was three, leaving him to spend much of his time alone on the streets. Although many fans assume he got his nickname, "Dr. J," as a tribute to his basketball skills, the name actually originated as a childhood joke. Erving had a friend who insisted he would become a professor and Erving had ambitions of being a medical doctor, and the two began calling each other by their imagined titles.

Julius found a focus for his life in basketball, at which he excelled early. He was especially gifted as a leaper and could dunk a basketball when he was in the seventh grade. After starring at Roosevelt High School in Long Island, Erving

Julius "Dr. J" Erving, who performed most of his magic in midair, introduced the slam dunk as an art form. *(Basketball Hall of Fame)*

was recruited by most national basketball powers. Concerned about the possibility of basketball's consuming his whole life, however, he chose the University of Massachusetts, where he believed he could focus on education as well as sports.

Erving performed spectacularly at Massachusetts; in his junior year he averaged 26.9 points a game and, despite being only six feet, six inches—merely average height for a basketball player—he led the nation in rebounding. But it was less what Erving did than the way he did it that awed sports fans and pro scouts alike. Dr. J was blessed with enormous hands that allowed him to grip the basketball easily in one hand. As a result, he could throw down slam dunks with style and ease. Spectators at U Mass games arrived at the gym early to watch Dr. J run through his assortment of dunks in warmups.

After his junior year, the family's bleak financial situation caused Erving to leave school, and he signed with the Virginia Squires of the American Basketball Association (ABA). He had no difficulty making the adjustment to the pros and tallied 27 points a game as a rookie in 1971–72. The following season he boosted his scoring average to a league-leading 31.9. The Squires, however, became mired in a deep financial mess and had to sell Erving's contract to the New York Nets.

Unphased by the turmoil, Dr. J again topped the league in scoring and displayed his all-around skill by ranking in the top seven in the ABA in steals, blocked shots, and rebounding. Capping off a perfect season, Erving led the Nets to the ABA championship and captured the league's Most Valuable Player (MVP) Award. He shared the MVP Award the following season and laid claim to his third straight trophy in 1975–76. That season Erving almost single-handedly carried the Nets to victory over a superior Denver Nuggets team to win the championship; in one crucial game of that series he scored 48 points, playing against the league's top defender, Bobby Jones. Erving's most spectacular moment, however, occurred in an exhibition slam dunk contest, when he became the first person to dunk a ball after taking off from behind the free throw line.

Unfortunately, the struggling ABA did not command the same attention as the National Basketball Association (NBA), and few people saw Dr. J in his prime. But nearly everyone had heard of his spectacular exploits, and it was at least partially because of Erving's fame that the NBA agreed to accept four teams from the ABA before the 1976–77 season. Recognizing that they did not have the resources to pay the game's hottest superstar in competition with established NBA teams, the Nets sold him to the Philadelphia 76ers.

Among the curious who watched Erving in his new league were many doubters who claimed that his skills were overrated because of the weak opposition in the ABA. Boston's legendary coach Red Auerbach was one of many who disparaged Erving, saying, "Over here, Erving is just another small forward."

Erving exploded that myth in the All-Star game that season. Playing against the best of the NBA stars, he dominated the game with 30 points and 12 rebounds to win the game's MVP trophy. Erving led the 76ers into the NBA finals that season, in which they lost to Portland in six games.

Dr. J did not reproduce the gaudy statistics of his ABA heyday; the closest he approached leading the league in scoring was in 1979–80, when he scored 26.9 points to finish fourth. Nonetheless, basketball fans and players held him in awe for the grace and style he gave to the game. "He played more than the required notes in his performance," said KAREEM ABDUL-JABBAR. "He invented in the open court." In addition, Erving displayed a dependable consistency in averaging more than 20 points a game through the 1985 season and leading his team deep into the playoffs nearly every year.

Dr. J earned the league's Most Valuable Player Award in 1981 for his outstanding all-around play. But his most satisfying NBA season, by far, was the 1982–83 campaign. A year after suffering yet another agonizing loss in the championship finals, the 76ers romped past their opposition in one of the most brilliant displays of playoff teamwork in history. Bolstered by the addition of strongman center MOSES EUGENE MALONE, Erving and his mates breezed through their first two playoff rounds by winning eight of nine games. They then disposed of the Los Angeles Lakers in four straight games to give Erving his elusive NBA championship. That same year, Erving showed the new generation of high-flying aerial acrobats that he was still the master of the art form by winning another All-Star MVP Award. He retired after the 1986–87 season and was voted to the NBA Hall of Fame in 1993.

Further Reading

Bell, Marty. *The Legend of Dr. J.* New York: Coward, McCann & Geoghegan, 1975.

"The First Guy to Fly," New York Times Biographical Service, April 1987.

Moritz, Charles, ed. *Current Biography, 1975.* New York: H. W. Wilson, 1975.

Evans, Lee Edward

(1947–   ) *track-and-field distance sprinter*

Lee Evans's world record in the 1968 Olympics was overshadowed by more charismatic performances of his teammates on the track and by political controversies off the track. Nonetheless, track historians regard his 400-meter effort in those games as one of the most remarkable examples of sheer determination in the history of sport.

He was born Lee Edward Evans on February 15, 1947, in Madera, California. Almost from the time he could walk, he worked in the fields of the San Joaquin Valley with his family, earning three cents an hour picking grapes and cotton. Evans shared a bed with two brothers in a cold cement house. All through school, he felt the stigma of poverty and race prejudice. Although he started out as an excellent student, teachers stereotyped him as stupid and he received little academic encouragement.

Evans became interested in sports because of his older brother, Doug, who was a high school All-American in football. Unlike Doug, however, who dropped out of school and ended up in trouble with the law, Lee was determined to make the most of his ability. His early success as a track star at Overfelt High School inspired him to train even harder.

The brutal workouts paid off when Evans graduated from high school and began running at San Jose City Junior College in 1966. Evans won every quarter-mile race he ran that year, including a stunning victory at the national Amateur Athletic Union (AAU) championships. Suddenly, he became a hot commodity and was welcomed at the powerhouse track program at San Jose State University, home of world champion sprinter TOMMIE C. SMITH.

Evans continued to rank as the United States's top quartermiler in 1967 even though his style of running was unorthodox. *The New York Times* commented that the stocky, broad-shouldered Evans "seems to beat up a track rather than glide over it." With his face a mask of determination, he outlasted foes in the stretch through sheer willpower, inspiring sportswriter David Wolf to hail him as "probably the most ferocious competitor in track and field."

In 1968, Evans captured the 400-meter title at the National Collegiate Athletic Association (NCAA) nationals and shattered the world record in the event at the U.S. Olympic trials with a time of 44.0. At the Mexico City Olympics, however, the furor surrounding his teammates Tommie Smith and John Carlos nearly sent Evans packing before he had even run. Upset that the two had been banished from the Games for their black-fisted salute on the victory stand, Evans refused to compete until Carlos persuaded him to go ahead.

Although emotionally drained by the situation, Evans went out and ran the race of his life in the 400-meter finals. He had to, because his teammate Larry James was running faster than any quartermiler in history. With typical tenacity, Evans forced one last surge out of his exhausted body to beat James to the tape with a world record time of 43.8.

Evans joined forces with James and two others to win gold and shatter the world record in the 4 × 400 relay in those same Olympics. He continued to compete and win into the early 1970s, gaining his fifth AAU title in 1972 before joining the short-lived track circuit that year. The passage of time showed how remarkable his Olympic effort had been. Whereas most other track records fell within a few years, more than a decade passed before anyone approached Evans's world record 400.

Further Reading

Page, James A. *Black Olympian Medalists*. Englewood, Colo.: Libraries Unlimited, 1991.

Silverman, Al. *The Best of Sport, 1946–1971*. New York: Viking, 1971.

Warner, J., and D. Wolf. "Amid Gold Medals, Raised Fists," *Life*, November 1, 1968, p. 64.

Ewing, Patrick Aloysius

(1962–) *basketball center*

Patrick Ewing was a fierce basketball warrior who carried Georgetown University to greatness and the New York Knicks to the edge of National Basketball Association (NBA) glory.

He was born Patrick Aloysius on August 5, 1962, in Kingston, Jamaica. His parents, Carl and Dorothy, immigrated to the United States when Patrick was young but left the children behind until they could earn the money to send for them. In 1974, Patrick arrived in Cambridge, Massachusetts, where his father had found work as a mechanic. The boy spoke with such a heavy Jamaican accent that other children could not understand him, and the only sports he knew were soccer and cricket.

But he made the adjustments and the following year was introduced to the sport of basketball in a neighborhood game. When Ewing shot up to six feet, six inches in eighth grade, he quickly began to dominate games. Ewing led Rindge and Latin High School to three straight state championships and was so impressive he was invited to try out for the 1980 U.S. Olympic basketball team.

The no-nonsense approach of Georgetown University coach John Thompson appealed to Ewing, who enrolled at the school in 1980. By this time, Ewing had filled out to a full seven feet. With his long arm span and solid frame, he immediately provided the Hoyas with an imposing presence as a freshman, primarily as an intimidating defender and rebounder. School was not easy for Ewing, and he was tempted with offers to leave school and turn pro. But having promised his mother, who

died in 1983, that he would graduate, Ewing stuck it out. The result was a National Collegiate Athletic Association (NCAA) championship and tournament Most Valuable Player (MVP) Award in 1984. Ewing then capped the season by playing a key role in the gold medal performance of the 1984 U.S. Olympic basketball team.

The New York Knicks made him the first selection of the 1985 draft. Although primarily noted as a defender in college, he averaged 20.0 points to go along with his nearly 10 rebounds a game and sterling defense, and he easily captured the NBA's Rookie of the Year Award. He improved steadily, until by the 1989–90 season he was a dominating force near the basket and the anchor of the New York team, which challenged for the divisional title every year. That season, he averaged a career high 28.6 points (third in the NBA), 10.9 rebounds (fifth), and 3.99 blocked shots (second). Ewing again ranked in the top five in the NBA in all three categories in 1990–91, and he finished in the top six in league scoring six consecutive seasons.

Ewing's efforts took the Knicks tantalizingly close to winning an NBA championship on several occasions. The closest he approached that goal was in 1993–94, when the Knicks lost the decisive seventh game in the finals against the Houston Rockets. The following year, the Knicks lost a chance to return to the finals when Ewing's last-second tip-in bounced off the rim against Indiana, and they lost again in the finals in 1999, when Ewing was sidelined by injury. Earlier that season, Ewing achieved the rare double feat of scoring more than 20,000 points and 10,000 rebounds in his career. His long career continued in Seattle in 2000 and with Orlando through 2002.

Further Reading

McCallum, J. "The Big Man Gets Bigger," *Sports Illustrated*, January 27, 1990, pp. 30–33.

Moritz, Charles, ed. *Current Biography, 1991*. New York: H. W. Wilson, 1991.

Phelps, Shirelle. *Contemporary Black Biography*. Vol. 17. Detroit: Gale Research, 1998.

F

Faggs, Mae
(Aeriwentha Mae Faggs, Mae Starr)
(1932–2000) *track-and-field sprinter*

Mae Faggs, the first U.S. woman to compete in three Olympics, was best known for her role in creating the legendary Tennessee State University Tigerbelles track team that held a stranglehold on women's sprinting in the 1950s and 1960s.

Aeriwentha Mae Faggs was born on April 10, 1932, in May's Landing, New Jersey, the only daughter among five children born to blue-collar workers, William and Hepsi Faggs. Mae discovered her love of sprinting in elementary school. She went on to compete at Bayside High School on Long Island, New York, and as a member of the New York Police Athletic League, in which her talent was spotted by Sergeant John Brennan. Brennan formed an Amateur Athletic Union (AAU) team made up of New Yorkers with Faggs as the centerpiece.

With Brennan's encouragement, 16-year-old Mae Faggs tried out for the 1948 U.S. Olympic team and qualified in the 200-meter dash and as a member of the 4 × 100 meter relay. Although she did not win a medal in either event at the London Games, the youngest member of the U.S. team enjoyed the experience and vowed to return. Over the next four years, Faggs won most of her races and even set a U.S. indoor record for the 220-yard dash with a time of 25.8. She returned to the Olympics in 1952 and was surrounded by a much better supporting cast than in the previous games. After Faggs gave the team a solid start with her leadoff leg, the U.S. women won the gold in the 4 × 100 meter relay.

At that time, Ed Temple was searching for a way to build up his women's track-and-field program at Tennessee State. The problem was solved when Faggs, by now a nationally known track star, agreed to accept a scholarship to attend the school. Although she stood only five feet tall, Faggs exuded a sense of confidence and leadership that rubbed off on her teammates. Coach Temple credited Faggs with being the "mother of the team," which eventually included world sprint champions WILMA GOLDEAN RUDOLPH and WYOMIA TYUS. Faggs enjoyed her finest day as a sprinter at the AAU championships in 1955 when she set a U.S. record in the 200-yard dash at 25.1 seconds and won the 100-yard event with an AAU record of 10.8. She also won AAU national championships in the 200 meters in 1954 and 1956, as well as the 100-meter title in 1956.

Faggs capped her career by leading an all–Tennessee State contingent in the 4 × 100-meter relay to the 1956 Olympics in Melbourne, Australia. Again running the leadoff leg, she helped her team win the bronze medal.

Faggs used her leadership skills in a 32-year career as a teacher. Known as Mae Starr after marrying Eddie Starr in 1958, she was inducted into the United States National Track and Field Hall of Fame in 1976. Faggs died on January 27, 2000.

Further Reading

Ashe, Arthur, Jr. *A Hard Road to Glory: A History of the African-American Athlete, 1919–45.* New York: Warner Books, 1988.

Davis, Michael D. *Black American Women in Track and Field.* Jefferson, N.C.: McFarland, 1992.

Temple, Ed. *Only the Pure in Heart Survive.* Nashville, Tenn.: Broadman Press, 1980.

Faulk, Marshall

(1973–) *football running back*

Marshall Faulk is widely regarded as the most versatile running back in National Football League (NFL) history. His ability to catch passes and run both inside and outside for the Saint Louis Rams has been a key element in developing the most explosive offense the NFL has ever seen.

Faulk was born on February 26, 1973, in New Orleans, Louisiana, to Roosevelt and Cecile Faulk. He was raised in a rough section of the city's public housing. He grew up with three brothers, and, according to Marshall, "They made me tough." Faulk also learned about hard work and about a life he did not want to lead by working as a janitor in the boiler room of his high school. His outlet was the football field, where he displayed the versatility for which he would become famous by playing quarterback, running back, wide receiver, and defensive back for Carver High School.

That achievement earned him a scholarship to the lightly regarded San Diego State University (SDSU). Any doubts about Faulk's ability to compete at the college level vanished in the second game of his freshman season when he ran for 386 yards and scored seven touchdowns. Faulk was named an All-American all three of his seasons

at SDSU, where he accumulated 4,589 yards rushing and an additional 773 yards receiving and scored 65 touchdowns.

Faulk's combination of running and receiving ability was exactly what many pro teams were seeking, and so he left school after his junior year. The Indianapolis Colts selected him in the first round of the 1994 draft and immediately installed him in the starting lineup. Faulk met the challenge by gaining 1,282 yards to become the NFL's Offensive Rookie of the Year.

After gaining 1,078 yards in 1995, Faulk found his effectiveness reduced by injuries the following year. In 1997 he bounced back to record his third 1,000-yard-rushing season in four years with 1,054 yards. But that was merely a prelude to the breakthrough effort he put forth in 1998, when, for the first time, the Colts made him an intricate part of their passing offense as well as their running game. Faulk ran for 1,319 yards and caught 86 passes, 30 more than his previous season's best, for another 908 yards to lead the league in combined yardage.

The Colts, fearing Faulk's probable salary demands after such a season, traded him to Saint Louis for two lower-round draft choices. Faulk was stunned and hurt. But the move turned out to be beneficial to him. As the linchpin of Saint Louis's racetrack offense, Faulk enjoyed a dream season in 1999. He rushed for a career-high 1,381 yards and caught 87 passes for 1,048 yards to set an NFL combined yardage record of 2,429 yards. The surprising Rams went on to win the Super Bowl.

Showing that his success was no fluke, Faulk ran for 1,359 yards, gained 830 more on pass receptions, and scored an astonishing 26 touchdowns in 2000, even when the rest of the Ram offense was not clicking on all cylinders. Faulk again led the Rams to the Super Bowl in the 2001 season with 1,387 yards rushing, 765 yards receiving, and 21 touchdowns. Although slowed by injuries he continued to lead the Rams ground gain, finishing the 2004 season with a career total of 11,987 yards rushing and 100 touchdowns.

Further Reading

Taylor, Phil. "The Frosh Prince," *Sports Illustrated,* November 18, 1991, p. 110.

Scott, David. "Breaking Away," *Sport,* November 1999, pp. 42–44.

Silver, Michael. "Star of Stars," *Sports Illustrated,* September 3, 2001, pp. 106–116.

Flood, Curt
(Curtis Charles Flood)
(1938–1997) *baseball outfielder*

Curt Flood quietly established himself as an outstanding fielder and valuable hitter in the 1960s. But his impact on baseball extends far beyond his on-field achievements. It was Flood who struck the first blow against the reserve clause that tied players to their teams, opening the door to the free agency system that has revolutionized sports.

He was born Curtis Charles Flood on January 8, 1938, in Houston, Texas. He was among the second wave of African-American ballplayers to hit the National League in the mid-1950s, after the success of the Brooklyn Dodgers in integrating baseball in the late 1940s. Flood initially played in the Cincinnati Reds organization and reached the major leagues in 1956. The Reds, however, were well-stocked in outfielders, and Flood saw action in only five games that year and only three the following season.

His chance occurred when the Reds traded him to Saint Louis before the 1957 season. Flood immediately worked his way into the starting lineup, primarily because of his range and dependability as a center fielder. After struggling at the plate for the better part of three seasons in Saint Louis, Flood finally developed the offensive skills to complement his defense. In 1960, he improved his average 85 points over his average of the previous season to finish at a surprising .322. It was the first of six seasons in which Flood surpassed the .300 mark.

Flood was a major factor in the Cardinals' two World Series championships in the 1960s. In the Cardinals' 1964 championship season, he led the National League in hits, and he achieved a career-best batting average of .335 when the Cardinals repeated in 1967. Despite such marks, he was always regarded as primarily as defensive player. Along with his skill at running down line drives and robbing batters of potential extra-base hits, he was a heady player who seldom made a mistake. He won the Gold Glove for defensive excellence seven times and played the entire 1966 season without making a single error.

After 12 years of solid play for Saint Louis, Flood was stunned when the Cardinals traded him to Philadelphia on October 7, 1969. The thought of having to uproot his family from their Saint Louis home infuriated him to the point that his wife, Maria, suggested, "Why not sue?"

Major league baseball's reserve rule binding a player to one team had been in effect since 1922, never seriously challenged despite its incompatibility with the nation's antitrust laws. Flood decided to take the matter to court. As he told the baseball players' union head Marvin Miller: "I want to give the courts a chance to outlaw the reserve system. I want to go out like a man instead of disappearing like a bottle cap."

The Supreme Court ruled against Flood. By acting on principle, he effectively ended his career and spent hundreds of thousands of dollars in attorney fees. However, the case raised the nation's consciousness of the issue and led directly to legal reforms that accomplished what he was asking, to the enormous benefit of future pro ball players. Flood died on January 20, 1997, of throat cancer.

Further Reading

Ballret, William. *Writing by the Rebels Who Changed Sports.* New York: Thunder's Mouth Press, 1999.

Miller, Marvin. *A Whole Different Ball Game.* New York: Birch Lane Press, 1991.

Foreman, George
(1949–) *boxer*

George Foreman underwent a remarkable transformation during his life from vicious young hood to intimidating world champion boxer to lovable symbol of middle-aged Americans.

He was born on January 10, 1949, in Marshall, Texas, to J. D. and Nancy Foreman. "Almost from the time I was born, anger and hunger shaped my youth," he recalls. Foreman grew up in a tough neighborhood in Houston. Although a good student, he ran with criminals while his mother worked hard to support her seven children. When he was 16, his sister told him about the Job Corps, a government program to teach skills to low-income youth. Eager for a new life, Foreman signed up for a program in Oregon. He took with him his hot temper, however, and was quick to use his fists when crossed. While listening to a Cassius Clay (MUHAMMAD ALI) fight, a coworker suggested he make use of his size and prickly disposition to become a boxer. Foreman took the advice and moved to a Job Corps center in California that had a boxing program.

Outstanding strength and uncanny quickness enabled him to make the U.S. Olympic team in 1968 after only 18 amateur fights. There he pounded the Soviet champion, Ionis Chepulis, into submission in the second round to win the gold medal.

Foreman then turned pro and began to display his frightening strength against a variety of foes. In 1969–70, he won all 25 of his fights, 22 of them by knockout. On January 22, 1973, he took on the rugged JOE FRAZIER and destroyed him. Foreman knocked Frazier to the mat six times in two rounds to score a quick victory. Many boxing experts consider Foreman to be the most powerful puncher of all time. He was not exaggerating when he said, "My opponents didn't worry about losing to me. They worried about getting hurt."

Most boxing fans feared for Muhammad Ali's health when the aging veteran entered the ring against Foreman in Zaire, on October 30, 1974. But by employing a clever strategy of covering up while Foreman punched himself into exhaustion, Ali neutralized the big champion and knocked him out in the eighth round.

The unexpected loss shattered Foreman's confidence and knocked his life off balance. He retreated to his ranch in Marshall, where he became violent and went on a huge spending spree. He attempted to pull himself back together back in the ring, but on March 17, 1977, he suffered another upset loss, to Jimmy Young, and was hospitalized for mental exhaustion.

Realizing his life was out of control, Foreman abandoned the ring and turned to religion. He started the Church of the Lord Jesus Christ in a rundown building in Houston, and he founded the George Foreman Youth and Community Center. Needing an influx of funds for his projects, Foreman shocked boxing fans by returning to the ring after a 10-year retirement at the age of 38. Most fans ridiculed his efforts as a publicity stunt. Playing the role of a jovial fat man, Foreman went along with the ribbing but was serious about his boxing. From 1987 to 1990 he recorded a string of 19 straight knockouts. In 1991, he took the champion, Evander Holyfield, to the limit in their fight. Three years later, the 45-year-old Foreman beat the British title-holder, Michael Moorer, inspiring a generation of middle-aged men to pursue their dreams. He then retired from boxing for good and returned to his church in Houston and ranch in Marshall, Texas.

Further Reading

Berger, P. "Body and Soul," *New York Times Biographical Service*, March 1991.

Foreman, George, with Joel Engel. *By George: The Autobiography of George Foreman*. New York: Villard, 1995.

Suster, Gerald. *Champions of the Ring*. London: Robson, 1994.

Frazier, Joe
(Joseph Frazier, "Smokin' Joe" Frazier)
(1944–) *boxer*

"Smokin' Joe" Frazier is best remembered for his three classic boxing matches with heavyweight legend MUHAMMAD ALI. Willing to absorb as well as deal out punishment, Frazier turned every fight into a battle of attrition.

Joseph Frazier was born on January 12, 1944, in Beaufort, South Carolina, the youngest of 13 children in a family of subsistence farmers. At the age of nine, Frazier earned his keep driving a tractor in the fields. Although a quiet boy, he was provoked into a fight in 10th grade by a boy who insulted his mother. The incident resulted in his suspension from school. At that point he decided to leave school altogether and went north to Philadelphia looking for work.

Frazier found employment as a meat cutter in a slaughterhouse. While working there, he decided he needed to lose weight and began to spend time at the Police Athletic League gymnasium. It was there that he discovered his interest in boxing and soon gained a reputation as "The Slaughterhouse Kid." As an amateur fighter, Frazier posted a 40–2 record, highlighted by national Golden Gloves titles in 1962, 1963, and 1964. At the 1964 Olympic trials, he was well on his way to fulfilling his dream of competing in the Olympics, notching six straight knockouts, when he lost a controversial close decision to Buster Mathis in the finals. Depression turned to excitement, however, when Mathis broke his thumb before the Olympics and had to step aside in favor of Frazier. Frazier made the most of his reprieve by defeating West Germany's Hans Huber to win the gold medal.

Frazier turned pro the following year and earned the nickname "Smokin' Joe" with his aggressive style. At 5 feet, 11 ½ inches, Frazier was shorter than most opponents, and to deal with their advantage in reach he developed a style of continually advancing, weathering his opponents' blows in order to connect with his more powerful punches. Frazier's powerful legs, dogged stamina, and unbending will kept him standing long enough to break down their defenses and knock them out.

When Muhammad Ali had his crown stripped in 1968 because of his antidraft stance, a host of lesser lights scrapped for the title. Frazier earned the World Boxing Council (WBC) version of the title that year by finally besting his old nemesis, Mathis. Two years later, he solidified his claim to the crown by beating the World Boxing Association (WBA) title holder, Jimmy Ellis. When Ali was reinstated, he and Frazier fought a titanic battle in Madison Square Garden in March 1971, which Frazier won. Smokin' Joe went on to devastate challengers such as light heavyweight champion Bob Foster, whom he dispatched in four rounds. However, just when Frazier appeared to have established himself as one of the great champions, GEORGE FOREMAN annihilated him in two rounds, knocking him off his feet six times.

Frazier and Ali offered two reprises of their thrilling match, and each was as hard-hitting and close as the first, although Ali came out on top in both cases. Although shaken by the fiasco with Foreman, Frazier retired in 1976, having knocked out 27 of the 32 men to face him.

Further Reading
Berkow, Ira. *Beyond the Dreams.* New York: Atheneum, 1975.

Kram, Mark. *Ghosts of Manila: The Fateful Blood Feud between Muhammad Ali and Joe Frazier.* New York: HarperCollins, 2000.

Suster, Gerald. *Champions of the Ring.* London: Robson, 1994.

Frazier, Walt
(Walter Frazier, Jr., Clyde Frazier)
(1945–) *basketball guard*

The New York Knicks have won only two National Basketball Association (NBA) championships, and Walt Frazier ran the show for both. A triple-threat star, the stylish Frazier worked his way up from an obscure small college player to one of the best in the business.

Walter Frazier, Jr., was born on March 29, 1945, in Atlanta, Georgia, the eldest of Walter, Sr., and Eula Frazier's nine children. A natural athlete, Frazier starred in three sports at segregated David T. Howard High School in Atlanta; he was a strong-armed baseball catcher, a polished football quarterback, and a tenacious basketball point guard. College scouts considered football his best sport, and he was offered scholarships to play at Kansas and Indiana. But when neither school guaranteed that he could play the quarterback position, he opted for a basketball scholarship at Southern Illinois University.

Frazier struggled with some of the academic work at college, to the point that he was declared ineligible for the 1965–66 season. Rather than giving up, however, he stayed in school, put in extra work on his studies, and improved his performance. Readmitted to the team the following year, he led the school to a magical season. With Frazier averaging 18.2 points a game, running the offense, and playing stifling defense, Southern Illinois soared to the number-one ranking among the nation's small schools. In 1967, they became the first small school to win the National Invitational Tournament (NIT) in New York, with Frazier picking up the Most Valuable Player (MVP) Award.

At that point, Frazier decided to skip his senior year of college and pursue a pro basketball career. The New York Knicks, impressed by his NIT performance, made him the fifth player selected in the 1967 draft. Frazier needed a year to adapt to the faster, more physical style of play in the NBA. But Frazier, whom teammates nicknamed Clyde (as in Bonnie and Clyde) for his flashy suits, took over the point guard role in his sophomore year and averaged 17.5 points and 7.5 assists while earning a reputation as a relentless defender. In 1969, he was voted to the NBA All-Defensive team, an honor that he held for seven consecutive seasons. In addition, the six-foot, four-inch, Frazier developed offensive post moves that he loved to use on smaller opponents.

In 1969–70, courageous center Willis Reed won most of the accolades for the Knicks' surprising NBA championship. But it was Frazier who led the way, averaging 20.9 points per game and dishing out 629 assists.

Two years later, the Knicks traded for offensive genius Earl Monroe. Frazier and Monroe teamed up to be one of the most effective and colorful guard tandems the league has ever seen. Frazier boosted his scoring average to a career-high 23.3 that season as Monroe adapted himself to the Knicks' system. The following year, the two led the undersized Knicks to a convincing four-games-to-one thrashing of the Lakers to win a second title.

Frazier averaged 18.9 points, 6.1 assists, and 5.9 rebounds in 13 NBA seasons, the final two spent with Cleveland. He retired in 1979 and was inducted into the NBA Hall of Fame in 1987.

Further Reading

Moritz, Charles, ed. *Current Biography, 1973.* New York: H. W. Wilson, 1973.

Phelps, Shirelle. *Contemporary Black Biography.* Vol. 19. Detroit, Mich.: Gale Research, 1999.

Fuhr, Grant Scott
(1962–) *hockey goalie*

While the stick-handling magician Wayne Gretzky controlled the headlines during the Edmonton Oilers' impressive run of five Stanley Cup titles in the 1980s, it was Grant Fuhr who manned the crucial last line of defense without which those titles would have been impossible.

He was born Grant Scott Fuhr in Spruce Grove, Alberta, Canada, on September 28, 1962, to teenaged parents and was immediately put up for adoption. His adoptive parents, Roberts and Betty Fuhr, were somewhat apprehensive about

Grant Fuhr's quick reflexes helped make the Edmonton Oilers the National Hockey League (NHL) dynasty of the 1980s. *(Bruce Bennett Studios)*

their ability to raise a black child in a white society but found most people to be accepting of their family.

Robert Fuhr was an insurance salesman who, like many Canadians, had a passion for hockey. When Grant was four, his dad bought him skates and turned his basement into a hockey rink.

Young Grant quickly caught the passion. He skated constantly outdoors, and at age seven, he announced his plan to become a professional hockey goalie.

Fuhr turned out to be such a fine all-around athlete that he entertained an offer to sign with the Pittsburgh Pirates' baseball team. He never swerved, however, from his dream of being a goalie. Since the sport originated in the cold northland, where few blacks live, ice hockey has been almost exclusively the domain of white athletes. Race was never an obstacle to his career, although some suggest that Fuhr was fortunate in this regard. "He was lucky he was out west," said one coach, who believed Fuhr would have suffered discrimination playing hockey in the eastern provinces. "And it's good he wears the mask."

In 1979, he dropped out of Composite High School in Spruce Grove to join the Victoria Cougars of the Western Hockey League. He showed such quick hands and great anticipation that the Edmonton Oilers claimed him as their top draft choice before his 18th birthday.

Fuhr broke into the starting lineup in his rookie season of 1982–83, performing well enough to be named a Second-Team All-Star. Fuhr proved to be the final piece in the puzzle as the Oilers figured out the way to take the Stanley Cup home to Edmonton on a regular basis. With Fuhr tending the goal, the high-scoring Oilers at last had someone who could shut down the opposition. The Oilers won Stanley Cup titles in 1984, 1985, 1987, 1988, and 1990, with Fuhr in the nets for nearly every game. Fuhr also shut down the Soviet Union's team to help Canada win a hotly contested three-game series between the fierce international rivals in 1987.

Fuhr's best individual season was 1987–88, when he led the league in games, wins, and shutouts, earning the Vezina Trophy as the National Hockey League's (NHL's) top goalie. At that time, Vancouver's Barry Pederson declared, "Bar none, Grant Fuhr is the best goalie in the league."

As do many young athletes, Fuhr had problems coping with the sudden rise to fame and fortune. In 1990, he admitted a drug abuse problem and received a 55-game suspension from the league that sent his career into a tailspin. In quick succession, Fuhr was traded to Toronto, Buffalo, and Los Angeles. Although he shared the Jennings Trophy for allowing the fewest goals with Dominik Hasek in Buffalo in 1993–94, he struggled so badly in Los Angeles that his career appeared to be over.

In 1995, however, he revived his career with the Saint Louis Blues. Fuhr set an NHL record that season by playing in 79 games, including 76 consecutive games. After three more stellar seasons with Saint Louis, he wound up his career in Calgary in 1999–2000. He won 400 games during his career and posted a playoff mark of 86 wins and 44 losses.

Further Reading

LaBlanc, Michael L. *Contemporary Black Biography*. Vol. 1. Detroit, Mich.: Gale Research, 1992.

Wiley, R. "The Puck Stops Here," *Sports Illustrated*, January 11, 1988, pp. 58–62.

G

Gervin, George
(Ice Gervin)
(1952–) *basketball guard*

George Gervin, the rail-thin, sleepy-eyed guard of the San Antonio Spurs, accumulated a wider variety of accurate shots, including an incredible array of his patented finger rolls, than any player of his time. Playing far from the media centers in a transplanted American Basketball Association (ABA) franchise, he became the National Basketball Association's (NBA's) most prolific scoring machine in the late 1970s.

Gervin was born on April 27, 1952, in a crumbling neighborhood on the east side of Detroit, Michigan. His father left home when George was two, and his mother, despite her best efforts, was not always able to keep food in the house. Fortunately, a janitor who befriended him let him use the school gym at nights. Gervin spent countless hours shooting up to 500 shots per session. Already a fine player as a five-foot, six-inch freshman, Gervin began to shine when he shot up to six feet, seven inches, over the next few years.

After starring at Martin Luther King High School, he received many scholarship offers and found the glamor of Long Beach State in California to be the most attractive. But the adjustment to a new culture proved too great and Gervin left school before the season began. He eventually enrolled close to home at Eastern Michigan, where he played well enough to earn an invitation to try out for the 1972 U.S. Olympic team. In a rare fit of temper, however, Gervin slugged an opponent, was kicked off the Eastern Michigan team, and had his Olympic invitation withdrawn.

Now an outcast in the basketball world, he had to settle for joining a semipro team in Pontiac, Michigan. But after he averaged more than 37 points a game, the Virginia Squires of the ABA signed him to a contract. Gervin played little the first year but came through in the play-offs with an average of nearly 19 points. The cash-poor Squires then sold him to the Spurs, for whom he averaged 23 points a game in his first full season. When four ABA teams joined the NBA the next year, in 1976, JULIUS ERVING warned the new league that Gervin was the man to watch out for. Few took him seriously.

But, moving to guard to take advantage of his height, Gervin calmly poured in points from all angles of the court. After scoring 23.1 points a game in 1976–77, he boosted his average to 27.2 the following year, the top mark in the NBA. Gervin kept improving hitting 29.6 in 1978–79 and 33.1 in 1979–80, both league-leading figures. After dipping to third place with 27.1 the following season, Gervin bounced back to tally 32.3 points in 1981–82 to capture his fourth NBA scoring title in five years. Most remarkably, Gervin accomplished this with an economy of shots. During his career, he sank 51 percent of his shots from his field, a remarkable average for a guard.

Known as "Ice" for his clutch shooting and calm demeanor, Gervin led his teams into the playoffs in all 10 of his NBA seasons. After nine years in San Antonio, he finished his career with Chicago in 1986 and left the court as the number eight scorer in NBA history. He has since organized the George Gervin Youth Center for troubled youth in San Antonio.

Further Reading

Great Athletes of the Twentieth Century. Vol. 6. Pasadena, Calif.: Salem Press, 1994.

Kirkpatrick, Curry. "Iceman Cometh and Scoreth," *Sports Illustrated,* March 6, 1978, pp. 12–15.

Gibson, Althea
(1927–2003) *tennis player*

Althea Gibson's dramatic rise from a habitual truant and ward of the New York City Welfare Department to a polished star in the traditionally elite social stratum of tennis remains one of the most inspirational stories in the history of African-American sports figures. After triumphing in a fierce struggle to break through the formidable barriers that excluded blacks from tennis competition, she repeated her pioneering efforts in breaking the color barrier in women's professional golf.

Gibson was born on April 25, 1927, in Silver, South Carolina, where her parents, Daniel and Anna, scratched a bare living out of the ground as sharecroppers. Repeated cotton crop failures left them destitute, and when Althea was one, they moved to a small apartment in the Harlem section of New York City.

Gibson noted in her memoirs that she always had a burning desire to "be somebody." This restless urge led only to frustration in her youth as she took on a tough kid image. She skipped school so

often that she barely passed junior high school. ("I think those teachers just made up their minds to pass me on to the next school and let them worry about me," she has said.)

Her problems grew worse when her request for a transfer to a downtown high school to be with friends was denied. Gibson soon dropped out of school altogether. She tried working at a number of jobs but was fired for such reasons as skipping work to watch movies, and she spent some time at a home for troubled youth.

Gibson's life began to turn around when she was introduced to the New York Police Athletic League, in which she learned to play paddleball, a game similar to tennis except that wooden paddles are used instead of strung racquets. For the first time in her life, she found motivation to succeed, and she spent hours hitting balls against a wall. Gibson won a local tournament and attracted the attention of Buddy Walker, a musician who worked part-time in the summer with the city recreation department. Recognizing her talent, Walker persuaded her to switch from paddleball to tennis; he even bought her a secondhand racquet and set up some matches with friends at tennis courts in Harlem.

Eventually, Gibson made an impression on tennis players at the integrated New York Cosmopolitan Tennis Club in Harlem, who agreed to sponsor private lessons for her, beginning in 1941. The initial lessons were somewhat stormy as Gibson, while soaking up the tennis instruction, balked at the coaches' insistence that she control her temper and develop some responsibility in her personal life.

She improved rapidly and, a year after beginning lessons, won the New York State Negro Girls Open. She went on to compete at the black American Tennis Association championships, in which she lost in the finals of the girls' competition. The event was canceled in 1943 because of World War II restrictions on travel, but when the tournament resumed in 1944, Gibson claimed the title, which she successfully defended the following year.

Gibson's performance caught the interest of yet another pair of mentors, surgeons Hubert Eaton, of Wilmington, North Carolina, and Robert Johnson of Lynchburg, Virginia. The doctors were interested in helping a young black tennis player develop the skills to attain a college scholarship and break color barriers in the sport, and Gibson seemed a likely candidate. Their plan grew more complicated, however, when they discovered that Gibson had barely completed junior high, much less high school. This led to an arrangement whereby Eaton and Johnson agreed to provide room and board and private tennis lessons if Gibson would complete her high school education. Gibson moved in with the Eaton family in Wilmington and found high school to be a far better experience the second time around, now that she had motivation. Gibson graduated 10th in her class at Williston Industrial High School in 1949. In the meantime, she began a string of nine consecutive black national women's championships in 1948, and she earned a tennis scholarship to Florida A & M University.

Once in college, Gibson had second thoughts about her career. Ever since childhood, she had dreamed of becoming a singer, and she debated about switching her focus to music. Advisers, however, persuaded her to stay with tennis.

Gibson dominated the competitions she entered, and by 1950 the only challenge left to her was the elite world of the United States Lawn Tennis Association, which sponsored the world's most prestigious tennis events. But her applications to compete in these tournaments were repeatedly denied strictly because of race; most of the host clubs of the top tournaments banned blacks from participation. Gibson expressed her disappointment with eloquence and restraint, which moved an influential ally to action. In 1950, Alice Marble, a four-time U.S. Open champion, wrote an editorial in a tennis magazine in which she blasted officials for refusing to allow Gibson to compete.

Althea Gibson broke racial barriers in two sports. (Library of Congress, Prints & Photographs Division, NYTW&S Collection [LC-USZ62-114745])

The article touched a nerve throughout the nation, and within months, Gibson began receiving invitations to tournaments previously closed to her. The first was the Eastern Grass Court Championships, in which Gibson won only one match before losing. She had more success at the National Clay Court Championships in Chicago, reaching the quarterfinals. Late in the summer, she became the first black player to step on the court at Forest Hills, New York, for the U.S. Open. Facing tremendous pressure in breaking the racial barrier, as well as a tough draw, she advanced only to the second round before succumbing to former U.S. Open champion Louise Brough in a fiercely contested match.

This began a long series of disappointing major tournaments, including the world's most famous tennis event, the Wimbledon Open in England, in which Gibson suffered relatively early losses. The frustration gradually wore her down; after being ranked as high as seventh among the world's women tennis players, by late 1953 she had dropped out of the top 10.

In fact, Gibson was ready to retire from competition. After graduating from college in 1953, she accepted a teaching position at Lincoln University in Jefferson City, Missouri. During the next two years, she played only sporadically, and even then only at the urging of a former Harlem coach. In 1955, her career recharged when the U.S. State Department invited her to represent the United States on a goodwill tour of Southeast Asia. While on this tour, Gibson regained her tennis touch and, more important, her confidence. She began blasting serves that few opponents could return and putting away opponents with crisp volleys at the net.

The rejuvenated Gibson swept through her opposition in 1956 as she won 16 of 18 tournaments around the world. Among these triumphs were victories in Sweden, Germany, England, Italy, Egypt, and her first major championship, the French Open. This performance raised expectations for her when she appeared at Wimbledon that year, but she reverted to previous form, experiencing a stunning first-round loss. Instead of collapsing under the disappointment, however, Gibson returned to the Wimbledon court in the doubles competition with her partner Angela Buxton and won the championship.

This victory gave Gibson a boost of confidence for a return visit to Wimbledon the following year. This time she crushed Darlene Hard in the singles finals, 6–3, 6–2, and then teamed up with Hard to win the doubles event as well. She returned to New York as a heroine and was honored with a ticker tape parade. For the next year and a half, Gibson was unstoppable. She beat her old rival Louise Brough to capture the U.S. Open in 1957, returned to Wimbledon and again swept the singles and doubles championships, and capped her brilliant run with another U.S. Open championship that same year.

At the height of her success, she shocked the tennis world by announcing her retirement from the sport before the 1959 season. Tennis at that time was primarily an amateur sport, and she needed a career in which she could earn income. Gibson pursued her childhood dream of becoming a singer, appearing on *The Ed Sullivan Show* and releasing several albums. She then embarked on a new sporting challenge—golf. In 1963, she broke a second color barrier by becoming the first woman to qualify for the Ladies Professional Golf Association Tour. This sporting endeavor was much less successful than her tennis career, and she gave it up after a few years without winning any tournaments or making much in prize money.

She spent most of her noncompetitive career in public relations and as a tennis coach before retiring in 1992. Gibson's efforts in breaking sports racial barriers had a lasting impact in creating a climate of acceptance for those who followed her. Typical of the tributes to her is basketball star CHERYL MILLER's statement: "What I remember today about her was that she refused to see herself as a Negro who made it in sports but as a human being whose talent, skill, and determination were at the core of her athletic success." Gibson died on September 28, 2003.

Further Reading

Ashe, Arthur, Jr. *A Hard Road to Glory: A History of the African-American Athlete, 1919–45.* New York: Warner Books, 1988.

Condon, Robert J. *Great Women Athletes of the 20th Century.* Jefferson, N.C.: McFarland & Company, 1999.

Candee, Majorie Dent, ed. *Current Biography, 1958.* New York: H. W. Wilson, 1958.

Gibson, Althea. *I Always Wanted to Be Somebody.* New York: Harper & Row, 1958.

Gibson, Bob
(Robert Gibson)
(1935–) *baseball pitcher*

One of the fiercest competitors baseball has ever seen, Bob Gibson terrorized major league batters with a blazing fastball and nasty disposition toward anyone with a bat in his hand. Teammates found Gibson relaxed and pleasant, but he took his profession so seriously that he refused even to talk to opponents. For impressive stretches in his career, particularly in World Series play, this competitiveness made him as close to unhittable as anyone who ever toed the pitching rubber.

His tenacious disposition was forged through bitter childhood experience. Robert Gibson was born on November 9, 1935, in Omaha, Nebraska, to Pack and Victoria Gibson. Three months later, Pack, a millworker, died of pneumonia, leaving Victoria to raise their seven children on her pay as a laundress. As an infant, Bob Gibson was so sickly with a series of illnesses including pneumonia, asthma, rickets, and rheumatic fever, that his mother "never thought he'd pull through."

He remained so thin during his years at Omaha Tech High School that he had to avoid physical sports such as football. Gibson, however, excelled at basketball and track and as a catcher in baseball. It was basketball that earned him a scholarship to Creighton University in Omaha, and he was talented enough to play one winter with the professional Harlem Globetrotters. But he chose to concentrate on baseball as a pitcher and left school in 1957 to sign with the Saint Louis Cardinals.

Although his athleticism and rocketing fastball impressed the Cardinals, Gibson was a raw talent. "He could throw the ball through the side of a barn, if he could only hit the barn," quipped one scout. Gibson spent the better part of four seasons in the minor leagues working on his control before earning a permanent spot on the Saint Louis roster in 1961. The right-hander posted a respectable 13–12 record in his rookie season.

Gibson was plagued with health problems through much of his career and—although one trainer said of him, "He has to have the highest threshold of pain I've ever seen in an athlete"— he lost a large number of starts as a result of injuries and illness. In 1962 he was sidelined for a time with a broken ankle suffered in batting practice but still managed to win 15 of 28 decisions. The following year, Gibson fought off asthma and an inflamed right elbow to win 18 games. In later years, he pitched well despite ruptured blood vessels, bone chips, and an arthritic condition that made it impossible for him to hold his arm straight.

After a slow start in 1964, Gibson bore down during the Cardinals' stretch run to win nine of his last 11 games. On the final day of the season, he won his 19th game of the year to clinch the pennant for his team. Gibson lost his first start in the World Series that year but returned to win his second start. Then, pitching on just two days' rest instead of the usual four, he gutted out a tough 7–5 victory to nail down the championship.

Few batters could catch up with Gibson's trademark high fastballs, and he frequently ranked among the league leaders in strikeouts, despite having only two basic pitches in his repertoire— fastball and slider. In 1965, he fanned a career best 270 batters as he joined the ranks of baseball's 20-game winners for the first time.

Gibson shrugged off a nerve injury to improve his record to 21–12 in 1966, with a sparkling 2.44 earned run average. The following year his season appeared to end in midsummer when he broke his ankle when struck by a line drive. But he returned in the final weeks of the season to spark the Cardinals to another pennant win. Gibson carried his momentum over into the postseason with a fabulous performance against the Boston Red Sox. He staked his team to an early World Series lead with a 2–1 win in game one. Gibson then blanked the Red Sox on five hits in his second start. The rest of the Cardinals' staff was not as effective, though, and Saint Louis was forced into a tense, winner-take-all seventh game. Again, they called upon Gibson and again he came through, allowing only three hits in a 7–2 win. His dominating performance in his three complete-game victories earned him the World Series Most Valuable Player Award.

All this was only a prelude to 1968, when opponents may as well have left their bats behind when facing Gibson. Enjoying perhaps the most dominating season of any pitcher in baseball history, Gibson pitched 304 innings, posting a staggering earned-run average (ERA) of 1.12 and 13 shutouts. He completed 28 of his 34 starts and in the other six was removed late in the game for a pinch hitter, in other words, his opponents never drove him out of a game. "As I recall," said the Cardinals outfielder Lou Brock, "he didn't make one bad pitch all year." During his hottest stretch, Gibson reeled off 15 straight wins and allowed only two runs over the course of 92 innings, more than 10 games. Only the Cardinals' woeful lack of hitting support held his won-loss record to 22–9 as he claimed the National League's Most Valuable Player Award as well as the Cy Young Award as the league's outstanding pitcher.

Gibson's dominance carried over to the World Series, as, matched against Detroit's 30-game-winner Denny McLain, he struck out 17 Tigers en route to a 4–0 win. Several participants called it the finest pitching performance they had ever seen. Gibson also won game four, allowing only one run. In the deciding game seven, he locked up with Mickey Lolich in a scoreless duel until the seventh inning, when a center fielder's misplay of a flyball led to a two-run triple and a Cardinal loss. Gibson's 35 strikeouts over the three games set a World Series record and his record, of eight complete games in nine starts stands as a formidable achievement.

In 1970 the 6-foot, 1½-inch, 200-pounder went on to win a career-high 23 games, which earned him his second Cy Young Award. Over his career, he posted a 251–174 record and 3,117 strikeouts. An all-around athlete, Gibson was one of the top fielding pitchers in the league and batted so well that the Cardinals seldom pinch-hit for him.

Further Reading

Gibson, Bob, with Lonnie Wheeler. *Stranger to the Game: The Autobiography of Bob Gibson.* New York: Viking, 1994.

Laird, A. W. *Ranking Baseball's Elite.* Jefferson, N.C.: McFarland, 1990.

Gibson, Josh
(Joshua Gibson)
(1911–1947) *baseball catcher*

Had Josh Gibson been born 20 years later, he would have ranked with Babe Ruth and HANK AARON as one of the most celebrated sluggers in baseball history. In the words of a contemporary Hall of Fame pitcher, Walter Johnson, "He can do everything. He hits the ball a mile. And he catches so easy I might as well be in a rocking chair. Throws like a rifle. . . . Too bad this Gibson is a colored player." Banned from major league baseball along with all other African Americans of his time, Gibson performed his legendary feats of strength and skill in the relative obscurity of the Negro Leagues, ignored by the vast majority of American sports fans.

Gibson was born on December 21, 1911, in Buena Vista, Georgia, near Atlanta, to Mark and Nancy Gibson, the oldest of three children. After years of struggling to eke out a living farming a poor plot of land, the family moved north in search of better economic opportunities in 1923. They settled in Pittsburgh, Pennsylvania, where they had relatives and where steel mill jobs were available.

Josh enrolled at Allegheny Prevocational School, preparing for a career as an electrician, but he dropped out after the ninth grade to work as an apprentice in an air brake factory. He showed an early talent for sports, especially in swim competitions at local pools. His favorite sport, though, was baseball, the most popular sport among the black population of the north side neighborhood of Pleasant Valley, where the Gibsons lived. When he could not find a baseball game to play, Gibson would roller skate as far as six miles to watch other top local players compete.

At age 16, Gibson started playing catcher in Pittsburgh's black sandlot leagues. In 1929, he began earning a few dollars a game playing for the semipro Crawford Colored Giants. While developing into an outstanding hitter, he dreamed of someday playing for the Homestead Grays, a team from a steel town a few miles upriver that was developing as one of the elite clubs in the National Negro League.

Unfortunately, the Grays already had a fine catcher, and so Gibson had to content himself with being a spectator at their games. On July 1929, however, the Grays were playing the Kansas City Monarchs when their catcher suffered a painful split finger and was unable to continue behind the plate. One of the Grays recognized Gibson in the stands, knew of his reputation, and asked him to fill in for the rest of the game. Gibson performed so well that he stayed with the team, batting a spectacular .441 for the season.

The six-foot, one-inch, 200-pound Gibson was a natural hitter. Unlike most power hitters, he did not overcommit himself by striding into the pitch and taking a long, hard swing. He used a quick, flat-footed swing that made contact with the ball nearly every time. Yet he was powerful enough that he was known to hit home runs accidentally while trying to halt his swing. The combination of power and contact hitting allowed him to hit for high average while belting tape-measure blasts out of the ballpark.

His defensive skills as a catcher did not come as easily. Although quick and agile for a big man, Gibson had trouble mastering the basics. Some critics claim he was never better than average behind the plate, but the more common view is

that through constant practice, he transformed himself into an outstanding receiver.

During his career, Gibson repeatedly switched teams. In 1932, he left the Grays and joined legendary pitcher SATCHEL PAIGE on a new Negro League powerhouse, the Pittsburgh Crawfords. In 1936, he rejoined the Grays. When owners of a team in Santo Domingo, Mexico, offered him $6,000 ($2,000 more than his salary for the Grays), to play for them in 1940, Gibson broke his contract and joined the team. Upset at losing the star slugger, the Grays' owners took him to court. The judge ruled in their favor and Gibson returned to the Grays in 1942.

Gibson was not so much a mercenary as a man who loved baseball so much that he was not particular about where he played or for whom. During his long career, he played year-round, joining teams in Florida, California, Mexico, and Venezuela during the winter months. Satchel Paige reported that their team once played three games in three days, traveling 950 miles by car between games. While sitting on the porch of their hotel after finishing the third game, Gibson saw some kids playing a pickup baseball game. Although the temperature was over 100 degrees, Gibson went out and joined the boys in the game.

The keeping of records and statistics in the Negro Leagues was haphazard at best; therefore, it is difficult to compare Gibson's accomplishments to those of his white counterparts in the major leagues. Nonetheless, Gibson did post some astounding numbers. During his 17 seasons, he slammed 962 home runs, compared to Babe Ruth's total of 714. In 1936, he hit 84 home runs. Although he played in about 20 more games than Ruth did in his record season, that total nonetheless dwarfs Ruth's long-revered mark of 60 in a season. His lifetime average of .354 ranks among the best of all time and includes several years in which he topped .400. Although the accuracy of the records is open to question, one widely reported home run leaves no doubt that Gibson was one of the most powerful sluggers of his time.

While playing in Ruth's own Yankee Stadium, Gibson hit a home run that struck the top of the stadium wall 580 feet from home plate, farther than any ball ever hit by Ruth or any batter since.

The outgoing Gibson liked to party, and he fell under the spell of alcohol midway into his career. Both physical and mental problems contributed to swiftly declining skills at the end of his career. In January 1943, Gibson was admitted to a mental hospital after suffering recurring headaches; he then fell into a coma. The problem was diagnosed as a brain tumor, which eventually killed him in 1947, a few months before JACKIE ROBINSON joined the Brooklyn Dodgers. Some claim that the heartbreak caused by his exclusion from the major leagues contributed to Gibson's decline. Close friends, however, say that, although he would have been thrilled at a chance to play in the majors, he loved his life as a baseball player so much that he did not harbor bitterness. Major league baseball belatedly recognized his contributions by making him the second player from the Negro Leagues inducted into its Hall of Fame.

Further Reading

Chadwick, Bruce. *When the Game Was Black and White.* New York: Abbeville, 1992.

Clark, Dick, and Lerry Lester, eds. *The Negro League Book.* Cleveland, Ohio: Society for American Baseball Research, 1994.

Holway, John. *Josh and Satch: The Life and Times of Josh Gibson and Satchel Paige.* New York: Meckler, 1991.

Pepe, Phil. *Talkin Baseball.* New York: Ballantine, 1998.

Peterson, Robert. *Only the Ball Was White.* New York: Gramercy, 1970.

Greene, Joe

(Charles Edward Greene, Mean Joe Greene)
(1946–   ) *football defensive tackle*

Mean Joe Greene was the swashbuckling defensive tackle who anchored the Pittsburgh Steelers' impenetrable Steel Curtain defense in the 1970s.

Playing with a rare combination of strength, quickness, and barely controlled rage, he terrorized opposing centers and guards for more than a decade.

Charles Edward Greene was born on September 24, 1946, in Temple, Texas. His parents divorced shortly after he was born, and he was raised solely by his mother, who worked as a domestic. Money was usually tight, and Joe, as his mother called him, spent enough time in cotton fields as a youngster to know he wanted to do something else with his life.

In eighth grade, Greene, a timid, somewhat overweight boy, found an outlet for his pent-up aggression by playing football. He was so large for his grade that opposing teams often questioned his age. Although Greene always had an intense desire to be successful, he was as undisciplined in football as he was in life in general. Shortly after joining the football team in eighth grade, he quit. He returned the following year as a 200-pound linebacker, but he displayed a hair-trigger temper, especially when his Dunbar High School team was losing, as it did frequently. Greene admits to having gained a reputation as the dirtiest football player ever and claims to have been ejected from nine games during his junior year. But his speed enabled him to excel as a 250-pound middle linebacker in his senior year.

Although an indifferent student at best, Greene went on to college at North Texas State University on a football scholarship. The green-shirted North Texas State defense was tagged with the nickname "Mean Green," which, given Joe's on-field personality, was inevitably transferred to him. Now playing defensive tackle at 275 pounds and sometimes heavier, Mean Joe Greene could manhandle opponents when the mood struck him. During his senior year he was named the Missouri Valley Conference Player of the Year. Unfortunately, pro scouts noticed that the mood did not always strike him. A scouting report of the Pittsburgh Steelers read, in part, "Puts on weight, tendency to loaf . . . only uses his ability in spurts."

Nonetheless, the Steelers recognized Greene's physical talents, and, with some trepidation, they selected him as their first pick in the 1969 college draft. Steeler fans, most of whom had never heard of Greene, bitterly criticized the selection. In truth, the Steeler management began to think they had made a big mistake when Greene at first held out in a contract dispute and then showed up for training camp late and overweight.

Steeler offensive linemen had the intention of teaching the cocky newcomer a lesson but soon discovered that Greene was a dangerous person to cross. None of them had ever seen a player so strong, quick, and fearless. Unfortunately, the Steelers were a bad team when Greene joined them, and losing always brought out the worst in him. The rookie was kicked out of two games and could have been tossed from several others for his violent outbursts. But when he was on the field, he tore through opposing linemen and harassed ball carriers so consistently that he was named the National Football League's (NFL's) Defensive Rookie of the Year.

The Steelers, who had been perennial losers for as long as many fans could remember, continued to struggle over the next two seasons. Greene developed into an All-Pro player in his second season, and the defense emerged as a formidable force, but the offense could not produce. Frustrated by losing, Greene on one occasion grabbed the ball before the opposing center could snap it, hurled it into the stands, and stormed off the field.

Such was Greene's physical strength and menacing aura that no one, coaches, teammates, or opponents, could do much to stop him. He took outrageous chances as a defender and usually had the ability to get away with them. As one teammate said of Greene, "He does what he wants out there." In a game against the Houston Oilers in 1972, Greene manhandled opposing linemen and recorded five sacks of the quarterback. Descriptions of Greene's accomplishments bordered on the incredible. Pittsburgh center Ray

Mansfield made this comparison when asked about Greene's ferocious play: "Have you ever seen a dog get a hold of a snake?"

As offensive players such as Terry Bradshaw and Franco Harris began to mature and make contributions, the Steelers began to win. But it was still the Steel Curtain defense, led by Greene, that carried most of the load. In 1972, when the Steelers won the first divisional title in their long history, Greene was named the NFL's Defensive Player of the Year. The following year, the relentless pressure on quarterbacks applied by Greene and his line mates allowed the Steelers' secondary to intercept 11 more passes than any other team in the league.

In 1974, Greene led a nearly perfect defense as the Steelers romped through the playoffs. That year, he experimented with a technique of lining up close to the opposing center but at an angle to disrupt the enemy attack before it got started. No one figured out a way to counter the move. In the first round of the play-offs, Pittsburgh handcuffed O. J. SIMPSON and the Buffalo Bills' vaunted ground game in an easy 32–14 win. In the American Football Conference (AFC) championship, they totally stifled the offense of the 13–2 Oakland Raiders to earn a berth in the Super Bowl. That contest belonged to Greene and the Steelers defense. Playing with a savage fury, the Steel Curtain shut down the Vikings' running attack, giving up only 17 yards. They harried Vikings quarterback Fran Tarkenton into 16 incompletions and three interceptions in 27 attempts and prevented the Vikings' offense from scoring a touchdown in a 16–6 victory. Greene, at the center of the chaos all day, had his most memorable moment when he stripped a running back of the ball and then recovered the fumble. Greene not only earned a Super Bowl ring that season but also picked up his second NFL Defensive Player of the Year Award.

Greene continued to be a major defensive force in the Steelers' run of four Super Bowl triumphs during the 1970s. However, after an injury in 1975, he never regained his dominating swagger. He retired in 1981 and was inducted into Pro Football's Hall of Fame in 1987.

Further Reading

Blount, Roy, Jr. "He Does What He Wants Out There," *Sports Illustrated*, September 22, 1975, pp. 96–100.

Harrington, Denis J. *The Pro Football Hall of Fame.* Jefferson, N.C.: McFarland, 1991.

Mabunda, L. Mpho. *Contemporary Black Biography.* Vol. 10. Detroit, Mich.: Gale Research, 2000.

Greene, Maurice

(1974–) *track-and-field sprinter*

From the time he was a child, Maurice Greene claimed he was going to be the world's fastest human. In 1999, that prediction came true. As of 2001, Greene had recorded the fastest three 100-meter times in history.

Greene was born on July 23, 1974, in Kansas City, Kansas, the youngest of four children of Ernest and Jackie Greene. All the Greene children competed in track, and, according to Jackie, "Maurice, being the baby, always said he was going to do it better." At the age of eight, he joined the KC Charger track club. By the time he reached F. I. Schlagle High School in Kansas City, Greene was dominating the sprint events. He won the 100 and 200 meters at the Kansas state meet from 1991 to 1993, and he added a championship in the 400 meters as a senior.

Although he was also a star football player, Greene focused on track instead of college. He attended Hutchinson Junior College, but spent most of his time training with his longtime coach, Al Hobson. In 1995, Greene beat the U.S. sprinting icon CARL LEWIS at the Texas Relays and finished second at the U.S. Championships. However, a hamstring pull hampered him the following year. He ran poorly at the U.S. Olympic trials and failed to make the team.

Greene then moved to Los Angeles, hoping to benefit from the coaching of the highly esteemed John Smith. Training with other world-class sprinters, Greene endured punishing practices. Always a fast starter, Greene learned to delay his acceleration so that he would have something left for the end of the race. But he grew frustrated at not seeing his hard work translate into faster 100-meter times. Seven months after moving to Los Angeles, he was ready to quit the sport until a scanning of the help wanted section of the paper convinced him he was lucky to have the opportunity for a track career.

With renewed energy, the five-foot, nine-inch, 175-pound Greene entered the 1997 U.S. championships and stunned himself by dropping 0.12 seconds off his previous best to win the race in a time of 9.96. Greene then demolished the field in the world championships at Athens that year with a world-record time of 9.86 seconds. The extroverted Greene told the press afterward, "It's time someone took responsibility for American sprinting." Two years later, Greene returned to the same track and lowered his own mark to 9.79.

Greene maintained his status as the world's premier sprinter into the Olympic year of 2000. This time Greene easily qualified for the 100 meters at the U.S. trials. His outspokenness, however, led him into a public feud with the world record holder, MICHAEL JOHNSON, at the 200-meter trials with the result that both men overexerted and injured themselves in the finals. At the Sydney Olympics, Greene surged ahead of the field with 25 yards to go to win the 100 meters in an Olympic record time of 9.87 seconds and added a gold medal as the anchor of the 4 × 100 meter relay. He retained his world championship in 2001 with a 9.80 clocking.

Further Reading

Deford, Frank. "Time Bandits," *Sports Illustrated*, August 6, 2001, pp. 56–67.

Henderson, Ashyia N. *Contemporary Black Biography.* Vol. 27. Detroit, Mich.: Gale Research, 2001.

Griffey, Ken, Jr.

(George Kenneth Griffey, Jr., "Junior" Griffey)
(1969–) *baseball outfielder*

Ken Griffey, Jr., has given a rare combination of grace and power to the game of baseball. Although the slick-fielding center fielder has never considered himself a power hitter, he clouted his 350th home run at a younger age than anyone else in baseball history.

"Junior," as the media dubbed him, was born on November 21, 1969, in Donora, Pennsylvania, to George, Sr., and Alberta Griffey. He grew up in a pro baseball environment. His father enjoyed a long and successful career in the major leagues, posting a career batting average of .296 and playing outstanding defense. Although Junior unquestionably inherited his father's athletic gifts, of equal importance was his understanding of the discipline and work ethic required to excel at the sport that he learned as a frequent visitor to the World Series champion Cincinnati Reds' dugout during his youth. Griffey's father, however, never pushed him to play the game. "The only thing Dad ever told me was to go out and have fun," says Junior. "Stay out of trouble and be a good kid."

Griffey showed promise as a young pitcher in Little League but was switched to the outfield at the age of 14 to take advantage of his exceptional range in the field. While attending Moeller High School in Cincinnati, he starred as a football tailback and wide receiver in addition to playing baseball. His potential in the latter sport was so evident that in 1987 the Seattle Mariners claimed him with the first selection of the draft.

Griffey's minor league apprenticeship with teams in Washington, California, and Vermont was marred by anxiety. In a fit of frustration due to the demands of the game and criticism of his play, he swallowed more than 200 aspirin early in 1988. But he recovered his equilibrium and, in 1989, surprised the Mariners in spring training by batting .359. Although he was slated to play in the team's top minor league club that year, the coaches recognized his ability and put him in Seattle's starting lineup. At 19 years of age, Griffey opened the 1989 season as the youngest player in the majors. But he played like a veteran, batting .287 and hitting 13 home runs before breaking his finger in July.

The next season, he led the Seattle offense with a .300 average and 22 home runs. Possessing an effortless, fluid swing, the left-handed batter packed deceptive power in his lean, six-foot three-inch frame. But it was as a center fielder that he won the most admiration. Griffey's speed, coordi-

With his trademark backward cap, Ken Griffey, Jr., represented a new generation of baseball stars in the 1990s. *(Brian Bahr/Getty Images)*

nation, fearlessness, and powerful throwing arm reminded veteran observers of the heyday of WILLIE MAYS. A special treat for Griffey that year was a midseason trade that brought his father to Seattle to finish his career. The two Griffeys became the only father-son combination in major league history to appear in the same lineup.

Junior's early success helped him relax and enjoy the game. His youthful enthusiasm, typified by his habit of wearing his cap backward on the practice field, endeared him to younger fans. In 1991, fans gave Griffey more All-Star votes than any other player. He rewarded them by winning the All-Star Most Valuable Player (MVP) Award for smashing three hits, including a home run, off Atlanta ace Greg Maddux. He finished the season with a .308 average and 27 home runs.

Griffey's power display began in earnest in 1993. Homering in eight straight games during a July stretch, he finished the season with 45 round-trips. Continuing the power surge, he won his first American League home run title the following year with 40, to go with a hefty .323 average.

Griffey's reckless abandon cost him in May 1995 when he broke his wrist crashing into the ouffield wall while making a game-saving catch. But after sitting out 73 games, he returned in mid-August to spark the Mariners' late-season charge that overtook the California Angels in the battle for the American League's Western Division. Griffey then pounded out five home runs and batted .391 to lead the Mariners to a dramatic upset victory over the New York Yankees in the playoffs. The Mariners, however, fell just short of the World Series, losing to Cleveland in the American League Championship Series.

Seattle rewarded their star in 1996 with a four-year, $34-million deal that made him the highest paid player in the game. Their money proved to be well spent, as Griffey solidified his status as the game's best player. His 49 home runs and .303 average in 1996 were just a preview. In 1997, Griffey terrorized opposing pitchers with 56 home runs and 147 runs batted in, both of which easily topped the league. In addition, he batted .304, led the league in runs scored, and continued his reign as the league's outstanding center fielder.

In 1998, Griffey smashed another 56 home runs, which made him the first American League batter to accomplish back-to-back 50-homer seasons since Babe Ruth. Few people noticed, however, because the performance was overshadowed by the media frenzy over the record-breaking home run contest between Mark McGwire and Sammy Sosa in the National League.

Griffey clouted 48 home runs in 1989, in a season clouded by controversy over questions about his future in Seattle. At the season's end, Griffey became the most highly pursued free agent in baseball. He opted to return to his hometown by signing with the Cincinnati Reds. The homecoming has been a source of frustration, however. The Reds have struggled since Griffey's arrival even as the Seattle Mariners have gone on to enjoy unprecedented success. Griffey, himself, was plagued by a season-opening slump in 2000 and a relentless spate of injuries over the next several seasons that all but destroyed his once promising quest to become the top slugger in the game's history.

Further Reading

Graham, Judith, ed. *Current Biography, 1996.* New York: H. W. Wilson, 1996.

Griffey, Ken, Jr. *Junior: Griffey on Griffey.* New York: Collins Publishers, 1997.

Griffey, Ken, Sr. "My Son, the Ballplayer," *Sports Illustrated,* June 21, 1999, pp. 32–37.

Griffith Joyner, Florence

(Florence Delorez Griffith, Flo Jo)
(1959–1998) *track-and-field sprinter*

At the end of the 20th century, Florence Griffith Joyner remained the fastest woman who ever lived. Her combination of graceful speed and flamboyant racing garb made her the star of the 1988 Olympics.

Florence Delorez Griffith was born on December 21, 1959, in Los Angeles, California. She was the seventh child of Florence, a seamstress, and Robert Griffith, an electronics engineer. In 1964, while they were living in the Mojave Desert, her mother grew frustrated with their situation and moved back to the Watts section of Los Angeles, in time to experience violent racial unrest in the neighborhood. She raised her children with a firm hand, allowing no television on weeknights and insisting on early bedtimes.

At the age of seven, Florence entered and won a sprint race as part of a Sugar Ray Robinson Youth Foundation competition, which started her on a track career. She set school records at Jordan High School in the sprints and long jump, but she was continually outshone by her city rival Valerie Brisco (later VALERIE BRISCO-HOOKS). At the same time, she exhibited a strong sense of style and independence with her creative hairstyles and her pet boa constrictor, which she carried around her neck.

After graduation in 1978, Griffith attended California State University at Northridge, where she joined her rival, Hooks, under the tutelage of coach Bob Kersee. Although she was a good student, financial struggles persuaded her to drop out to work full-time after her freshman year. However, Kersee insisted she stay and helped her find the financial aid she needed. When he was offered a job as track coach at the University of California at Los Angeles (UCLA), one of the premier track schools in the nation, Griffith followed him there. She ran well enough to qualify for the 1980 Olympic trials, where Brisco edged her out for the third and final spot in the 200 meters.

Griffith hovered near the top echelon of women sprinters over the next four years. In 1982, she won the women's 200 meters at the National Collegiate Athletic Association (NCAA) championships with a time of 22.39. A year later, she was the NCAA women's 400-meter champion. In

Photogenic Florence Griffith Joyner poses with her three gold medals from the 1988 Seoul Olympics. *(Tony Duffy/Getty Images)*

1984, she made the U.S. Olympic team at 200 meters, turning heads in the process by competing in a shimmering bodysuit. "Fluorescent Flo," as some called her, won the silver medal at the Los Angeles Olympics. Nonetheless, the experience was not completely satisfying. Again, Valerie Brisco had beaten her out, this time claiming the gold. In addition, the East Germans, who fielded the best women's sprint team in the world, had boycotted the Olympics, making her accomplishment somewhat hollow. As the crowning blow, the U.S. team coaches refused to let her run in the 4 × 100 relay unless she cut her six-inch fingernails, which, they believed, would hinder the passing of the baton. Stubbornly, Griffith refused and it cost her a gold medal.

Griffith's enthusiasm for training waned, especially when she landed an employee relations job. But at about that time, she began dating Al Joyner, Olympic gold medal winner in the 1984 triple jump, who was the brother of her former UCLA teammate, track star Jackie Joyner (later JACKIE JOYNER-KERSEE). They encouraged her to give the sport another try. Her comeback was a success, as she finished second in the 200 meters at the 1987 world championships in Rome, wearing another of her track fashion innovations, a hood.

After marrying Joyner that fall, Griffith Joyner set her sights on a higher goal. As she described it, "When you've been second best for so long, you can either accept it or try to become the best. I made the decision to become the best in 1988." At first, she worked days in a bank and trained at night. Then she found a job with a company that helped Olympic athletes by allowing her to work four hours and train the rest of the day.

Although she had recorded the fastest 100-meter time among Americans in 1987, she went into the 1988 U.S. Olympic trials as an underdog to such sprinters as the defending Olympic gold medalist EVELYN ASHFORD. Confident in her abilities after a rigorous training routine, she showed up for the competition in Indianapolis in the gaudiest costumes anyone had ever seen on a track. They included brilliant colors, one-legged tights, and an all-white-lace bodysuit. A rival sprinter, Gwen Torrence, commented, "If you're going to wear outfits like that, then you'd better do something in them."

Flo Jo, as the press began to call her, certainly "did something." She stunned her rivals and the crowd by exploding out of the starting blocks in the quarterfinals and shattering the world record of 10.76 with a winning time of 10.49. It so anni-

hilated the previous record that many observers refused to believe that she had not been aided by a brisk tail wind. Flo Jo followed this up by easily defeating Ashford in the finals in 10.61. She then won the 200 meters as well, in a U.S. record time of 21.77.

Flo Jo's stunning performance made her a marked woman at the 1988 Olympics in Seoul, Korea. Rather than tightening up under the pressure, she seemed to thrive on it. She breezed through the preliminary rounds of the 100 meters with a best time of 10.62 that obliterated Ashford's previous Olympic mark of 10.97. She then rocketed to victory in the final by a huge margin in 10.54, a time that was disallowed because of a tail wind. Moving on to the 200 meters, she appeared to be floating on air as she glided to decisive victory in a world record time of 21.34, flashing a brilliant smile as she crossed the finish line.

In a show of class, Flo Jo ran the third leg of the 4 × 100 relay for the U.S. team, allowing the team's veteran star, Ashford, the honor of running the anchor leg. Ashford responded with a come-from-behind effort that gave Joyner her third gold medal. Flo Jo nearly won an unprecedented fourth gold medal in the 4 × 400 relay. It took a world-record effort by the Soviet team to beat out the U.S. team.

The disqualification of the men's 100-meter winner Ben Johnson for steroid use and the incredible improvement Flo Jo made in 1988 led to widespread rumors that she had taken steroids. Those close to her vigorously denied all allegations and no evidence linking her with steroid use was ever presented.

Griffith Joyner was named the Associated Press Female Athlete of the Year in 1988 and also won the Sullivan Award as the nation's top amateur athlete. She retired in 1989, owning the fastest seven times ever run in the 100 meters. She moved on to her other interest in life, fashion designing, until her sudden death of heart failure on September 21, 1998.

Further Reading

Condon, Robert J. *Great Women Athletes of the 20th Century.* Jefferson, N.C.: McFarland & Company, 1999.

Griffith Joyner, Florence, and John Hane. *Running for Dummies.* Foster City, Calif.: IDG Books, 1999.

Moore, Kenny. "Very Fancy, Very Fast," *Sports Illustrated,* September 14, 1988, pp. 158–161.

Gwynn, Tony

(Anthony Keith Gwynn)
(1960–   ) *baseball outfielder*

Playing his entire career for the low-profile San Diego Padres, Tony Gwynn did not gain the public recognition of many lesser contemporaries. Nonetheless, he stands with ROD CAREW as the best pure hitters in major league baseball over the past half-century.

He was born Anthony Keith Gwynn on May 9, 1960, in Los Angeles. His was a close-knit family supported by his mother, Vendella, who worked for the post office, and his father, Charles Gwynn, Sr., a warehouseman for the state of California. The family moved to Long Beach when Tony was eight. There he and his two brothers spent many hours playing baseball in the backyard with a whiffle ball. All three ultimately played either collegiate or professional ball.

Tony was the best athlete of the three. Although only five feet, 11 inches, he showed such talent as a point guard at Long Beach Polytech High School that he earned a basketball scholarship to San Diego State University. There he won a starting job and set a school record for assists. But during his sophomore year, he began to realize that his size limited his chances of going on to the pros, and, while continuing to play basketball, he switched his main focus to baseball. After some experimentation, Gwynn switched to a lighter, thick-handled bat and saw his average soar to over .400 during his last two seasons.

In 1981 Gwynn had the rare distinction of being drafted by pro teams in two different sports on the same day. He chose the offer of the San Diego Padres over that of the San Diego Clippers and reported to their minor club at Walla Walla, Washington. Although confident in his batting, Gwynn was concerned about his fielding. In the minors he worked constantly to improve his throwing and his outfield play.

Gwynn played so well at Walla Walla, Amarillo, and Hawaii that the Padres called him up to the majors in 1982. His progress was thwarted, however, when he broke both wrists that year and returned to the minors. Gwynn returned to the Padres for good on June 21, 1983. As a teaser of what was to come, he put together a 25-game hitting streak, best in the majors that year, and finished with a .309 average. Few, if any batters have been so totally consumed by the science of hitting as Tony Gwynn. During a rare slump in 1983, he began to use a video recorder, which he had bought to document his son's childhood, and his wife, Alicia, recorded his at bats. By carefully analyzing every detail of his swing, and then using 600-swing workouts to correct the flaws, Gwynn was able to make the adjustments needed to get himself back on track. He went on to compile an extensive library of video, not only of his own swing, but of the pitching motions of each pitcher in the league. He disciplined himself to become the best pure hitter in the National League, resisting the urge to smash home runs. That meant using the smallest bat in the majors and letting the location of the pitch dictate whether he pulled the ball or slapped it to the opposite field. A left-handed batter, Gwynn also used his speed to beat out infield grounders for hits.

The result of Gwynn's effort was that in 20 seasons, he never failed to reach the .300 mark. He earned his first batting title in 1984 with a .351 average, leading the league in hits with 213. His effort helped the surprising Padres win the National League's Western Division title. Gwynn then contributed a .368 average as the Padres defeated the Chicago Cubs to earn a berth in the World Series, which they lost to the Detroit Tigers.

It was the last taste of team success Gwynn would enjoy for more than a decade, as the small-market Padres lacked the resources to keep pace with the high payrolls of the wealthier teams.

Although Gwynn continued to bat over .300, he did not win batting titles in 1985 and 1986. His long hours of defensive work paid off, however, as he earned the Gold Glove as the National League's top defensive right fielder in 1986. In 1987, Gwynn scorched major league pitchers for a .370 average, the highest total in the National League in 30 years. He stole 56 bases, scored 119 runs, and won a second Gold Glove, yet, because the Padres played dreadfully as a team, he was ignored in the league Most Valuable Player (MVP) voting. Over the years, Gwynn was constantly advised to move on to a larger-market team so he could gain more recognition and team success. Gwynn, however, enjoyed the San Diego community and saw the lack of attention as a benefit. "You've got to have time and room to work at your craft," he responded, and the relative lack of demands on his time gave him that freedom.

The only season in which Gwynn seemed in danger of breaking his streak of .300 seasons was in 1988, when he was mired at .246 in early July. He managed to right himself, however, and boosted his average to .313 by season's end to win his third batting title. After repeating as batting champion in 1989 with a .336 mark, Gwynn went through a four-year drought. He broke out of it with a vengeance in 1994. During the strike-shortened season, he batted .394, the best achieved in the major leagues in over half a century.

During his 20-year major league career, Gwynn captured eight batting titles, the last in 1997 at the age of 37. Such was his reputation for hitting that few fans realize he has won five Gold Glove awards for fielding.

Injuries took an increasing toll on Gwynn at the end of his career, forcing him to sit on the bench for most of his final two years. But he retired after the 2001 season with his string of .300 seasons unbroken. Gwynn has long been regarded as one of the true gentlemen in baseball. As OZZIE SMITH said of him, "The bottom line is that Tony's a better person than he is a hitter, and you know, he's a pretty good hitter."

Further Reading

Graham, Judith, ed. *Current Biography, 1996.* New York: H. W. Wilson, 1996.

Gwynn, Tony, with Roger Vaughn. *The Art of Hitting.* New York: GT Publishing, 1998.

Stevenson, S. "Tony Gwynn: A Portrait of the Scientist in the Batter's Box." *New York Times Biographical Service,* June 1991, p. 168.

H

Hagler, Marvin
(Marvelous Marvin Hagler)
(1954–) *boxer*

During the height of Marvin Hagler's career, the *London Observer* noted, "There are two middleweight divisions, Hagler and the rest." After being denied a shot at the title for several years, he reigned for nearly a decade as undefeated champion.

Marvin was born on May 23, 1954, in Newark, New Jersey, to Robert Sims, who left when Marvin was small, and Ida Mae Hagler. Violent riots in the summer of 1968 scared Ida Mae into moving the family to Brockton, Massachusetts. Marvin, the oldest of six children, was a shy youngster. He walked into a boxing gym and stood silent until someone finally asked whether he wanted to box. Hagler nodded and his career was born.

In the ring, the left-handed Hagler displayed power, speed, stamina, long reach, and intelligence. After winning 48 of 50 amateur fights and the national Amateur Athletic Union (AAU) title in 1973, he turned pro in the middleweight division. With his head shaved for good luck, he scored some impressive knockouts before upsetting the Olympic gold medal champion Ray Seales in a 10-round decision in August 1974. Although he lost two close decisions in 1976, his talent was so obvious at that point that champions avoided

him for years. Hagler channeled his frustration into relentless training. "People may have thought they were cutting out my heart," he said, "but they were only making me meaner."

Hagler demolished 20 of the best-quality opponents he could find before he was finally offered a title fight against Vito Antuofermo in November 1979. Hagler came out uncharacteristically flat in the fight and finished with a draw. But he was given a second chance a year later against Alan Minter, who had wrested the crown from Antuofermo. Fighting before a rowdy crowd of supporters in his native England, Minter tried to take the fight to Hagler. A master at counterpunching, Hagler methodically dismantled his opponent, who was counted out in the third round.

For most of the decade, Hagler put his title on the line against the best challengers and battered them into submission. His most memorable fight took place on April 15, 1985, against THOMAS HEARNS. This dream match between two of the top middle division fighters in history was several years in the making, and during that time animosity had grown between the two proud fighters. According to one observer, the boxers "tore from their corners like greyhounds released from their traps." For two rounds they slammed each other with thunderous blows, which left Hagler bleeding from two serious cuts.

When asked whether he could see his opponent, Hagler snarled, "I'm hitting him, aren't I?" He then knocked out Hearns in the third round.

During many years of title defenses, only the great Roberto Duran managed to go the distance with Hagler. The champ's streak came to an end in 1987 against SUGAR RAY LEONARD. Even then, against such a high-quality opponent, Hagler frequently staggered his foe, and when the split decision was announced, he stood in stunned disbelief. It was a bitter end to the career of a man who, for nearly a decade, was perhaps the most feared fighter in the world.

Further Reading

Mullan, Henry. *Boxing*. London: Chartwell Books, 1996.
Telander, Rick. "With Friends Like These, Who Needs Sugar Ray?" *Sports Illustrated*, July 20, 1990, pp. 40–42.
Walsh, Peter. *Men of Steel*. London: Robson Books, 1993.

Hawkins, Connie

(Cornelius Hawkins)
(1942–) *basketball forward*

Despite relatively unimpressive National Basketball Association (NBA) statistics, Connie Hawkins remains a legend among his peers. As KAREEM ABDUL-JABBAR said of him, "Hawk represented an entire subculture of competition and playground excellence."

Cornelius Hawkins was born on July 17, 1942, in the Bedford-Stuyvesant district of New York City to Dorothy and Isaiah Hawkins. Isaiah abandoned the family when Connie was small, leaving Dorothy to struggle with raising and supporting six children.

Connie was a tall, shy youth who developed an early taste for basketball on the playgrounds and at the local Young Men's Christian Association (YMCA). It was on these playgrounds that he acquired an unmatched reputation. During the summers, the high school kid would challenge and often beat top NBA stars who dropped by to play the local talent. The six-foot, eight-inch Hawkins had huge hands and used them to create an endless variety of swooping, one-handed moves to the basket. He also displayed his skills on an organized level, leading Boys High School to 40 straight wins and earning praise as a *Parade Magazine* High School All-American.

Hawkins accepted a scholarship to attend the University of Iowa, where his pro aspirations were derailed. Early in his college career, he was rumored to have been involved in a betting scandal. Although charges were never brought against him, he was forced to leave Iowa in 1961. At the same time, his pro options were choked off when the NBA declared that the league would never accept any college player associated with betting scandals. Although no case was ever presented against Hawkins, the league considered him stained by the scandal and banned him.

Hawkins was left scrambling to find alternatives to a once-bright career. He joined the Pittsburgh Rens of the American Basketball League in 1962 and was easily the star of the league until it folded at the end of the season. Hawkins then played four seasons with the Harlem Globetrotters, before he jumped at a chance to play competitive ball with the formation of the American Basketball Association (ABA) in 1967. In his first year, Hawkins led the league in scoring with a 26.8 average, finished second in rebounding, captured the ABA's Most Valuable Player (MVP) Award, and led his team to the league championship.

The team moved to Minneapolis the following year, and there Hawkins averaged 30 points per game, including an ABA record 57 against the New York Nets.

In 1969, Hawkins won a lawsuit against the NBA for unjustly barring him. After an eight-year exile he was admitted to the league and signed with the Phoenix Suns. Although already slowed by injuries that would continue to take their toll, Hawkins averaged more than 24 points a game in his first season, sixth in the league, and grabbed more than 10 rebounds a game. He was selected for the NBA All-Star game that year, an honor that was repeated the following year.

Hawkins played only seven seasons in the NBA before injuries forced his retirement in 1976. Although circumstances prevented him from showing his best playground wizardry basketball in the NBA, he was voted into the basketball Hall of Fame in 1992.

Further Reading

Great Athletes of the Twentieth Century. Vol. 7. Pasadena, Calif.: Salem Press, 1994.

Wolf, David. *Foul! The Connie Hawkins Story.* New York: Holt, Rinehart & Winston, 1972.

Hayes, Bob

(Robert Lee Hayes)
(1942–2002) *track-and-field sprinter, football wide receiver*

Bob Hayes, perhaps the most powerful sprinter of all time, reigned without challenge as the world's fastest human in the early 1960s. He then capitalized on his speed to enjoy a rewarding pro football career.

He was born Robert Lee Hayes on December 20, 1942, in Jacksonville, Florida, the son of a disabled war veteran and a domestic worker who separated early in his life. Raised primarily by his mother in a tough neighborhood of Jacksonville, he helped the family make ends meet by shining shoes as a teen.

Hayes played high school football well enough to win a scholarship to play the sport at Florida A & M. During an early football practice, Hayes flew by the team's fastest players, including the future pro running back Hewritt Dixon. When the coach chewed out his players for loafing, a stunned Dixon responded, "Coach, I never ran faster in my life." Later that spring, Hayes ran a near–world record time of 9.3 in the 100-meter dash, which con-

vinced both the runner and his coaches that he could contend for an Olympic medal.

During the last three years of college, Hayes ranked as the number-one sprinter in the world. Running in his churning, pigeon-toed style, the heavily muscled Hayes captured Amateur Athletic Union (AAU) championships in the 100-yard dash in both 1962 and 1963 and the 100-meter dash in 1964. Despite being a notoriously slow starter, Hayes displayed such acceleration that he set a world record of 5.9 seconds in the 60-yard dash, blazed a world record 9.1 in the 100-yard dash, and showed surprising stamina in capturing the 200-meter dash at the National Collegiate Athletic Association (NCAA) finals.

Hayes went into the 1964 Tokyo Olympic Games as a heavy favorite in the 100 meters, having won more than 100 consecutive races at that distance. He quickly destroyed all suspense by obliterating all opponents in the earlier heats, and he won the finals in a time of 10.0, tying the world record.

Most observers, however, cited the 4 × 100 relay as Hayes's most spectacular moment. Running the final leg for the U.S. team, he took the baton handoff in sixth place, a good four yards behind the leading French team. With a stunning burst of speed, Hayes caught the leaders within 30 yards and breezed home with a three-yard margin of victory.

Having accomplished all he could in track, the burly six-foot, 185-pound Hayes returned to football. Whereas many world-class sprinters have washed out in pro football tryouts, Hayes showed tremendous aptitude for the wide receiver position. Signed by the Dallas Cowboys in 1965, he immediately provided the Cowboys with the most dangerous long pass threat in the game. In his rookie season, he caught 46 passes for 1,003 yards, for a league-leading average of 21.8 yards per catch, and 13 touchdowns. Hayes continued to burn defenders in 1966 with 64 catches, for 1,232 yards and 13 more touchdowns, and added 10 more touchdowns in 1967: an eye-popping three-year total of 33 touchdowns. Hayes stayed with the Cowboys until 1975, when he joined the San Francisco 49ers for one final season. He finished his National Football League (NFL) career with 76 touchdowns, 71 of them coming on pass receptions.

Hayes was convicted and jailed on drug charges in the 1970s but turned his life around before his death from prostate cancer in 2002.

Further Reading

Hayes, Bob, and Robert Pack. *Run, Bullet, Run: The Rise, Fall, and Rise Again of Bob Hayes.* New York: Harper & Row, 1990.

Moritz, Charles, ed. *Current Biography, 1966.* New York: H. W. Wilson, 1966.

Hayes, Elvin Ernest
(The Big E)
(1945–   ) *basketball forward*

Although overshadowed through most of his career by KAREEM ABDUL-JABBAR, Elvin Hayes enjoyed phenomenal success as a collegian and proved one of the most versatile and durable big men in the National Basketball Association (NBA).

Elvin Ernest Hayes was born on November 17, 1945, in Rayville, a small town in northeastern Louisiana. He is somewhat of a genetic anomaly, as his father was only five feet, five inches, and none of his five siblings grew taller than five feet, seven inches. Elvin grew up with so little money that the family had no indoor plumbing or telephone. He spent much of his summers picking cotton all day and dreaming of becoming a major league baseball player.

In eighth grade he was rescued from a bad crowd of friends by the Reverend John Calvin, an eighth-grade teacher at Eulah Britton High School, who took an interest in him and put him on his basketball team. Hayes disliked the game at first because he knew so little about it. But as he learned, he grew into an imposing physical speci-

men, reaching six feet, five inches, and still growing fast as a high school senior. By his senior year he had developed to the point where he led Eulah Britton to 53 consecutive wins and scored 45 points in the team's state championship win.

In 1964 Hayes boldly accepted a scholarship from the University of Houston, which had never before invited an African American into its basketball program. He led the Cougars to two National Collegiate Athletic Association (NCAA) Final Four appearances and held center stage in the most publicized college basketball game of his time. It was his 39-point, 15-rebound performance in a 71–69 victory over seemingly invincible University of California-Los Angeles (UCLA) on January 20, 1968, that made "The Big E" a household name among the nation's basketball fans.

Influenced by the impression he created in that game, the San Diego Clippers made Hayes the first player selected in the 1968 NBA draft. He got off to a blazing start as a pro by leading the NBA in scoring with a 28.4 average and finishing second in rebounds at 17.1. Incredibly, he lost the Rookie of the Year balloting to Wes Unseld.

Despite giving up several inches to opposing centers, the six-foot, nine-inch Hayes continued to rank among the league's best in scoring, reboundings, and blocked shots. He finished second in scoring in 1969–70 and third the following season with a career best 28.7 average. Hayes claimed rebounding titles in both 1970 and 1974.

Continually underappreciated, Hayes was traded to Houston in 1971 and ended up with the Baltimore Bullets the following year. With the Bullets, who soon moved to Washington, Hayes played power forward and teamed with center, Unseld, to form a solid inside presence. Their efforts culminated in a hard-fought, seven-game victory over Seattle in the championship series of 1978. Hayes later reflected, "Out of my 16 years of playing, I had waited for that moment, and that moment came and it was tremendous." The Big E finished his career in Houston in 1984 as the fourth leading rebounder in NBA history.

Further Reading

Henderson, Edwin B. *The Black Athlete: Emergence and Arrival.* New York: Publishers Company, 1968.

Hayes, Elvin, and Bill Gilbert. *They Call Me the Big E.* New York: Prentice-Hall, 1978.

Haynes, Marques Oreole
(1926–) *basketball guard*

Marques Haynes has been basketball's unparalleled showman. In a career that lasted 40 years, Haynes played more basketball games than any person in history and helped lay the foundation for the growth of the professional game.

He was born Marques Oreole Haynes on October 3, 1926, in Sand Springs, Oklahoma, the son of Matthew and Hattie Haynes. Matthew left the family when Marques, the youngest of the couple's four children, was four. All the Haynes children were fine athletes and Marques followed in the footsteps of his older siblings. In junior high he played on a team coached by his older brother, Wendell, who taught him dribbling skills. At segregated Booker T. Washington High School in Sand Springs, Marques played football and led the basketball team to the state high school championship as a senior.

Haynes then followed his older brothers to Langston University, a black university in Oklahoma. The six-foot guard broke into the starting lineup as a freshman and directed the offense of one of the most successful teams of the time. Langston posted a 112–3 record with Haynes in charge, including a 51-game winning streak. Haynes was named the league's Most Valuable Player (MVP) in each of his final three seasons.

Among Langston's victims was a barnstorming professional team known as the Harlem Globetrotters. Haynes scored 21 points in his team's shocking upset over the pros and so impressed the Globetrotters' owner, Abe Saperstein, that when Haynes graduated in 1946, he signed him to play for Harlem. Along with the forward, Goose

Marques Haynes entertained fans for 37 years with his dribbling wizardry. *(Basketball Hall of Fame)*

Tatum, Haynes became the centerpiece of a Globetrotter team that was to gain international fame. Haynes's specialty was dribbling, and he captivated crowds by maintaining three bounces per second while keeping the ball an inch off the floor. He and his teammates were so talented that they defeated the National Basketball Association (NBA) champion Minneapolis Lakers in both 1947 and 1948. Two years later, Haynes and the Globetrotters performed before 75,000 fans in Berlin, Germany, the largest crowd ever to watch a basketball game. The touring Globetrotters were such enthusiastic and fun-loving ambassadors that they generated national and international interest in the sport, which spilled over to the fledgling NBA.

In 1953, Haynes left the team in a contract dispute with Saperstein and formed his own barnstorming club, The Fabulous Magicians, which for a time rivaled the Globetrotters in popularity. Meanwhile, in the early 1950s, the NBA dismantled its color barrier and began signing blacks. Haynes was wooed by several NBA teams. But by this time, he had a considerable investment in his own team and was having too much fun entertaining crowds to join the NBA.

As the NBA began attracting the most skilled black players, the Magicians and the Globetrotters focused more on entertainment than on pure competition. Haynes continued to play an exhausting schedule for the Magicians from 1953 to 1972, for the Globetrotters again from 1972 to 1979, and for the revived Magicians in the 1980s. By the time of his retirement in 1992, he had played an estimated 12,000 games, in all 50 states and in 97 countries. In 1994 the state of Oklahoma honored him by renaming a 12-mile stretch of highway Marques Haynes Highway, and in 1998 he was inducted into the pro basketball Hall of Fame.

Further Reading

Mitchell-Powell, Brenda, ed. *African American Biography.* Vol. 2. Detroit: UXL, 1994.

Phelps, Shirelle. *Contemporary Black Biography.* Vol. 22. Detroit, Mich.: Gale Research, 1999.

Hearns, Thomas
(Hit Man Hearns)
(1958–) *boxer*

Thomas "Hit Man" Hearns, one of boxing's most feared punchers, was the first man to win world championships in five different weight divisions.

Hearns was born on October 18, 1958, in Memphis, Tennessee. At age five, he moved with his mother, Lois, to Detroit, where he grew up on the city's east side. Painfully shy by nature, Hearns developed an interest in boxing by watching the sport on television. After taking lessons at a neighborhood gym for a year, 11-year-old Hearns began riding the bus across town to work out at the more boxing-intensive Kronk Gym on the west side. Hearns weighed only 55 pounds at the time, and trainers advised him he was too thin to be a fighter.

Hearns kept at it, however, and through sheer determination made himself into a ferocious and effective puncher. During his senior year, he dropped out of high school to work at his craft full-time. Hearns started slowly as an amateur, losing two of his first six fights. But he gained experience through a busy schedule of activity and eventually reached the finals in the 132-pound class at the 1976 Amateur Athletic Union (AAU) tournament. He suffered a crushing disappointment, however, by losing that fight, which eliminated him from contention for the U.S. Olympic team. In 1977, Hearns bounced back to win both the AAU and the Golden Gloves tournament to earn recognition as the nation's top amateur boxer. After winning 155 of 163 amateur bouts, he turned professional in November 1977.

The lanky Hearns easily dispatched his first 28 opponents, knocking out 26 of them, generally in the first three rounds. "Hit Man" Hearns, as he became known, was given his first title shot in August 1980 against welterweight champion Jose Cuevas. The champ failed to last two rounds against Hearns's onslaught. The Hit Man further solidified his reputation as a puncher by becoming the first man to flatten Panamanian star Roberto Duran. In December 1982, Hearns showed another side of his talent when he fought crafty Wilfred Benitez for the junior middleweight crown. In a more controlled, strategic fight, he earned a 15-round decision to claim his second title.

As he continued to mature, Hearns kept moving up in weight class. In 1987 he captured the light heavyweight title by defeating Dennis Andries of Great Britain. He claimed the middleweight title the same year and then went on to take the light heavyweight championship in 1988.

Ironically, Hearns's most memorable fights were two of his losses. In September 1981, he squared off against undefeated SUGAR RAY LEONARD. Hearns battered his famous rival in the early rounds and forged a commanding lead on points. But as Hearns wilted in the blistering Las Vegas heat, Leonard mounted a desperate comeback in the 14th round to gain a knockout victory. Four years later, Hearns stood toe-to-toe with Marvelous MARVIN HAGLER in a middleweight bout with a similar result. Hearns rocked the champion with thunderous punches only to be knocked out in the third round.

Further Reading

Henderson, Ashyia N. *Contemporary Black Biography*. Vol. 25. Detroit: Gale Research, 2001.

Walsh, Peter. *Men of Steel*. London: Robson Books, 1993.

Henderson, Rickey
(Rickey Henley)
(1958–   ) *baseball outfielder*

Rickey Henderson ranks as baseball's top base stealer of all time. The controversial outfielder has also set the standard for runs scored, joined the exclusive 3,000-hit club, won a Gold Glove for defense, and set a major league record for lead-off home runs.

He was born Rickey Henley in a car on the way to the hospital on Chicago's South Side on December 25, 1958. His father, John Henley, left the family when Rickey was two, and Rickey never saw him again. His mother, Bobbie, then moved with her four boys to her mother's farm in Pine Bluff, Arkansas. There Rickey learned to play baseball at the urging of his older brother, Tyrone. After Bobbie married Paul Henderson, the family moved to a working-class neighborhood in Oakland, California, where Rickey was adopted by his stepfather and took his last name.

Rickey spent most of his free time at nearby Bushrod Park, playing with older boys whatever

sport was in season. He showed exceptional speed at a young age, and in sixth grade was named Bushrod Park's Athlete of the Year. He went on to become a four-sport star at Oakland Technical High School. Football was his favorite sport, and he was named first-team all-city as a running back and second-team as a linebacker. Area fans proclaimed him the city's best running back since O. J. SIMPSON.

However, Henderson's mother, concerned about his health, insisted that Rickey turn down scholarship offers at major football schools and instead pursue a professional baseball career. In 1976, Henderson signed with the Oakland A's, the team he had idolized since moving to Oakland. He spent several years in the minor leagues before moving up to the majors on June 23, 1979.

Unfortunately, by that time the once-powerful A's had disintegrated into baseball's worst team. Oakland lost 108 games in Henderson's first year and played in a virtually empty stadium. Henderson took it upon himself single-handedly to give Oakland fans a reason to go to the ballpark the following year. In his first full season in the majors, he batted .303, drew 117 walks, scored 111 runs, and broke Ty Cobb's American League record for steals, finishing with an even 100. He followed that up with a .319 average in 1981 to lead the surprising A's back into the play-offs.

During spring training in 1982, Oakland's manager, Billy Martin, approached his star and said, "Rickey, we're going to break the record this year." The mark in question was LOU BROCK's major league stolen base record of 118. From the opening pitch, Henderson was off and running, barreling into bases with his reckless, head-first slide. By the end of April he had 22 steals; a month later he was already up to 49. At the end of July, Henderson's total stood at 99, and he still had two months to go. Henderson swiped record-setting base number 119 on August 27 and finished the season with 130, a record that has never been challenged. He stole 108 more bases the

Rickey Henderson's ability to read pitchers' motions helped him become baseball's top base stealer. *(National Baseball Hall of Fame Library, Cooperstown, N.Y.)*

following season, giving him three seasons of more than 100 stolen bases in four years.

In 1984, Oakland traded Henderson to the New York Yankees for six players. The Yankees, in need of a center fielder, switched Henderson to that position from his accustomed spot in left field. While at New York, the thickly muscled Henderson began hitting with power for the first time in his career. In 1985, he blasted 24 home

runs. At the same time, he hit and stole his way into scoring position for powerful hitters such as Don Mattingly to drive him in. Henderson stole 80 bases and scored a staggering 146 runs that year.

Despite Henderson's efforts, however, the Yankees could not manage to get into postseason play. The frustration of falling short of the high Yankee expectations took its toll on Henderson in 1987. For the first time in his career, he suffered a leg injury that kept him out of the lineup for several weeks. Yankee officials, however, were not convinced that he was hurt and the battle that raged in the press over the rest of the season angered Henderson.

Before that time, Henderson had acquired a reputation as a showoff and an egotist. Part of the problem was that he viewed himself as an entertainer as well as an athlete. Having grown up watching WILLIE MAYS's unique basket catch, he worked to perfect his own trademark catch— snatching fly balls with a quick swipe that appeared to purists to be needlessly risky. Also, since speed was his main asset, he was especially protective of his legs and did not run full speed when he thought the situation did not warrant it. Baseball enthusiasts viewed this as laziness. Therefore, even though Henderson was indeed struggling with a torn hamstring, many fans began to regard him as a malcontent and a bad influence on the club, a label that has clung to him ever since.

In view of his problems in New York, Henderson was pleased to be traded back to the Oakland A's in 1989. He provided exactly the spark the up-and-coming A's needed to win their division. In the American League Championship Series against Toronto, Henderson batted .400 and scored eight runs to lead the A's to victory. He went on to bat .474 in the World Series as the championship returned to Oakland.

Henderson followed this up by batting .325, hitting 28 home runs and leading the league in steals and runs scored in 1990, an effort that earned him the American League's Most Valuable Player Award. In May of that season, he also broke Ty Cobb's American League record of 892 stolen bases in a career. Continuing his assault on the record books, he surpassed Brock's major league steals mark of 939 on May 1, 1991.

Henderson then began a long odyssey through the league, playing for Toronto, going back to Oakland, then to San Diego, Anaheim,

back to Oakland, to the New York Mets, Seattle Mariners, and back to San Diego. Remarkably, he maintained his speed and batting eye into his 40s. This allowed him to finish the 2001 season with a remarkable flourish: In the final week of the season, Henderson achieved his 3,000th hit and scored his 2,248th run to set an all-time major league mark in that category. Henderson began the 2002 season with yet another new team, the Boston Red Sox, with whom he continued to add to his record totals in steals and runs scored.

Further Reading

Gammons, Peter. "Man of Steal," *Sports Illustrated,* October 1, 1990, pp. 60–68.

Henderson, Rickey, with John Shea. *Off Base: Confessions of a Thief.* New York: HarperCollins, 1992.

Hill, Grant Henry
(1972–) *basketball forward*

Grant Hill is known as the reluctant superstar. In a pro basketball era of strutting and trash talking, the polite and modest Hill has impressed observers both on and off the basketball court.

He was born Grant Henry Hill on October 5, 1972, in Dallas, Texas, an only child surrounded by fame and accomplishment. His father, Calvin, starred at running back for the Dallas Cowboys, while his mother, Janet, a college roommate of Hillary Rodham Clinton, founded her own consulting firm. Young Grant was forever trying to melt into the background, desperate to prove that, despite his lofty lineage, he was just one of the guys.

He grew up in Reston, Virginia, after his father was traded to the Washington Redskins in 1975. His parents were extremely strict, to the point that Hill says, "I didn't make any mistakes as a kid because I couldn't." His father refused to let him play football until he was in high school for fear of injury and the pressure of living up to his dad's reputation; by that time he had no interest in the sport. Instead, he played soccer, winning a state championship at the ages of 10 and 12, and basketball.

Still concerned about fitting in with his peers, Hill begged off when his coach at South Lakes High School put him in the starting lineup as a sophomore. Under pressure from his parents, though, he relented and was named Northern Virginia's High School Player of the Year three seasons in a row.

He went on to Duke University, where, as a defensive ace, he played a key role in the team's national championships in both his freshman and sophomore years. Although six feet, eight inches, Hill was so quick and had such good ball control that Duke occasionally asked him to fill in at point guard. Because he preferred to blend in with his teammates, he got few headlines. But after Hill's graduation in 1994, the Duke coach, Mike Krzyzewski, head of college basketball's most successful program, declared, "Grant Hill is the best player I ever coached, period."

The Detroit Pistons claimed him with their first choice in the 1993 draft. Hill's all-around skill and selfless, likable personality attracted droves of fans in his first months as a pro. They made him the first rookie ever to receive the most All-Star votes, an honor that genuinely embarrassed Hill.

Hill averaged 19.9 points per game and shared the Rookie of the Year Award with the Phoenix star Jason Kidd. The following year he was the only player in the National Basketball Association (NBA) to lead his team in scoring, rebounds, assists, and steals. Yet it was not until he began practicing with the top pros as a member of the gold-medal-winning U.S. Olympic team that he started believing he could hold his own against the NBA's best.

A model of consistency, Hill averaged 21 points per game from 1996–97 to 1998–99. But because he had little support from a weak team, the Pistons had only modest success. Hill ratcheted his scoring up to 25.8 points per game in 1999–2000, but it still was not enough to make

Detroit a winner. Frustrated, Hill left Detroit and in 2000 signed as a free agent with Orlando, when an injury sidelined him for most of the 2000–01 season and all of the next three seasons before he finally regained the court in 2004.

Further Reading

Hill, Grant. *Change the Game: One Athlete's Thoughts on Sports, Dreams, and Growing Up.* Princeville, Hawaii: Lightning Source, 1997.

Thomsen, I. "Come Hill or High Water," *Sports Illustrated*, July 17, 2000, pp. 46–48.

Holdsclaw, Chamique
(1977–   ) *basketball player*

No woman basketball player has ever inspired the hype that accompanied Chamique Holdsclaw before she had graduated from college. Hailed as the MICHAEL JORDAN of women's basketball, Holdsclaw has compiled an unparalleled record of success and has been described by basketball experts as having fundamentally changed the sport of women's basketball.

Holdsclaw was born on August 9, 1977, in New York City. Financial struggles led to her parents' divorce, and they sent the 11-year-old Chamique to live with her grandmother June in Queens. Holdsclaw credits her grandmother with holding her life together.

Holdsclaw's talent at basketball was such that her teams almost never lost, beginning with her eighth-grade team. She immediately cracked the starting lineup at Christ the King High School as a freshman and helped the team to the state championship. The school never lost a postseason game during her tenure, winning the state title all four years. College scouts hailed her as the best female high school player ever. At six feet, two inches, she could dominate teams in the paint, and yet she was quick enough and had such polished dribbling and passing skills that she could play point guard.

Holdsclaw decided to join the powerhouse program of the University of Tennessee, where Coach Pat Summit reigned as the most respected women's coach in the nation. The two clashed at first but grew to admire and respect each other's competitiveness. Easily making the transition from high school to college, Holdsclaw averaged more than 18 points per game, won All-American recognition, and sparked the Volunteers' National Collegiate Athletic Association (NCAA) championship run. During her four seasons at Tennessee, the team won three national titles, giving her a nearly flawless streak of seven championships in eight years of play. Holdsclaw became the Southeastern Conference's career scoring and rebounding leader and the first woman ever to win ESPN's College Player of the Week Award. She beat out all competitors, male and female, to win the 1999 Sullivan Award as the nation's finest amateur athlete; grateful Volunteer fans named a street after her.

The Washington Mystics made Holdsclaw the top choice in the 1999, Women's National Basketball Association (WNBA) draft. At about the same time, she signed the most lucrative endorsement deal ever offered a woman athlete, one that guaranteed her an annual six-figure income, with Nike.

Holdsclaw's streak of championships came to an end with the talent-poor Mystics, and her statistics as a pro have not been as eye-popping as her reputation predicted. Except for a 31-point, 13-round effort against the New York Liberty on June 10, 2001, her performances have been solid rather than spectacular. She was remarkably consistent, averaging 16.9, 17.5, and 16.7 points per game in her three seasons, and she increased her rebounding average from 7.9 in 1999 to 9.8 in 2001. Holdsclaw enjoyed a breakout season in 2002, leading the WNBA in scoring (19.9) and rebounding, and leading the Mystics to the league finals. Holdsclaw again led the league in rebounding and finished second in scoring in 2003. Prior to the 2005 season, she was traded to the Los Angeles Sparks.

But for Holdsclaw, statistics tell only part of the story. With her quickness and court awareness, experts say she can dominate a game without scoring a point. Coach Nancy Lieberman-Cline, the top woman player of the early 1970s, has noted, "Her mental capacity to play in the big games, to compete at the highest level—and never lose—is unique."

Further Reading

Giri, P. "She's Got Next," *Life*, April 1991, pp. 108–112.

Howerton, D. "Be Like 'Mique," *Sport*, April 1998, pp. 90–92.

Oblender, David G. *Contemporary Black Biography*. Vol. 24. Detroit: Gale Research, 2000.

Hyman, Flo

(Flora Jean Hyman)
(1954–1986) *volleyball player*

Flo Hyman, widely regarded as the top U.S. women's volleyball player ever, was the major force in making the U.S. team competitive in Olympic competition.

Flora Jean Hyman was born on July 29, 1954, in Inglewood, California, where her father worked as a janitor for the Southern Pacific Railway and her mother cleaned houses. Two older sisters introduced her to the game of volleyball. As a freshman at Morningside High School in Inglewood, she walked into the gym to try out for the volleyball team, got scared, and walked out. She developed enough poise over the next year, however, to make the varsity team. Towering over all others on the court, Hyman improved rapidly to become the team's top hitter by her senior year.

Hyman played with various club volleyball teams after graduation, including the South Bay Spikers, which won the national championship. She was asked to join the U.S. national team in 1974 and enrolled at the University of Houston at about the same time on a volleyball scholarship. She won All-American honors three years in a row and was named the nation's top player in 1976.

The women's team, however, failed to qualify for Olympic competition that year. Hyman quit school to devote her full time to the U.S. team training camp in Colorado. "You can go to school when you're 60," she explained. "You're only young once, and you can only do this once." With Hyman playing a key role, the team rose dramatically in the world rankings, to number five in 1978 and number two the following year. In 1980, however, their dreams of an Olympic medal were dashed by the U.S. boycott of the Moscow Games.

Hyman was one of seven team members who set aside their frustration and stuck with the team. She may have reached her zenith as an overpowering spiker in 1981, when she was named Best Hitter of the World Cup tournament. One commentator described her as "one of the world's strongest hitters at the net, who spikes the ball the way JULIUS ERVING dunks a basketball."

Hyman stayed with the team long enough to realize her goal of Olympic competition in 1984. As the oldest player on the team, she provided leadership and maturity for her teammates. Hyman proved to be the star of an inspired U.S. squad that attracted a large audience of television viewers in the United States through their excit-ing play. The team defeated favored China in preliminary competition only to lose a heartbreaking series to the Chinese in the gold-medal game, therefore settling for the silver.

Because of lack of professional opportunities for women athletes in the United States, Hyman signed with a Japanese semipro team sponsored by the supermarket chain Daiei, shortly after the Olympics. There, on January 24, 1986, after pulling herself from a game, she collapsed on the sidelines and died. The cause of death was determined to be a genetic heart disorder, known as Marfan's syndrome, which frequently affects extremely tall, long-limbed people. In 1987 the Women's Sports Foundation honored her by initiating an annual Flo Hyman Award given to the woman athlete "who captured Flo's dignity, spirit, and commitment to excellence."

Further Reading

Demak, Richard. "Marfan Syndrome: A Silent Killer," *Sports Illustrated*, February 17, 1986, pp. 30–35.

Great Athletes of the Twentieth Century. Vol. 8. Pasadena, Calif.: Salem Press, 1994.

Woolum, Janet, *Outstanding Women Athletes*. Phoenix, Ariz.: Oryx Press, 1998.

I

Iverson, Allen
(1975–   ) *basketball guard*

Allen Iverson has made a remarkable transition from being a symbol for everything that was wrong with the modern athlete to becoming the most courageous and exciting young player in basketball.

Iverson was born to a 15-year-old high school student, Ann Iverson, on June 7, 1975. The family often lived in squalor in Hampton, Virginia; at one point he lived in a two-bedroom house with 13 other people, none of whom was older than a teenager, and where street fights were an accepted fact of life. When he was 14, the family was evicted from their home and moved into a homeless shelter. Allen moved in with a football coach.

Iverson surmounted his depressing circumstances to become the star athlete at Bethel High School. He quarterbacked the football team to the state championship and starred on the basketball team. But his sports career seemed doomed when a racial brawl at a bowling alley ended with Iverson in jail, convicted of felony assault. The charges were suspicious, however, and Iverson's conviction was eventually overturned by the courts.

In 1994, he enrolled at Georgetown University to play under the firm hand of Coach John Thompson. Seemingly playing at a different speed than everyone else on the floor, he led the Hoyas to two successful seasons, and then, feeling ready for new challenges, he entered the National Basketball Association (NBA) draft.

The Philadelphia 76ers selected him in the first round, but over the first few years of his career, many people both inside and outside the organization feared it was a mistake, for although Iverson displayed waterbug quickness, he played an undisciplined game. A point guard's main job is to set up teammates for scores, yet Iverson shot at will. He averaged 23.5 and 22.0 points in first two years. When respected coach Larry Brown arrived, he found Iverson nearly impossible to coach because of the player's furious sense of pride, which carried over to his heavily tattooed hip-hop image.

Brown, however, made the adjustment of moving Iverson to shooting guard, a position at which his star could rain his shots down on the opposition without upsetting the team flow. Iverson responded by increasing his scoring to 26.8 in 1998–99 and 28.4 the following season. Nonetheless, tensions between the two ran so high that Brown tried desperately to trade Iverson before the 2000–01 season.

Early in the year, however, the two developed a mutual respect. Iverson proved to be a fearless battler, intensely loyal to his teammates. Although he weighed only 165 pounds, he repeatedly charged into the lane to take his lumps and get to the free throw line. That season, Iverson led the NBA in scoring with a 31.1 average and also topped the league in steals. The resilient Iverson bounced back from a battering in the conference finals against Milwaukee to throw a challenge at the powerful Los Angeles Lakers. He scored 48 points in the 76ers' first-game win before the superior Laker team wore down the challengers. Such performances thrilled fans throughout the league, and Iverson was rewarded by becoming the smallest man ever to win the league's Most Valuable Player Award. He repeated as the NBA's scoring leader in 2002, with a 31.4 average, and he regained that honor with a 30.7 average in 2004–05.

Further Reading

Edelson, Matt. "You Don't Know the Answer," *Sport,* April 2000, pp. 32–34.

Perlman, J. "It's About Time," *Sports Illustrated,* November 14, 2000, pp. 44–47.

Smallwood, John. *Fear No One.* New York: Pocket, 2001.

J

Jackson, Bo
(Vincent Edward Jackson)
(1962–) *football running back and baseball outfielder*

Many sports observers rate Bo Jackson the finest raw all-around sports talent in the past quarter-century. He was the first modern athlete to succeed on the pro level in two major professional sports: baseball and football.

Vincent Edward Jackson was born on November 30, 1962, in Bessemer, Alabama, a working-class suburb of Birmingham. His mother, Florence Jackson, was a single parent who worked 12 to 16 hours a day as a cleaning woman to provide a bare living in a one-bedroom house for her 10 children.

Vincent was the only one of her children who gave her trouble. Known as "Boar," Jackson spread terror throughout the neighborhood as a vicious bully and leader of a gang of toughs. Even his own brothers and sisters were scared of him. Jackson's activities nearly landed him in prison when he and his gang entered a pen full of pigs and killed them with rocks and baseball bats. The owner agreed not to press charges if Jackson paid the pigs' value of $3,000. Chastened by his close call with the law, Jackson worked to pay off the debt and straightened out his life. On entering McAdory High School, he sought new, more

stable friends, who shortened his nickname to "Bo" and persuaded him to try out for football. Although Jackson had shown astounding athletic ability (he threw so hard that he was not allowed to play Little League for fear he would hurt someone), he had never cared for football. But he quickly emerged as a star on both offense and defense. During his high school career, he also batted .450 with 20 home runs for the baseball team, won the Alabama state title in the decathlon, and set a state high school record of 9.54 seconds in the 100-yard dash.

Heeding his mother's request, Jackson turned down the New York Yankees' offer of a $250,000 signing bonus and instead attended Auburn University, where he continued to play three sports. Jackson started for the football team as a freshman. In four years of competition, the six-foot, two-inch, 225-pound speedster gained 4,303 yards and scored 43 touchdowns. During his senior year, he won the Heisman Trophy as college football's top player. For a time he quit baseball to focus on track, but after narrowly missing a place on the U.S. Olympic team in 1984, he returned to baseball.

Always pursuing his own dreams regardless of economic benefits, Jackson passed up a $7 million contract with football's Tampa Bay in order to play baseball with Kansas City for $200,000. In 1987, he broke into the Royals' lineup and led the team in home runs, although his average was a paltry .235. By the end of the year, however, his hankering for football returned. Jackson worked out a deal with the Oakland Raiders, who agreed to let him play for them after the end of the baseball season.

Jackson performed so well that he supplanted All-Star MARCUS LEMARR ALLEN as the Raiders' main running back. He put on one of the most memorable shows in National Football League (NFL) history on a Monday night game when he ran over Seattle's tough-guy linebacker Brian Bosworth on a two-yard touchdown run, sprinted 91 yards on another touchdown romp, and finished with 221 yards, the most ever accumulated by a Raider back.

Jackson became a national phenomenon by being the first athlete in modern times to play two major pro sports at the same time. National shoe ad campaigns featured him as the ultimate athlete with a "Bo Knows," campaign. Although Jackson never reached his potential as a baseball player, he gradually improved his average from .246 in 1988 to .272 in 1990. He enjoyed a brief moment of glory when he made the American League All-Star Team that year and proceeded to blast a 448-foot home run, steal a base, and drive in another run with a hit.

He had better luck with football. Although his baseball obligations prevented him from ever playing a full football season, Jackson's contributions during his final seasons repeatedly propelled the Raiders into the playoffs, and he posted some of the best yards-per-rush averages in modern league history.

Throughout his career, both baseball and football executives warned that he was trying to do too much by playing both sports. Remembering the long hours of hard work his mother put in to support him as a child, Jackson scoffed at such fears. Sports experts agree, however, that Bo had the potential to be one of the finest football players or one of the finest baseball players of all time had he chosen to concentrate on one or the other.

The Bo Jackson phenomenon, however, ended in 1991, when during an NFL playoff game against Cincinnati, Jackson fell awkwardly on his hip at the end of a 34-yard gain. The severe hip damage he suffered abruptly ended his football career and, despite a couple of seasons of trying to play through pain and rehabilitation for the Chicago White Sox, he had to give up baseball as well. He went back to Auburn to finish his degree and began work as president of a national sports health care company.

Further Reading

Devaney, John. *Bo Jackson.* New York: Walker, 1992.

Gutman, Bill. *Bo Jackson: A Biography.* New York: Pocket Books, 1991.

Jackson, Bo, and Dick Schaap. *Bo Knows Bo.* New York: Doubleday, 1990.

Jackson, Madeline Manning

(Madeline Manning, Madeline Manning Mims)

(1948–   ) *track-and-field middle-distance runner*

Whether she played the role of the teenage phenomenon or the "grand old lady of track," Madeline Manning Jackson did so with class and grace. She remains to this day the only U.S. woman to win a gold medal in a middle-distance event and one of the most admired Olympic athletes of her generation.

Madeline Manning was born on January 11, 1948, in Cleveland, Ohio, the daughter of an inner-city minister. During childhood, she barely survived a bout of spinal meningitis and overcame poverty to be a well-adjusted student at John Hay High School. Her performances during physical education classes attracted the interest of the school's track coaches. Although Manning showed promise in the longer sprints, she had no idea of the depth of her talent until she ran a relay race at a large meet in 1964. Running the anchor leg, she received the baton in sixth place, seemingly well out of contention, yet her coaches were encouraging her, telling her that she could win the race. Pressed to the limit by the challenge, Manning did overtake her opponents with a quarter-mile time four seconds faster than she had ever run before.

A similar challenge spurred her to victory at her first international meet, which was held in Toronto in 1966. A bad case of nerves caused her to sprint out in a near-panic at the start of the race, far faster than she had intended. Instead of paying the price for her reckless pace, she kept up that pace and won.

Such efforts caught the eye of the Tennessee State track coach Ed Temple, the famed coach of WILMA GOLDEAN RUDOLPH, who continued to run one of the nation's few competitive women's track programs. He awarded Manning a scholarship, part of which she had to repay by working in the school's mail room.

As the 1968 Olympics approached, Manning won the 800 meters at U.S. Olympic trials and began training in New Mexico to acclimate to the high altitude she would encounter in the Mexico City. The 20-year-old advanced to the Olympic finals, when she again took the risk of sprinting to an early lead. Although her rivals caught up to her, the five-foot, nine-inch Manning demolished them with a furious finishing kick. She won the race and the gold medal by more than 10 meters in an Olympic record time of 2:00.9.

Manning retired several times, first in 1970, but she kept being bitten by the competitive bug as the Olympics rolled around. She returned to win the 800 at the U.S. Olympic trials in 1972. Although she failed to make the finals, she earned a gold medal as part of the women's 4 × 400 relay team. After another retirement, she returned in 1976 to become the first U.S. woman to run 800 meters in less than two minutes, with a 1:57.9 clocking in a meet pitting the United States against the Soviet Union. She won the U.S. trials in that event again that year and, remarkably, won

the trials a fourth time in 1980. A popular athlete who went on to become an ordained minister, Jackson was elected a captain on three Olympic teams and voted into the U.S. Track & Field Hall of Fame in 1984.

Further Reading

Gilbert, Bill. "See How They Run," *Saturday Evening Post*, October 19, 1968, pp. 84–86.
Wallechinsky, David. *The Complete Book of the Olympics*. Boston: Little, Brown, 1991.

Jackson, Peter
(1861–1901) *boxer*

The earl of Lonsdale, a noted boxing historian, once commented, "Personally, I always think that the best man—the quickest, most scientific, and the hardest hitter—that I have ever seen was Peter Jackson."

Jackson was born in Saint Croix, Virgin Islands, on July 3, 1861. His father grew weary of fishing in the Caribbean, and the family emigrated to Australia when Peter was 12. Three years later the disillusioned family returned to the Virgin Islands, but Peter stayed behind and became a sailor. He never saw his parents again.

The ship owner for whom Jackson worked was a boxing enthusiast. Recognizing Jackson's athletic gifts, he put him in touch with Larry Foley, an expert boxing coach, in Sydney. Jackson began his fighting career in 1882 but almost immediately suffered a knockout at the hands of a blacksmith. Discouraged, Jackson returned to Foley and spent two years in training. When he returned to the ring, the quick six-foot, 200-pound Jackson was nearly unbeatable. In 1886, he won the Australian heavyweight championship with a clear-cut 30-round decision over Tom Lees.

Searching for new challenges, he sailed to San Francisco in 1888, only to find that the great American fighters such as John L. Sullivan and

Bob Fitzsimmons refused to fight him. "I will not fight a Negro," insisted Sullivan. "I never have and never shall." According to some accounts, Sullivan's manager later said he kept the champion away from Jackson to protect the proud Irish-American from humiliation at the hands of a black man.

Jackson had to scrounge for fights against black fighters and occasional journeyman whites who were desperate for a paycheck. As many black fighters did, Jackson developed a defensive style of boxing and was careful not to offend audiences by hurting his white opponents too badly. Depressed by lack of opportunity, Jackson lapsed into drinking and fought uninspired fights.

In 1891, however, top heavyfight contender Gentleman Jim Corbett agreed to take on Jackson for what at that time was a staggering purse of $10,000. The two fought a dull, defensive fight for four hours and 61 rounds before the referee called it a draw.

Jackson then traveled to England, where he managed to get a match against British Empire champion Frank Slavin. Slavin was an outspoken racist, and his slurs against Jackson created tremendous animosity. The result was that Jackson abandoned his normal defensive posture and savagely battered Slavin before scoring a 10th-round knockout.

Still discouraged by lack of opportunities in the heavyweight division, Jackson turned to acting for a brief time but showed no aptitude for it. He returned to the ring, but by the time he got an opportunity for a major fight, against Jim Jeffries in March 1898, his skills and reflexes had eroded. Jackson was beaten badly by Jeffries. The great boxer, who was described by contemporaries as "a pleasant, softly spoken, modest fellow, utterly unspoiled, unassuming, intelligent, cultured," died three years later of tuberculosis.

Further Reading

Henderson, Edwin B. *The Black Athlete: Emergence and Arrival.* New York: Publishers Company, 1968.

Wiggins, David K. *Glory Bound: Black Athletes in White America.* Syracuse, N.Y.: Syracuse University Press, 1997.

Jackson, Reggie
(Reginald Martinez Jackson, Mr. October)
(1946–   ) *baseball outfielder*

Critics have said there is not enough mustard in the world to cover the hot dog in the baseball slugger Reggie Jackson. Commanding the spotlight wherever he went, Jackson played his best when the pressure was the greatest, thus earning respect as baseball's "Mr. October."

He was born Reginald Martinez Jackson on May 18, 1946, in Wyncote, Pennsylvania. His parents divorced when he was a child, and his father Martinez, a tailor, primarily raised him. Reggie starred for his Cheltenham Township High School in both baseball and football. It was as a running back that he accepted a scholarship to attend Arizona State University, and his coach there, Frank Kush, was certain he had pro potential. But the school was primarily noted for its baseball program, and Jackson took advantage of this to learn more about the game. He ended up switching sports and showed such home run ability that the Kansas City A's selected him in the first round of the 1966 draft.

After spending most of two years in the minor leagues, Jackson joined the A's for the final 35 games of the 1967 season. Despite batting only .178 with one home run, Jackson showed enough potential to crack the starting lineup the following year. In between his record-setting 171 strikeouts in 1968, Jackson batted .250 with 29 home runs for the team, which had moved to Oakland.

The extroverted Jackson made a major impact on the sport in 1969 when he went on an early-season home run tear. By late July, he had clouted 40 round-trips and was on pace to challenge Roger Maris's home run record of 61. A serious late-season slump defused his challenge to history, but Jackson still ended the season with 47 homers, 118 runs-batted-in (RBIs), and a .275 batting average.

Jackson's slump carried over into the 1970 season, when he managed only a .237 average and 23 home runs. But he snapped out of it in 1970 and reestablished himself as a drawing card for Oakland in the All-Star game that year. In front of a national audience, Jackson crushed a pitch from Dock Ellis that landed more than 520 feet away, the longest home run in All-Star history. Better yet, the once hapless A's finally improved to the point where they won the divisional title.

This was the first of five consecutive divisional titles, which gave Jackson the chance to participate in the media-saturated postseason on a regular basis. To his immense frustration, Jackson missed his first opportunity to shine in the World Series when Oakland made the big stage in 1972. Sidelined with a hamstring injury, he had to sit out Oakland's seven-game triumph over Cincinnati. But, with Jackson, who won the American League home run title in 1973 with 32, providing much of the offensive clout, Oakland returned to the Fall Classic the following two seasons. Jackson was a major contributor as the A's repeated as champions both years, particularly in 1973 against the Mets, when he was voted the Series's Most Valuable Player (MVP).

In 1975, Jackson shared the American League home run title with Milwaukee's George Scott at 36. But the fiscal belt tightening and eccentricities of the Oakland A's owner, Charles Finley, began to ruin one of baseball's finest teams. Finley began selling off his stars, beginning with Jackson, who was traded to Baltimore in 1976.

Jackson spent one year with the Orioles before winding up in the venue most attractive to his attention-craving personality—New York. At first, life in the big city was a nightmare. Jackson insulted established Yankee stars and disgusted fans by declaring that, among the Yankees, only he was "the straw that stirs the drink." Jackson's ego also irritated the fiery Yankee manager, Billy

Martin, and the two had a much-publicized blowup during a midseason game. Feeling ostracized and misunderstood, Jackson nonetheless contributed to the Yankees' divisional title by hitting 32 home runs and driving in 119 runs.

The humbling continued when Martin benched Jackson during the Yankees' American League championship series victory over Kansas City to qualify for the World Series. It was at this Fall Classic, however, that he forged his "Mr. October" legacy. On his final plate appearance in game five of the series against the Los Angeles Dodgers, Jackson smashed a home run. In the following game, on October 18, he walked on four pitches. In his next plate appearance, Jackson drove the first pitch from Dodger hurler Burt Hooten into the stands. One inning later, he hit the pitch from Elias Sosa out of the park. In the eighth inning, he slammed Charlie Hough's pitch for a monstrous drive over the fence. Under the most intense pressure that baseball has to offer, Jackson had hit home runs on four consecutive swings to clinch the title for New York. The opposing manager, Tommy Lasorda, called Jackson's feat "the greatest single performance I've ever seen."

The following season, Jackson cemented his claim to be Mr. October in a repeat World Series matchup with the Dodgers. The series was in doubt until Jackson clouted a home run off Dodger ace Bob Welch to win a dramatic victory in game six. It was, however, Jackson's final appearance on the World Series stage. Although he enjoyed perhaps his finest all-around season in 1980, winning a third home run title with 41 and batting .300 for the only time in his career, the Yankees could not qualify for the playoffs. In 1982, Jackson moved on to play for the California Angels, whom he led to the playoffs but not the World Series. As an Angel, he also captured his fourth home run title, when he topped the league with 39 in 1982. After five seasons in California and a final year in Oakland, he retired in 1987.

Although Jackson's need for attention could be insufferable at times (in the mistaken belief that the Baby Ruth candy bar was named after slugger Babe Ruth, Jackson promoted his own "Reggie" candy bar) he provided more than his share of entertainment and clutch hits. He batted well in all five World Series in which he participated, accumulating 10 home runs and 24 RBIs and posting a .357 batting average. Indicative of his all-or-nothing approach to the game, Jackson struck out more than anyone else in major league history, 2,597 times, while hitting 563 career home runs, to rank sixth among major league players.

Further Reading

Allen, Maury. *Mr. October: The Reggie Jackson Story.* New York: Time Books, 1981.

Jackson, Reggie. *Reggie.* New York: Villard, 1984.

Jackson, Reggie, with Bill Libby. *Reggie: A Season with a Superstar.* Chicago: Playboy, 1975.

Waxler, C. "Mr. October Becomes Mr. Rainmaker," *Forbes,* September 20, 1999, pp. 126–127.

Jeter, Derek Sanderson

(1974–   ) *baseball shortstop*

Derek Jeter has quietly become the latest in the long line of New York Yankee superstars. At the turn of the 21st century, the slick-fielding shortstop clearly assumed leadership of the Yankees' turn-of-the-century dynasty.

He was born Derek Sanderson Jeter on June 26, 1974, in Pequannock, New Jersey, to Dorothy (who is an accountant) and Charles Jeter (who has a Ph.D. in substance abuse counseling). The family moved to Kalamazoo, Michigan, when Derek was small. Derek and his sister were raised strictly; Derek remembers having the earliest curfew of all his friends and being required to sign a contract detailing his expectations for school with his parents each year.

From the time he first tried T-ball, Derek loved to play baseball. His best position was shortstop, the same position his father had played at Fisk University. Derek played it so well at Kala-

mazoo Central High School that the New York Yankees made him the sixth selection in the first round of the 1992 draft.

After spending a period of apprenticeship in the Yankees farm system, Jeter made the parent club in 1996 and did it so convincingly that the Yankees made him the first rookie to start for them at shortstop in 34 years. Showing a poise and charm far beyond his years, Jeter instantly became a key contributor and one of pro sports' most sought-after bachelors. In his first season, the six-foot, three-inch, 185-pounder showed soft hands, marvelous range, and a powerful throwing arm at shortstop while batting .314. That made him a clear choice as the American League's Rookie of the Year. Seemingly immune to the championship jitters, Jeter paved the way for the Yankees' first World Series victory in 15 years that season by collecting five hits and five runs.

After tailing off slightly to a .291 average in 1997, Jeter established himself as one of the game's finest hitters as well as fielders with a .324 average and 127 runs scored in 1998. Continuing his improvement, Jeter raised his average to .349 with a league-high 219 hits, including 24 home runs, in 1999. He continued his offensive surge in 2000 with a fine .339 mark, before dropping off the following season.

But it was for his postseason play that Jeter gained the most recognition. It was Jeter who anchored the defense and jump-started the offense in the Yankees' championship seasons in 1998, 1999, and 2000. Firmly established as the leader of the Yankee club, Jeter strung together a World Series record 14-game hitting streak. Perhaps his greatest example of leadership occurred in the 2001 play-offs when he single-handedly kept the Yankees in the playoffs with a retrieval of an errant throw and backhand flip of the ball to the catcher to nail a startled A's runner at the plate. Unphased by his New York celebrity status, Jeter has remained one of the most admired men in sports and has been active in establishing the Turn 2 Foundation for at-risk drug abusers.

Further Reading

Giles, Patrick. *Derek Jeter: Pride of the Yankees.* New York: St. Martin's Press, 1999.

Jeter, Derek, with Jack Carey. *The Life You Imagine: Life Lessons for Achieving Your Dreams.* New York: Crown, 2000.

Silver, Michael. "Prince of the City," *Sports Illustrated,* June 21, 1999, pp. 100–6.

Johnson, Jack
(John Arthur Johnson, Papa Jack)
(1878–1946) *boxer*

Jack Johnson fought through racial barriers to become the first African-American world heavyweight boxing champion. However, he left a controversy in his wake that inflamed white prejudices and complicated the efforts of two generations of black athletes to pursue their careers.

He was born John Arthur Johnson in Galveston, Texas, on March 31, 1878, one of five children of Henry and Tiny Johnson. From the age of 13, he bounced about from one short-term job to another, working as a painter, baker, and dockworker. He began fighting for fun and soon found himself good enough at it to earn some money.

Boxing was a humiliating sport for blacks at that time. Johnson began fighting in battle royals, contests that pitted as many as eight black men against each other for the entertainment of white crowds who laughed and screamed racial taunts during the fight. The only rule was that the last man standing was the winner, and for variety, promoters sometimes blindfolded the contestants or tied them together. Even when he advanced to more conventional boxing competition in 1897, he had to fight other blacks for little money, and he had to cope with cruel spectators who tossed lit cigars at his back between rounds.

Johnson's best break occurred after a local fighter named Joe Choynski knocked him out. The two found themselves thrown together in a jail cell, where Choynski began teaching Johnson some of his boxing expertise. Johnson picked up his tutor's defensive style of boxing and became a master at patiently luring an opponent into an attack and then counterpunching effectively. Since few whites would fight blacks, Johnson had to settle for low-paying repeat matches against a small pool of boxers. He steadily improved, losing only three fights in three years, and in 1903, he advanced to the top of the black ranks by defeating Denver Ed Martin.

Johnson felt that he deserved a shot at the world heavyweight title, but the champion, Jim Jeffries, proclaimed, "When there are no white men left to fight, I will quit the business." Johnson forged enough name recognition that some white contenders went for the large paycheck that resulted with taking him on, and he beat them all.

After Jeffries's retirement, Tommy Burns won the title. As he was a rather uninspiring fighter, the nation's sportswriters attempted to spark interest by pushing for a match between Burns and Johnson. For his part, Johnson chased Burns across the United States and then followed him overseas to England. There Johnson decisively won two matches, which encouraged more international support for a Burns-Johnson title fight. When Burns continued to ignore him, Johnson followed him to Australia, demanding that he stand and fight. Finally, the offer of a huge sum of money and a concession to let Burns's manager referee the fight induced Burns to enter the ring.

On December 26, 1908, the two met in Sydney before 25,000 fans. Burns was heavily favored to win, but according to writer Jack London, a boxing enthusiast, "There was no fight. No Armenian massacre would compare with the hopeless slaughter that took place in the Sydney stadium today." Venting years of persecution, Johnson knocked down the champ in the first round and then played with him, laughing and taunting as he pummeled him without mercy. The police finally stepped into the ring and stopped the fight in the 14th round.

Nearly a century after he fought, Jack Johnson remains one of sports' most controversial figures. *(Library of Congress, Photographs & Prints Division [LC-USZ6-1823])*

Johnson's victory generated impassioned pleas from whites in the United States for a champion to defend the honor of their race. The more challengers Johnson demolished, the greater the outcry. Many people insisted that the retired Jeffries was the real heavyweight champion and called for him to return to the ring.

Johnson's behavior exacerbated the general discomfort about a black man's being champion.

Having beaten the odds and fought his way to the top, he considered himself beholden to neither persons nor conventions. He constantly grinned in the ring, displaying his gold teeth, and mocking opponents. Calling himself "Papa Jack," he drank, spent money wildly, played around with women, and infuriated whites by marrying two white women and often beating them. His arrogance offended nearly everyone, including blacks, when he declared, despite firsthand knowledge of the injustice, "I won't box any of those colored boys now."

The boxing world, meanwhile, was riddled with corruption. Johnson agreed to stage a fight with a middleweight, Stanley Ketchel, that would end in a draw. But when Ketchel double-crossed Johnson and decked him in the 12th round, Johnson got up and knocked him out with his next punch.

The campaign of hatred against Johnson finally goaded Jeffries into fighting him. The two fought on July 4, 1910, in Reno, Nevada, in the most publicized bout in boxing history up to that time. Relying on his counterpunching skills, Johnson battered the ex-champ before ending the fight with three knockdowns in the 15th round. Celebration and bitterness over the result led to riots in every southern and many northern states.

Johnson was finally chased out of the country by an all-white jury that convicted him of violating a vague law against transporting women across state lines for "immoral purposes." Johnson relocated in Europe, where he fought three title defenses. In 1915, he met Jess Willard in a fight in Havana, Cuba. Underestimating his rival, Johnson undertrained, and although he was ahead on points after 20 rounds, the fight was scheduled to go 40. Johnson wilted in the 100-degree heat and was knocked out. He later claimed he threw the fight in exchange for a false promise of a pardon, a claim that few observers take seriously.

Tired of exile, Johnson surrendered to the U.S. authorities in 1920 and served a year in jail. Although long past his prime, he continued to fight until 1928. Having squandered his earnings, he eked out a living making personal appearances until he lost control of a speeding car on June 10, 1946, and was killed, leaving behind a mixed legacy. Although some admired his courage in defying convention and breaking through boxing's racial barrier, black athletes for many years paid the price for his excesses. Most went out of their way to distance themselves from any comparison with Johnson's behavior.

Further Reading

Johnson, Jack. *Jack Johnson Is a Dandy*. New York: Chelsea House, 1969.

Lipsyte, Robert, and Peter Levine. *Idols of the Game*. Atlanta: Turner Publications, 1995.

Roberts, Randy. *Papa Jack*. New York: Free Press, 1983.

Vecchione, Joseph, ed. *The New York Times Book of Sports Legends*. New York: Random House, 1991.

Johnson, Magic
(Earvin Johnson, Jr.)
(1959–) *basketball guard*

Basketball experts credit Magic Johnson with igniting the explosion in popularity that the National Basketball Association (NBA) enjoyed during the 1980s. A consummate team player with an infectiously enthusiastic personality, Johnson served as the triggerman in the creative, racehorse pace of Laker basketball that became known as "Showtime."

He was born Earvin Johnson, Jr., on August 14, 1959, in Lansing, Michigan, one of 10 children in a working-class family. His father, Earvin, Sr., worked two full-time jobs, as a 5 P.M. to 1 A.M. assembly worker at a General Motors plant and as an operator of his own hauling service. A strong work ethic was ingrained in the Johnson children; even when he became a national high school star, Earvin still had to get up early on Saturday mornings to help with the hauling.

Earvin, Sr., had a passion for the game of basketball, which he passed on to his son. When Earvin, Jr., was a youngster in elementary school, his father drilled him in the fundamentals of ball handling. Junior later said, "I was very fortunate to have been coached at an early age by the best teacher in the world. He's the reason I'm playing the way I am now."

Johnson dominated his early leagues, scoring at will and winning every game. But parents of his teammates complained that he scored so much that none of the other children got a chance to shoot. Johnson listened to the criticism and began concentrating more on setting up his teammates to score, a skill that he later described as "passing out the sugar." It was the beginning of a style of unselfish floor generalship that would be unmatched in his generation.

Although Johnson grew to nearly six feet, nine inches, in high school, his ball handling and passing skills were so exceptional that his coaches kept him at point guard instead of forward or center. Playing for Everett High School, Johnson put on basketball clinics that left opponents and observers gaping. One evening, a reporter, Fred Stabley, Jr., of the *Lansing State Journal* searched for a nickname that would adequately describe the incredible 36-point, 18-rebound, 20-steal, 16-assist effort he had just seen from the gangly point guard. The only word that came to mind was *magic*. From the time Stabley wrote his story, Earvin, Jr., would forever more be Magic Johnson.

With Magic at the controls, Everett won the state tournament in 1977. Although recruited nationally, Johnson opted to stay in Lansing and attend Michigan State University in 1977. His statistics were unexceptional as a Spartan—he averaged only about 17 points a game during his two years with the team. But his leadership skills and spectacular passing made him one of the most famous college players in the land. In the spring of 1979, he led the Spartans to the finals of the National Collegiate Athletic Association (NCAA) tournament against Larry Bird's undefeated Indiana State Sycamores. The marquee matchup between the two superstars of college

Magic Johnson introduced a sense of joy as well as consummate skill to the NBA. *(Tim DeFrisco/ Getty Images)*

ball created a sensation that is widely recognized as having established the tournament as one of the top events in all sports. Johnson scored 24 points and handed out 10 assists in sparking Michigan State's 75–64 win.

After winning the title, Johnson left school and moved on to the challenge of professional basketball. The Los Angeles Lakers had the first choice in the 1979 draft and they eagerly spent it on Magic. Magic responded with such polished play that he became the first rookie in 11 years to start in the All-Star game.

Johnson's glowing personality and youthful exuberance at first took the veteran Lakers by surprise. Seasoned pros were not expected to leap into KAREEM ABDUL-JABBAR's arms, as Johnson did after one last-second victory. But the enthusiasm was contagious, and the recharged Lakers fought their way to the NBA finals against Philadelphia. There Los Angeles took a 3–2 lead, only to lose their star scorer, Abdul-Jabbar, to an ankle injury in that fifth game.

On the plane ride home, the Lakers were grim as they contemplated the untimely loss of their center. Johnson, however, had a surprise in store for them. When the Lakers took the floor for game six, it was Magic who strode out to play center against Philadelphia's seven-foot Caldwell Jones. Playing undersized and out of position, the rookie put on a stunning performance. He made 14 of 23 field goals and sank all 14 of his free throws for a total of 42 points. In addition, Johnson collected 15 rebounds and dished out seven assists as the Abdul-Jabbar–less Lakers upset the 76ers, 123–107, to win the championship.

Having experienced such phenomenal success in his past two seasons, Johnson was unprepared for the trials of the 1980 season. Coach Paul Westhead risked tampering with success by installing a new offense for the champion Lakers. This offense was a slowed-down, disciplined approach in which Johnson was supposed to walk the ball up court and run the Lakers through set plays. It was a far cry from the freewheeling, think-on-the-run offense to which Magic was accustomed. Although the Lakers continued to win, the game lost its fun for Johnson. Playing uninspired ball, Los Angeles was knocked out of the playoffs by Houston in the first round. When the team started out dismally in 1981, Johnson could stand it no longer. He publicly asked to be traded to a team that ran an offense to his liking. The Lakers responded by firing the coach.

At the time, Johnson took a barrage of criticism as a selfish athlete who got a coach fired just because he did not like the offense. But, in fact,

Johnson's speaking out rid the team of a style of play not conducive to his talents and resulted in the hiring of Pat Riley, under whose leadership Magic and the Lakers established their Showtime dynasty. This fast-break style of play, with Magic threading no-look passes to graceful leapers such as James Worthy, amazed fans and was one of the reasons why basketball developed into the sport of the 1980s. Although Magic epitomized this modern style of play, Coach Riley reminded reporters, "Earvin is in a lot of ways an old-fashioned player in that he is so fundamentally sound in all aspects."

Another factor in the pro game's new popularity was Johnson's rivalry with Bird, which continued in the pros. Bird led the resurgence of the Lakers' traditional rival, the Boston Celtics. Over the past decades, the Celtics had repeatedly broken the hearts of Laker fans with narrow victories in championship competition. In 1984, Los Angeles and Boston met in the finals again. Magic's uncharacteristic mistakes in the closing minutes of two of those games helped the Celtics prevail yet again. Johnson took the defeat so personally that some Laker brass feared he might never recover.

Johnson was given a chance for redemption the following year when the two teams again met in the finals. After suffering through an embarrassing 148–114 loss in game one, Johnson rallied his team for a four-games-to-two victory that final broke the Celtics' hex on the Lakers.

Asked to take on additional scoring responsibilities in 1986, Johnson responded by boosting his average 4 points to a career-high 23.9. In 1987, he showed that he could come through with the key shot under pressure. With the Lakers and Celtics again battling in the finals, Los Angeles took two of the first three games but fell behind in game four by a single point with seconds remaining. Magic calmly lofted his "baby hook" over Robert Parish and Kevin McHale to win the game and propel the Lakers to another championship. That capped a season in which Johnson won the Most Valuable Player (MVP) Awards in both the regular season and the playoffs. Under Johnson's

leadership in 1988, Los Angeles became the first NBA champions in more than a decade to defend their title. Their quest for a third straight championship, however, ended when Johnson injured his hamstring in the finals.

Three games into the 1991 season, Johnson stunned the sports world by announcing that he had contracted human immunodeficiency virus (HIV), the virus that causes acquired immunodeficiency syndrome (AIDS). The condition forced him to retire, except for a fling on the 1992 U.S. Olympic team, when Magic added an Olympic gold medal to his trophy collection, and a brief comeback effort in 1995–96.

Individually, Magic won three MVP Awards in four seasons, the last in 1990. That same year, he passed OSCAR PALMER ROBERTSON as the NBA's career assist leader. Underrated as a shooter, Johnson shot nearly 85 percent from the free throw line and made more than 52 percent of his shots from the field.

Yet statistics fell far short of telling the story of the effervescent Johnson's value to his team and to this sport. Basketball experts say that he could take only three shots in a game and still dominate it from start to finish. Johnson proved that far from being an undisciplined recipe for failure, an up-tempo style of play could provide both thrills and championships. Perhaps the greatest tribute was that of his longtime rival, Larry Bird, who said of Magic, "He played the game the way I want to play it."

Further Reading

Johnson, Earvin, Jr., with Richard Levin. *Magic*. New York: Signet, 1991.

Johnson, Earvin, Jr., with William Novak. *My Life*. New York: Random House, 1992.

Johnson, Earvin, Jr., and Roy S. Johnson. *Magic's Touch*. Reading, Mass.: Addison-Wesley, 1989.

Gutman, Bill. *Magic: More Than a Legend*. New York: Harper, 1992.

Pascarelli, Peter. *The Courage of Magic Johnson*. New York: Bantam, 1991.

Johnson, Michael

(1967–   ) *track-and-field sprinter*

Before Michael Johnson, no one had ever won both the 200- and 400-meter races in a major track meet. Running in his trademark, ramrod-straight posture, Johnson not only accomplished this in the 1996 Olympics, but annihilated the existing 200-meter world record.

Michael was born on September 13, 1967, the youngest of five children born to Paul, Sr., a truck driver, and Ruby Johnson, a teacher, in Dallas, Texas. He first felt the exhilaration of racing as a 10-year-old, when he won a 50-yard dash sponsored by the Dallas Parks & Recreation Department. But even though he ran track and played football in junior high school, he thought of himself more as a student than as an athlete. Education was so important to the Johnson family that in ninth grade Michael did not compete in any sports so that he could concentrate on his studies.

Johnson went out for track as a sophomore at Skyline High School in Dallas, and he dabbled in long jumping and sprints. His track coach thought of him as "just another skinny kid" who had no special ability. But suddenly during his junior year, Johnson began posting some of the top 200-meter times in the state. By his senior year, college track coaches had taken an interest in him. Pleased that a track scholarship would help him pursue his studies in business administration, Johnson, an honor roll student at Skyline, enrolled at Baylor University.

In Johnson's first 200-meter race in college, he broke Baylor's school record for the distance. At the same time, he became aware, through meeting other track stars, that there was money to be made as a top sprinter. A planner and organizer by nature, Johnson set a goal of becoming a world-class runner and embarked on a regimen of spartan self-discipline in his effort to reach the top ranks of his sport. While his classmates partied late at night, Johnson regularly went to bed at 8

P.M. While teammates called off practice rather than run in torrential rainstorms, Johnson splashed through his rugged workouts alone on the track. In all his years of training, Johnson never missed a scheduled day of practice.

Unfortunately, his dedication yielded frustrating results. Near the end of 1987, his freshman year, Johnson fell victim to a leg injury. A year later, he was leading his 200-meter race at the National Collegiate Athletic Association (NCAA) outdoor finals when he suffered a stress fracture. The injury not only cost him his collegiate title but ruined his chances of making the 1988 U.S. Olympic team. The following year, Johnson suffered a season-ending leg injury for the third straight year.

Rather than feeling sorry for himself, Johnson determined that he needed to concentrate on improving his strength and flexibility. Following his conviction that "plans are the strings holding the pearls together," Johnson carefully retooled his training program and vowed to make one last effort to succeed as a sprinter.

This time Johnson stayed healthy and his times improved enough that he decided, at the end of the 1990 college season, to test his skill on the lucrative European track-and-field circuit. To his surprise, and almost everyone else's, he proved unbeatable, winning nearly a dozen races. Then, just as he was reaching the pinnacle of success in track, he stunned experts by backing off his training and returning to school in the fall to complete the credits he needed to graduate.

Having accomplished that goal, Johnson turned his attention back to the track. In 1991 he won the world championship in the 200-meter event. A year later, he returned to defend his world title only to receive a bad break. A stiff head wind in his qualifying heat and luck of the draw put him out in lane eight for the finals. In the staggered start of the 200, a runner in the eighth lane cannot see his opponents to gauge his progress through the turn. Undaunted by the bad draw, Johnson burst out of the blocks and rocketed through the turn well ahead of his rivals. He cruised the final

Michael Johnson's intense discipline elevated him from an unknown college runner to the dominant athlete of the 1996 Olympics. *(Brian Bahr/Getty Images)*

yards to win the race in a time of 19.79, the fastest time anyone had run in four years.

The victory established him as the favorite in the Olympic 200 meters. But a brief illness he suffered just before the Games, probably caused by food poisoning, weakened him more than anyone suspected. Johnson could place no better than sixth in his semifinal heat and failed to qualify for the finals. The gold medal that he won as part of the United States' winning 4 × 400 relay team was small consolation—Johnson ran the slowest leg on the team.

The disappointment only fanned the flames of Johnson's competitive nature. After winning the world championship in the 400, Johnson toyed with the idea of trying for an unprecedented Olympic double in the 200 and 400. First, he had to prove that he was physically capable of such a demanding feat. This he accomplished by winning both races at the U.S. championships in 1995 and then at the world championships later that season. Then he had to persuade Olympic officials to reschedule the events so that heats were not held too closely together to allow him any recovery time.

Given the excitement generated by Johnson's dominance of both events, the Olympic officials agreed to accommodate him. That put the pressure squarely on Johnson to live up to the hype that he had invited. Johnson responded by easily winning the 400 at the U.S. trials and then running 19.66 in the 200 to break a world record that had stood for 17 years.

In the Olympics, Johnson's dominance destroyed all suspense. The powerful Texan easily captured the 400-meter title, then ran the race of his life in the 200. Flying down the track faster than any human has ever run, Johnson left the world's top sprinters in his wake. "The finish line seemed to reach out and grab me," a euphoric Johnson later marveled. In a race in which margins of victory are normally measured in hundredths of a second, Johnson breezed to the finish line 0.36 second ahead of second place. His time of 19.32 obliterated his own world record.

Although an injury prevented him from qualifying in the 200 meters, Johnson returned to the Olympics in 2000 and defended his 400-meter title. He retired in 2001, widely regarded as the greatest endurance sprinter of all time.

Further Reading

Graham, Judith, ed. *Current Biography 1996*. New York: H. W. Wilson, 1996.

Johnson, Michael. *Slaying the Dragon: How to Turn Your Small Steps to Great Feats*. New York: Regan Books, 1996.

Moore, Ken. "The Man," *Sports Illustrated*, August 12, 1996, pp. 26–32.

Johnson, Rafer Lewis
(1935–   ) *track-and-field decathlete*

Continuing his nation's tradition of excellence that began with the legendary Jim Thorpe, Rafer Johnson succeeded MILT CAMPBELL as the Olympic gold medalist in the decathlon and thus gained the distinction of being the world's greatest athlete.

Rafer Lewis Johnson was born on August 18, 1935, in Hillsboro, Texas, to Lewis and Alma Johnson but spent most of his younger childhood in a poverty-ridden section of Dallas. Johnson hated those years and was pleased when, at the age of 10, he moved with his family to the small town of Kingsburg, California, near Fresno, where his father found work with the railroad. During the first year of their stay in California, the Johnsons lived in a boxcar near a peach-canning factory. A year or two later, Rafer caught his foot on a conveyor belt in the factory and came perilously close to being crippled for life.

Eventually, the Johnsons moved into town, where Rafer developed into a star athlete in high school and baseball was his favorite sport. But his combination of strength, speed, and coordination in all sports led to comparisons with the great decathlete Bob Matthias, who grew up in Tulare, just 25 miles from Kingsburg. During his junior year, he saw Matthias compete in the decathlon in a local meet. Aside from being impressed with Matthias, Johnson was unimpressed with the competition and thought he could beat most of them. He decided to give the event a try and was so successful that in his senior year he finished third in the Amateur Athletic Union (AAU) national meet, which earned him an athletic scholarship from the University of California at Los Angeles (UCLA).

While at college, Johnson broke Matthias's world decathlon record, took first in the 1955 Pan American Games, and finished second behind Milt Campbell in the 1956 Olympics. He also became close friends with his college teammate C. K. Yang of Taiwan. In 1960, the two staged one of the most inspiring battles ever seen in Olympic competition. Yang, representing China, used his superior speed and athleticism to beat Johnson in the sprints and the jumps, while Johnson took advantage of his strength to rack up points in the throwing events. On the second day of competition, Johnson's hopes suffered a blow when he hit the first hurdle and stumbled to a subpar performance. However, he quickly made up for that with a personal best in the pole vault.

With only the 1,500-meter run remaining, Johnson held a slim lead over Yang. If Yang could beat Johnson by 10 seconds in this event, the gold would be his. That seemed likely, as Yang's personal best in this event was 4:36, whereas Johnson had managed only a 4:54.

After two full days of grueling competition, both competitors were exhausted. Grimly, Johnson clung to Yang's heels while Yang desperately tried to shake him. Running his best time ever—4:49.7—Johnson finished within two seconds of Yang and claimed the gold. The two fierce but friendly competitors then collapsed into each other's arms.

Johnson's engaging personality and leadership skills have been evident throughout his life. As a college senior, he was voted student body president, and at the Rome Olympics, he was the first African American selected to carry the U.S. flag at the opening ceremonies. After his retirement from sport, he carved out successful careers in acting, politics, community work, and broadcasting.

Further Reading

Nelson, Cordner. *Track's Greatest Champions*. Los Altos, Calif.: Tafnews Press, 1986.

Johnson, Rafer. *The Best That I Can Be*. Thorndike, Maine: G. K. Hall, 1998.

Jones, Deacon
(David Jones)
(1938–   ) *football defensive end*

David "Deacon" Jones may be more responsible than anyone else for creating hazardous working conditions for quarterbacks in the National Football League (NFL). Combining strength, speed, and iron will, Jones introduced a new dimension to the art of rushing the passer.

Jones was born on December 9, 1938, in Eatonville, Florida, one of eight children of Ishmael and Mattie Jones. Although his father worked as a carpenter, Jones and his family struggled to make ends meet. One escape for the Jones boys was sports. All were exceptional football players at Orlando's Hungerford High School.

Professional football was not nationally popular in the early 1950s; nonetheless Jones followed the sport and dreamed of someday being an unstoppable force in the league. In addition to football, Jones played basketball and ran track. In fact, his best time of 9.7 in the 100-yard dash made him one of the fastest players in the state. But as he continued to grow into a six-foot, four-inch, 250-pound giant, he found himself placed in the defensive line with other larger players. Once that happened, football observers tended to forget how fast he was.

At the time, few college coaches in the South paid attention to black high school football players. Unable to attract any scholarships to traditional football schools, he resigned himself to getting an education at Mississippi Vocational School. Eventually, he transferred to South Carolina State. There he became one of the team's defensive stars and earned the nickname "Deacon" in honor of his leading the team in prayer before games.

Despite his overflowing talent, Jones's chances of playing pro football were virtually nil. No NFL team scouted small black colleges such as South Carolina State, and so none of them had heard of Jones at the time of his graduation. Fortunately for Jones, the Los Angeles Rams obtained some film of a running back for one of South Carolina State's rivals who had attracted their attention. While studying the film, they noticed a lightning-quick lineman who kept running down speedy backs from behind. Being well-stocked with defensive linemen, they were not particularly interested in picking up a new talent, but the scouts could not get over the combination of speed and power that they had witnessed on film. They decided to take a chance on this lineman, Jones, by selecting him in the 14th round of the 1961 draft.

At training camp, which Jones later described as the worst experience of his life, he discovered just how far behind his lack of coaching at an underfunded college program had put him. He found that he did not know even the basic fundamentals of line play that were taught at larger universities. Lessons in humiliation from the more experienced were frequent, and only Jones's undying faith in his ability and determination to succeed allowed him to survive the period.

The Rams had intended to give Jones time to learn and develop his raw talent before throwing him into league play. But when the team's top defensive tackle, Gene Brito, contracted a fatal illness, they had no choice but to play Jones. Undersized at the position, Jones tried to bulk up. His weight ballooned to 290 pounds and his speed and stamina suffered. His play was so unimpressive those first few years that the Rams debated trading him.

Jones, however, studied films of the best defensive linemen, particularly Baltimore's Gino Marchetti, and learned their techniques. He slimmed down to a lean and powerful 250 pounds and was installed at left end, where he could make better use of his speed. In 1964, his preparation paid off as Jones became one of the top linemen in the league. By 1965, he was the unquestioned star of the NFL's first celebrity defensive line, dubbed "The Fearsome Foursome." Jones, tackles Merlin Olsen and Roosevelt Grier (soon replaced by the equally effective Roger Brown), and right end Lamar Lundy began ravaging opposing offenses with a ferocious pass rush and punishing run defense. Olsen and Jones worked particularly well in tandem as they consistently caved in the right side of the offensive line.

Of the four, Jones was by far the superior pass rusher. His speed and quickness often allowed him to race by offensive tackles before they could set up. When he developed the technique of stunning his opponents with a ferocious head slap, he began to beat a regular path into the enemy backfield. Many pass rushers copied the head slap, which was soon banned as being too brutal a technique.

Deacon Jones played in 143 consecutive games for the Rams until an injury forced him out of action in 1971. During that time he was named All-Pro six times, went to the Pro Bowl eight

years, and was named NFL Defensive Player of the Year in both 1967 and 1968. Unfortunately, the Rams' offensive never matched their defensive performance. As a result, despite their overpowering defensive line, Jones won only two divisional titles during his career in Los Angeles, in 1967 and 1969, and never played in a championship game. After his injury in 1971, he was traded to San Diego, where he played for two years before finishing his career with the Washington Redskins in 1974. He was voted to the Pro Football Hall of Fame in 1980.

During Jones's career, the NFL did not keep official records of the number of times an individual tackled the quarterback for a loss. But unofficial reviews of NFL game films have credited him with anywhere between 172 and 180 sacks during his career, the most of any player of his time. It was Jones, in fact, who gave the sports world his pet name for this accomplishment, the "sack," which was adopted as an official NFL statistic in 1982.

Jones took pride in his role as a pass-rushing innovator. "Forever more as long as time stands, I am registered as the guy who moved this era along," he has said. "To me that's worth more money than all the gold in Fort Knox."

Further Reading

Allen, George. *Pro Football's 100 Greatest Players*. Indianapolis, Ind.: Bobbs-Merrill, 1982.

Henderson, Edwin B. *The Black Athlete: Emergence and Arrival*. New York: Publishers Company, 1968.

Klawitter, John. *The Book of Deacon: The Wit and Wisdom of Deacon Jones*. Santa Ana, Calif.: Seven Locks Press, 2001.

Jones, Marion

(1975–) *track-and-field sprinter, jumper*

Marion Jones's contagious smile and valiant effort to win an unprecedented five gold medals in a single Olympics made her the star of the 2000 U.S. Olympic track-and-field team. Although she fell short of her goal, she nevertheless succeeded in making Olympic track-and-field history.

Jones was born on October 12, 1975, in Los Angeles, California. Her mother, Marion Toler, an immigrant from Belize who worked as a medical legal assistant, divorced her husband, George Jones, when Marion was very young. At the age of nine, Jones and her family were living in Palmdale, north of Los Angeles, when the 1984 Olympics came to town. Marion was so inspired by the competition that she wrote on a chalkboard her goal of someday becoming an Olympic champion.

Having spent much of her younger childhood trying to keep up with her older brother, Albert, Jones found competing with girls her own age easy in comparison. She began running track almost immediately and added basketball in sixth grade. As a freshman at Rio Mesa High School in Oxnard, she captured the California state championship in both the 100 and 200 meters, and she repeated as a sophomore. After moving to Thousand Oaks as a junior, she again repeated in both events, came within 0.01 second of making the 1992 U.S. Olympic team in the 200 meters, and set a national high school record of 11.17 in the 100 meters. As a senior, she added the long jump title to her sprint successes, giving her a total of nine state titles. She was twice voted Gatorade's National Female High School Athlete of the Year and broke her own national high school record for the 200 meters four times.

Despite her world-class potential in track, however, Jones put the sport on the back burner to play basketball at the University of North Carolina. The 5-foot, 10-inch, Jones switched from forward to shooting guard and cracked into the starting lineup as a freshman. She averaged 14.1 points as a freshman as North Carolina rolled to the National Collegiate Athletic Association (NCAA) championship in 1994. The following season, she led the offense with over 24 points per game. During her three seasons on the hard court at North Carolina, Jones scored 1,716 points while her school posted a 92–10 record.

Sprinter Marion Jones set an impossible goal in the 2000 Olympics and very nearly accomplished it. *(Allsport/Getty Images)*

Although she tried to continue her track career at the same time, basketball consumed so much time and energy that she failed to win a single NCAA title during her college track career. In fact, she was not even able to equal her best high school times and distances. As the 1996 Olympics approached, however, Jones felt the lure of the promise she had made as a youngster. She intended to sit out the 1995–96 basketball season to train for the Olympics, but in August 1995, she broke a bone in her foot while playing basketball. Because of the injury, she was not able to compete in either basketball or the 1996 Olympic trials. She returned to basketball for the 1996–97 season and then abruptly announced she was quitting basketball to concentrate on track for the rest of her athletic career.

Focusing only on track produced immediate results. Just months after resuming her training, Jones won the 100-meter race at the 1997 U.S. track-and-field championships and upset JACKIE JOYNER-KERSEE to claim the long jump title as well. She went on to capture the 100-meter title at the world championships that year in Athens, Greece, with a personal record of 10.83.

Her performances continued to improve in every event. During one stretch of competition, Jones won 36 consecutive finals in the long jump, 60-meter, 100-meter, 200-meter, and 400-meter events, before losing to Olympic champion Heike Drechsler of Germany in a long jump competition. In 1998, she became the first female athlete since Stella Walsh in 1936 to win the 100 meters, 200 meters, and long jump at a U.S. championship competition. After gaining the number-one ranking in the world in all three events, which included a sizzling 10.65 time in the 100 meters and 21.62 at 200 meters, that year, Jones set her sights on a goal far greater than anyone had ever achieved in her sport. She openly spoke of her "Drive for Five"—winning gold medals in five events at the 2000 Olympics. The press picked up on her ambition, and Jones found herself under a media barrage as the 2000 Olympics approached. But she maintained a sunny disposition in the face of press demands and steeled herself for an exhausting schedule of her three individual events plus two relays, the 4 × 100 and 4 × 400.

Running with fluid grace at the Sydney Olympics, Jones started her quest with a shockingly easy victory at 100 meters. In an event normally decided by hundredths of a second, her winning time of 10.75 seconds put her a full 0.36 second ahead of the field.

Jones's exuberant quest then took a severe hit when her husband, shot putter C. J. Hunter, was disqualified from Olympic competition for testing positive for steroids. The disgrace posed a huge distraction to Jones's effort and increased the already intense media focus. But she managed to put it behind her as she flew to another easy victory, this time in the 200 meters. Again, her time of 21.84 seconds was impressive and her margin of victory (0.43 second) phenomenal.

The weakest link in her Drive for Five was the long jump, in which the defending champion Drechsler posed a formidable challenge. It was in this event that Jones's dream unraveled. She fouled on four of six jumps and had to slow considerably on one of the others. Even so, in setting for third place, she still managed to leap 22 feet, 8 ¼ inches, to come within 3 ½ inches of Drechsler's gold medal leap. Another gold medal slipped away from Jones when her teammates in the 4 × 100 relay botched a baton exchange that doomed the team to third place despite Jones's strong effort.

Jones finished the Olympics strongly, however. Running the third leg of the 4 × 400 relay, she broke open a close race to ensure her team a convincing victory. That gave her a grand haul of three gold medals and two bronze, the best performance by a female track-and-field athlete in Olympic history.

Further Reading

Montville, Leigh. "Back to Earth," *Sports Illustrated*, October 18, 2000, pp. 77–78.

Rapaport, Ron. *See How She Runs: Marion Jones and the Making of a Champion*. Thorndike, Md.: Thorndike Press, 2000.

Schick, Elizabeth, ed. *Current Biography 1998*. New York: H. W. Wilson, 1998.

Jordan, Michael
(Michael Jeffrey Jordan)
(1963–) *basketball guard*

Michael Jordan emerged in the 1980s as the most famous athlete on the planet. His ability to leap high and perform acrobatic maneuvers while in the air inspired an entire line of athletic shoes known as "Air Jordan." His overall skill and competitive drive carried him to a record 10 National Basketball Association (NBA) scoring titles and six league championships. His warmth, humor, and accessibility made him a marketing gold mine. Jordan's accomplishments are so impressive that no less a basketball artist than Larry Bird has said of him, "I think he's God disguised as a basketball player."

Michael Jeffrey Jordan was born on February 17, 1963, in Brooklyn, New York, the fourth of five children of James and Delores Jordan. The family moved to Wallace, North Carolina, when Michael was an infant and settled in Wilmington when he was seven. There James worked his way up from mechanic to supervisor at a General Electric plant and Delores made a similar advancement working at a bank.

Jordan's first love as a child was baseball, which was also his father's favorite sport. He has said that his favorite childhood memory is winning the league Most Valuable Player (MVP) trophy for his Babe Ruth League team with his lively fastball. He also dabbled in track as well as in football, until he was scared away by an injury. But eventually, he and his brother, Larry, who was a year older, began to concentrate on basketball. James Jordan accommodated them by building them a full-sized basketball court on their property.

During his early days at Laney High School, Jordan appeared to have made the wrong choice of sports. As a 5-foot, 11-inch, sophomore, he failed to make the varsity team. But after adding four inches and improving his skills over the next year, he was able to join Larry on the varsity for a season. Jordan's admiration of his older brother was evidenced by his choosing number 23 for his uniform—as close as could get to half of Larry's number 45. He was further inspired by the aerial artistry of JULIUS ERVING and began creating his own repertoire of slam dunks.

Jordan's potential became evident in his senior year, and he was recruited by the University of North Carolina, one of the nation's elite basketball schools. He spent much of his freshman year learning Coach Dean Smith's system and

Michael Jordan's incredible body control and fierce competitiveness led many to call him the greatest athlete of his time. *(Andrew D. Bernstein/NBAE/ Getty Images)*

working on his defense. He finished third in scoring on the talented Tarheels, who reached the finals of the 1982 National Collegiate Athletic Association (NCAA) tournament. Few basketball fans knew who Jordan was until the final seconds of that game against Georgetown. With his team trailing by 62–61, it was Jordan—and not his veteran teammates and future NBA stars James Worthy and Sam Perkins—who was called on to nail the jump shot that gave North Carolina its first national championship.

Jordan never achieved gaudy scoring numbers in Coach Smith's team-oriented offense. But even though he averaged barely 20 points per game his sophomore and junior years, *The Sporting News* voted him College Player of the Year both seasons. Jordan then skipped his senior season to play in the NBA. Before turning pro, however, he led the U.S. Olympic team to a surprisingly easy gold medal victory in the 1984 Olympics. The Spanish Coach, after watching him lead the dismantling of his team in the finals, muttered of Jordan, "He's a rubber man. He's not human."

Jordan was the third player selected in the 1984 NBA draft. His new team, the hapless Chicago Bulls, had modest expectations for Jordan. One team executive warned the public, "Jordan isn't going to turn this franchise around. He's a very good offensive player but not an overpowering offensive player." It did not, however, take Jordan long to prove him wrong. Finding the faster-paced, wide-open NBA game more suited to his talents than college ball, Jordan poured in 22 points in a single quarter in just his third game of the season. He scored so often and with such gravity-defying flair that he quickly became the league's top drawing card. He won the NBA Slam Dunk contest and finished the season with an average of 28.2 points, six assists, and six rebounds to beat out HAKEEM ABDUL OLAJUWON easily as the league's Rookie of the Year. The only sour note his first year was at the All-Star game, when the veteran players on his team, apparently jealous of Jordan's popularity, deliberately kept the ball away from him.

Just as the six-foot, six-inch, guard was establishing himself as the NBA's refreshing new star, disaster struck when he fractured his foot in October 1985. After missing most of the season, he stubbornly insisted on coming back to play,

against the advice of Bulls' management and medical staff. Jordan sparked a late-season rally that pushed the Bulls into the playoffs. Then, against the Boston Celtics, Jordan put on an incredible one-man show. He scored a play-off record 63 points in one game and averaged more than 43 points for the series, in a losing effort. The Boston coach, K. C. Jones, remarked, "I thought he was awesome the last time we played against him. I don't have a word for him this time."

Jordan's domination of the NBA scoring title began in the first game of the 1986–87 season when he scored 50 points. He finished the year with a 37.1 average, the highest ever by an NBA guard and second only to WILT CHAMBERLAIN in league history. Jordan repeated as scoring champ the following year with an average of 35.0. Almost lost in the excitement over his offensive displays was the fact that Jordan had become one of basketball's top defensive players. He led the league in steals that season and became the first person ever to win the scoring title and be voted Defensive Player of the Year in the same season. Jordan also reeled in his first MVP Award.

Jordan continued to win scoring titles over the next several years, but the Bulls kept bowing out early in the postseason playoffs despite Jordan's heroics. The Bulls' star came under criticism for being a ball hog who could not blend in with his teammates to be successful. Such perceptions stung Jordan, who was fiercely competitive and a tireless perfectionist in practice.

The Bulls gradually gathered a strong supporting cast for Jordan, who then showed he could be both a scoring star and a team player. In 1990–91, the Bulls won 61 games, best in the league, and then beat their longtime nemesis, Detroit, to make the finals. There, Jordan sank 12 consecutive shots in one game and buried a last-second shot to send another game into overtime to lead the team past the Los Angeles Lakers for their first title. Chicago then went on to win the next two championships, silencing Jordan's critics once and for all.

Jordan's wonderful world was rocked in the summer of 1993, when his father was reported missing and found weeks later, murdered. Jordan abruptly announced his retirement before the next season, then stunned fans even more by attempting a widely publicized baseball career. The venture met with limited success in the Chicago White Sox minor league organization, and in March 1995, Jordan pulled another stunning about-face by returning to basketball. The effects of the year-and-a-half layoff were too great to overcome that season, but Jordan returned to his old form in 1995–96. He regained his scoring title with a 30.4 average and led the Bulls back to the NBA championship. Jordan retained his scoring title as the Bulls repeated as NBA champions the following two seasons.

Jordan's performance against the Utah Jazz in the finals of 1998 solidified his exalted status in sports. With the Bulls trailing by a point in game six of the finals with seconds to go and the ball in the hands of Utah's Karl Malone, Chicago appeared to be doomed to defeat. But, taking a reckless gamble, Jordan left his man and stripped Malone of the ball, then calmly drained a jump shot to win the game and the title.

It was a perfect note on which to finish the most illustrious career in NBA history. In addition to his 10 scoring titles, Jordan led the NBA in steals three times, was named to the All-Defensive team nine times, won the NBA MVP Award five times, and won the NBA Finals MVP Award another five times. He retired from basketball again, well set for life as the most recognizable pitchman in the nation with an income from endorsements exceeding $30 million per year.

Unable to stay out of basketball, Jordan became president of the Washington Wizards in January 2000. The team's inept performances eventually pushed Jordan's competitive nature to its limit, and in 2001 he again shocked the basketball world by announcing he would play for the Wizards. Most experts thought the 38-year-old Jordan, who had been out of the game three years,

was taking on too great a challenge this time, and many feared he would embarrass himself. But after a rough start, Jordan performed yet another miracle by guiding the once-woeful team back to respectability.

Further Reading

Greene, Bob. *Hang Time: Days and Dreams with Michael Jordan.* New York: Doubleday, 1992.

———. *Rebound: The Odyssey of Michael Jordan.* New York: Viking, 1995.

Halberstam, David. *Playing for Keeps: Michael Jordan and the World He Made.* New York: Random House, 1998.

Jordan, Michael. *For the Love of the Game.* New York: Crown, 1998.

Naughton, Jim. *Taking to the Air: The Rise of Michael Jordan.* New York: Warner, 1992.

Smith, Sam. *The Jordan Rules.* New York: Simon & Schuster, 1992.

———. *Second Coming: The Strange Odyssey of Michael Jordan from Courtside to Homeplate and Back Again.* New York: HarperCollins, 1995.

Joyner, Florence Griffith   See GRIFFITH JOYNER, FLORENCE.

Joyner-Kersee, Jackie
(Jacqueline Joyner)
(1962–) *track-and-field pentathlete and heptathlete*

Al Joyner, a superb athlete who won an Olympic gold medal in the triple jump, was once humiliated in front of his peers when his younger sister beat him in a sprint race. As the years passed, however, Al began to see that he had little reason for shame. Speaking of Jackie, the Olympic high jumper and television commentator Dwight Stones was moved to declare, "There's no argument that she is the greatest female athlete of all time."

Jacqueline Joyner was born on March 3, 1962, in East Saint Louis, Illinois, to Al and Mary Ruth Joyner. Al and Mary had been married early in high school and had four children, of whom Jackie was the second, which made them unable to continue school. As a result, they struggled to make ends meet with low-paying jobs while living in a neighborhood overrun with drugs, gangs, and criminals. Their flimsy house had no working furnace, so Jackie was forced to sleep in the kitchen next to the stove in winter. Al said of their childhood, "I remember Jackie and me crying together in a back room in that house, swearing that we were going to make it. Make it out."

The one thing the community did offer was the Mary E. Brown Community Center. Jackie tried virtually every sport and craft the center offered, but her favorite activity was dance. When her instructor told her that her talent and long legs would carry her far in dance, she dreamed of a professional dance career. That dream was shattered, however, when her teacher was shot to death and the classes were discontinued.

Joyner became involved in track and field because she wrote her name down on every sign-up sheet that was passed around at the building, including one for a track team. Even though she finished last or near last in almost every race, Jackie refused to quit. At the same time, she became so fascinated with long jumping that she and her younger sisters took potato chip bags to a nearby park and filled them with sand from the playground to make a sand pile in their front yard. Then Joyner would practice leaping out into the pit from the porch.

Her coach never imagined the slow-footed girl could do well at long jumping and so did not enter Jackie in the event. But one day while she was waiting for a ride home from the coach, she took a try at the long jump pit. Her coach happened to arrive just as her long legs stretched far out into the sand. In stunned disbelief, he measured the 12-year-old's distance at nearly 17 feet, a good distance for a high school athlete!

As Joyner grew, her long legs began to carry her past opponents in races as well as in the long jump. Her coach recognized her versatility would make her an ideal candidate for the five-event pentathlon competition. Not only did she train hard for the event, but she and her teammates worked tirelessly at car washes, bake sales, and other fundraising events to raise money so they could attend the National Junior Olympics in 1976. Joyner made her national debut a success by winning the pentathlon in the 13- to 14-year age group.

Her combination of intense dedication with natural ability made the 5-foot, 10-inch Joyner a multisport star at Lincoln High School in East Saint Louis. Although she did not start playing basketball until her sophomore year, she was named an All-American in basketball and led her team to a state title. She was an All-Metro selection in volleyball. In track and field, she won four consecutive national junior championships in the pentathlon and was the star of a team that won three straight state high school titles. She not only won the 400-meter dash at state but set an Illinois state high school record in the long jump with a leap of 20 feet, 7 ½ inches, which qualified her for the Olympic trials. Facing world-class athletes for the first time, she placed a respectable eighth.

Joyner, who ranked 13th in her class academically, was heavily recruited both as a basketball player and as a track athlete. She accepted a basketball scholarship at the University of California at Los Angeles (UCLA) in 1980, on the condition that she could also compete in track and field. Her freshman year, however, started off as a nightmare. First, she and her mother broke off relations with her increasingly abusive father. Then in January 1981, her mother contracted meningitis and died. Meanwhile, the UCLA track coaches looked at her as a basketball player who was only competing in the long jump for fun. They gave her little coaching, and Joyner began to struggle. As if that were not enough, Joyner began experiencing severe breathing problems during workouts. It was determined that she had asthma, a condition she would have to battle throughout her career.

During this difficult period, the assistant coach Bob Kersee took her under his wing. Although hired to coach sprinters and hurdlers, he recognized Joyner's potential, advised her to take up the seven-event heptathlon (which consisted of the 100-meter hurdles, high jump, shot put, 200-meter dash, long jump, javelin, and 800-meter run), and gave her individual coaching in track-and-field techniques. Under Kersee's supervision, Joyner improved quickly, finishing third in her first heptathlon competition. By the end of her sophomore year, she had mastered the skills well enough to win the National Collegiate Athletic Association (NCAA) title.

In the winter of 1983–84, she took a leave of absence from the basketball team to focus on the Olympics. After working out for eight hours a day, she set a national record in the heptathlon with 6,520 points and made the U.S. Olympic team in the long jump. However, during the 1984 Olympics, she grew preoccupied with a strained hamstring and lost her focus even though she was leading the competition. On the same day that her brother won a gold medal in the triple jump, Joyner finished the final event, the 800 meters, an agonizing 0.33 second short of victory and had to settle for the silver medal.

After the 1984 Olympics, Joyner went back to playing basketball and studying. She made First-Team All-Conference her senior year and finished her career as the school's fourth-leading rebounder and sixth-leading scorer. But her main love was track and field, which also happened to be Bob Kersee's life. The two began spending more time together and eventually married in January 1986. Meanwhile, Jackie proved her versatility by trying some new events. In 1985, she ran the 400-meter hurdles in 55.05, the fourth-best women's time in U.S. history, and recorded the top woman's triple jump in the nation—43 feet, 3 inches.

Moving back to the heptathlon, Joyner-Kersee broke the world record at the Goodwill Games in

Jackie Joyner-Kersee has garnered strong support for recognition as the best female athlete of all time. *(Tony Duffy/Getty Images)*

Moscow on July 7, 1986, with 7,148 points. Previously, experts had doubted a woman could ever break 7,000 points. A month later, she topped that performance with 7,158 points. Joyner-Kersee then tied the world record in the long jump that same month with a leap of 24 feet, 5 ½ inches. For her efforts, she was named winner of the Sullivan Award as the United States' top amateur athlete, only the eighth woman to win the award in its 67-year history.

At the 1988 Games in Seoul, Korea, the only drama focused on how high Joyner-Kersee could push the record. The competition was virtually over by the end of the first day when Joyner-Kersee blazed to a time of 22.56 in the 200 meters, a full 1.5 seconds faster than she had run in 1984. So confident was Joyner-Kersee of victory that she deliberately jumped off the wrong foot to avoid stress on her injured knee and still managed a distance of 7.27 meters (23 feet, 10 ¼ inches), an Olympic record for the long jump. She then uncorked one of her best javelin throws ever (45.66 meters) and finished nearly five seconds faster than her 1984 time. That gave her the staggering total of 7,291 points. To put that in perspective, Sabine John of East Germany and Irina Belova of the Soviet Union both topped the previous Olympic record, yet Joyner-Kersee beat both by nearly 400 points.

While she celebrated her victory, as well as the three gold medals won by her sister-in-law, FLORENCE GRIFFITH JOYNER, Joyner-Kersee stayed focused on her next task—the long jump. No American woman had ever won the event since it was introduced to the Olympics in 1948. But she hit the target her husband had set for her, jumping 7.40 meters to claim the Olympic record and the gold medal.

The 1992 Olympics in Barcelona, Spain, were more of a coronation than a competition for Joyner-Kersee in the heptathlon. Although her performances tailed off slightly in most areas from those of 1988, she won easily with 7,044 points and added a bronze medal in the long jump.

The battle-scarred veteran of the U.S. track team continued to train, fighting through severe asthma attacks that almost killed her at the 1995 U.S. championships. She fought through an ankle injury to earn spots in both the heptathlon and long jump at the 1996 Olympics, finishing her Olympic career with a courageous bronze medal effort on a severely pulled right thigh in the long jump. After that, she retired and started youth clubs in East Saint Louis.

Further Reading

Condon, Robert J. *Great Women Athletes of the 20th Century.* Jefferson, N.C.: McFarland, 1999.

Deford, Frank. "Jackie! Oh!" *Newsweek,* June 10, 1996, pp. 72–3.

Joyner Kersee, Jackie. *A Kind of Grace: The Autobiography of the World's Greatest Female Athlete.* New York: Warner, 1997.

Moore, Ken. "Head to Head: Heike Drechsler and Jackie Joyner-Kersee," *Sports Illustrated,* July 22, 1992, pp. 66–7.

Kemp, Lee
(Leroy Percy Kemp)
(1956–   ) *wrestler*

Lee Kemp ranks as one of the greatest competitive wrestlers (not to be confused with pro wrestlers, who are popular choreographed entertainers) the United States has ever produced. He won more than 400 matches and is the only U.S. wrestler to have won three world championships.

He was born Leroy Percy Kemp on December 24, 1956, in Cleveland, Ohio. Had he been even a moderately skilled basketball player, he would never have become involved in wrestling. But after being cut from his eighth-grade basketball team, he looked for a replacement activity. The next year, he watched some competitive wrestling and decided to give it a try. By the time Kemp began wrestling, the presence of African Americans in the sport had been established. In 1957, a few months after Kemp's birth, 147-pound Simon Roberts of the University of Iowa had become the first black National Collegiate Athletic Association (NCAA) wrestling champion.

At first, wrestling seemed to be a great deal of work for little benefit. But Kemp showed some early promise. He liked the natural high he enjoyed in his occasional victories and stayed with the sport. As a 10th-grader, Kemp made the varsity and fashioned a respectable 11–8 record. That

An Olympic boycott prevented the wrestling legend Lee Kemp from going after the gold medal for which he had worked so hard. *(University of Wisconsin-Madison)*

summer he attended a clinic put on by Dan Gable, a man who had come within one match of an undefeated college career and had won an Olympic gold medal. Kemp was so motivated by what he heard at the camp that he began training with fanatical dedication. He spent hours studying other wrestlers to learn some of their techniques. The work paid off as Kemp shocked even his own coach with his undefeated season as a junior and his victory over the defending champion at the state tournament. Kemp then continued his unbeaten streak through his senior season.

Kemp enrolled at the University of Wisconsin in the fall of 1974. Although he experienced five defeats early in his freshman season, he set a goal of surpassing the great Gable to become the first four-time NCAA champion. Showing his trademark explosive quickness and strength, he wrestled his way to the final of the 150-pound weight class that year. There his dream slipped away by the narrowest of margins when he battled to a 1–1 tie in overtime, only to lose a referee's decision. That would be the last match Kemp would lose as a collegian. Over his final three years of collegiate competition, Kemp won 108 matches with one tie while wrestling at 150 and 158 pounds, thus gaining three NCAA titles.

After graduating in 1978, Kemp became the youngest U.S. wrestler to win a world freestyle championship. He repeated the following year and was a heavy favorite to win a gold medal at the 1980 Olympics. However, the U.S. boycott of the Moscow Games denied him this ultimate triumph.

Kemp overcame his disappointment and in 1982 became the first American to win three world championships. Unfortunately, he had lost just enough of his edge to slip to second place in the 1984 U.S. Olympic trials, and thus he never was able to enjoy the Olympic experience. Kemp then retired from the sport, having won more than 400 matches and six national freestyle championships in his career. He was inducted into the National Wrestling Hall of Fame in 1990.

Further Reading

Great Athletes of the Twentieth Century. Vol. 9. Pasadena, Calif.: Salem Press, 1994.

Looney, D. S. "Suppression of His Aggression," *Sports Illustrated,* February 21, 1977, p. 28.

L

Lane, Night Train
(Richard Lane, Dick Lane)
(1928–2002) *football defensive back*

Often the only time a National Football League (NFL) cornerback gets noticed is when a wide receiver beats him on a long touchdown pass. Dick "Night Train" Lane was the first cornerback to gain more fame than receivers. He remains the consensus choice of football experts as the best cornerback of all time.

Richard Lane was born on April 16, 1928, in Austin, Texas. He began playing football at L. C. Anderson High School in Austin and continued at Western Nebraska Community College in Scottsbluff. His college career lasted only a year, however, before Lane dropped out of school and joined the army. During his four years of service, he played for the army's football team at Fort Ord, California, primarily on offense.

Having had no experience at a competitive level, Lane did not see football as a career option. After leaving the army, he stayed in California and found work in an aircraft factory. But he soon found himself dreaming of a football career, and, armed with a few press clippings from his limited playing days, he walked into the office of the Los Angeles Rams in the summer of 1952 and asked for a tryout. There must have been at least the look of an athlete about the six-foot, 195-pound

Lane because the Rams agreed to consider the 24-year-old rookie. They liked his quickness and thought he showed potential as a wide receiver.

The Rams, however, already had two of the NFL's best wide receivers, Tom Fears and Elroy "Crazy Legs" Hirsch. Lane and the Rams soon found that his talents could be put to better use on the other side of the ball. Before he made the switch, though, he was tagged with one of football's most colorful nicknames. While Lane roomed with Fears, the veteran had repeatedly played the popular song "Night Train" in his room, but it was Lane who became associated with the song and given the moniker.

Despite his lack of experience, Lane immediately made an impact as cornerback. He was extremely quick in reacting to the ball and he loved to take chances in hopes of getting on interception. Although he was occasionally burned by a wrong guess, he intercepted 14 passes in his rookie season, which still stands as the NFL season record even with the schedule expanded from 12 games in Lane's time to 16 today. He returned two of those scores for touchdowns. Opponents continued to test Lane in 1954, when he again led the NFL in interceptions. After that, Lane often spent a lonely afternoon during games as teams refused to test him. Even legendary Green Bay coach Vince Lombardi instructed his quarterback Bart Starr not to throw to Lane's side of the field.

Incredibly, Lane never made All-Pro until after he was traded to the Chicago Cardinals in 1954, after which he won the honor five times. He enjoyed his best seasons with the Detroit Lions from 1960 to 1965, during which he developed a reputation as a fierce hitter. Although foes rarely challenged him, Lane finished his career in 1965 with 68 interceptions, the third highest in NFL history. He died January 29, 2002.

Further Reading

Allen, George. *Pro Football's 100 Greatest Players*. Indianapolis: Bobbs-Merrill, 1982.

Great Athletes of the Twentieth Century. Vol. 10. Pasadena, Calif.: Salem Press, 1994.

Leonard, Buck

(Walter Fenner Leonard)
(1907–1997) *baseball first baseman*

With his spectacular hitting and solid fielding, Buck Leonard frequently drew comparisons to New York Yankees legend Lou Gehrig. Most Negro League experts list him with SATCHEL PAIGE and JOSH GIBSON as the best players of their era.

Walter Fenner Leonard was born in Rocky Mount, North Carolina, on September 8, 1907, to Jon and Emma Leonard. Jon Leonard, a railroad fireman, died when Buck was 11, and the boy worked at shining shoes to help support the family. After finishing eighth grade, Leonard began working for the railroad, primarily as a mechanic. In his spare time, he joined his brother, Charlie, in playing baseball in a local league. Leonard began as an outfielder, but when he was made the team's manager, he found it inconvenient to keep running in from the outfield to argue. As a result, he switched to first base, the position at which he stayed his entire career.

Leonard never would have played pro ball except that, after nine years on the job, the Great Depression forced the railroad to lay him off his job in 1933. "I had almost given up baseball," he later recalled. "I had gotten too old to play around here." But with no alternate source of income, the 25-year-old Leonard accepted a meager offer to join a traveling semipro team. After struggling to eke out a bare living with teams in Portsmouth, Baltimore, and Brooklyn that year, he was signed at the beginning of the 1934 season by the Homestead Grays of the Negro League to fill in for a few days while they waited for their first baseman to arrive from the Midwest. Leonard so impressed the team in his first two days that the Grays installed him as their regular first baseman instead.

Unlike most of his African-American contemporaries, Leonard played his entire Negro League career with one team, the Grays. The left-handed-hitting Leonard was widely regarded as both a power hitter and a high-average, line-drive hitter. According to a rival pitcher, Dave Barnhill, "You could put a fastball in a shotgun and you couldn't shoot it by him." When Josh Gibson joined the Grays in 1937, they formed the most explosive power-hitting duo in the history of black baseball. Although records from that era are spotty and unreliable, Leonard is generally credited with winning at least two home run titles and two batting titles. As for his fielding prowess, one contemporary commented, "Buck makes the hard plays look easy."

Leonard was widely respected as a no-nonsense competitor on the field and a gentleman off the field. He was selected for the league All-Star team in 11 of the 14 years he played for the Grays. As did most black ball players of the time, he played year-round, traveling to Mexico or Cuba to play during the winter months. He continued to play at Homestead until the team disbanded in 1950, after which he played in the Mexican League until he retired in 1955 at the age of 48. Along with Gibson and Paige, Leonard was inducted into baseball's Hall of Fame in 1972, the first year that Negro League ballplayers were considered for the honor.

Further Reading

Chadwick, Bruce. *When the Game Was Black and White.* New York: Abbeville, 1992.

Clark, Dick, and Lerry Lester, eds. *The Negro League Book.* Cleveland, Ohio: Society for American Baseball Research, 1994.

Leonard, Buck, with James A. Riley. *Buck Leonard: The Black Lou Gehrig.* New York: Carroll & Graf, 1995.

Leonard, Sugar Ray
(Ray Charles Leonard)
(1956–   ) *boxer*

Sugar Ray Leonard was a charismatic and intelligent boxer who only reluctantly embarked on a fighting career. In a series of memorable matches with all-time greats, he lived up to the nickname that invited comparisons with the legendary SUGAR RAY ROBINSON.

Ray Charles Leonard was born on May 17, 1956, in Wilmington, North Carolina, one of six children born to Cicero and Getha Leonard. His mother, hoping he would become a singer, named him after recording artist Ray Charles.

Ray was introduced to boxing at a boys' club at age seven, but he hated it. Seven years later, after the family moved to Palmer Park, Maryland, a suburb of Washington, D.C., he took up the sport again and this time showed both interest and great aptitude. He won numerous Golden Gloves bouts and, at age 16, was invited to try out for the 1972 U.S. Olympic team. He failed to make the team that year but continued his stellar amateur career into the next Olympics. An articulate man with a flair for public relations, Leonard became the most famous member of a strong U.S. boxing contingent in the 1976 Montreal Olympics. With his superior hand speed, balance, and reflexes, he had no trouble dispatching his opponents, and he won his gold medal by pounding Andres Adlama of Cuba in the final. Boasting a 145–5 record as an amateur, Leonard then shocked the boxing world by announcing his

retirement from the sport. It was his intention to live off his celebrity product endorsements from his Olympic fame and work toward a business degree at the University of Maryland.

However, the endorsements never materialized, his parents became ill, and his girlfriend Juanita Wilkerson applied for welfare to support their three-year-old son. Faced with this responsibility, Leonard trained under MUHAMMAD ALI's former handler, Angelo Dundee, and made his pro debut in May 1977.

His big chance occurred in 1979, when he fought the welterweight champion, Wilfred Benitez, finally scoring a 15th-round technical knockout (TKO) to gain the title. Leonard then suffered his first pro defeat to Panama's brawling Roberto Duran. With his ability to adjust to any style of boxing, Leonard was ready for Duran when they fought a rematch in November 1980. This time, he so thoroughly outboxed Duran that the champion quit in frustration midway through the bout. In September 1981, Leonard took on the feared THOMAS HEARNS in a ferocious match. After being rocked on his heels in the early rounds, Leonard launched a frantic comeback to gain a 14th-round TKO.

Leonard's flair for the dramatic and unexpected put his fans on a rollercoaster of emotions in the 1980s. In 1982, an injury suffered in a sparring match persuaded him to retire. He then made the equally unexpected decision to reenter the ring in 1984 but quit again after one lackluster fight.

Although it appeared certain that Leonard's career was over, he could not shake the urge to compete. "I truly love boxing," he once said. "There is nothing to compare to the feeling you get from winning." In 1986, Leonard pulled yet another surprise by going back into serious training, this time with the aim of beating MARVIN HAGLER. Leonard pulled another surprise by winning the controversial 12-round bout. In 1988, he added the supermiddleweight and light heavyweight crowns to his collection by beating the champion, Donny Lalonde.

Leonard was inducted into boxing's Hall of Fame in 1997, after becoming the first boxer to earn more than $100 million in prize money.

Further Reading

Goldstein, Alan. *A Fistful of Sugar: The Sugar Ray Leonard Story.* New York: Coward, McCann & Geoghegan, 1981.

Walsh, Peter. *Men of Steel.* London: Robson, 1993.

Leslie, Lisa Deshawn

(1972–) *basketball center*

After a decade as one of the most recognizable stars of women's basketball, Lisa Leslie enjoyed a breakthrough season in 2001 that carried her to the pinnacle of her profession. That year, the graceful, six-foot, five-inch center swept the Women's National Basketball Association's (WNBA's) Most Valuable Player (MVP) Awards in the regular season, All-Star Game, and championship.

Lisa Deshawn Leslie was born on July 7, 1972, in Compton, California, to Christine and Walter Leslie. Her father, a semipro basketball player, left the family two months after her birth. Christine, a tough-minded, independent woman, raised her daughter by working at the post office until 1982 and then learned to drive a truck and bought her own 18-wheeler. This job took her away from home for all but a few days each month, leaving Lisa in charge of the home front.

Lisa grew quickly, reaching six feet at the age of 12. Other children teased her about her size, but Lisa's six-foot, three-inch, mother constantly told her to be proud of her height; to keep her head up; and to avoid slouching. Yet even when she sprouted up to six feet, five inches, Leslie had no intention of being a basketball player. Her sights were set on becoming a model. She agreed to go out for the sport in junior high only because she was lonely and one of the more popular girls in the school begged her to do it. But, as she

remembers, "I didn't want to break a sweat . . . I was so prissy."

Leslie's height gave her a tremendous advantage even when she knew nothing about the game. Her education in the sport was supplied by her cousin, Craig Simpson. Recognizing her potential, Simpson set about teaching her the basics of the game. He also helped toughen her up and gave her a strict regimen of exercises to improve her strength and coordination. By the time she was in ninth grade, Leslie not only could handle herself on the court but could dunk the basketball.

At Inglewood Morningside High School in Los Angeles, Leslie played so well that fans began to speak of her as the next CHERYL DEANNE MILLER. Leslie further invited comparisons when she broke Miller's record of 100 points in a game by scoring 101 points in only two quarters of action. Leslie enjoyed the media attention but remained so likable that she was voted her class president at Morningside three times.

Leslie continued to follow the Miller legend when she attended the University of Southern California (USC). In her freshman year, she led the team with 19.4 points and 10.1 rebounds a game. She stumbled somewhat the following two seasons when opponents began to take advantage of her tendency to foul, which forced her to sit on the bench for long stretches, yet continued to win All-Conference honors. After learning to play with more control during her senior year, she set Pac10 Conference records in scoring, rebounds, and blocked shots, and she won the Naismith Award as the college woman player of the year in 1994.

As there were few opportunities for women basketball players in the United States, Leslie went to Italy after graduation. There the slender center gained valuable lessons in playing the rugged style of international basketball, and she adjusted well enough to average more than 22 points and nearly 12 rebounds per game. The experience helped her immensely when she joined the U.S. Olympic women's team in 1996. The team garnered an unusual amount of publicity by being undefeated in 52 consecutive games leading up to the Olympics. Leslie led the team in both scoring and rebounding, and the towering would-be model became one of the most popular players on the team.

In the 1996 Olympics, Leslie again led the way for Team USA. She connected on a sizzling 74.5 percent of her shots and *averaged* more points per game than the previous Olympic single-game record, with a high of 35 points against Japan. In the championship game against Australia, Leslie poured in 29 points in a 118–87 pounding that earned the team their gold medal.

Leslie intended to capitalize on her success by pursuing her longtime dream of becoming a career model. But she quickly returned to basketball when the WNBA organized its inaugural season in 1997 and assigned her to the team in her hometown of Los Angeles. Leslie continued to enjoy success as a WNBA pro as she led the Sparks in scoring with a 15.9 average, topped the league in rebounding with 9.5 per game, and was voted to First-Team All-WNBA. Although she again led the league in rebounding in 1998 and increased her scoring to 19.6, she was relegated to All-WNBA Second Team. Leslie's play slumped the following season when she averaged just 15.6 points and 7.8 rebounds. But she regained her touch, with 17.8 points and 9.6 rebounds, in 2000, earning both the All-Star Most Valuable Player (MVP) Award and First Team All-NBA honors, while collecting a second gold medal in the 2000 Olympics.

Yet despite her success, the Sparks failed to challenge the Houston Comets, who won four consecutive WNBA championships, and many observers felt that Leslie lost her poise at crucial times. Aware of the talk, Leslie entered the 2001 season with a renewed focus. As she later admitted, "Players would say, 'If you get into Lisa's head, you've got them.' I wanted to make sure I defied that."

Lisa Leslie wanted to be a model but instead became the Women's National Basketball Association's (WNBA's) top player in 2001. *(Al Bello/Getty Images)*

Defy that she did, showing a newfound confidence and determination by sweeping the MVP Awards in the regular season, All-Star Game, and championship. Her 24 points, 13 rebounds, six assists, and seven blocked shots in the final game of the playoffs led Los Angeles to a 82–54 thrashing of the Charlotte Sting to claim their first title and establish Lisa Leslie as the WNBA's most dominant player. Leslie led the Sparks to a repeat championship in 2002.

Further Reading

Anderson, Kelli. "Woman Possessed," *Sports Illustrated*, September 10, 2001, pp. 46–47.

Corbett, Sara. *Venus to the Hoop*. New York: Doubleday, 1997.

Schick, Elizabeth, ed. *Current Biography 1998*. New York: H. W. Wilson, 1998.

Lewis, Carl
(Frederick Carlton Lewis)
(1961–   ) *track-and-field sprinter, jumper*

Carl Lewis is the longest-reigning sprint star in track-and-field history. He achieved fame both for winning four gold medals in a single Olympics and for winning the same event, the long jump, in four consecutive Olympics.

He was born Frederick Carlton Lewis into an extremely athletic family in Montgomery, Alabama, on January 1, 1961. His mother, Evelyn, had been a star hurdler in the 1950s, his brother Cleveland was a standout soccer player, and his brother Mack was All-State in track. Carl, who was much smaller than the others, appeared to be the non-athlete of the family—he regularly lost races to his younger sister, Carol, who became a national-caliber track competitor.

At the height of the civil rights tension in Montgomery in 1963, the family moved to Willingboro, a New Jersey suburb of Philadelphia. There his father, William, and his mother were track coaches at rival schools and organized the Willingboro Track Club. Living all his life around track, Carl tried hard to fit in. He gradually improved, especially after experiencing a growth spurt, and managed a 22-foot long jump as a sophomore. He became obsessed with the sport after being ridiculed by his high school teammates when he lost a lead in a relay race and made a vow to himself: "I was not going to be humiliated on the track again. I was either going to quit or I was going to dedicate myself to work harder than I had been."

He chose the latter, after first transferring from Kennedy High School to Willingboro High School. There, as a junior, he jumped 24 feet, 9 inches, the third-best distance by a prep athlete that year. At the same time, he dropped his time in the 100-yard dash from 10.6 to 9.3. After leaping 25 feet, 9 inches, the summer after his junior year, Lewis was highly recruited by colleges. He chose the University of Houston, where he enrolled in 1979. There, Coach Tom Tellez altered Lewis's jumping technique, which resulted in Lewis's winning the National Collegiate Athletic Association (NCAA) indoor championship as a freshman with a jump of 26 feet, 4 ½ inches. He followed up with an even more impressive victory at the NCAA outdoors, with a 27-foot, 4 ¾ -inch leap.

Lewis then won the 1980 U.S. Olympic trials in the long jump and finished a surprising fourth in the 100 meters to make the relay team, but the U.S. boycott of the Moscow Olympics prevented him from taking part in this first international competition. He created an international stir when he broke the world indoor long jump record at the 1981 NCAA championships. Then he became the first person, since his childhood hero JESSE OWENS in 1936, to win a track event and a field event in the U.S. national championship when he won the outdoor 100 meters and long jump later that season. Lewis then uncorked a leap of 28 feet, 3 ½ inches, over the summer, the longest jump since BOB BEAMON's monumental effort. Lewis capped off the year by winning the long jump at the world championship.

Such performances made Lewis the main event at the 1984 Olympics, especially when it became known that he planned to try to duplicate Owens's unprecedented feat of winning four gold medals in a single Olympics. The weight of expectations was nearly unbearable as he began his quest in the 100 meters. "I really get anxious in the blocks," he admitted. "That is the moment of truth." Although the Eastern European boycott of the Los Angeles Games took some of the luster off the event, Lewis came through as advertised. He

Carl Lewis matched Jesse Owens's Olympic performance, then held on to the long-jump title for 16 years. *(Mike Powell/Getty Images)*

easily sprinted to victory in the 100 meters with a time of 9.99. In the long jump, he unleashed a leap of 28 feet, ¼ inch, on his first try to win that event by nearly 1 foot. Gold medal number three was in the 200 meters as he breezed to a clear-cut win over his teammate Kirk Baptiste in an Olympic record 19.80. He then matched Owens by running anchor on the world-record-setting gold medal run of the United States's 4 × 100 relay team.

Unfortunately, a number of misunderstandings led to a negative press reaction, and rather than being heralded as the next great U.S. track star, Lewis was criticized as a selfish prima donna. Only after battling back from a knee injury in 1986 and the death of his father (with whom he buried his 100-meter gold medal) in 1987, did Lewis manage to rehabilitate his image.

Lewis set out to repeat his record-tying performance in the next Olympics. He tuned up for the event with career bests of 28 feet 8 ½ inches, in the long jump and 9.93 in the 100 meters. However, a dangerous rival had emerged, the Canadian sprinter Ben Johnson. An explosive starter, Johnson opened up early leads that Lewis was hard-pressed to make up.

At the 1988 Olympics in Seoul, Korea, Johnson catapulted out of the blocks in the 100-meter final. Although he ran a U.S. record 9.92 seconds, Lewis could not close the gap and he had to yield his title as world's fastest human. However, two days later, testing determined that Johnson had been using illegal steroids. His world record was erased and the gold medal given to Lewis. Lewis then achieved the four best jumps of the long jump competition, winning with a best of 28 feet, 7 ½ inches. His Olympic winning streak came to an end, however, in the 200 meters when his U.S.A. teammate Joe DeLoach nosed him out at the tape. The relay team was then disqualified for an illegal handoff and Lewis had to settle for two golds.

Lewis experienced disappointment when it was his rival Mike Powell and not Lewis who finally topped Beamon's long-standing long jump record. As the effects of aging began to take their toll in the early 1990s, Lewis's reign as a track-and-field champion appeared to be at an end. He failed to qualify for the 1992 U.S. Olympic team in the sprints and settled for second in the long jump. But he showed his competitive fire by pulling an upset in the long jump at the Barcelona Olympics, winning his seventh gold medal and then adding an eighth by anchoring the 4 × 100 relay team to victory. Even more stunningly, he returned four years later to win the 1996 Olympic long jump in Atlanta, his fourth consecutive triumph in that event. It was a fitting end to the competitive career of a man who, had the United States not boycotted in 1980, might have held the Olympic long jump title for two solid decades.

Further Reading

Lewis, Carl, with Jeffrey Marx. *Inside Track: My Professional Life in Amateur Track and Field.* New York: Simon & Schuster, 1990.

Moore, Ken. "Chasing the Dream," *Sports Illustrated,* August 29, 1988, pp. 20–25.

Nelson, Cordner. *Track's Greatest Champions.* Los Altos, Calif.: Tafnews Press, 1986.

Lott, Ronnie
(Ronald Mandel Lott)
(1959–   ) *football defensive back*

Ronnie Lott earned a reputation as the hardest-hitting defensive back in football while patrolling the secondary for the San Francisco 49ers during the team's Super Bowl victories of the 1980s.

He was born Ronald Mandel Lott on May 8, 1959, in Albuquerque, New Mexico, the oldest of three children of Roy and Mary Lott. When he was age five, the family moved to Washington, D.C., where his father had been assigned by the air force. He was nine when they moved back to California and settled in Rialto.

Ronnie enjoyed the contact of Pop Warner youth football (a national program like Little League), but such was his love of basketball that he once said of football, "If I had the slightest indication that I could have played basketball in the [National Basketball Association] NBA, you'd never see me play it [football]." Lott played and made All-Conference in both sports at Eisenhower High School. He went to the University of Southern California in 1977 on a football scholarship, where he had as a mentor the senior safety Dennis Thurman, who soon joined the pros. Lott made several All-America teams his junior year while also making the varsity basketball team. As a senior he led the conference with eight interceptions and was the Most Valuable Player on a team that featured four future pros in the defensive backfield.

The San Francisco 49ers drafted Lott in the first round in 1981. He paid immediate dividends by intercepting seven passes at cornerback and running back three of them for touchdowns. He not only made All-Pro as a rookie, but was also a key contributor on San Francisco's rise from also-ran to Super Bowl champion that year. Lott showed his versatility by moving to free safety in 1984 and continuing to make All-Pro. In 1986, he led the National Football League (NFL) with 10 interceptions.

Lott's toughness and positive attitude were a source of inspiration to his teammates. In a game in 1985, he so mangled a finger that he was forced to make a decision to have the tip of it amputated so he could continue to play. Despite his relatively small size at six feet, one inch, 200 pounds, punishing hits were his trademark. Lott's seismic tackle of Ickey Woods in the 1988 Super Bowl so slowed the Cincinnati star running back that the 49ers coach, George Seifert, said, "Ronnie Lott had a direct impact on us winning that game." With Lott guarding the deep middle of the field, San Francisco went on to win its third Super Bowl the following season.

After injuries hampered Lott's play in 1990, the 49ers' coaches believed his effectiveness had been compromised and urged him to retire. Unwilling to end his career, Lott signed with the Los Angeles Raiders. Playing yet another new position, strong safety, Lott made his case by leading the league in interceptions again, with eight. The following season, he led the Raiders in tackles.

Lott finished his career with the New York Jets in 1994. He retired owning the San Francisco club record for interceptions and a record of nine consecutive Pro Bowl appearances.

Further Reading

Graham, Judith, ed. *Current Biography 1994.* New York: H. W. Wilson, 1994.

Leiber, Jill. "Hitter with a Heart," *Sports Illustrated,* January 23, 1989, pp. 44–48.

Louis, Joe

(Joseph Louis Barrow, "The Brown Bomber")
(1914–1981) *boxer*

Although JACKIE ROBINSON's breaking of the race barrier in baseball stands as the most important event in the integration of sports, Joe Louis may have been an even more inspirational figure than Robinson to African Americans. In the words of historian Thomas Sowell, Louis "appeared at a time in American history when blacks were not only at a low economic ebb, but were also the butt of ridicule . . . how he fared in the ring mattered more to black Americans than the fate of any other athlete in any other sport, before or since."

Joseph Louis Barrow was born on May 13, 1914, in rural Lafayette, Alabama, the son of Munroe and Lilly Barrow. When Joe was two, Munroe was committed to a mental institution; the boy was told his father was dead and did not learn the truth until many years later. The family struggled to survive in Alabama until Joe turned 12, then moved north to Detroit. Joe attended Bronson Vocational School, hoping to learn a trade as a cabinet maker. But by the age of 17, he was out of school and working in an automobile factory.

Joe claimed to be so timid that he was regularly beaten by bullies until his sister forced him to stand up for himself. He took up boxing only because friends pressured him to do so, using the money his mother gave him for violin lessons to rent a locker at Brewster East Side Gym. To prevent his mother from discovering his deception, he fought under the name Joe Louis.

Although most fans later assumed he was a natural boxer, Louis's career began with a humiliating defeat in which he was knocked down three times. In his own words, "I was a badly beaten and bruised boy when I slipped into the house that night."

He proved to be a fast learner who never made the same mistake in the ring twice. By 1933 he improved so much that he advanced to the finals of the Amateur Athletic Union (AAU)

national tournament in the light heavyweight division. A year later, he won all 26 of his fights, 22 of them by knockout, including the AAU championship. After compiling a 54–5 record as an amateur, Louis turned professional on July 4, 1934.

His managers warned him of the difficulty of what he was doing. After the furor stirred up by the controversial JACK JOHNSON, the white boxing establishment had worked hard to prevent black boxers from advancing in the sport. Louis was told that he had to do two things in order to be successful in boxing. First, since he could not

Boxing champion Joe Louis became a symbol of hope to African Americans in the World War II era. *(Library of Congress, Prints & Photographs Division, Carl Van Vechten Collection [LC-USZ62-42521])*

count on judges to render a fair decision, he had to win his fights over white fighters by knockout. Just as important, he needed to distance himself from Johnson's contentious legacy by conducting himself with an air of dignity and professionalism. To that end he even had tutors to help him polish his speech.

For a man who began his career weighing only 175 pounds, the task of knocking out heavyweight opponents was no small order. But Louis packed a powerful punch; one opponent said, "When you're hit by Louis, it's like a light bulb breaking in your face." He easily dispatched his first foe, Jack Kracken, in one round. He followed that with 10 more victories in 1934 and 14 the following year. With a 22–0 mark, he felt he was ready for a big-time fight, but he could not break into the elite level of boxing without a reputable sponsor. Veteran fight manager Mike Jacobs signed on with Louis in 1935 and opened the door for a fight in New York against Primo Carnera on June 25. Louis repeatedly rocked the hulking ex–world champion and finally knocked him out in the sixth round. Next up was another former champion, Max Baer, whom Louis dispatched in four rounds.

Louis's quick rise to the top ranks of the boxing world inspired blacks throughout the country, those who had been ridiculed for decades as being beneath the level of white sportsmen. According to the author Richard Wright, "Two hours after the (Baer) fight, the area . . . was jammed with no less than 15,000 Negroes, joy-mad and moving to they didn't know where."

Louis's sudden rise to fame as "The Brown Bomber" went to his head and he began to spend more time partying and celebrating than training. As a result, he was in poor shape when he stepped into the ring with another Max, this time Max Schmeling of Germany, on June 19, 1936. The poorly prepared Louis lost a 12-round decision, the first defeat of his professional career. The racist rhetoric of the German Schmeling's Nazi government made the defeat particularly distasteful. According to one German magazine,

Schmeling "checked the arrogance of the Negroes and clearly demonstrated to them the superiority of the white race."

Louis recovered his focus and obtained a title fight against James J. Braddock on June 22, 1937, in Chicago. The fight started poorly as Louis suffered a knockdown in the first round. But he came back strong to win the fight and the heavyweight title with an eighth-round knockout. Then he set his sights on a return match with Schmeling. This time, Louis trained hard. By this time, the Nazis had grown into a worldwide menace and their claims to be a superrace had disgusted most Americans. The desire for Louis to stand up for U.S. values in the face of the Nazi claims put tremendous pressure on him. Louis, however, used both the Nazi insults and a late blow by Schmeling in their previous fight as extra motivation, and he confessed to being an angry man when he entered the ring in Yankee Stadium with the German on June 28, 1938.

By this time, the 6-foot, 1 ½-inch Louis had filled out to a powerful 197 pounds and he put all of it to effective use. At the opening bell, Louis exploded across the ring and lit into Schmeling. Overwhelmed by the rage of his quicker-fisted opponent, Schmeling managed to throw a total of two punches in the entire fight. Louis battered him, knocking him down twice before pounding him senseless and ending the fight at two minutes, four seconds, into the first round. As evidence of Louis's charisma among African Americans, an estimated 20,000 of the 45,000 fans at the fight were black. Yet because of the political implications of the German-American fight, patriotic white Americans also rejoiced in Louis's triumph.

Louis went on to defend his championship 25 times without a loss, while millions of black Americans cheered him on. Some disparaged the quality of the fighters he defeated in his frequent title defenses, deriding them as the "bum of the month club." In reality, it was Louis's skill, intelligence, and power that made the opponents look bad. Included among his victims was yet a third ex–heavyweight champion, Jack Sharkey, who succumbed in the third round of their fight. Louis's toughest title fight opponent was the light heavyweight champion Billy Conn. Conn and Louis waged a ferocious battle on June 18, 1941. Conn, in fact, was ahead on points after 12 rounds, but Louis rallied to knock him out in the 13th.

The champ's reign was interrupted by World War II. Continuing to serve as a national symbol of strength and honor, Louis joined the army in 1942. In an effort to boost military morale, he traveled over 70,000 miles and boxed 96 exhibitions before his discharge from the service in October 1945. The following year, he defeated Conn in a rematch, and he continued to box until announcing his retirement on March 1, 1949. Not only had Louis retired undefeated in championship bouts, but only three of his 25 opponents had managed to last the full 15 rounds.

Unfortunately, Louis was not adept at handling money. The millions of dollars he earned during his career quickly evaporated. At one point, he discovered that he owed the U.S. government $1.25 million in back taxes. Louis contributed to his problems with an unstable social life that went through four marriages and led to a cocaine addiction. Always desperate for money, Louis attempted a comeback in 1950, but his skills had eroded and he lost badly to Ezzard Charles and Rocky Marciano. He stumbled through a variety of failed careers and ended up as a celebrity greeter at Las Vegas night clubs.

By the time Louis died on April 12, 1981, of cardiac arrest, the sports world had changed dramatically. African Americans had achieved superstar status in many sports. Although many of the new generation of athletes had heard Louis's name, few were aware of his impact on the nation. But as much as anyone, it was Louis who, reigning as world heavyweight champion for 12 years, opened the doors for future generations of blacks in American sport. In the words of writer Chester Higgins, in an *Ebony* magazine article, "He gave inspiration to downtrodden and despised people. When Joe Louis fought, blacks in ghettos across the land were indoors glued to their radios, and when Louis won, as he nearly always did, they hit the streets whooping and hollering in celebration."

Further Reading

Astor, Gerald. *. . . And a Credit to His Race: The Hard Life and Times of Joseph Louis Barrow, a.k.a. Joe Louis.* New York: E. P. Dutton, 1974.

Bak, Richard. *Joe Louis: The Great Black Hope.* New York: Da Capo Press, 1998.

Barrow, Joe Louis, and Barbara Munder. *Joe Louis: 50 Years an American Hero.* New York: McGraw-Hill, 1988.

Louis, Joe. *My Life.* New York: Harcourt, Brace, Jovanovich, 1978.

Mead, Chris. *Champion Joe Louis: Black Hero in White America.* New York: Scribner, 1985.

Mullan, Harry. *The Ultimate Encyclopedia of Boxing.* London: Chartwell, 1996.

M

Malone, Karl
("The Mailman")
(1963–   ) *basketball forward*

With his size, granite physique, feathery shooting touch, and surprising speed, Karl Malone emerged as arguably the finest power forward in National Basketball Association (NBA) history. He teamed with John Stockton to form the league's most consistent duo, one that led the Utah Jazz into the playoffs for more than 15 years.

Malone was born on July 24, 1963, in the small town of Summerfield, in northwestern Louisiana, the second youngest child of Shirley and J. P. Malone. When J. P. abandoned the family four years later, Shirley refused welfare despite her desperate situation. Believing that "every tub should sit on its bottom," she worked two jobs, as a forklift operator and a poultry cutter. On weekends, she took the children hunting and fishing for food.

When Karl developed an interest in basketball, there was no money for a hoop, so Shirley would stand with her arms held out like a hoop for him to shoot at. One thing she would not let him do was play football, which she considered unsafe. As Karl grew older, he began taking after his maternal grandfather, who stood six feet, nine inches. The rough play of his older brothers toughened him up, and a job wrestling hogs (with

the goal of inserting nose rings on them) helped him develop enormous strength. These traits made him unstoppable as a basketball player at Summerfield High School. Averaging 30 points and 20 rebounds a game, Malone carried the team to three straight State Class C championships.

Unfortunately, Malone ignored his studies. His grades dropped so low that few colleges would accept him. Then, when he did enroll at Louisiana Tech in 1981, poor grades made him ineligible for his freshman year. Learning his lesson, Malone boosted his grades and made All-Conference three years in a row. Local sportswriters dubbed him "The Mailman" because he could always be counted on to deliver.

Although pro scouts admired his body-builder's physique, they were concerned that Malone's performance at Louisiana Tech dropped from his sophomore to his senior year and that he had failed to make the 1984 U.S. Olympic team. This caused Malone to fall to 13th in the draft's first round, to the Utah Jazz. At first, Malone played down to expectations as a serviceable but flawed power forward. Especially discouraging was his inability to make even half of his free throws.

But the truth was Malone was a small-town kid who needed some time to get used to the fast-paced life of the NBA. By the end of the year, with some experience under his belt, he improved his performance so much that the Jazz felt they could afford to trade away their top-scoring forward Adrian Dantley. Impressed that the Jazz were depending on him, Malone accepted responsibility for improving his play. When asked whether he expected to get better as a player, he commented, "I can improve but I'm not going to talk about improving. I'm just going to do it." One of the most relentless workout warriors in sports (he preferred sweating in heat and humidity to working out in air-conditioned gyms), he made himself into the strongest person in the NBA. At the same time, he began to perfect his shooting touch.

One of the key events in Malone's career was the insertion of guard John Stockton into the starting lineup. One of Malone's few weaknesses was difficulty in creating his own shot, and Stockton's uncanny ability to pass him the ball in scoring position made that unnecessary. Malone averaged 21.7 points and 10.4 rebounds in his second pro season, and he then established himself as an NBA star in 1987–88 by ranking fifth in the league in scoring (27.7) and fourth in rebounding (12.0). Although prone to temper outbursts and controversial off-the-cuff statements, Malone became a model of consistency in production. From 1988 to 2000, a total of 13 consecutive seasons, he finished in the top five in scoring in the NBA. Only MICHAEL JORDAN's presence prevented him from capturing four consecutive scoring titles from 1989 to 1992; despite averaging 29 points over those years with a high of 31.0 in 1990, he finished second to Jordan each year.

Malone could score many different ways. Jack McCallum of *Sports Illustrated* wrote, "There is no defensive player in the league who can beat Malone to the blocks when he has a running start nor is there one who cares to impede Malone's progress by stepping in front of him." His hard work lifting weights and working on his feathery touch paid off at the foul line. Few defenders could keep six-foot, nine-inch, 265-pound Malone away from the basket without fouling him; when they did, he made them pay by increasing

his once-woeful shooting percentage to better than 77 percent. Eight times in his career, Malone led the NBA in free throws made.

Despite most experts considering Malone and Stockton to be the NBA's best at their positions, the Jazz frequently faltered in the playoffs. For a number of years, he enjoyed more success outside regular NBA competition than in it. In 1979, he won the Most Valuable Player (MVP) Award at the NBA All Star Game, and he was cowinner of the same award in 1993. He made up for his failure to make the 1984 Olympic team by winning a starting position on the United States's gold-medal-winning "Dream Teams" of 1992 and 1996.

In 1996–97, several years after basketball observers had begun writing off Malone and Stockton as aging veterans, the two finally made a pair of determined runs at the championship. Malone paved the way with a 27.4 scoring average and 9.9 rebounds a game to win, in his 12th season, the NBA's Most Valuable Player Award. But both that year and the following, Utah fell to Jordan's Chicago Bulls in hard-fought championship series. In 2003, Malone signed with the Los Angeles Lakers. But, he suffered a late-season injury and was severely hobbled as the favored Lakers disintegrated in the championship series against Detroit.

Still the same small-town, backwoods person he has always been, Malone retains a passion for hunting and for driving enormous semis. A leading critic of the showboating, lazy, selfish style of play he sees in younger players, he has described scoring a basket to help Stockton set the all-time NBA assist record as his greatest thrill in sports.

Further Reading

Howerton, D. "The Greatest Power Forward of All Time?" *Sport*, March 1996, pp. 20–2.

Latimer, Clay. *Special Delivery: The Amazing Career of Karl Malone.* Lenora, Kansas: Addax Publishing, 1999.

Lewis, Michael C. *To the Brink: Stockton, Malone, and the Utah Jazz's Climb to the Edge of Glory.* New York: Simon & Schuster, 1998.

Malone, Moses Eugene
(1955–) *basketball center*

Moses Malone was a man of prodigious talent and an even more impressive work ethic. He was the first person to show that a high school basketball player could skip college and make an immediate impact as a pro.

He was born Moses Eugene Malone on March 25, 1955, in Chesterfield County, Virginia. His height is a genetic miracle, as he eventually grew to 6 feet 11 inches, despite having parents who were 5 foot 6 and 5 foot 2. He grew up in poverty in Petersburg, Virginia, raised by a single parent, Mary Malone.

Although a shy, socially awkward boy, Moses knew what he wanted in life. At age 14, he wrote a promise to become the best high school basketball player in America and placed it in the family Bible. Then he set about working to make it come true. In his first game as a freshman at Petersburg High School, Malone snared 30 rebounds. He went on to average 39 points, 26 rebounds, and 10 blocked shots over his high school career, as he led his team to two state titles. Few observers doubted that he was, indeed, the best prep player in the land.

On graduation in 1974, he signed a letter of intent to attend the University of Maryland but instead accepted an offer from the Utah Stars of the American Basketball Association (ABA). Immediately dispelling doubts about whether such a young player could hold his own against pros, he averaged 18.8 points and finished fourth in the league in rebounds with 14.6. The following season was continual chaos as first the Stars folded, then the ABA folded. Malone was bounced from Utah to Saint Louis to Portland to Buffalo before finally landing with the Houston Rockets.

Malone's relentless hustle and quick reflexes immediately established him as the best rebounder in the game and the best offensive rebounder of all time. As a National Basketball Association (NBA) rookie in 1976–77, he set a league record of 437 offensive boards, which he topped in 1978–79 with 587. That year he also led the league in total rebounds with an average of 17.6, finished fifth in scoring with 24.8 (largely on rebound put backs), and was voted league Most Valuable Player (MVP). During his career, he led the NBA in rebounds six times and finished in the top five every year from 1976–77 to 1985–86.

Malone also worked on other aspects of his game. After he had perfected a jump shot, his scoring average soared to 31.1 in 1981–82, second best in the league, and he claimed his second MVP Award. Malone's greatest value, however, was not as an individual but as a team player. Twice Malone led relatively weak teams to the NBA championship as a Houston Rocket. In 1982, he was traded to the Philadelphia 76ers, with whom he proved to be the missing piece to the puzzle that had frustrated the talented 76ers for years. With Malone performing the grunt work under the basket, the 76ers rolled to the best record in basketball in 1982–83. Malone then led the team to an NBA title, winning the championship Most Valuable Player Award for his 25.8 points and 18 rebounds per game.

Malone retired after the 1983–84 season. He took immense satisfaction in excelling at the blue-collar parts of the game. Many fans would agree with his statement, "I'm not the greatest player, but . . . I have always tried to be the greatest worker."

Further Reading
Cotton, A. "I Can Do So Many Things," *Sports Illustrated*, November 1, 1982, pp. 46–9.
Moritz, Charles, ed. *Current Biography, 1986*. New York: H. W. Wilson, 1986.

Mays, Willie
(Willie Howard Mays, Jr., "The Say Hey Kid")
(1931–) *baseball outfielder*

Had Willie Mays not lost two prime years of his baseball career to military service, it likely would

Many baseball experts consider Willie Mays (left) to have been the finest all-around player in the sport's history. Here he visits with another African-American Hall of Famer, Roy Campanella. *(Library of Congress, Prints & Photographs Division, NYTW&S Collection [LC-USZ62-112029])*

have been he and not his fellow Alabaman HANK AARON who broke Babe Ruth's career home run record. A more spectacular fielder and swifter base runner than Aaron, the flamboyant Mays is considered by some baseball experts to have been the finest all-around baseball player in major league history.

Willie Howard Mays, Jr., was born on May 6, 1931, in Westfield, Alabama, a working-class suburb of Birmingham. His parents, Willie, Sr., and Ann Mays, were only 18 at the time, and they separated when he was three. Willie lived with his father from that point, along with two older orphan girls Willie, Sr., had taken in who helped raise him.

Willie, Sr., worked as a porter before landing a job in Birmingham's steel mills. In his spare time, he enjoyed playing baseball with the Birmingham Black Barons. His son inherited his athletic talent, along with the gift of speed from his mother, who had been a high school track star. By the time he reached Fairfield Industrial High School, Willie, Jr., was a star quarterback and an excellent basketball player. In baseball, he showed exceptional talent as a pitcher, but his father refused to let him pitch for fear that he might hurt his arm. He showed such promise as a hitter and fielder that the Black Barons offered him a chance to play in the outfield alongside his father, even though he was only 16. Playing professional ball would make him ineligible to play sports at his high school, and Fairfield coaches put pressure on him to reject the opportunity. But the idea of getting paid to play baseball, even at the low wages of the Black Barons, struck Mays as "just about the nicest that anyone ever thought up—like getting paid for eating ice cream." In 1947, the year that JACKIE ROBINSON broke major league baseball's racial barrier, Mays became the youngest professional ball player in the country.

Although Robinson's breakthrough was good news for top black ballplayers, it spelled the end of Negro League baseball. In 1948, Mays played in what turned out to be the final Negro League

World Series. He remained in high school, preparing for a career in laundry, one of the limited employment opportunities for southern blacks, while he continued to play for a Black Barons team that struggled to survive. In June 1949 a Boston Braves scout on a tour of the area saw Mays play and was impressed. But a second scout called in for further evaluation saw nothing special in this young prospect. Thus, the Braves missed the chance to have Aaron and Mays playing together in the same outfield. A short while later, New York Giants scout Eddie Montague traveled to Birmingham to look at the Barons' power-hitting first baseman, Alonzo Perry. But it was Mays who caught his attention. Montague reported that the youngster was the best player he had ever seen. The Giants waited until he graduated from high school and then signed him to a contract on June 20, 1950.

Mays was assigned to the Giants' Class B club in Trenton, New Jersey, where he batted .353. That performance prompted them to skip him up to their top AAA team in Minneapolis. In 35 games with the Millers in 1951, Mays batted .477, showing the Giants he was more than ready for the big time. Mays had become so popular during his brief stay with the Millers that Giants owner, Horace Stoneham, took out newspaper ads apologizing for taking him to the majors.

Mays found the jump to New York intimidating at first, however. He managed only one hit in his first 25 at bats and was so embarrassed by his failure that he sobbed uncontrollably. But after encouraging words from his manager, Leo Durocher, Mays quickly righted himself. He finished the season with a .274 average and 20 home runs and won the National League's Rookie of the Year Award. He was a key factor in the Giants' miracle finish, in which they came back from 13 ½ games behind the Dodgers to defeat them for the pennant in a playoff game.

Although they lost the World Series to the New York Yankees, Mays captured the hearts of the New York fans. He could do everything on the field: run, catch, throw, and hit for both average and power, and he did it with flair and enthusiasm. New York broadcaster Red Smith remarked, "I don't think any ballplayer ever related to the fans as quickly as Willie." He became known as "The Say Hey Kid," after his manner of addressing teammates whose names he had not yet learned. A born entertainer, Mays found ways to stamp his own unique brand of play on the public mind. Before long, his basket catches in center field and the sight of his hat flying off as he dove for a ball or stole a base became his trademarks.

The military duty of the Korean War years, however, interrupted his burgeoning career. Thirty-four games into the 1952 season, Mays was called into the army. The Giants felt his absence greatly during his two-year hitch at Fort Eustis, Virginia, as the rival Dodgers captured the pennant both years. But Mays returned with a vengeance early in the 1954 season. Despite his late start, he led the National League in hitting with a .345 average, clouted 41 home runs, scored 119 runs, drove in 110, won the National League's Most Valuable Player (MVP) Award, and led the Giants back into the World Series.

It was there that he performed a defensive feat so spectacular that it became known in baseball lore simply as "The Catch." With the score tied 2–2 in the eighth inning of game one, and two runners on base, Cleveland's Vic Wertz slammed a pitch deep into the cavernous center field of the Polo Grounds. Sprinting all out with his back to the plate, Mays caught up with the ball 450 feet away from home, then immediately spun and fired the ball to the infield to prevent the runners from advancing. Cleveland never recovered from the shock. The underdog Giants won the game in 10 innings and went on to a stunning four-game sweep.

The following year, Mays showed that his 1954 campaign had been no fluke. He batted .319 and captured his first home run crown with 51, drove in 127 runs, and led the league in outfield

assists with 23, yet was beaten out for MVP by the Dodgers' ROY CAMPANELLA.

At one time or other, Mays proved himself to be the best in nearly every phase of hitting, fielding, and baserunning. In 1956, he led the National League with 40 stolen bases, the first of four consecutive base-stealing titles. In 1957, he led the major leagues with 20 triples, while batting .333 and belting 35 home runs. When the Giants moved to San Francisco in 1957, Mays had no problem adjusting, as he batted .347, just shy of Stan Musial's league-leading .351. On April 30, 1961, he tied a major league record by belting four home runs in a single game. At the same time he kept alive his incredible streak of winning the Gold Glove 12 straight times as the National League's best defensive center fielder.

Nonetheless, the Giants fell into a decline after their World Series win of 1954. It was not until 1962, when Mays blasted a league-leading 49 home runs, that the Giants returned to baseball's Fall Classic. This World Series ended in heartache as San Francisco lost to the New York Yankees by a score of 1–0 in the seventh and final game of the series. Mays continued to slam home runs over the next several seasons, winning the National League crown in 1964 with 47 and following that up with a league-leading and career-best 52 in 1965. That season, at the age of 34, he won his second Most Valuable Player Award.

Mays continued to roam center field for the Giants through the 1971 season and then finished his career back where it started in New York with the Mets in 1972–73. During his long career, he hit 660 home runs, third only to Aaron and Ruth, and collected 3,283 hits. Had Mays enjoyed only modestly successful seasons during the two years in which he was in military service, he would rank as the major league leader in both home runs and RBIs. But perhaps the greatest sign of the respect with which Mays was held was the fact that he was named to the National League All-Star team 22 consecutive times.

Further Reading

Einstein, Charles. *Willie's Time: A Memoir.* New York: Lippincott, 1979.

Honig, Donald. *Mays, Mantle, and Snider: A Celebration.* New York: Macmillan, 1987.

Mays, Willie, with Lou Sahadi. *Say Hey: The Autobiography of Willie Mays.* New York: Simon & Schuster, 1988.

Smith, Ron, and Willie Mays. *The Sporting News Selects Baseball's Greatest Players.* St. Louis, Mo.: The Sporting News, 1999.

McCovey, Willie Lee
("Stretch" McCovey)
(1938–) *baseball first baseman*

Although he spent much of his career in the shadow of his teammates WILLIE MAYS and Orlando Cepeda, Willie McCovey so earned the respect of San Francisco Giant fans for his hard hits to right field that the bay beyond the right field fence at the Giants' stadium is known as McCovey's Cove.

Willie Lee McCovey was born on January 10, 1938, in Mobile, Alabama, the seventh of 10 children of a railroad worker, Frank McCovey, and his wife, Esther. McCovey loved to play first base in baseball, and as a high school player he attracted the attention of Giants scouts. Even though he quit school at 16 and moved to Los Angeles to live with his older brother, the scouts found him. When he was 17, they signed him and gave him a bus ticket to report to their Florida training camp.

McCovey rose rapidly through the minor league ranks but had the misfortune of playing the same position as the Giants' Orlando Cepeda, the National League's Rookie of the Year in 1958. Unsure of where to play McCovey, the Giants did not call him up to the parent club until July 1959, and then they platooned him in left field. McCovey blasted four hits in his first game and finished the year with a sparkling .354 average

and 20 home runs. Although he played in just 52 games that season, he was voted the league's Rookie of the Year. For the next two seasons, though, McCovey struggled as a part-time player at the plate as well as in the unfamiliar outfield position.

He became part of baseball legend when, in the seventh game of the 1962 World Series, he hit a screaming line drive on the game's last pitch that would have won the series had it not been snared by New York Yankee second baseman Bobby Richardson. The following season, he finally earned a full-time starting position in left field and responded with a league-leading 44 home runs. "Stretch" McCovey, as he was dubbed because of his lanky six-foot, four-inch frame, finally took over at first base from Cepeda in 1965 and teamed up with Mays to be baseball's top long-ball duo in the middle 1960s. In 1968, McCovey took over from the aging Mays as the Giants' main weapon. He won his second home run title that year with 36 and also led the league with 105 runs-batted-in (RBIs). The following season he reached his peak as he batted .320 and again led the league in home runs (45) and RBIs (126). This earned him his first National League Most Valuable Player (MVP) Award.

When McCovey was in a groove, no pitcher could get him out. He clouted two home runs facing the American League's top pitchers in the 1969 All-Star game and twice belted two home runs in a single inning. By 1970 he was so feared by pitchers that he was walked intentionally 45 times, a league record.

After his production declined in the 1970s, the Giants angered fans by trading McCovey to San Diego in 1974. They reacquired him, however, in midseason in 1976, and he thrilled his old fans by batting .280 and hitting 28 home runs to win honors as the league's Comeback Player of the Year. McCovey retired in 1980 with 521 career home runs, the most ever by a National League left-handed batter, and he was elected to the Hall of Fame in 1986.

Further Reading

Moritz, Charles, ed. *Current Biography 1970.* New York: H. W. Wilson, 1970.

Mulvoy, M. "Pursuit of Willie and Clyde," *Sports Illustrated,* September 15, 1969, pp. 22–25.

Miller, Cheryl Deanne

(1964–) *basketball forward/center*

Cheryl Miller was the first female basketball player to win widespread recognition for playing a powerful inside game. She had the combination of height, strength, athleticism, desire, and flamboyance that made her the top player of her era and the leading spokesperson for the women's game as it progressed from a novelty to a respected sport in the 1980s.

Miller was born on January 3, 1964, in Riverside, California, the only daughter among Saul and Carrie Miller's five children. Both parents had been fine basketball players but had played at a time when few opportunities were available for African-American athletes. Cheryl began playing with her brothers at age four, with some coaching from her father.

When Cheryl was 13, she tried out for a basketball team in a boys' league. The coach said that if she could beat his son in a one-on-one contest, she could be on the team. She trounced the youngster, 11–1, but the coach reneged on his promise and told her to get lost. Miller went home in tears, wanting to quit the sport, but Saul told her, "I didn't raise any quitters. Tomorrow you will try out for the girls' team and become the best who ever played."

Miller did just that, improving her play with countless hours of competition against her younger brother, Reggie, who went on to become one of the National Basketball Association's (NBA's) deadliest outside shooters. Because of battles with her brothers, Miller developed a rugged style of play that had seldom been seen in girls' basketball. As she grew to a towering six feet, three inches, she focused even more on playing in the low post and began to admire the play of Lusia Harris of Delta State, one of the first talented centers to play on the college level.

Playing at Riverside Poly High School beginning in 1979, Miller utterly overwhelmed her opponents, even as a freshman. She became the only person ever named a *Parade* magazine All-American four years in a row. Averaging almost 33 points per game, she set state records of 1,156 points in a year and 3,405 points for a career. Miller drew national attention when she scored 100 points in a single game, although the achievement against an obviously overmatched team drew as much criticism as praise for its questionable sportsmanship. A fierce defender and rebounder as well as scorer, she led her team to a four-year mark of 132–4.

Miller's favorite NBA player was high-flying dunkmaster JULIUS ERVING. She did her best to emulate his graceful artistry and is credited by many as the first woman to dunk in a competitive basketball game.

Although recruited by more than 100 colleges, Miller chose to stay close to home at the University of Southern California (USC). Continuing her phenomenal success, she led the team in scoring, blocked shots, steals, and rebounds. The Trojans advanced to the finals of the National Collegiate Athletic Association (NCAA) tournament. There, in the title game against the defending champion Louisiana Tech, Miller scored 27 points and grabbed nine rebounds to lead the team to victory and capture the tournament Most Valuable Player (MVP) Award.

In 1983–84, Miller paced Southern Cal to a 24–4 record, another conference championship, and their second straight national title. She then took center stage as the most famous player on a talented U.S. Olympic women's basketball team. Miller led the team in scoring during the Olympics with 99 points, including a game-high 16 points to go with 11 rebounds in the team's gold medal victory over Korea. For many U.S.

fans, that Olympics was their first exposure to the talent of female hoopsters.

After such an auspicious beginning, Miller's career had nowhere to go but down. Although she enjoyed her finest individual season in 1984–85, averaging 26.8 points and 15.8 rebounds, she was disappointed that the team failed to defend its national title. The disappointment continued the following year as she averaged 25.4 points but experienced a heartbreaking defeat in the NCAA finals.

At this time, there were no professional opportunities for women basketball players in the United States. Despite being a three-time college Player of the Year, Miller had to settle for staying on at USC as an assistant coach. As the 1988 Olympic year drew near, she prepared for another Olympic run. This time, however, a severe knee injury knocked her out of the trials and effectively ended her playing career. She tried to come back again in 1992 for the Olympics but suffered a similar injury.

Miller's competitive nature and demonstrative style of celebrating success attracted a great deal of criticism by opponents and observers. Never did she face more controversy than when the USC coach, Marianne Stanley, was fired after accusing USC of sexual discrimination. Instead of backing her mentor, Miller agreed to take Stanley's job. Labeled a traitor by many, Miller nonetheless did an admirable job, leading her team to a 26–4 record.

A communications major with major star appeal, Miller left USC after a brief run as coach to work as a network basketball analyst. She also helped launch the Women's National Basketball Association (WNBA) by serving as coach of the Phoenix Mercury. There is no doubt that had such a league been in existence when she graduated from college, Cheryl Miller would have been its star and main attraction. She is widely credited with helping women's basketball establish the credibility it needed to get a successful league into operation.

Further Reading

Jackson, R. "She May Well Be the Best Ever," *Sports Illustrated*, November 11, 1982, pp. 90–91.

Mabunda, Mpho, ed. *Contemporary Black Biography*. Vol. 10. Detroit, Mich.: Gale Research, 1996.

McCormick, J. "A Heroine Who Plays Ball Like a Man," *Newsweek*, August 13, 1984, p. 27.

Morgan, Joe Leonard
(1943–) *baseball second baseman*

Although his teammates Johnny Bench and Pete Rose garnered more press, it was actually the fireplug second baseman Joe Morgan who made the Cincinnati Reds' "Big Red Machine" run smoothly in the mid-1970s.

Joe Leonard Morgan was born on September 19, 1943, to Leonard and Ollie Morgan in Bonham, Texas, north of Dallas, and moved to Oakland when he was five. His father was a baseball buff who took Joe to see the minor league Oakland Oaks play whenever they were at home and encouraged him to play the game. Joe played in organized leagues from a very young age through his years at Castlemont High School.

After a year of junior college, Morgan signed with the Houston Astros in November 1962. Morgan advanced quickly through the Astros' minor league system; he joined the big league club in 1963 and became a starter by 1965. He played solid but unspectacular ball for Houston when he was healthy; his most noteworthy accomplishment was 49 stolen bases in 1969. Morgan made the All-Star team in 1970 and showed exceptional reliability in the field, but his best batting average at Houston was .285 in 1966, and he showed little power.

On being traded to the Cincinnati Reds in 1972, however, Morgan blossomed into one of the top players in the league. A keen student of the game, Morgan improved himself in all phases of play. In 1972 he batted .292, led the National League in walks with 115, scored 122 runs, and topped the league's second basemen in fielding percentage. The following year, Morgan discovered surprising power in his five-foot, seven-inch, 160-pound frame and became the first major leaguer to hit more than 25 home runs while stealing 60 bases.

Morgan became the key cog in the greatest offensive team the National League had witnessed in years. In 1975, he led the league in both batting average (.327) and walks (132), which gave him a staggering on-base percentage of .471. Added to his 17 home runs, his speed on the base paths, and his third consecutive Gold Glove for his defensive work, Morgan easily won the National League's Most Valuable Player (MVP) Award. He capped his season by slapping the winning hit in the deciding game of the World Series with two outs in the ninth inning.

Morgan and the Reds did even better the following season. He batted .320, slammed 27 home runs, scored 113 runs, drove in 111, stole 60 bases, and won yet another Gold Glove Award, all of which added up to a second consecutive MVP honor. With Morgan leading the way, the Reds demolished all opposition in the postseason without a loss.

In 1977, Morgan set a record for second basemen by playing 91 games without making an error. His offensive production gradually declined over the years as he moved about from team to team, finally finishing his 22-year career in Oakland in 1984. Morgan's blend of speed and power is best shown by his career mark of 689 stolen bases and his 268 home runs, which surpassed Rogers Hornsby's mark as the most ever hit by a second baseman. Morgan, who was voted to the Hall of Fame in 1990, has since put his knowledge of baseball to use in the television booth, where he is regarded as one of television's most insightful analysts.

Further Reading

Mabunda, Mpho, ed. *Contemporary Black Biography.* Vol. 9. Detroit, Mich.: Gale Research, 1995.

Morgan, Joe, with Rich Lally. *Long Balls, No Strikes: What Baseball Must Do to Keep the Good Times Rolling.* New York: Crown, 1999.

Mulvoy, M. "Little Big Man," *Sports Illustrated,* April 12, 1976, pp. 52–54.

Moses, Edwin Corley
(1955–) *track-and-field hurdler*

Edwin Moses was the epitome of the self-made athlete. Working out on his own while studying for a physics degree at a college that did not even have a track, Moses made himself into the finest 400-meter hurdler in history.

He was born Edwin Corley Moses on August 31, 1955, in Dayton, Ohio, to Irving and Gladys Moses. The family was far more interested in academics and fine arts than in sports. Edwin, who was small for his age, had no desire to compete against larger boys and never gave a thought to an athletic career. In high school he began running hurdles in track just to have fun and to stay in shape while he concentrated on his studies. As Moses remembers of his high school track career, "I was competitive, but nowhere near national caliber."

Moses's classroom efforts paid off, earning him an academic scholarship to Morehouse College, a school primarily for African Americans, in Atlanta, Georgia. He debated skipping track altogether in college, but, as in high school, he found the training to be a welcome and healthy break from his demanding course load as a physics major. The sport was so low-key at Morehouse that the college had no weight room and did not even have its own track. Moses had to drive 30 miles a day to get to a track on which he could train.

As a freshman, he ran the high hurdles and intermediate sprints. A late bloomer physically, Moses grew several inches in college, to six feet, two inches, and found that his exceptionally long legs could then easily glide over the hurdles in the

Self-made hurdler Edwin Moses compiled a winning streak that lasted 11 years. *(Bob Martin/Getty Images)*

400-meter race. During his sophomore year in 1975, he planned to add the 400-meter hurdles to his repertoire at the conference meet but scratched because the event followed the open 400 meters too closely. He settled for winning conference championships in the 400 meters and the 110-meter hurdles. Moses competed in no official meets at the longer hurdle distance until the spring of 1976, when he entered the Florida Relays and finished second in a time of 50.1.

Although it was an amazing performance for a beginner, it was hardly world class. Looking forward to the Olympic trials later that spring, a track expert compiled a list of 18 hurdlers with a chance to make the U.S. team; Moses was not on it. But over the next few weeks, Moses lowered his time to 48.86, which qualified him for the tri-

als. Moses then astounded the track-and-field world by not only winning the 400-meter hurdles at the trials but setting a U.S. record of 48.3.

At the 1976 Olympics, an anticipated match-up between Moses and world-record-holder John Akii-Bua of Uganda failed to materialize when the African nations boycotted the meet. In the final, Moses overcame his lack of international race experience as well as a slow start that left him off balance at the first hurdle. Showing remarkable stamina, he maintained a rhythm of 13 long strides between hurdles (14 or 15 is average), something no athlete in the event had ever done before. Moses totally outclassed the remainder of the competition, winning by more than a full second in a world record time of 47.64. Typically, although elated over his triumph, Moses regretted that his more intense training for the Olympics had interfered with his studies, causing his grade point average to slip below 3.6.

In the summer of 1977, Moses competed on the European circuit. While running his third competition in five days, he broke his stride on the ninth hurdle of a race and lost to Harold Schmid of Germany. The race was significant because it would be the last 400-meter hurdle race Moses lost in a decade of racing. Returning from Europe, he took a break from competition to complete his physics degree. But when he resumed training, he honed his craft to a level of perfection seldom seen. In 1979 Moses posted 21 consecutive finals victories and was never challenged in any of them. The following year he was a virtual lock to win another gold medal, only to be disappointed when the United States boycotted the Moscow Games in response to Russian policy in Afghanistan. He gained a measure of satisfaction on July 3, 1980, however, when he easily won a rematch with Germany's Schmid in a blistering world-record time of 47.13.

In 1981, Moses so outshone the competition that the top 12 times in the 400-meter hurdles that year were his. Two years later, still riding his undefeated streak, he posted a lifetime best of

47.02. In 1984, Moses returned to the Olympics after an eight-year hiatus and breezed to his second gold medal in a relaxed time of 47.75. It was not until June 4, 1987, that the old veteran finally lost a 400-meter hurdle event, by .12 seconds, to Iowa State University runner Danny Harris, who was 11 years younger than him. Moses continued training and placed a respectable third in the 1988 Olympics. Two years later, he decided to dabble in a sport completely foreign to him. Running as the brakeman on a U.S. four-man bobsled team, he won his first international race in Germany in 1990, but he gave up the sport before the 1992 Winter Olympic competition.

For Moses, track and field was always a pleasant diversion to his real career pursuits. Not only did he earn his degree from Morehouse, but he became a licensed pilot and an aerospace engineer. Throughout his running career, Moses was widely admired for his consistency, his tremendous self-discipline, and his gracious, soft-spoken nature.

Further Reading

Deford, Frank. "Sportsman and Sportswoman of the Year," *Sports Illustrated*, December 24, 1984, pp. 32–34.

Kirkpatrick, Curry. "The Man Who Never Loses," *Sports Illustrated*, July 30, 1984, pp. 52–58.

Nelson, Cordner. *Track's Greatest Champions*. Los Altos, Calif.: Tafnews Press, 1986.

Will-Weber, M. "Edwin Moses," *Runners World*, December 2000, pp. 44–45.

Motley, Marion
(1920–1999) *football running back*

Marion Motley was among the first African-American men to play professional football, after a 13-year informal ban that was justified on the grounds that it protected them from injury at the hands of racist opponents. He played both offense and defense, and the *Sports Illustrated* writer Paul Zimmerman has rated him the best football player of all time.

Motley was born on June 5, 1920, in Lessburg, Georgia, to Shakeful and Blanch Motley. When he was three, the family moved to pro football's birthplace, Canton, Ohio, where his father got a job as a foundry worker. Marion played both basketball and football at McKinley High School in Canton; the football team lost only three games in the three years that he played.

After graduation in 1939, he enrolled at South Carolina State; after one year he transferred to the University of Nevada at Reno. There he was a standout running back and linebacker for a mediocre team until he suffered a knee injury in 1943. Convinced that he would never be able to play again, Motley returned home, where he found work in the steel mills.

He joined the U.S. Navy the following year and, after discovering that his knee had healed, joined the Great Lakes Naval Training Station football team coached by Paul Brown. Motley became a standout player in a powerful football machine that destroyed heralded Notre Dame 39–7.

When Coach Brown began organizing a team in Cleveland as part of the new All-American Football Conference (AAFC) in 1946, he decided to discard the gentleman's agreement excluding African Americans that had been in force since 1933. But after signing the standout lineman Bill Willis in August, he faced the dilemma of who would room with the black man. His answer was to sign another African American, and he remembered Motley from the Great Lakes team. The 26-year-old Motley was invited to try out, and he made the team.

Motley, though used sparingly as a running back his rookie season, gained 601 yards in only 73 carries for a whooping 8.3 average. In addition, he was a tremendous blocker who provided pass protection for the quarterback, Otto Graham, and helped anchor the Browns' defense from his linebacker spot. At six feet, one inch, 238 pounds,

Marion Motley's determined power running opened the door for a generation of African-American running backs. *(Henry Barr/Diamond Images)*

he was larger than most linemen, and few opponents could tackle him one-on-one. Yet he had the explosive quickness to burst through small holes in the line, particularly on delayed running plays such as draws and traps.

With Motley providing strong support on both sides of the ball, the Cleveland Browns dominated the AAFC. They lost only four games in the league's four years of existence and won the championship every season. Motley became the league's all-time leading rusher with 889 yards for a 6.9-yard average in 1947, 964 yards for a 6.1 average in 1948, and 570 yards for a 5.0 average in 1949. Ironically, the Browns' complete superiority helped bring about the demise of the league, as it eliminated the competitive aspect of the game. The AAFC disbanded in 1950, and Cleveland and two other teams were enfolded into the established National Football League (NFL).

Many experts expected the Browns would flounder now that they were facing "real" competition. For Motley and Willis, however, the most difficult challenge was dealing with cheap shots from racist opponents, to which officials turned a blind eye. "Players stepped on my hands so much that I still have scars on the backs of them," reported Motley. He and Willis fought back with bone-crunching but legal blocks and tackles on the offenders.

Highlight films of that era show Motley looking distinctly out of place with his size, skin color, and lineman's number 76. Shrugging off tacklers like flies, leaving a trail of prone defenders in his wake, Motley led the NFL in rushing that season with 810 yards in only 140 carries for an average of better than 5.8 yards per rush. At the same time, he continued his devastating blocking and linebacker play. Cleveland went on to embarrass the haughty NFL by winning the league championship game, 30–28, over the Los Angeles Rams.

Such success earned Motley immediate respect. His peers voted him to the Pro Bowl game at the end of the year, and officials began enforcing unsportsmanlike conduct penalties against flagrant cheap shots from the opposition.

As the Browns began to rely more on the throwing arm of Otto Graham and as Motley's battered knees began to fail, his rushing production dwindled. In his final years, he added pass receiving to his many talents. Motley caught 85 passes in his career for 1,107 yards and seven touchdowns in his career, to go with his 4,712 yards and 31 touchdowns rushing. His all-around play helped the Browns remain title contenders every season. Few players can match Motley's achievement of playing in eight consecutive league championship games.

Injuries finally forced Motley to the sidelines in 1954. He attempted a comeback with the Pittsburgh Steelers the following season but, unable to overcome a rash of injuries, retired. Motley hoped to land a coaching or scouting job in football but was denied. "They were ready to let me run with the ball," he recalled. "But they weren't ready to pay me—or let me think."

Many credit Motley and Bill Willis with proving to Brooklyn Dodgers executive Branch Rickey that African Americans could succeed in sports, thus paving the way for the integration of baseball in 1947, the year after Motley's rookie pro season. "What we did helped get JACKIE ROBINSON into the major leagues," Motley insisted. Motley was inducted into pro football's Hall of Fame in 1968, the first African American so honored. He died on June 27, 1999, of cancer.

Further Reading

Great Athletes of the Twentieth Century. Vol. 13. Pasadena, Calif.: Salem Press, 1994.

Oblender, David G., ed. *Contemporary Black Biography.* Vol. 26. Detroit, Mich.: Gale Research, 2001.

Young, A. S. *Negro Firsts in Sports.* Chicago: Johnson Publishing Company, 1963.

Murphy, Isaac
(Isaac Burns)
(1861–1896) *jockey*

Isaac Murphy was the first nationally known African-American sports figure. Racing at a time before black jockeys were barred from prestigious horse races, he made headlines across the country by winning consistently with style and class.

He was born Isaac Burns on a farm in Fayette County, Kentucky, on January 1, 1861. During the Civil War, his father enlisted in the Union Army and was killed while in the service. This forced his mother to move in with her father, Green Murphy, in Lexington, where she supported her two young children by doing laundry. Green Murphy worked as a horse groom and trainer, a common profession for black men during the post–Civil War era. One of his customers, Richard Owens, raced horses. Through his connection with Green Murphy, he hired young Isaac to break yearlings under the tutelage of the veteran trainer Eli Jordan. Isaac began riding the mounts in races and won his first race at age 14. As he became successful, he began racing under the name Isaac Murphy in honor of his grandfather.

At that time, black jockeys were common in the sport. In the 1875 Kentucky Derby, for example, 14 of the 15 horses were ridden by black riders. But they were so little regarded by the public that they were not even named in race programs. Murphy began to change that after he started riding for J. W. Reynolds in 1879. Murphy started modestly by placing second in the Kentucky Derby that year but then raised eyebrows by winning four races in one day in Detroit on July 4, 1879. He then went on to Saratoga, New York, where his dramatic, come-from-behind victories drew admiration from New York race critics. They interviewed him for a magazine article, which made him one of the first athletes of any race ever profiled in the U.S. press. Murphy's honesty and charm captivated his audience. When asked in the interview about his racing strategy, he responded, "I had no instructions, except that I was to win the race."

Murphy reached his peak as a jockey during the 1880s. In 1882, he won 49 of 51 races he rode at Saratoga. The following season, he posted an overall record of 51 victories in 133 starts. In 1884, Murphy captured his first Kentucky Derby title riding a horse, Buchanan, that was so volatile and high-spirited that Murphy refused to ride him until he was threatened with suspension. By 1887 Murphy was probably America's best-known athlete. He was certainly the highest paid, earning an estimated $20,000 a year, a fortune in those days.

Murphy won accolades for his success, his tremendous work ethic, and his unflinching honesty. In a sport in which bribery was rampant, Murphy not only refused bribes but refused to ride in races when he suspected dishonesty. As he told an aspiring young jockey, "A jockey that will sell out to one man will sell out to another. Just be honest and you'll have no trouble and plenty of money." That integrity was crucial not only to his personal success but also to helping establish public confidence in the sport.

Murphy's greatest strength as a rider was his uncanny sense of pace. He could tell, to the split second, how fast his horse was running and so was able to distribute the horse's energy evenly over the course of the race. Such expert pacing left his horses with enough strength for a furious finishing kick; he won so many races in the home stretch that rivals accused him of laying back so he could show off with a dramatic victory.

Murphy's main problem was that, as he grew older, he found it increasingly difficult to keep off the weight. Fearful of being too heavy for his mounts, he often starved himself to the point of endangering his health. "I have seen him get off his horse in such a weak condition after the finish of a race that the attendants would have to support him from falling," said one contemporary, "and all this weakness caused by reducing."

Murphy maintained his dominance and celebrity status into the next decade. In 1890 he eked out a hair's breadth win over his main rival, Snapper Garrison, in Sheepshead Bay, New York. The race, the first to be decided by the rapidly improving art of photography, left thousands of spectators breathless. That same year he won the Kentucky Derby for a second time, riding a mount named Riley. In 1891, he became the first jockey to post back-to-back Kentucky Derby wins, this time on Kingman.

At about the same time, however, his radical fasting began to take its toll. After finishing dead last in one race, he had such trouble dismounting that rumors spread about a supposed drinking problem. "When I won it was all right," noted Murphy, "but when I lost, and when not on the best horse, they would say, 'There, that n _ _ _ _ _ is drunk again.'" At the same time, horse racing had grown so popular and jockeys had begun earning so much money that whites became interested in riding. Before long, black jockeys were shuffled into more menial tasks and the roster of jockeys, which had once been overwhelmingly black, became a fraternity of whites only. With the rumors of Murphy's supposed addiction floating around, Murphy was an early candidate for the phase-out. He raced sparingly and rarely won after his 1891 Kentucky Derby win.

Murphy died of pneumonia less than five years after that victory, on February 13, 1896. Known as the best of the black jockeys of the 19th century, he posted a career record of 530 victories in 1,538 races for a sparkling 34 percent winning rate. More important, he promoted the sport of horse racing both in his carriage as one of its first stars and his pride and professionalism. "I was as proud of my calling as I am of my record," he once said. That attitude helped establish a foundation for horse racing that has lasted well over a century.

Further Reading

Hotaling, Edmund. *The Great Black Jockeys*. Rocklin, Calif.: Forum, 1999.

Wiggins, David K. *Glory Bound: Black Athletes in White America*. Syracuse, N.Y.: Syracuse University Press, 1997.

N

Newcombe, Donald
(Newk)
(1926–   ) *baseball pitcher*

Don Newcombe was the first African-American pitcher to star in major league baseball. Along with JACKIE ROBINSON and ROY CAMPANELLA, he was one of the Big Three who integrated the Dodgers and made them a contender for a decade.

Donald Newcombe was born on June 14, 1926, in Madison, New Jersey, one of five children of Roland and Sadie Newcombe. He grew up in Elizabeth, New Jersey, where, at the age of nine, he began taking batting practice with a semipro team managed by an older brother. Because his school had no baseball team, Newcombe's baseball was restricted to pitching in informal leagues in which, according to his report, "I was lightning fast but I seldom knew where my next pitch was going."

Newcombe was preparing for a career as a truck driver when the Negro League New Jersey Eagles offered him a contract in the spring of 1944. There he was spotted by Brooklyn Dodgers scouts who signed him before the 1946 season under the pretense of forming a new Negro League team. In reality, they were preparing to scoop up the cream of the Negro Leagues in preparation for integration.

After a successful stint in Brooklyn's minor league organization, Newcombe arrived in the majors in May 1949. He hurled a shutout in his first start and at one point tossed 32 consecutive shutout innings. Newcombe made the All-Star team, posted a 19–11 record and five shutouts, and was the National League's Rookie of the Year. On September 6, he showed incredible stamina by starting and winning both games of a doubleheader against Philadelphia. Newcombe firmly established himself as Brooklyn's ace pitcher the following year by improving to 20–9.

At the prime of his career, Newcombe lost two years of play when he was drafted into the army in 1952. When he returned in 1955, he showed plenty of rust and managed only a 9–8 mark with a mediocre 4.56 earned run average (ERA). But he found his groove in 1956. Newcombe started the year by winning 14 of his first 15 decisions and finished the season at 20–5. He also established a claim as one of the best hitting pitchers of all time by batting .359 that season with seven home runs, a record for National League pitchers.

In 1956, Newcombe and his hopping fastball gathered momentum as the season progressed. He won 18 of his final 20 decisions to finish the year at 27 wins and seven losses, including five shutouts, boasting a sparkling 3.06 ERA in the process. Not only was Newcombe voted the first winner of the Cy Young Award as baseball's top pitcher, but he became one of the rare pitchers to win a league Most Valuable Player (MVP) Award.

Sadly, Newcombe began struggling with alcohol addiction at that time, and his career plummeted. He managed only an 11–12 mark in 1957 and was ineffective until he finished his career with Cleveland in 1960. Since that time, he has overcome his alcoholism and has been in demand as one of baseball's top motivational speakers.

Further Reading

Golenback, Peter. *Bums: An Oral History of the Brooklyn Dodgers.* New York: McGraw-Hill, 2000.

Moritz, Charles, ed. *Current Biography, 1957.* New York: H. W. Wilson, 1957.

Olajuwon, Hakeem Abdul
(1963–) *basketball center*

Within three years of first picking up a basketball, Hakeem Olajuwon was on his way to leading U.S. colleges in blocked shots. The cat-quick seven-footer developed into a brilliant all-around center who led the Houston Rockets to two consecutive National Basketball Association (NBA) championships in the early 1990s.

Hakeem Abdul Olajuwon was born on January 21, 1963, in Lagos, Nigeria. His parents, Salaam and Abike, owned a cement business that provided a comfortable middle-class life for their six children. As a child, Hakeem enjoyed playing goalie in soccer. But when he grew to six feet, nine inches, at the age of 16, a U.S. coach, who had been hired to promote basketball in Nigeria, introduced him to the game. Although painfully awkward at first, Olajuwon possessed a natural coordination that helped him to improve rapidly. He began playing the sport, as well as team handball, at Lagos State and in summer adult amateur leagues.

U.S. college scouts who saw him lead the Lagos junior team to a bronze medal at the 1980 All-African Games arranged for him to visit U.S. colleges that year. Overwhelmed by the winter weather on arriving in New York, he sought a warmer location and settled on Houston University. After red-shirting a year to gain strength and

experience, Olajuwon began his college career in 1981–82. He spent much of his freshman season in foul trouble, but in 1982–83 he developed into an intimidating defensive force on Houston's colorful "Phi Slamma Jama" squad. He scored 21 points and pulled down 22 rebounds in the National Collegiate Athletic Association (NCAA) semifinals and blocked 11 shots in a losing effort in the finals to be named the tournament Most Valuable Player (MVP). With Olajuwon emerging as an offensive threat, Houston again reached the finals the following year before losing to PATRICK ALOYSIUS EWING's Georgetown team.

When Olajuwon entered the 1984 National Basketball Association (NBA) draft, Houston made him the draft's top pick, ahead of MICHAEL JORDAN. He joined Houston's seven-foot, four-inch, Ralph Sampson as basketball's tallest frontcourt tandem. By this time, he had learned to use his soccer footwork to his advantage in gaining position near the basket. He averaged 20.6 points per game and finished fourth in the league in rebounds and second in blocked shots his rookie season. The following year, he led the Rockets to the NBA finals against the Boston Celtics, in which they lost in six games.

In 1989–90 Olajuwon averaged 24.3 points and led the NBA in both blocks and rebounds. He boosted his scoring average to 26.1 in

1992–93. The following season, he scored 27.3 points per game, while remaining dominant on the defensive end, and led Houston to the championship series. In that series, with his team on the verge of elimination in game six, he blocked a last-second shot by the New York Knicks to preserve victory. He followed up on this by scoring 25 points and grabbing 10 rebounds to help Houston win the deciding seventh game. That season, Olajuwon became the first player in history to win the NBA's MVP, Defensive Player of the Year, and finals MVP Awards in the same season.

Olajuwon remained at the top of his game in 1994–95. First, he soundly outplayed DAVID MAURICE ROBINSON, the league's MVP, in their play-off series, scoring 42 and 39 points in the final two games. Then, he scored the crucial tip-in that gave Houston an overtime win over SHAQUILLE RASHAUN O'NEAL and the Orlando Magic in game one of their series, setting the stage for Houston's four-game sweep of the championship. He continued to play at a high level for Houston until he was traded to Toronto in 2001.

Further Reading

McCallum, Jack. "Double Trouble, Houston Style," *Sports Illustrated*, November 5, 1984, pp. 18–21.

Montville, Leigh. "The Stuff of Dreams," *Sports Illustrated*, June 12, 1995, pp. 28–32.

Olajuwon, Hakeem, with Peter Knobler. *Hakeem Olajuwon: Living the Dream*. Boston: Little, Brown, 1996.

O'Neal, Shaquille Rashaun
(Shaq)
(1972–) *basketball center*

Shaquille Rashaun is Arabic for "little warrior." Whereas the *warrior* part of the name fits him perfectly, *little* is a complete misnomer. For sheer size combined with footwork and offensive moves, there has never been a basketball player like Shaquille O'Neal. Once regarded as a one-dimensional brute who lacked the mental toughness to

win championships, O'Neal built himself into an unstoppable force that has powered his team to three consecutive titles.

O'Neal was born on March 6, 1972, to Lucille O'Neal in Newark, New Jersey. His natural father, Joe Toney, was never part of his life. When Shaquille was two, his mother, a clerk at city hall, married Philip Harrison. Harrison, a stern disciplinarian who was determined to make his large stepson tough, joined the army, and subsequently the family frequently moved to wherever he was stationed. In fifth grade, they moved to Fort Stewart, Georgia, and the following year to Germany.

Having trouble fitting in overseas, O'Neal spent most of his free time playing basketball with a German friend. It took him a while to learn to coordinate his rapidly growing size, however. Already a tall 12-year-old at five feet, 10 inches, he sprouted nine inches in the next four years. Although he was six feet, nine inches as a high school sophomore, he could not dunk and was cut from the team. Self-conscious about his size and wishing to fit in, O'Neal began acting out. This led to violent confrontations with his stepfather, who was determined to keep the youngster in line.

The family moved back to San Antonio, Texas, in February 1987, and O'Neal gradually began to develop hard court skills. He became a starter at Cole High School in San Antonio, but as his junior year was ending the seven-footer had attracted interest from only a few colleges. In a high school All-Star game that summer, though, O'Neal completely overpowered his opponents, and suddenly mobs of recruiters were after him. O'Neal continued to improve as a senior, averaging nearly 30 points and more than 21 rebounds per game as he led his team to a 36–0 record and a state title.

He chose to attend Louisiana State University (LSU) to play for Dale Brown, whom he had met while he was a struggling 13-year-old in Germany. During his freshman season he posted respectable numbers: 14 points and 12 rebounds per game. As he began to bulk up in the weight room, however, he became nearly unstoppable. In

The most massive presence in pro sports, Shaquille O'Neal powered the Los Angeles Lakers to NBA titles in 2000 and 2001. *(Barry Gossage/NBAE/Getty Images)*

his sophomore year he averaged 27.6 points and 14.7 rebounds, figures that he nearly matched during his junior year. Both seasons ended in disappointment, however, when LSU failed to advance in the National Collegiate Athletic Association (NCAA) tournament.

Realizing that the constant triple-teaming O'Neal attracted from opponents was hampering his development, Coach Brown encouraged him to turn pro after his junior year. The Orlando Magic selected him as the first pick of the 1992 draft. Now at an imposing height of seven feet, one inch and more than 300 pounds, O'Neal made an immediate impact in the pros, being named National Basketball Association (NBA) Player of the Week in his first week. He easily earned Rookie of the Year honors as he finished the season eighth in scoring (23.4 points), second in rebounding (13.7), and second in blocked shots (3.53).

O'Neal worked tirelessly to expand his offensive game from power dunks to an assortment of hook shots and short jumpers. He was so quick and developed such nifty footwork that when the NBA's bulkiest centers tried to push him out of position, he drove around them.

In 1995, O'Neal joined guard Penney Hardaway to lead the young Orlando Magic into the NBA finals. There, he played Houston star HAKEEM ABDUL OLAJUWON to a draw, but the rest of the veteran Rockets shot their team to a four-game sweep of the Magic. Expected to improve on their title challenge the following year, Orlando instead suffered another embarrassing playoff sweep in 1996, this time at the hands of MICHAEL JORDAN and the Chicago Bulls.

At the end of the season, O'Neal joined the U.S. gold-medal-winning Olympic team and signed a contract with the Los Angeles Lakers. O'Neal was named as one of the NBA's 50 Greatest Players that year after only four seasons in the league.

But even though he continued to rank among the league leaders in scoring and rebounding, the Lakers kept getting bounced out of the play-offs with surprisingly inept performances. Basketball insiders pointed to O'Neal's outside interests such as cutting rap records and acting in motion pictures as evidence that he was more interested in being a star than being a champion.

The accusations hurt O'Neal, who continued to work tirelessly on his game, including his most glaring weakness—free-throw shooting. In 1999, the Lakers hired coach Phil Jackson to help in their title quest. Although O'Neal experienced some difficulties adjusting to both Jackson and young star guard KOBE BRYANT and missed several games as a result of injuries, he established himself as the NBA's dominant player. Enjoying his finest season, he led the league in scoring with 29.7 points, including a high of 61 in a game against the Los Angeles Clippers. He not only won the NBA Most Valuable Player Award but was the Most Valuable Player (MVP) of the All-Star Game as well.

However, in the Western Conference finals, it appeared the season would end in the usual disappointment for O'Neal when the Lakers trailed a talented Portland team by 15 points in the fourth quarter of their deciding game. Miraculously, Los Angeles roared back to win the game and earn a spot in the NBA finals against the Indiana Pacers. O'Neal established himself as the best player in that series by averaging 38.0 points and 16.7 rebounds. Pacer coach Larry Bird summed up his team's problem when he said, "We can't stop Shaq. He's just too good." O'Neal won MVP honors for the finals, as the Lakers won the series, four games to two.

O'Neal warned opponents that this was only the beginning of a new dynasty. "The first championship was just to get people off my back," he said during the 2000–01 season. "This one? It's gonna be for me." Sure enough, he was more overpowering than ever as he carried Los Angeles to a spectacular 15–1 playoff record on their way to a second championship in 2001. Said Larry Brown, coach of Philadelphia, the Lakers' victim in the finals, "I've never seen a better player in my life."

O'Neal captured his third consecutive finals MVP Award in 2002 as he averaged 36.3 points in the Lakers champion triumph over the New Jersey Nets. O'Neal was traded to Miami in 2004–05 where he led his team to the best record in the Eastern Conference and finished a close second in the voting for league MVP.

Further Reading

Hunter, Bruce. *Shaq Impaq.* Chicago: Bonus Books, 1993.

O'Neal, Shaquille. *Shaq Attack!* New York: Hyperion, 1993.

———. *Shaq Talks Back.* New York: St. Martin's Press, 2001.

Owens, Jesse
(James Cleveland Owens)
(1913–1980) *track-and-field sprinter, jumper*

Few confrontations in sport have been as dramatic as Jesse Owens's challenge to the racist policies of

Nazi Germany in the 1936 Olympics. His talent and grace under pressure made a mockery of Adolf Hitler's Aryan superiority theories, won over thousands of German spectators, and made him a hero in his home country.

James Cleveland Owens was born on September 12, 1913, in Danville, Alabama, a grandson of slaves. J. C., as the family called him, was the youngest of 12 children born to Henry and Mary Emma Owens, who worked as sharecroppers on a farm in Oakville. Throughout his childhood, J. C. was a sickly child, susceptible to pneumonia. At age six he had to walk nine miles to school with his brothers and sisters, and at seven he was expected to spend much of his spare time picking cotton.

Despite working hard, Henry Owens was able to wring so little from the land that he owned nothing but a mule and the clothes on his body. In 1923, Mary Emma persuaded him to move to Cleveland, where relatives had informed them of employment opportunities. Moving from rural Alabama to a crowded eastside Cleveland neighborhood was a severe culture shock to the Owens family. On the first day of class at racially mixed Bolton Elementary School, a timid J. C. mumbled his name to the teacher, who heard it and recorded it as "Jesse." From that time on, Jesse Owens was his official name.

Owens continued to spend his free time working at jobs such as delivering groceries and loading freight cars. His track potential might never have been developed had not a high school track coach, Charles Riley, timed him in a 60-yard dash during a junior high physical education class. Although Owens was too young to join the track team, Riley invited him to train with them. When Owens's work schedule prevented that, Riley agreed to coach him in early morning workouts before school.

Owens was 13 when he was able to compete for the first time. Before the year was over, he broke the world record for his age group in both the high jump and the long jump. Taking Riley's

At the 1936 Olympics in Germany, Jesse Owens convincingly demonstrated the fallacy of Adolf Hitler's notions of racial superiority. *(Allsport Hulton Deutsch/Getty Images)*

advice to focus on keeping his feet on the ground for as short a time as possible, he also blazed a time of 9.9 in the 100-yard dash.

Despite his potential, Owens nearly had to give up track in high school. The Great Depression hit his family particularly hard, throwing his father and several brothers out of work. There was pressure on Jesse, who was never interested in or adept at schoolwork, to drop out of school and work longer hours to make money, especially when his girlfriend (whom he later married) became pregnant. But his family let him stay in school and, at age 15, he high jumped more than 6 feet and long jumped 22 feet, 11 inches—both world records for his age group. His long jump mark was so outstanding that he was invited to the 1932 Olympic trials. There his youth and inexperience showed and he was unable to make the team. But he returned to Cleveland's East Technical High School and during his senior year in 1933 set a world record in the long jump with a leap of 24 feet, 3 1/6 inches. At a national interscholastic meet that June, he upped that mark to 24 feet, 6 inches; blazed a world record time of 20.7 in the 220-yard dash, and tied the world record in the 100-yard dash at 9.4 seconds. At the same time, he was so outgoing and popular that his 95 percent white high school class elected him student body president.

At a time when major universities did not recruit black athletes, Owens was such an exceptional talent that he attracted the interest of more than two dozen colleges. He chose to attend Ohio State University in 1933, disappointing the national black press, which was irked by the school's racial policies. At Ohio State, Owens had to live off-campus in housing for blacks only and eat in blacks-only dining areas. But even though he was not awarded an athletic scholarship (such scholarships were unknown in those days), he was provided with easy, decent-paying jobs such as elevator operator and page in a state office building.

The adjustment to college classes proved to be the most difficult part of college life. A poor student at a high school that did not offer a college-preparation curriculum, Owens struggled and was put on academic probation in the spring of his freshman year. He regained his eligibility in time for the 1935 outdoor track season during his sophomore year and made the best of it. Unveiling a new, compact start that allowed him to burst out of the blocks more quickly in the shorter races, Owens quickly dominated his college competition. The week before the Big Ten Conference

championship, however, he fell down a flight of stairs and hurt his back. The injury left him unable to work out and he appeared to be out of the conference competition.

But on May 25, 1935, he decided to give it a try, although he was hurt too badly to warm up or stretch. His back loosened up enough for Owens to put on what many regard as the greatest track-and-field performance of all time. In the space of little more than an hour, he set or tied six world records. His time of 9.4 equaled the world record in the 100-yard dash, followed by world marks of 20.3 in the 220-yard dash and 22.6 in the 200 low hurdles. Independent watches in those two races also indicated that he had exceeded the world record in the metric equivalents (200 meters) of those events. But his most remarkable performance was a long jump of 26 feet, 8 1/4 inches, a distance so far beyond that of his peers that it was to stand for 25 years.

Sprint competition in the United States, however, was fierce at that time. After his Big Ten triumph, Owens had trouble beating his rival sprinters Eulace Peacock of Alabama and Ralph Metcalfe of Marquette University. Beginning in the summer of 1935, Peacock beat Owens five consecutive times in the short sprints. Going into the 1936 U.S. Olympic trials, Owens was a prohibitive favorite in the long jump but an underdog in the sprints. But Peacock tore a hamstring muscle that eliminated him from competition, and at the trials, Owens edged Metcalfe in both the 100 and the 200 meters.

There had been considerable debate as to whether the United States should send a team to the 1936 Berlin Olympics in light of Germany's repugnant policies. The Nazis had openly boasted of their Aryan superiority and ridiculed the United States for using black "auxiliaries" to represent their country. But the heavily African-American U.S. track-and-field contingent used the opportunity to deal an embarrassing blow to Hitler's pride. In the 100 meters, Owens tied the world record of 10.3 in a qualifying round, then held off a fast-closing Metcalfe to capture the gold and the record in 10.2. The pressure nearly got to Owens in the long jump, and he lost his rhythm and nearly fouled out of the competition. But he recovered in time to fight off a spirited challenge from Germany's Luz Long, with whom he had become friends, to win the event with a jump of 26 feet, ½ inch. Owens then breezed to victory in the 200 meters with a time of 20.7. Although he protested against what many regard as a political decision by U.S. team officials to placate the host Germans by replacing two Jewish sprinters in the 4 × 100 relay, he was ordered to run the race. The U.S. team gained an easy victory, thus giving Owens a record four Olympic gold medals in track and field in a single Olympics.

German fans so admired Owens that they followed him to his apartment in the Olympic village, begging for autographs. Back in the United States, his courageous performance in a hostile environment made him a legend among many Americans, black and white. But he was snubbed by U.S. President Roosevelt on returning home and by the U.S. sports establishment, which inexcusably failed to vote him the Sullivan Award as the nation's best amateur athlete. In response to a question about Germany's treatment of minorities, Owens noted, "I came back to my native country, and I couldn't ride in the front of the bus.

I had to go to the back door. I couldn't live where I wanted. Now what's the difference?"

In spite of his brilliant performance in the Olympics, his athletic fame did him no good monetarily. After finishing his career at Ohio State, he worked as a playground instructor, became involved in a chain of cleaning stores that went bankrupt, and had to endure the humiliation of publicly racing dogs and horses to earn a living. In later years, however, he showed an inspirational gift for public speaking that led *Track and Field News* to note, "When he enters a room, he doesn't so much take over it as envelop it." A lifelong smoker, Owens died of cancer on May 31, 1980.

Further Reading

Baker, William. *Jesse Owens: An American Life*. New York: Free Press, 1986.

Nelson, Cordner. *Track's Greatest Champions*. Los Altos, Calif.: Tafnews Press, 1986.

Owens, Jesse. *Jesse*. Plainfield, N.J.: Logos International, 1978.

Owens, Jesse, with Paul Neimark. *Blackthink*. New York: Pocketbooks, 1970.

———. *I Have Changed*. New York: William Morrow, 1972.

Vecchione, Joseph J., ed. *The New York Times Book of Sports Legends*. New York: Times Books, 1991.

P

Page, Alan Cedric
(1945–) *football defensive tackle*

"Football was a job and often a tedious one," remembers Alan Page. Nonetheless, despite his disdain for the sports world, he combined catlike quickness, intelligence, creativity, and competitiveness to wreak havoc on opposing offenses in the late 1960s and early 1970s.

Alan Cedric Page was born on August 7, 1945, in Canton, Ohio, the birthplace of pro football. Although Page could play the sport with the best of them, his heroes were not sports figures but social activists and professionals such as Justice Thurgood Marshall and Martin Luther King, Jr. His size and skill as a football player at Catholic Central High School in Canton earned him a scholarship to prestigious Notre Dame University. There he played defensive end on a Notre Dame team that won the national championship in his senior year of 1966. The Minnesota Vikings then selected him in the first round of the 1967 draft, with designs of switching him to defensive tackle.

Page caught on so quickly to the Viking defensive scheme that he became the first rookie ever to start for Coach Bud Grant. In just his second season, Page's explosive charge at right tackle formed the catalyst for one of the most dominating defensive lines in football history. Page joined ends Carl Eller and Jim Marshall and tackle Gary Larsen to form a front four that became feared throughout the National Football League (NFL) and known as the Purple People Eaters. The Vikings shocked the league by winning the NFL championship that year, although they fell to the Kansas City Chiefs in the Super Bowl.

Page continued to improve each season. In contrast to most pro lineman, who bulk up over their years in the sport, Page recognized that a lighter weight gave him even more quickness without detracting greatly from his strength. He slimmed down from 278 pounds as a rookie to 245 during his peak years. He became the most disruptive force in the game as he shot past linemen into the backfield, generating sacks, lost yardage, and fumbles. No other lineman has perfected the art of blocking kicks as Page did; he recorded 28 blocks during his career to go with his 23 fumble recoveries and (unofficial) 173 sacks.

Page's prowess is evidenced by the fact that he was named to the Pro Bowl nine straight seasons, won the National Football Conference (NFC) Most Valuable Defensive Player four times, and in 1971 was one of the few defensive players ever to win the overall Most Valuable Player Award. He was a prime reason why the Vikings won six division titles and four NFC championships from 1968 to 1976. His linemate Jim Marshall claimed that Page was so good that he changed the way referees called penalties.

"They stopped calling holding because Alan was so quick and elusive, and he was so disruptive of the other teams," says Marshall.

Fiercely independent and annoyed by the exalted status of sports in society, he repeatedly clashed with Coach Grant, who wanted him to stop losing weight. Six games into the 1978 season, Minnesota released him. He was promptly claimed by Chicago, for whom he played three more seasons before retiring.

Page went on to earn a law degree and in 1992 became the first African American elected to the Minnesota Supreme Court. Typical of his emphasis on education over sports, he chose his school principal as his presenter at his induction into the NFL Hall of Fame in 1988.

Further Reading

Bernstein, Ross. *Fifty Years, Fifty Heroes.* Hopkins, Minn.: Self-published, 1997.

Bigelow, Barbara Carlisle, ed. *Contemporary Black Biography.* Vol. 7. Detroit, Mich.: Gale Research, 1994.

Paige, Satchel
(Leroy Robert Paige)
(1906–1982) *baseball pitcher*

Satchel Paige was easily the most flamboyant and, by most accounts, the most talented of the Negro League pitchers. Long past the age when most pitchers retire, Paige finally was given a chance to pitch in the major leagues. He had enough left in his arm to win the American League's Rookie of the Year Award. Baseball fans can only imagine what Paige in his prime would have done to big league hitters. The Olympic star and politician Ralph Metcalfe called Paige "a supremely talented athlete and showman with a personality perfectly suited to a life of carefully walking the race line without compromising his dignity or disowning his heritage."

Leroy Robert Paige was born in Mobile, Alabama, on July 7, 1906, the son of John and Lulu Paige. In order to help feed a family that included 10 brothers and sisters, seven-year-old Leroy earned money at a railroad station carrying travelers' bags or satchels, which he slung on a pole. It was from this activity that he acquired his nickname "Satchel."

Satchel frequently tangled with the law and truant officers as a youngster and ended up being sentenced to four years at the Alabama Reform School for Boys. There he discovered his talent for throwing a baseball. After his release, Paige started his career with the semipro Mobile Tigers in 1924. By 1927 he had moved to the upper echelons of Negro League baseball when he joined the Birmingham Black Barons, the first of many teams for whom he toiled in his long career.

As a youngster, Paige relied almost exclusively on his explosive fastball, which he generated from a high leg kick, fluid motion, and exceptionally long arms. The rail-thin, six-foot, three-inch, hurler enjoyed being the center of attention, not only with his pitching skill but with his colorful and often outrageous speech. "I threw my trouble ball, and they just wet their pants or cried," he once said. "They thought of passing a law against me." As the years went on, he developed a crafty assortment of breaking pitches, including what he called his "hesitation" pitch, which he claimed caused batters to swing before it left his hand. His boasting evolved into an entertaining eccentricity that made him a legend both on and off the ball diamond. For example, in 1931 Paige was supposed to pitch a championship game for the Pittsburgh Crawfords against the Homestead Grays. He failed to arrive for the start but made a dramatic appearance at the ballpark in the fourth inning and proceeded to strike out six in a row.

Paige frequently played barnstorming games against major league players, many of whom conceded he was the best pitcher of their era. In 1936, after managing a weak infield hit against Paige, a young Joe DiMaggio commented to teammates, "Now I know I can make it with the Yankees. I finally got a hit off ol' Satch." Paige struck out Rogers Hornsby, one of the greatest hitters of all time, five times in a game; fanned Babe Ruth; and outdueled Bob Feller. The Hall of Fame pitcher Dizzy Dean openly declared, "If Satch and I were pitching on the same team, we'd cinch the pennant by July 4 and go fishing until World Series time."

One Chicago Cub player who did not show Paige respect paid for it with a public humiliation. After hearing that the player had slurred him, Paige deliberately walked three batters to load the bases for the offender. After calling in his outfielders and telling his infielders to sit down, Paige then struck out the batter on three pitches.

Over time, Paige's actions and tales were so incredible that it was hard to tell truth from fiction. For example, the story that Paige, so confident in his laser-like control, would empty a cigarette of its tobacco, unfold it, and use it as home plate during warmups is regarded as true. His claim that he had to the dodge machine-gun fire of fans in Mexico who had bet against him is viewed as less credible.

Because of the irregularity of both Negro League schedules and record keeping, it is difficult to document Paige's dominance in raw statistics. Among the claims made about him are that he recorded 55 no-hitters during his career and won 104 of 105 games in 1934.

What is not in dispute is that Paige likely pitched in more games than any other hurler who ever lived. As Negro League baseball's best drawing card, he was in such demand that his teams often had him pitch with little or no rest to satisfy the paying customers. Best estimates are that Satchel took the mound in at least 2,500 games. Such overwork nearly destroyed his arm in 1939. It was then that Paige developed off-speed pitches, relieving stress on his arm and making him more effective than ever.

In 1948, after JACKIE ROBINSON had broken the color barrier, Cleveland's Bill Veeck signed the 42-year-old legend in midseason to a major

Rubber-armed hurler Satchel Paige talked as good a game as he pitched, leaving behind him a trail of legendary feats and fascinating quotes. *(National Baseball Hall of Fame Library, Cooperstown, N.Y.)*

league contract. More than 72,000 fans showed up to see Paige's first appearance, a flawless two innings of relief. In 73 innings of work, Paige notched a 6–1 record, including two shutout victories versus Chicago, and sported a fine 2.47 earned run average (ERA). In a typical response, the oldest rookie in league history admitted to being "a little tired from underwork." Paige's contributions provided a margin of victory that enabled Cleveland to win the pennant by a single game. He then became the first black pitcher to play in a World Series, although he was restricted to one relief appearance.

Paige pitched for five seasons in the American League, winning 28 games and saving 32 others. At the age of 46, he won 12 games for the Saint Louis Browns and was named to the All-

Star team. The final chapter of the Satchel Paige legend took place in 1965, when the Kansas City A's signed him as a publicity stunt. Incredibly, the 59-year-old hurler pitched three competitive innings in his final professional appearance.

Paige became something of a folk hero in his later years, spouting his unique home-spun advice such as jangling the arms to get juices flowing, avoiding running, and issuing his most famous caution: "Never look back; something may be gaining on you." In 1971, he was the first Negro League athlete voted into major league baseball's Hall of Fame. He died of emphysema on June 5, 1982.

Further Reading

Bruce, Janet. *The Kansas City Monarchs: Champions of Black Baseball.* Lawrence: University of Kansas Press, 1985.

Chadwick, Bruce. *When the Game Was Black and White.* New York: Abbeville, 1992.

Clark, Dick, and Lerry Lester, eds. *The Negro League Book.* Cleveland, Ohio: Society for American Baseball Research, 1994.

Holway, John. *Josh and Satch: The Life and Times of Josh Gibson and Satchel Paige.* Westport, Conn.: Meckler, 1991.

Sterry, David, and Arielle Eckstut, eds. *Satchel Sez: The Wit, Wisdom, and World of Leroy "Satchel" Paige.* New York: Three Rivers Press, 2001.

Parker, Jim
(James Thomas Parker)
(1934–   ) *football offensive tackle*

Jim Parker broke the mold for offensive football linemen. His unprecedented blend of size and speed made him the bastion of the Baltimore Colts line in the late 1950s and early 1960s and the prototype of today's giant blockers.

James Thomas Parker was born on April 3, 1934, in East Macon, Georgia, where his father, Charles, worked as a track laborer for a railroad.

Jim was one of six Parker children raised in a strict Baptist family. After his junior year of high school, Parker traveled north in hopes of finding a summer job. After landing construction work in Detroit, he decided he liked the North well enough to stay with his aunt in Toledo, Ohio, and finish high school there. While he was attending Scott High School, Parker began playing football, and he did it well enough to make All-State in Ohio, one of the high school football hotbeds of the nation.

Coach Woody Hayes recruited him to play as a two-way lineman at Ohio State University. In 1954 during his sophomore year, Parker earned starting positions on both offense and defense, and his team went undefeated, beat Southern California in the Rose Bowl, and claimed a share of the college national championship. The following year, the All-American lineman paved the way for his teammate Howard "Hopalong" Cassidy to gain enough yards to win the Heisman Trophy as the nation's top college football player, and he continued to play stout defense. In 1956 Parker was awarded the Outland Trophy as the best lineman in college football.

The Baltimore Colts made him their first selection in the 1957 draft of college players. At six feet, three inches, and 272 pounds, Parker was one of the most physically imposing players of his time. Yet he was light on his feet and showed exceptional quickness. Faced with a decision of whether to play their giant rookie on offense or defense, the Colts decided to install him at left tackle to protect the blind side of their star quarterback John Unitas. As Parker remembered later, "It didn't take long to learn the one big rule: just keep 'em away from John." Parker provided key pass protection that gave Unitas time to pick apart pass defenses. Unitas won the National Football League's (NFL's) Most Valuable Player trophy that season.

Parker also proved to be a stalwart run blocker who cleared paths for the Colts' running backs Alan Ameche and Lenny Moore. His blocking was a key factor in Baltimore's winning the NFL championship in 1958 and 1959. He demonstrated his versatility by maintaining his string of eight consecutive Pro Bowl honors after switching to guard in 1962.

Parker was such an intense competitor that he frequently broke into a rash psyching himself up for the game. "Jim Mutschellar used to say that he wouldn't come near me before a game because he was afraid I'd kill him," Parker admitted.

After suffering a knee injury in 1967, Parker retired. Most defensive linemen of his time rated him the best blocker they had faced, and in 1973, he became the first offensive lineman voted into the Pro Football Hall of Fame.

Further Reading

Berkow, Ira. *Beyond the Dream.* New York: Atheneum, 1975.

Gildea, William. *When the Colts Belonged to Baltimore.* Baltimore: Johns Hopkins University Press, 1996.

Hanks, Stephen, and Stewart Richardson. *The Game That Changed Pro Football.* Charleston, S.C.: Birch Lane, 1989.

Payton, Walter Jerry

("Sweetness")
(1954–1999) *football running back*

Walter Payton was a running back of exceptional talent, and he holds the National Football League (NFL) record for career rushing yardage. Yet it was not his statistics but his heart that made him one of the sport's most inspirational figures.

He was born Walter Jerry Payton on July 24, 1954, in Columbia, Mississippi, to Peter and Alyne Payton, the youngest of three children. By working separate shifts at a parachute plant, the major employer in a town of about 7,500, his parents were able to provide the basics for their family, which did not include indoor plumbing. Walter learned a strong ethic from his parents, who oversaw many hours of work in the family garden. He

and his older brother, Eddie, spent most of their free time playing sports of one kind or other. Their father laid down a basic rule when it came to sports: They could play only if they gave 100 percent all the time.

Yet it was not sports but music that interested young Walter. Although he played Little League and joined pickup football games in the neighborhood, he bypassed high school football in favor of playing the drums. Eventually, though, he succumbed to the pressure of living up to his brother's exploits as a football running back and teasing about his drumming. In his junior year at all-black Jefferson High School, he went out for football for the first time and became an instant star at running back. Although he was not big and had never lifted weights, he was incredibly strong and had good balance and exceptional speed. His natural athletic ability allowed him to play baseball, basketball, and football in high school as well as run track. In track he set a school long jump record without ever practicing the event.

Just before his senior year, the schools in his area finally moved to integrate. Payton was among the black football players transferred to previously white Columbia High School. Payton's outstanding running skill, his work ethic, and his friendly nature helped make the transition a smooth one.

Payton was voted All-State in football and was a fine student, yet few people outside Columbia took any notice of him. Only the University of Kansas and two primarily black schools, Alcorn State and Jackson State, offered him football scholarships. Payton decided to follow his brother Eddie to Jackson State. As a freshman, Walter played alongside Eddie in the same backfield. Their coach, Bob Hill, had no patience with prima donna running backs. He made sure Walter learned to block and catch passes as well as run with the ball. In Walter Payton, Hill found a back who was willing to work hard to master all the skills.

During his career at Jackson State, Payton gained 3,563 rushing yards, for an average of 6.1

yards a carry, and scored 66 touchdowns. Many football experts regarded him as the best college player in the nation during his senior year, but again he received little national publicity. In fact, the most recognition he received while in college was for his dancing—Payton won a dance contest that earned him a trip to Los Angeles to appear on the show *Soul Train*. As further evidence that he was far more than a one-dimensional jock, he graduated at the age of 20 with a 3.5 grade point average with a major in special education.

Although Payton had little name recognition around the country, he did attract the attention of the Chicago Bears. In 1975, they claimed him with the fourth selection in the first round of the draft. The big city and the cold weather proved to be a bit of a culture shock for Payton. Furthermore, the Bears were a dreadful team with a weak offensive line. In his first game as a pro, Payton carried the ball eight times for zero yards. However, he managed to keep a positive attitude and used the failure as motivation to work harder. As he later said, "Sometimes you learn more through adversity than through success and my rookie year was proof of that." The hard work began to pay off in the final game of the year when Payton finally broke loose for 134 yards, giving him 679 for the season.

In his second season, Payton had a better chance to display the aggressive, relentless style of running for which he became famous. When he could not twist and dance away from tacklers, Payton attacked them. He exploded into opponents like a grenade, bounced off, maintained his balance, and kept driving forward. Although he weighed only 205 pounds, his huge upper legs made him feel like a 250-pounder to defensive backs. Payton's refusal to quit impressed the Hall of Fame running back JIM BROWN, who described Payton as having "as great a heart as anyone who ever lived. He would fight you for every inch, all day long, with no thought of running out of bounds to get away from a hit."

Known throughout the NFL as "Sweetness," the career rushing leader Walter Payton stood as the epitome of class and determination. *(Jerry Elder/Getty Images)*

Payton gained 1,390 yards in 1976, second only to O. J. SIMPSON, and scored 13 touchdowns. The following season, he again showed his courage when he fought off a bad case of flu to gain an NFL record 275 yards in a single game against the Minnesota Vikings. Payton finished the season with a league-leading 1,852 yards and 14 rushing touchdowns, and he won the NFL's Most Valuable Player Award.

Playing at a position and with a running style in which he absorbed a great deal of physical punishment, Payton seldom missed a game in his career. ERIC DEMETRIC DICKERSON, himself a fitness fanatic, regarded Payton as "arguably the best-conditioned football player of all time." With remarkable consistency, Payton churned out yardage for a Bears team that had few offensive weapons to complement him, thus forcing him to run into the teeth of stacked defenses designed specifically to stop him. He gained 1,395 yards in 1978, 1,610 in 1979, 1,460 in 1980, and 1,222 in 1981. His streak of 1,000-yard seasons was stopped only by a leaguewide strike that shortened the season in 1982. Payton returned the following year to gain 1,421 yards.

Payton displayed his versatility with his blocking and pass receiving. Many experts rated him as far and away the best-blocking running back in the league, and he was frequently among the Bears' leading receivers. In 1984, Payton even played quarterback one game and tossed two touchdown passes against the New Orleans Saints.

His consistently outstanding performances racked up yardage at an unprecedented rate. On October 7, 1984, he gained six yards on an end sweep, thus passing Jim Brown as the leading career rusher in NFL history. Typically modest, Payton refused to allow the game to be stopped to honor him for the accomplishment. That season, the Bears made the playoffs, only to lose in the first round to the Washington Redskins. The disappointment typified Payton's career to that point. No matter how hard he played, Chicago just could not seem to win. He had gained more yards than any other running back in NFL history and yet the Bears' record during his first nine years was 58–71, and they had lost the only two playoff games in which they played.

In 1985, Payton's luck changed. Driven by a marauding defense, the Bears swept through their league opponents with ease. At this point in his career, Payton was so battered he could hardly walk or lift his arms. But he stayed in the lineup and played with his usual reckless abandon. As the recognized leader of the team, he led by example and was instrumental in soothing some

of the turmoil created by a volatile coaching staff. "The man taught me what a professional was," declared Mike Singletary, the leader of the team's defense.

Chicago sported a 15–1 record in 1985 and then trampled the New York Giants and Los Angeles Rams in the playoffs to gain a Super Bowl berth. There, the New England Patriots were so concerned about stopping Payton that they left everything else vulnerable to attack. The Bears demolished the Patriots, 46–10, to earn the championship.

With Payton still leading the way, Chicago posted a 14–2 mark the following year but were upset by Washington in the playoffs. Payton began sharing running duties with Neal Anderson in 1987 and then retired after the 1988 season. True to form, he went down battling, as he led the team with 85 yards rushing in its playoff defeat. The man his teammates called Sweetness finished his career with 16,728 yards rushing and 110 touchdowns, much of it accomplished behind a mediocre offensive line.

Shortly after retiring, Payton attempted to become the first black NFL owner, but his bid to win a franchise in Saint Louis was refused. In 1998, five years after his induction into the NFL Hall of Fame, he was diagnosed with a rare liver disease. After a courageous battle with this illness and the cancer that followed, Payton died on January 1, 1999. As an indication of his inspirational qualities, fans and fellow players packed Chicago's Soldiers Field for a memorial service in his honor.

Further Reading

H & S Media. *Sweetness: The Courage and Heart of Walter Payton.* Chicago: Triumph Books, 1999.

Payton, Walter, with Don Yeager. *Never Die Easy.* New York: Villard, 2000.

Towle, Mike. *I Remember Walter Payton: Personal Memories of Football's Sweetest Superstar by the People Who Knew Him Best.* Nashville, Tenn.: Cumberland House, 2000.

Pollard, Fritz
(Frederick Douglas Pollard)
(1894–1986) *football running back*

Fritz Pollard was the first African-American star in football, but his exploits are virtually unknown to sports fans today because he played professional ball at a time when the National League was still in its formative stages.

Frederick Douglas Pollard was born on January 27, 1894, in Chicago, Illinois, the seventh of eight children of John and Catherine Pollard. John Pollard, a Civil War veteran, established a successful barber shop and moved the family to the affluent, all-white Rogers Park neighborhood. Discrimination was a fact of life for young Frederick; he remembered that his mother never answered the front door without a handgun in her apron pocket.

John Pollard, who had been frustrated in his dream to be a lawyer, was adamant about his children's receiving the best education they could. Frederick, who was nicknamed Fritz at an early age by his German neighbors, excelled academically at Lane Technical High School, where he also achieved fame as one of the best high school football players in the nation.

At that time, although blacks were barred from major league baseball, college football had no such prohibitions. Roughly two dozen African Americans had played the sport at major colleges and universities by the time Pollard left high school, and he was actively recruited by several programs. His brother, Leslie, in fact, had played football for Dartmouth several years earlier. In 1915 Pollard enrolled at prestigious Brown University, where he immediately took over as the team's quarterback. That year he earned the grudging respect even of blatantly racist opponents by leading his team to victories over football powers Harvard and Yale on consecutive weekends with his throwing, running, and punt returning. One Yale rival conceded, "You're a n _ _ _ _ _, but you're the best goddam football player I ever saw."

In 1915, Pollard led Brown to the Rose Bowl, its first (and only) major bowl appearance, in which the team lost to Washington State. The following season, Pollard switched to running back. For the rest of his college career, he was widely regarded as the best college player at his position. In the words of sports historian Edwin Bancroft Henderson, "No more brilliant comet ever streaked across a turfed gridiron than flashy Fritz."

Pollard joined the professional Akron Pros in 1919 and was so highly regarded for his knowledge of the game that he was named player-coach, becoming the first African-American head coach in professional sports (half a century would pass before the second). His Akron team not only went through the 1920 season undefeated but did not yield a single point.

Despite his status as coach, Pollard suffered the usual indignities heaped upon African Americans at the time. He was forced to dress for games in the club owner's cigar factory rather than in the locker room and could not stay with the team in many hotels or eat in the same restaurants. Rough and even dirty play was commonplace. Yet, even though he stood only five feet, six inches and weighed 160 pounds, Pollard never had to leave a game with an injury.

Pollard played and coached at Akron through the 1926 season. He then founded the first African-American investment firm in New York City and formed a short-lived all-black pro football team. He died on May 11, 1986.

Further Reading
Carroll, John M. *Fritz Pollard: Pioneer in Racial Advancement.* Champaign: University of Illinois Press, 1999.
———. "Fritz Pollard and the Brown Bombers." Professional Football Researchers Association. Available online. URL: http://www.geocities.com/Colosseum/sideline/5960/pollard.htm. Downloaded on November 12, 2002.
Young, A. S. *Negro Firsts in Sports.* Chicago: Johnson Publishing Company, 1963.

Puckett, Kirby
(1961–   ) *baseball outfielder*

By far the most popular athlete in Minnesota history, Kirby Puckett gave both joy and success to a struggling Twins franchise. His performance in the 1991 World Series firmly established him as one of the legends of baseball.

Puckett was born on March 14, 1961, the youngest of nine children of William and Catherine Puckett. He spent his early years living on the 14th floor of the Robert Taylor housing project in one of Chicago's roughest neighborhoods. When he was 12, his father's postal job enabled them to move to a better neighborhood. Puckett became the star third baseman at Calumet High School, but his short, stocky build and lack of power turned off scouts. After graduating in the top 20 percent of his class, he began working in a Ford assembly plant. He refused to give up on his dream of playing baseball, however, and answered an ad to participate in a Kansas City Royals tryout camp. The Royals were not impressed, but a coach from Bradley University saw enough in him to offer him a scholarship.

Puckett switched to center field at Bradley to take advantage of his speed and in 1982 he made All-Conference as a freshman. But after his father's sudden death that year, he transferred to Triton Community College, closer to home. While he was playing in a summer league, his enthusiasm drew the admiration of a Minnesota Twins scout, who signed him. By May 1994 Puckett worked his way to the major leagues. He whacked four hits in his first game and earned the starting center fielder job.

Although Puckett batted .296 his rookie season, he failed to hit a home run. The 1995 season was similar to his first: a .288 average and only four home runs. Former Twins batting champion Tony Oliva told him he was swinging too early. Exercising the patience that Oliva preached, Puckett stunned the league by belting 11 home runs in his first 24 games of 1986. He finished the season with a .328 mark, 223 hits, 33 home runs, and a Gold Glove for outstanding fielding. Just as important as his production was Puckett's positive influence. The manager Tom Kelly said of him, "There's something about the guy that makes you feel good." Puckett's love of baseball was contagious; he always wore a smile, and he made a point of personally welcoming every rookie into the league. His approach to batting was simple: "I just go up there hacking."

In 1987, Puckett's .332 average and 28 home runs led the Twins into the playoffs, in which they won their first World Series championship. The following year he collected 234 hits, the most by a right-handed batter in 42 years, and batted .356 with 24 home runs. In 1989, he won the American League batting title with .339.

After leading the Twins into the World Series again in 1991, Puckett single-handedly staved off elimination in game six. He drove in both Twins' runs, and robbed Atlanta's Ron Gant of a home run to send the game into extra innings. In the 11th inning, Puckett clouted the winning home run and the Twins went on to win the series.

Puckett continued as the modern game's most prolific right-handed hitter, racking up more hits in his first 10 years than any player since Willie Keeler nearly a century earlier. His career was tragically cut short by damage to his retina at the end of the 1996 season, and he finished his 12-year career with a lifetime .318 average and six Gold Gloves.

Further Reading
Carlson, Chuck, and George Brett. *Puck! Kirby Puckett: Baseball's Last Warrior.* Lenexa, Kansas: Addax Publishing, 1997.

Puckett, Kirby. *I Love This Game!* New York: Harper-Collins, 1993.

Santa Maria, Michael. *In the Shadow of the Diamond.* Madison, Wis.: Brown & Benchmark, 1992.

Ribbs, Willy
(William Theodore Ribbs, Jr.)
(1956–   ) *automobile racer*

Willy Ribbs has struggled for much of his life to break into the traditionally white, corporate realm of automobile racing. Battling a chronic lack of financial backing, he became the first African American to qualify for the Indianapolis 500.

He was born William Theodore Ribbs, Jr., on January 3, 1956, in San Jose, California to Geraldine and William Ribbs, Sr. His father ran a successful plumbing business that earned enough money to allow him to indulge his hobby of racing motorcycles and sports cars on the amateur circuit on the West Coast. Having spent much of his childhood around racetracks, Willy became interested in being a professional race driver. He saved up enough money by working in his father's business that in the mid-1970s he traveled to Europe to study racing. He won 6 of the 11 races in the Star of Tomorrow racing series in England, which made him the overall champion of the competition. While in London, he sought out visiting U.S. celebrity MUHAMMAD ALI and followed the champ's advice to take up a boxer's regimen as training for racing.

Flushed with success, Ribbs returned to the United States and began to race on the NASCAR circuit. His attempts to imitate some of Ali's

boastful flair (including victory dances on the hood of the car), however, brought down the wrath of the conservative auto racing world. "As a newcomer, I didn't know how the racing fraternity expected me to carry myself," Ribbs later commented. "I was, in effect, blacklisted."

Unable to attract sponsorship money for the expensive sport, Ribbs quit racing and went back to work for his father. In 1981 he grudgingly agreed to accompany a friend to a race in Southern California, where he met a man who remembered his early racing promise and offered him support. Ribbs rejoined the racing competition in the Trans-Am series. In 1983 he won five of 12 races in the series to finish second overall in the competition. The following season, he again took second place, after which he attempted to move up to auto racing's highest echelon, the Indy Car circuit. Unfortunately in 1986, his Winston Cup NASCAR team had to disband after three races when the sponsor pulled out.

In 1987 Ribbs caught on with a Toyota-sponsored Dan Gurney team on the GTO circuit. Although his aggressive driving frequently led to blown engines, he managed to win seven of 24 starts to earn Driver of the Year honors in the circuit. The following year, with entertainer Bill Cosby's backing, he began racing in the prestigious CART series. By 1991, he had advanced to 17th in the CART standings. That same year, he became the first African American to race in the Indianapolis 500, although he completed only five laps before his engine failed. He returned to Indianapolis two years later and finished 21st in the 33-car field.

After achieving five top 10 CART finishes in 1994, he dropped out of racing to spend time raising his children. He returned to professional racing in 1999. Although critical of the barriers that auto racing imposes on minorities, Ribbs maintains that he has experienced no racial problems on the racing teams themselves, "When you slide down into the cockpit and get strapped in," he has noted, "you'd better believe in the people around you. You'd better be color-blind."

Further Reading

Garret, J. "Tell 'Em Willy T. Is Back!" *Car & Driver*, July 2000, p. 123.

Thompson, Clifford, ed. *Current Biography 2000.* New York: H. W. Wilson, 2000.

Rice, Jerry Lee

(1962–   ) *football wide receiver*

Jerry Rice is the most efficient touchdown machine the National Football League (NFL) has ever seen. It took the San Francisco 49ers receiver only eight years to break the NFL career mark for touchdown passes that Hall of Famer Steve Largent fashioned in 14 years, and he has continued to widen the gulf between him and the rest of the league ever since.

He was born Jerry Lee Rice on October 13, 1962, in Starkville, Mississippi, the sixth of eight children of Joe and Eddie B. Rice. He grew up in the small town of Crawford, where Joe worked as a brick mason. Joe expected the boys to help out with the family business, and so Jerry spent his summers laboring with bricks in the Mississippi heat. "Catching bricks taught me the meaning of hard work," Rice has said. It also helped him develop the vise-grip fingers that would later be his trademark. Jerry was always good with his hands, and he often thought about opening a repair shop once he finished high school.

At B. L. Moor High School, Rice was a good student who also participated in basketball and track. He did not try football until his sophomore year, when the vice principal caught him skipping class and Rice, in a panic, ran away. Impressed with the boy's speed, the vice principal offered to ease up on his punishment if Rice would put it to use on the football field. Since the Rices had no way to transport him from school after practice, Jerry had to run the five miles home every day. The exercise helped him build speed and power in his legs.

Rice quickly developed into an outstanding wide receiver. During his senior year, he caught 80 passes for 35 touchdowns. Yet because he played at such a small school, those impressive numbers did not attract the interest of Division I colleges, not even Mississippi State, which was only 20 miles away. In 1981 Rice enrolled at Mississippi Valley State in tiny Itta Bena, Mississippi, hoping to major in electronics.

The Delta Devils of Mississippi Valley State played at the Division 1-AA level, a step below the better-known schools. The low-key atmosphere was just what Rice needed to develop, and the wide-open aerial attack of Coach Archie "Gunslinger" Cooley was tailor-made for his talents. After adjusting to the college game in his freshman year, Rice caught 66 passes as a sophomore. In 1983, the junior wide receiver ran wild in a game against Southern University. He snared 24 passes for 279 yards, both of which were Division 1-AA records. During his senior year, Rice continued his attack on the record books with 103 catches on the year and a five-touchdown, 294-yard performance against Kentucky State. That gave him college career totals of 301 receptions, 4,693 yards, and 50 touchdowns, all division records.

Yet because he played at a small school, Rice continued to fall beneath the radar of most football experts, among them San Francisco 49ers

Jerry Rice shattered most NFL receiving records early in his career and has been putting them out of reach ever since. *(Allsport/Getty Images)*

coach Bill Walsh. Walsh happened to be in Houston preparing for a game when Mississippi Valley was playing in town against Southern University. Unable to sleep at night, he flipped through some local sports channels and saw a highlight clip of Rice scoring two long touchdowns. Impressed, he sent a scout to check out the prospect. The scout returned raving, and the 49ers were convinced they had uncovered a golden secret.

That secret began to leak out when Rice scored two touchdowns and earned the Most Valuable Player (MVP) Award at the postseason Blue-Gray All-Star Game. At draft time in 1985,

San Francisco had to trade up in the draft to claim Rice with the 16th selection of the first round.

Although the small-town Rice was intimidated by big-city life among the pros, he entered training camp bursting with confidence. In his first game, he caught four passes. But then, the normally glue-fingered receiver, of whom his college coach said, "He could catch BBs in the dark," suddenly developed a case of the jitters. Rice dropped 10 passes in his next 13 games, a result of trying to run with the ball before he caught it.

It was not until the 14th game of the season, a Monday night game against the Los Angeles Rams, that Rice gave a display of his potential by setting a 49ers record of 241 receiving yards on 10 receptions. That performance boosted his totals for the year to 49 catches and 927 yards, and it clinched Rookie of the Year honors for him.

Teammates discovered that Rice did his most impressive work during the offseason. Rice studied the 49ers' complex play book until he had mastered every nuance of it. As soon as one season ended, he trained fanatically for the next season, running torturous workouts up and down the San Francisco hills. Thus prepared, Rice got off to a great start in 1986 and carried it through to the end. He led the NFL in pass-receiving yards with 1,570 and began a streak of 13 consecutive games with at least one touchdown pass reception. *Sports Illustrated* named him its NFL Player of the Year. The year ended poorly, however, when Rice committed an unforced fumble in the play-offs, triggering a disastrous San Francisco defeat. The memory of the blunder goaded him on through another brutal training regimen.

In 1987, Rice demonstrated an astounding ability to reach the end zone. His ability to score on long bombs baffled many observers, who noted that Rice's speed was only average for a receiver. More than one defender, however, noted that Rice seemed to find an extra gear when the ball was in the air. At six feet, three inches, and 205 pounds, Rice was fairly large for a receiver and he frequently broke tackles to reach paydirt. One of his favorite pass patterns was the slant into the middle of the field, a route dreaded by many receivers because it leaves them open to violent hits. Showing courage, intense concentration, iron discipline in running precise routes, and elusiveness in the open field, Rice repeatedly turned short slants into long touchdown runs. "I feel like the fun is just starting when I catch the football," he said. Rice experienced more than his share of fun in 1987. He scored an NFL record 22 touchdowns in a season shortened to 12 games because of a players' strike and easily won the voting for NFL Most Valuable Player (MVP).

Injuries diminished his statistics the following year, but he more than made up for it in the playoffs. Frustrated by his subpar postseason performances, Rice stepped up to the challenge with three touchdown catches in San Francisco's first-round match with Minnesota. Then, despite having lived his entire life in warm climates, he caught two touchdown passes on a freezing afternoon in Chicago to bounce the Bears out of the playoffs. Rice's sprained ankle was so sore that he doubted he could play in the Super Bowl against Cincinnati two weeks later. But he fought through the pain to catch 11 passes for 215 yards. His clutch grabs helped San Francisco to pull out a 20–16 comeback victory, and Rice was honored as the game's Most Valuable Player. The following year, San Francisco romped through the regular season and playoffs, finishing the year with a 55–10 dismantling of the Denver Broncos in the Super Bowl. Rice contributed seven catches for 148 yards and a Super Bowl record three touchdowns of those receptions.

Working well with both Joe Montana and his successor at quarterback, Steve Young, Rice continued to terrorize defenses. In 1990, he tied a league record by scoring five touchdowns against the Atlanta Falcons. He recorded a league-leading 100 receptions that year for 1,502 yards, which earned him another NFL Player of the Year Award. Two years later, he scored his 101st career touchdown to break the record held by Seattle's

Steve Largent. In 1994, touchdown number 126 put him ahead of JIM BROWN as the most prolific touchdown scorer in NFL history. Solidifying his reputation as a big-game player, he blitzed the San Diego Chargers with a touchdown catch in the first minute of that season's Super Bowl, and he added two other touchdown catches in earning his third Super Bowl ring.

Showing no signs of slowing down, Rice enjoyed his finest statistical season in 1995 with 122 receptions for an NFL-record 1,848 yards. That year he passed both James Lofton's career record of 14,004 yards and Art Monk's career mark 934 career receptions.

A severe leg injury in 1997 appeared to put an end to Rice's record rampage. But Rice rebounded to grab 82 passes for 1,157 yards in 1998. Then, when the 49ers gave up on him after diminishing performances in 1999 and 2000, Rice again proved himself by gaining more than 1,000 receiving yards and nine touchdowns with the Oakland Raiders in 2001. Rice finished his career with the Seattle Hawks where he pushed his career totals far out of reach of any aspiring challengers: 2,895 yards and 197 touchdowns as a receiver.

Further Reading

Axthelm, Pete. "The 49er with the Golden Hands," *Newsweek*, January 11, 1988, p. 62.
Hunter, E. "The Legacy," *Sports Illustrated*, August 14, 1995, pp. 36–38.
"The San Francisco Treat," *Gentlemen's Quarterly*, October 1989, p. 121.

Robertson, Oscar Palmer

("The Big O")
(1938–   ) *basketball guard*

Today the achievement of a "triple double" (double figures in scoring, rebounding, and assists) in a National Basketball Association (NBA) game is regarded as exceptional: Oscar Robertson averaged a triple double over his first five years in the league! Many experts regard him as perhaps the finest all-around player in the game. In the words of rival coach Dick Harp, "He had unbelievable control of a basketball game, and many times he looked like he was taking a walk in the country while he did it."

Oscar Palmer Robertson was born on November 24, 1938, in Charlotte, Tennessee, to Henry and Mazell Robertson, the youngest of three sons. After spending the first five years of his life living in a shack, he and his family moved to Indianapolis, where his father found work in the sanitation department. There, at a local Young Men's Christian Association (YMCA) facility, he was introduced to the hallowed Indiana rite of basketball. His parents were divorced in 1949, about the time when Oscar obtained his first regulation basketball. For years, he lived with that ball until it became almost an extension of his hand.

Oscar followed his older brother, Bailey, to basketball fame at Crispus Attucks High School. Not only was Oscar voted All-State three straight years, but he led his team to two state championships, including the first undefeated season in Indiana high school history. In addition, he was a fine student who graduated 16th in his class.

"The Big O," as he became known throughout his career, went on to the University of Cincinnati in a unique program that allowed him to alternate seven weeks of class with seven weeks of work at a gas and electric company. As a sophomore he led the nation in scoring with an average of 33 points per game. He increased that to 35.1 as a junior and maintained a 32.6 mark as a senior to give him a school record 2,973 points as he led his team to an 89–9 record during his tenure. Despite his success, he was bothered by the hypocrisy of American sports. Although hailed as a basketball hero, he had to endure racial slurs during many games and suffered the indignity of using separate facilities from his white teammates on road trips. The experience reinforced his tendency to be a loner and somewhat

aloof from the media. Yet among his peers, Robertson showed such leadership qualities that he was elected cocaptain of the 1960 U.S. Olympic basketball team that was undefeated in winning a gold medal.

In 1961, Robertson signed with a struggling local NBA franchise, the Cincinnati Royals (now the Sacramento Kings). In his first season, the graceful six-foot, five-inch guard romped through the NBA as if it were his own personal playground. He finished third in the league in scoring with a 30.5 average, more than 7 points better than any guard had ever achieved. He also led the league in assists with a 9.7 average and averaged 10.1 rebounds, an unheard of total for a guard.

In 1961–62, Robertson enjoyed a season that may never be matched. He increased his scoring average to 30.8, his assists to 11.4, and his rebounding to 12.5. K. C. Jones, a defensive expert for the champion Boston Celtics, who drew the task of guarding Robertson, said of him, "Oscar made everything simple. Nobody ever wants to admit they're afraid of another player, but it was scary the things Oscar could do to you." Taller than most guards and with long arms, he could move in close to the basket and score at will over most defenders. Yet he had the quickness to scoot around taller defenders. In addition, Robertson was among the most accurate shooting guards in the league, frequently ranking near the top in both field goal and free throw percentages.

Like all players of that era, however, Robertson played in the shadow of the amazing Boston Celtics. Although he frequently led the Royals into the playoffs, the Celtics always stood in the way of advancement. In 1963, Robertson and his teammates made a valiant effort, extending the Celtics to the maximum seven games of their playoff series before bowing out. It was the closest they would ever be to dethroning Boston.

Robertson maintained his unprecedented triple-threat play in 1963–64, with averages of 31.4 points, 11.0 assists, and 9.9 rebounds. The following season he led the league in assists with an 11.5 average, finished second in scoring at 30.4, and averaged 9.9 rebounds. This time he was finally rewarded with the NBA's Most Valuable Player (MVP) trophy. As time went on, he began to leave more of the rebounding load to his larger teammates but kept up his 30-point scoring average and double-digit assist average through the 1966–67 season.

Despite Robertson's efforts, the Cincinnati franchise went into a decline in the late 1960s from which it never recovered. After 10 years of struggling against impossible odds to win a championship, Robertson got a break in 1970. That year he was traded to the Milwaukee Bucks, who were looking for an experienced guard to complement their brilliant young center, Lew Alcindor (later known as KAREEM ABDUL JABBAR). With the scoring load taken off his shoulders and some of his quickness eroded by age, as a Buck, Robertson never approached his former scoring averages. But he provided the stability and guidance the young team needed. The Bucks cruised through their schedule with a league-best 66–16 mark and then washed away years of frustration for Robertson by breezing through the playoffs and thrashing the Baltimore Bullets in four straight games in the championship series.

Robertson went on to play three more successful seasons with the Bucks before retiring in 1974. Robertson was highly respected by his peers, as evidenced by his 11 years as president of the NBA Player's Association. Among the honors he garnered in his career were six assist titles, three MVP Awards in All-Star Games, and nine consecutive selections as first-team All-NBA. He was elected to the Hall of Fame in 1979 and continues to rank all-time number three in assists and free throws.

Further Reading

Berkow, Ira. *The Golden Year: 1964.* New York: Prentice-Hall, 1971.

Moritz, Charles, ed. *Current Biography 1966.* New York: H. W. Wilson, 1966.

Roberts, Randy. *But They Can't Beat Us: Oscar Robertson and the Crispus Attucks Tigers.* Indianapolis: Indiana Historical Society, 1999.

Robinson, David Maurice

("The Admiral")
(1965–   ) *basketball center*

David Robinson may be the fastest and most intelligent big man ever to play in the National Basketball Association (NBA). A courteous gentleman who has broad and varied interests, he is thought by many experts to have lacked the single-mindedness and killer instinct needed to fulfill his potential as a basketball player.

He was born David Maurice Robinson on August 5, 1965, in Key West, Florida, where his father, Ambrose, was stationed as a U.S. Navy sonar radar technician. He spent most of his childhood in Virginia Beach, Virginia, with his mother, Freda, while Ambrose was away on duty for months at a time. David was a precocious youngster who read the dictionary, played classical piano by ear, and built his own television from scratch. As a freshman, he tried out for basketball but quit rather than languish on the bench.

Robinson suddenly began growing at age 14, sprouting from five feet, five inches to six feet, six inches by the time the family moved to Manassas, Virginia, for his senior year of high school. His height led to pressure to try basketball again, and he did, merely hoping to earn a letter. He became the team's most valuable player.

Robinson continued to grow after being accepted into the U.S. Naval Academy. After playing basketball reluctantly as a freshman, he began to realize his potential when he reached seven feet as a sophomore. With newly developed bulk from the weight room, he averaged 23.6 points and 11.6 rebounds. During his junior year, he shattered the National Collegiate Athletic Association (NCAA) record for blocked shots with a 5.9 average. Nicknamed the Admiral, he was named College Player of the Year as a senior after averaging 28.2 points and 11.8 rebounds, as well as scoring 50 points against Michigan in the NCAA tournament.

The San Antonio Spurs made him their first selection in the 1987 draft, despite the knowledge that he had two years of active duty to serve before playing pro ball. When he finally reported to the Spurs in 1989–90, he ranked in the top 10 in the NBA in scoring, rebounds, and blocked shots, and he was a unanimous choice as Rookie of the Year. The following season, the hook shot and jump shot that he added to his repertoire helped him boost his scoring average to 25.6, to go along with his league-leading rebounding and blocked shot totals.

Robinson had entered the league worrying, "It's hard to be a good person if you're rich. My biggest fear is that I won't be a good person." With those ideals in mind, in the early 1990s he became a charismatic Christian. At the same time, however, he developed a bitter rivalry with the NBA's new star center, SHAQUILLE RASHAUN O'NEAL. Robinson scorched the Los Angeles Clippers for 71 points in the final game of the 1993–94 season to edge O'Neal for the scoring title with a 29.8 average. The following year Robinson reached the zenith of his game, earning the NBA's Most Valuable Player (MVP) Award for combining a 27.6 scoring average with spectacular defense.

In 1999, Robinson finally quieted criticism of his lackluster playoff performances with the help of a newcomer, TIM DUNCAN. After bouncing O'Neal's Lakers in four straight games, Robinson and Duncan led the Spurs to their first NBA championship, in a 4–1 series over the New York Knicks. Robinson retired from the sport in 2003 after winning his second NBA title with the Spurs.

Further Reading

Montville, Leigh. "The Trials of David," *Sports Illustrated*, April 29, 1996, pp. 90–94.

Taylor, Phil. "Rear Admiral," *Sports Illustrated*, April 12, 1999, pp. 40–41.

Robinson, Frank, Jr.

(1935–) *baseball outfielder*

Frank Robinson ranked just behind his more famous outfield contemporaries, WILLIE MAYS and HANK AARON, in combining power, speed, and high average. Although not their equal on defense, he cultivated better leadership skills and was the first player to win Most Valuable Player (MVP) Awards in both the National and American Leagues.

Frank Robinson, Jr., was born on August 31, 1935, in Beaumont, Texas, the youngest son of Ruth Shaw and her third husband, Frank Robinson, Sr. His parents separated when he was an infant and at the age of four, he moved with his mother to California, settling in a rough, mixed neighborhood of Oakland. Robinson excelled in many sports; in fact, he outshone the future legend BILL RUSSELL when the two were basketball teammates at McClymonds High School. But he considered basketball and football only ways to kill time until baseball season came around. Immediately after graduating in 1953, he signed with the Cincinnati Reds.

When Robinson was assigned to the Reds' minor league club in Ogden, Utah, he had his first exposure to institutionalized racism. Movies were his favorite pastime, and the only theater in Ogden was for whites only. Robinson tended to withdraw from others in his early years and was basically a loner when he was called up to the Reds in 1956.

During his minor league stint, he had moved from third base to left field, and he quickly won the starting left field job in Cincinnati. The right-handed-hitting Robinson flexed his muscles that year, tying a league record for rookies by blasting 38 home runs. This, along with his .290 average, earned him National League Rookie of the Year honors. In 1957, he upped his average to .322 with 29 home runs and made the first of his 11 All-Star Game appearances.

Robinson posted solid but unspectacular numbers over the next three seasons, but he began to get a reputation as a troublemaker. Part of the problem was his loner status, but more of it stemmed from his refusal to back down from anyone. At the plate, Robinson refused to stop crowding the plate despite fastballs aimed at his head. Six times while at Cincinnati, he was hit by more pitches than any other player in the league. He also stood firm on salary demands and other issues, and a rift developed between him and management.

The low point in his career was in February 1961, when he was jailed for carrying a concealed weapon. Instead of circling the wagons against the world, however, Robinson took the bold step of changing his attitude. According to his teammate Jim Brosnan, "I've never seen such a dramatic change in one player. Frank became the club's leader that year." Robinson enjoyed a breakout season in which he batted .323, slugged 37 home runs, drove in 124 runs, and stole 22 bases in 25 attempts. Just as impressive was his leadership in focusing the Reds on winning their first National League pennant in 21 years, and Robinson was recognized as the league's Most Valuable Player (MVP). He then topped that season with his most productive year in 1962. He batted a sizzling .342, hit 39 home runs and 51 doubles, drove in 136 runs, scored 134 more, and yet lost out in the MVP voting to the base stealer MAURY WILLS.

In 1963 injuries hampered Robinson, who never quite returned to his performances of 1961 and 1962. Nonetheless, he still produced All-Star–caliber numbers hitting .306 with 29 home runs in 1964 and .296 with 33 home runs in 1965. Therefore, Reds fans were stunned when Cincinnati traded Robinson to the Baltimore Orioles before the 1966 season, claiming that he was an "old 30." The trade, for three players who produced little at Cincinnati, is widely regarded as one of the most one-sided in baseball history. Robinson proved he was far from over the hill by unleashing the greatest power explosion of his career. He hit 49 home runs, batted .316, and drove in 122 runs, leading the American League in all three categories and thus becoming one of

Frank Robinson followed a Hall of Fame career by becoming major league baseball's first black manager. *(National Baseball Hall of Fame Library, Cooperstown, N.Y.)*

baseball's rare Triple Crown winners. His Orioles won the pennant and then swamped the Los Angeles Dodgers in four straight games to win the World Series. Robinson contributed two home runs, including the game winner, in a 1–0 victory in the final game.

After batting .310 with 30 home runs in 1967, Robinson slumped in the following year. But he recovered to bat .308 with 32 homers in 1969. His bat paced the Orioles as they won three straight pennants from 1969 to 1971, including another World Series victory. Robinson made history on June 26, 1971, by clouting grand slam home runs in two consecutive plate appearances against the Washington Senators.

At that point Robinson's offensive production faded, and he was traded to the Los Angeles

Dodgers in 1972. But by this time, people began to take more interest in Robinson's potential as a manager. Starting in 1968, Robinson had managed a Puerto Rican team during the offseason and had performed well. This record, plus his widely recognized skills as a clubhouse leader, made him the prime candidate to become the major league's first African-American manager.

The Cleveland Indians made this a reality when they traded for Robinson in 1975 and installed him as their player-manager. After a brief time, Robinson hung up his spikes and stuck to managerial duties. He did not achieve great success in Cleveland nor in a subsequent stop at San Francisco, but he gained redemption by winning the 1989 Manager of the Year Award with the Baltimore Orioles.

Robinson finished his 21-year career with 586 home runs, behind only Aaron, Mays, and Babe Ruth among career sluggers. In addition, he posted a .294 lifetime average, stole 204 bases, and was hit by 203 pitches. Those numbers easily earned him entry into baseball's Hall of Fame in 1982. He has continued managing with the Montreal Expos and the new Washington Nationals, leading these talent-poor teams to records far beyond expectations.

Further Reading

Mabundi, L. Mpho. *Contemporary Black Biography.* Vol. 9. Detroit: Gale Research, 1995.

Robinson, Frank, with Al Silverman. *My Life in Baseball.* New York: Doubleday, 1968.

Schneider, Russell J. *Frank Robinson.* New York: Coward, McCann, Geoghegan, 1976.

Robinson, Jackie

(Jack Roosevelt Robinson)
(1919–1972) *baseball second baseman*

Jackie Robinson is universally recognized as the man most responsible for creating opportunities for African-American athletes in professional sports. As the subject of major league baseball's great experiment, he had to survive the crushing burden of expectations while living in public isolation, and to endure without complaint insults and ridicule at every turn. Robinson's grace under this pressure shattered most of the remaining social barriers for African Americans in sports and led longtime sports broadcaster Howard Cosell to say, "Who was the greatest all-around athlete this nation has ever produced? I say Jackie Robinson, also the greatest all-around man."

He was born Jack Roosevelt Robinson on January 31, 1919, in a cabin in Cairo, Georgia, the youngest of five children of poor sharecroppers, Mallie and Jerry Robinson. Jerry disappeared before Jackie reached his first birthday. Left to fend for herself, Mallie packed up her family in the spring of 1920 and moved to Pasadena, California, where she found work as a maid for a wealthy family.

The Robinson children had to learn to deal with racial discrimination in many forms. Pasadena's public swimming pool, for example, was open to blacks only on Tuesdays. After spending four years in a segregated neighborhood, the Robinsons moved into an exclusively white area of town, where the neighbors, at first, tried to circulate a petition to get them to leave. Growing up, Jackie got into many fights while defending himself against racial slurs.

Robinson drew inspiration in his athletic endeavors from his older brother, Mack, who won a silver medal in the 200 meters in the 1936 Olympics, finishing second to JESSE OWENS. Jackie actually began surpassing Mack's feats at John Muir High School and then at Pasadena Junior College, where he competed in baseball, football, and basketball in addition to track. He then moved on to the University of California at Los Angeles (UCLA), where he became the school's first four-sport letterman. Football was his highest-profile sport. As a junior, he averaged 11 yards per carry while playing running back, and he led the conference in scoring. As a senior, he finished second in the conference in total offense (running and passing combined) and repeated as scoring champ. He also earned national recognition by winning the National Collegiate Athletic Association (NCAA) title in the long jump in 1940. As a measure of his versatility, he even captured his conference's golf championship one year.

However, Robinson could not see a stable future for a black athlete in professional sports, and he was skeptical about the opportunities a college education might offer him. As a result, he left school before graduation and got a job as an assistant playground director. He then moved to Hawaii, where he played on a semipro football team, working on a housing construction crew during the week to support himself. With World War II heating up in the Pacific, he was then drafted into the army in 1942. Aware of his athletic reputation, his army post asked him to play on their football team, but after being threatened with a court-martial for refusal to sit in the back of the army bus, the proud Robinson declined.

After his discharge from the service in 1945, Robinson signed a contract with the Kansas City Monarchs baseball club of the Negro League. He hated the constant travel and meager pay, and he had made up his mind to quit at the end of the year when he received an unexpected offer. Branch Rickey, general manager of the Brooklyn Dodgers, had decided to defy major league baseball's unwritten 60-year ban on hiring black ball players, and he was looking for an exceptional player to lead the way. He focused on Robinson because of Jackie's tremendous all-around athletic talent, his strong character, and his experience in sports with whites as a college running back.

Before offering him a contract, Rickey described the pressure and abuse Robinson would have to face. If Robinson was not strong enough to hold up under this treatment without losing his temper or fighting back, then, Rickey said, it would not be worth the effort. Robinson agreed to give it his best shot and signed a contract in 1946. He was assigned to the Montreal Royals of the

Jackie Robinson's courageous pioneering efforts in major league baseball in 1947 opened the door to African-American success in pro sports. *(National Baseball Hall of Fame Library, Cooperstown, N.Y.)*

Class AAA International League for the season. Although Montreal was fairly accepting of Robinson, he experienced exactly what Rickey had envisioned for him on the road. At one ballpark a fan threw a black cat onto the field and screamed, "Here's your cousin." As he had promised Rickey, Robinson kept his cool. He doubled in his next at bat and scored. As he passed the fan he remarked, "Guess my cousin's happy now." Such episodes, however, took a severe emotional toll.

Many longtime baseball experts derided Robinson's signing as merely a publicity stunt and predicted Robinson would fail because blacks simply were not as skilled as whites. Robinson shattered that myth by leading the league in batting with a .349 average and topping the league in fielding percentage at a position he had never played before—second base.

The next step was the major leagues, but there were rumblings that baseball would never allow a black man to play. Some of the Dodgers said they would quit if Robinson joined the team, and the Saint Louis Cardinals tried to organize a boycott. But although the former commissioner Kenesaw Landis had strongly opposed integration, the new commissioner, Happy Chandler, supported it. He squelched opposition to Robinson by threatening stiff penalties for players who refused to play with him.

When Robinson made his major league debut with the Dodgers on April 15, 1947, he went hitless in four at-bats and hit into a double play. Critics smugly crowed that he could not play at the major league level. Robinson and his family received hate mail and verbal abuse from opposing players that was relentless. In his autobiography, *I Never Had It Made*, Robinson said, "I had to fight hard against loneliness, abuse, and the knowledge that any mistake I made would be magnified because I was the only black man out there." Robinson, who had always fought back at any affronts to his dignity, was sorely tempted to fight back against his tormentors and to quit the sport altogether.

The virulence of the racists backfired on them. The Philadelphia Phillies were so vicious in their heckling of Robinson that they shocked and outraged even Jackie's southern Dodger teammates. The Dodgers sympathized with Robinson and gradually united around him, particularly when they saw how well he could play baseball. With his speed and daring, Robinson played an exciting brand of baseball. The Dodgers set major league attendance records as fans flocked to see Robinson play. By the end of his first season, one national poll found him to be the second most popular man in the United States. Robinson led the National League in stolen bases with 29 that year, batting .297 with 12 home runs to earn the league's Rookie of the

Year honor and helping the Dodgers win the National League pennant.

Robinson enjoyed his finest season in 1949, when he led the National League in batting with a sizzling .349 average, drove in 124 runs, and was voted the league's Most Valuable Player. Having established that he belonged in the major leagues, he no longer meekly accepted slurs and fought back. "I never cared about acceptance as much as I cared about respect," he explained.

Once Robinson exploded the myths about African-American inferiority, the door was immediately opened for other black athletes in pro baseball. The Dodgers, having anticipated the result, were ahead of their rivals in scouting blacks. Robinson and those black athletes who followed him to Brooklyn, such as ROY CAMPANELLA and DONALD NEWCOMBE played a vital role in propelling the Dodgers to the top of the National League; Brooklyn won six pennants between 1947 and 1956.

Of all Robinson's skills, it was his baserunning that most electrified fans. According to longtime broadcaster Red Smith, "He [Robinson] was the only base runner of his time who could bring a game to a stop just by getting on base." In an era when few teams employed base stealing as a weapon, Robinson stole 197 career bases. He perfected the difficult art of stealing home, accomplishing the feat 11 times in his 10-year career.

Robinson retired in 1956 rather than accept a trade to the rival New York Giants. Despite his legendary status, no one in baseball offered him a job. He spent his remaining years involved in various business enterprises, such as a construction company specializing in housing for blacks, and in social and political causes. In 1962 Robinson became the first African American elected to baseball's Hall of Fame. He died of a heart attack in 1972 at the age of 53. Elston Howard, himself the first African American to play for the New York Yankees, summed up the debt of gratitude that minority professional athletes owe to Robinson: "He meant everything to a black ballplayer. I don't think the young players today would go through what he did."

Further Reading

Falkner, David. *Great Time Coming: The Life of Jackie Robinson from Baseball to Birmingham.* New York: Simon & Schuster, 1995.

Frommer, Harvey. *Rickey and Robinson.* New York: Macmillan, 1982.

Rampersad, Arnold. *Jackie Robinson: A Biography.* New York: Knopf, 1997.

Robinson, Jackie, as told to Alfred Duckett. *I Never Had It Made.* New York: Putnam, 1972.

Robinson, Rachel, with Lee Daniels. *Jackie Robinson: An Intimate Portrait.* New York: Abrams, 1996.

Tygiel, Jules. *Baseball's Great Experiment: Jackie Robinson and His Legacy.* New York: Oxford University Press, 1983.

Robinson, Sugar Ray
(Walker Smith, Jr.)
(1921–1989) *boxer*

Sugar Ray Robinson was the fighter who inspired the common sports cliché "Pound for pound, the best." Even HENRY ARMSTRONG, himself ranked among boxing's elite, admitted after losing a fight to Robinson, "I couldn't have handled Robinson on the best night I ever had."

Robinson was born on May 30, 1921, as Walker Smith, Jr., to Walker Smith, Sr., and Leila Smith, Georgia sharecroppers who had moved to Detroit, Michigan, seeking work and had found little success. Smith's first exposure to boxing was as a youngster when he hung around the Brewster Gym, where the neighborhood hero, JOE LOUIS, worked out. His parents separated, and in 1932, Smith moved with his mother and two sisters to live in Harlem, New York.

Fascinated by the dancing of Bojangles Robinson, Smith began dancing his own routines on the streets to earn money for his cash-strapped

Boxing experts rank Sugar Ray Robinson as the greatest boxer of all time. *(Allsport Hulton Deutsch/Getty Images)*

family. At age 13, he drifted into boxing under the supervision of the Police Athletic League and eventually joined the Salem-Crescent Boxing Club. On one occasion, his coach took him to a boxing match where they discovered that one of the fighters had canceled at the last minute. His coach volunteered Smith as a substitute. Since he needed to be an Amateur Athletic Union (AAU) member to participate in the event, the coach gave him the AAU card of the recently retired Ray Robinson. Fighting under that name, he won, and he decided to continue boxing under that name. Later a reporter provided his famous nickname by remarking to his coach, "You got a mighty sweet boy there, sweet as sugar," inspiring the name "Sugar Ray Robinson."

Robinson fought 125 amateur fights, winning the Golden Gloves featherweight title in 1939 and the lightweight title in 1940. He turned pro in October 1940 and won his first 40 bouts, 28 of them by knockout. Among his victories was a win over lightweight champion Sammy Angott in their title fight of July 1941.

In his boxing style, Robinson combined the nimble footwork of his dancing talent with an ability to mix powerful punches in deadly combinations. Randolph Sugar, author of *The Hundred Greatest Boxers of All Time*, wrote, "Robinson could deliver a knockout blow going backward. His footwork was superior to any that had been seen in boxing up to that time. His hand speed and leverage were unmatchable."

Robinson's 40-bout streak came to an end on February 5, 1943, when he fought rugged Jake LaMotta for the second time and lost. After this defeat, Robinson launched an even more impressive unbeaten streak of 89 fights over the next eight years. This streak was sandwiched around his induction into the U.S. Army at the end of 1943. Because of his fame, he was assigned to join heavyweight champion JOE LOUIS in a series of exhibition matches to entertain the troops. When he discovered that the segregated army had arranged an exhibition for a whites-only audience, he refused to box until blacks were allowed to attend. He was discharged from the service in June 1944.

Although he started out as a lightweight, Robinson reached his peak as a welterweight in the mid-1940s. He earned the welterweight title in December 1946 by gaining a 15-round decision over Tommy Bell and held it until he moved up to the 160-pound middleweight class a few years later. In 1950 he added the middleweight title to his collection by defeating champion Robert Villemain.

On February 14, 1951, Robinson took on Jake LaMotta in a renewal of their fierce rivalry. In one of boxing's most memorable bouts, the two waged a furious, even battle until the 10th round, when

Robinson began to take over; he finally stopped LaMotta in the 13th round. The two fought six times in their career; Robinson won five times.

Robinson lost and regained the title four times in the highly competitive middleweight division. In 1951 he lost a decision to Randy Turpin but avenged the defeat the following year with a dramatic come-from-behind knockout in the 10th round. After losing to Joey Maxim in 1953, he won back his title with a seventh-round knockout of Bobo Olson in 1955. After a loss to Gene Fullmer in 1957, the 35-year-old Robinson came back to score a fifth-round knockout in their rematch four months later. In 1957 he lost a 15-round decision to Carmen Basilio only to win back his title the following year in another 15-round marathon.

As a handsome, flashy celebrity with a good business mind, Robinson acquired a string of outside business interests including a night club, dry cleaning shop, lingerie shop, and barber shop. Yet he was such a generous, free-spending individual that he was constantly short of money and, as a result, had to continue boxing to earn a living far past his prime. "I went through four million dollars," he once said, "but I have no regrets. I didn't gamble away my money; I used it to let people live." His late-career losses, including five defeats in his last six months at the age of 44, marred an otherwise sparkling career record. Even so, he finished his pro career with 175 victories and only 19 losses. During a long career that lasted until 1965, Robinson was never knocked out. He prided himself both on his defensive skills and on his ability to take a punch; the only time he did not finish a fight was when he was far ahead on points but collapsed of exhaustion in the 100-degree heat in the 14th round against a larger light heavyweight opponent at Yankee Stadium.

In 1969 he took advantage of his fame to found the Sugar Ray Robinson Youth Foundation in inner city Los Angeles. The effects of diabetes and Alzheimer's disease took their toll on Robinson in his later years and he died on April 18,

1989. But he left a legacy and a style of boxing that inspired fighters such as MUHAMMAD ALI. Both the Boxing Writers of America and the editors of *Ring* magazine rank him as the best boxer of all time.

Further Reading

Robinson, Sugar Ray. *Sugar Ray.* New York: Viking, 1970.

Robinson, Sugar Ray, and Dave Anderson. *Sugar Ray.* New York: Da Capo, 1994.

Rothe, Anna, ed. *Current Biography 1951.* New York: H. W. Wilson, 1951.

Rudolph, Wilma Goldean
(Wilma Glodean Rudolph)
(1940–1994) *track-and-field sprinter*

Like many girls her age, Wilma Rudolph had never heard of the Olympics until she was asked to try out for the U.S. Olympic team in 1956. By the time her running career was finished, millions of young girls throughout the world dreamed of competing in the Olympics. It was Rudolph who was largely responsible for the change. The speed, grace, and beauty she displayed in the first internationally televised Olympic Games in 1960 inspired a generation of black girls to begin dreaming of gold medals.

Wilma Goldean Rudolph had to overcome tremendous odds to earn athletic success. She was born on June 23, 1940, in Saint Bethlehem, Tennessee, the 20th of 22 children of Edward and Blanche Rudolph. Shortly after Wilma was born, the family moved to nearby Clarksville. Ed worked as a porter on the railroads, and Blanche worked as a housekeeper for wealthy families. The income they made was barely enough to keep the family fed. Their house had an outhouse in the back for a bathroom and no electricity. Blanche sewed the children clothes out of flour sacks.

During her younger years, Wilma was sick almost constantly. Before she reached age five, she battled double pneumonia, whooping cough, scarlet fever, and, worst of all, polio, which cost her the full use of her left leg. At five, she was fitted with a heavy steel brace and special shoes to help her walk. She continued to get sick so often that she was unable to attend school until second grade.

In her autobiography, Rudolph states, "I think I started acquiring a competitive spirit right then and there, a spirit that would make me successful in sports later on. I was mad, and I was going to beat these illnesses no matter what." Her family helped fight. For two years, her mother scheduled regular day-long trips to Nashville, where Wilma endured four hours of therapy. Each day, her mother, brothers, and sisters took turns giving her leg massages to stimulate its development. On her own, Rudolph practiced walking without a limp.

The efforts paid off. As a nine-year-old, Rudolph left her brace at home and walked unaided down the church aisle, a day she remembered as one of the happiest of her life. She continued to wear the brace and the special shoes off and on for a few more years whenever her legs hurt. One day, her mother went home to find her 11-year-old daughter playing basketball barefoot. Within a year, Wilma discarded the brace and shoes for good. Rudolph entered the seventh grade at segregated Burt High School feeling as though she had been released from a lifelong prison.

Rudolph joined the basketball team along with an older sister. During the 1950s, girls were not encouraged to play sports in the United States. Burt High School had only one girls' basketball team, and it included players from 7th to 12th grade. This meant that younger players like Rudolph, unable to compete with much older girls, had to spend their early years sitting on Coach Clinton Gray's bench. When Rudolph cracked into the starting lineup in 10th grade, though, she did so with a vengeance. Her long arms and legs, along with her relentless defense, earned her the nickname "Skeeter." She used her

Wilma Rudolph's spectacular performance at the 1960 Rome Olympics sparked a tradition of gold-medal success for African-American women sprinters. *(Allsport/Getty Images)*

speed to race past defenders and average more than 32 points a game. Not only did she win All-State honors, but she led her team to the state championship.

Among the referees who watched her play was Ed Temple, a track coach, who had built a powerhouse women's track team at Tennessee State University. Impressed with her speed, he visited her home in the spring of 1956 to offer her the chance to participate in his summer track program, all expenses paid.

The program culminated in a trip to the Amateur Athletic Union (AAU) national cham-pionships in Philadelphia. In her first visit to a large city, Rudolph overcame her awe to place first in the 75-yard dash, the 100-yard dash, and the 4 × 110 relay. This led Temple to urge her to participate in the U.S. Olympic trials later that year. Although she had never heard of the Olympics, Rudolph followed his advice and qual-ified for the team in both the 200 meters and the 4 × 100 relay.

The 1956 Olympics in Melbourne, Australia, was a humbling experience for the 16-year-old prodigy. Accustomed to winning all her races, she was stunned when she finished third in the second round of preliminaries for the 200 meters, elimi-nating her from further competition. She salvaged her pride somewhat by running the third leg on the United States's bronze-medal-winning relay. But she returned home determined to make her-self the best female sprinter in the world.

Rudolph's quest was nearly derailed by a series of unexpected events. Shortly after gradua-tion from high school, she discovered she was pregnant by her boyfriend. Then, after delivering the baby and enrolling at Tennessee State, she suf-fered a leg injury that sidelined her for most of the 1958 season.

Rudolph recovered in 1959, winning another national AAU title in the 100-yard dash. But as the 1960 Rome Olympics drew near, injury and illness struck again. She pulled a hamstring mus-cle in a dual meet between the United States and Soviet Union, then fell violently ill after having her tonsils removed. Rudolph fought through those setbacks with her usual tenacity and showed up for the U.S. Olympic trials at Texas Christian University in the best shape of her life. She easily won the 100-meter race and then shattered the world record while capturing the 200 meters in a time of 22.9. Rudolph also earned the right to run the final leg of the 4 × 100 relay.

Temperatures at the Stadio Olimpico in Rome soared over 100 degrees Fahrenheit, but the heat did not bother Rudolph, who had been train-ing all her life in hot Tennessee summers. For the first time in history, television cameras were recording the events of the Olympics and relaying them by satellite to a curious audience back in the United States. The television producers could not have dreamed up a better performer than Rudolph. With her long, graceful strides; blazing speed; and sunny disposition, she quickly captured the viewers' hearts.

Rudolph breezed through the preliminaries of the 100 meters, tying the world record of 11.3 seconds in the semifinals. In the finals, she started slowly, as usual. While her shorter opponents blasted out of the starting blocks, Rudolph took a few seconds to get her long legs into a rhythm. Once she did, she glided past her opponents so easily that she appeared to have another gear beyond the normal sprinter. Rudolph broke the tape in 11.0 seconds, far ahead of the second-place finisher, Dorothy Hyman of Great Britain. Her time would have smashed the world record except that the tail wind was over the allowable limit.

Rudolph then set an Olympic record of 23.2 in the opening heat of the 200 meters. By this time, she was so relaxed that she fell asleep waiting for her semifinal heat. Rudolph won the 200 meters even more convincingly than she had won the 100, beating Jutta Heine of Germany by 0.4 seconds, although a muddy track slowed her time to 24.0.

Nicknamed "La Gazella Nera" (The Black Gazelle) by the admiring Italian crowds, she capped her Olympics with a furious sprint in the 4 × 100-meter relay. After nearly dropping the baton and disqualifying the team in the final baton exchange, she came from behind to give her Tigerbelle teammates the gold medal in a world-record-tying 44.4 seconds. The victory made Rudolph the first U.S. woman to win three track-and-field gold medals in one Olympics.

Her stunning performance made her famous, and she was honored with parades and ceremonies in a number of cities around the world. None meant more to her than the parade held in

her honor back at her hometown of Clarksville. It was the first racially integrated event in the city's history.

Rudolph went on to set world records of 6.8 seconds in the 60-yard dash and 11.2 seconds in the 100 meters. The Associated Press named her Female Athlete of the Year in both 1960 and 1961, and she won the Sullivan Award as the United States's top amateur athlete in 1961. After retiring from the sport, she raised four children and formed a foundation that worked with the Indianapolis school system to help the disadvantaged through sports and education. "I wanted to leave behind a legacy, and I thought this would be ideal," she said. A more visible legacy is the long string of outstanding black American women sprinters, from EVELYN ASHFORD to FLORENCE GRIFFITH JOYNER, who were inspired by Rudolph's courageous efforts to take up the sport. Rudolph died on November 12, 1994, of a brain tumor.

Further Reading

Condon, Robert J. *Great Women Athletes of the 20th Century.* Jefferson, N.C.: McFarland, 1999.

"Fastest Female," *Time,* September 9, 1960, pp. 74–75.

Moritz, Charles, ed. *Current Biography 1961.* New York: H. W. Wilson, 1961.

Temple, Ed. *Only the Pure in Heart Survive.* Nashville, Tenn.: Broadman Press, 1980.

Russell, Bill
(William Felton Russell)
(1934–) *basketball center*

Bill Russell demonstrated the value of a strong interior defense in basketball; indeed, many sports authorities credit him with inventing it. A proud, defiant figure who neither catered to fans nor hid behind any false modesty, he nonetheless emerged as the "good guy" in his classic rivalry with WILT CHAMBERLAIN. Most of all, Russell is remembered for his unyielding will to succeed. "They can talk about individual players in any sports," said bas-

Although he did not have an outstanding individual record, Bill Russell enjoyed more team success than any other athlete in pro sports history. *(Basketball Hall of Fame)*

ketball Hall of Fame guard Jerry West. "But I tell you that when it comes to winning, there is no one like Bill Russell."

William Felton Russell was born on February 12, 1934, in Monroe, Louisiana, where his father, Charles, worked as a laborer in a paper bag factory. Despite his lowly status, Charles Russell bristled at the indignities heaped upon him by society, such as an incident in which his wife, Katie, was ordered out of town for "dressing like a white woman," and his resentment made a lasting impression on Bill. Fed up with degrading treatment, the Russell family moved to Oakland, California, when Bill was young. They started out living in an eight-room house with eight other families until Charles was able to establish a trucking business.

Katie and Charles Russell, however, soon separated. When Katie then died at the age of 32,

Charles had to give up the business to care for his two sons, nine-year-old Bill and his older brother, Charlie.

The two brothers became close, and Bill tried to follow in Charlie's footsteps as a star basketball player. The problem was, however, that he apparently had no aptitude for the game. At Hoover Junior High School, the gangly youngster failed to make the team. With little supervision from his harried father, who was now working at a foundry, Russell drifted into trouble. He credits George Powles, basketball coach at all-black McClymonds High School, with saving him from a criminal life. Although Russell did not show the ability to make the 15-person basketball roster, Powles saw enough raw ability to allow him to share the 15th spot on the team with another player; the two even shared a single jersey.

Russell's hard work and his eventual height of six feet, nine inches, helped him finally crack into the starting lineup as a senior. Even then, however, Russell appeared to have little future in the game. He made no all-star teams. According to Russell, an offer from the local University of San Francisco (USF), a tiny school with so little basketball tradition that it did not even have its own gym, "was the only scholarship I was offered, and I took it because I couldn't have gone to college any other way."

Russell began attending USF in 1952. He and his roommate, K. C. Jones, soon propelled the school's basketball program out of obscurity. With Jones providing perimeter defense and Russell dominating the paint, the Dons won two straight National Collegiate Athletic Association (NCAA) championships amid an astounding run of 55 consecutive victories. By the time he graduated in 1956, Russell was widely regarded as one of the top college players in the land. Before turning pro, he joined the U.S. Olympic team and was a key factor in the team's gold medal victory in the 1956 Melbourne Olympics.

Boston Celtics coach Red Auerbach recognized that Russell's ability to control the lane was the key to the type of fast-break basketball he wanted the Celtics to play. In 1956, he swapped two starters, Ed McCauley and Cliff Hagan, to the Saint Louis Hawks for their second-round draft choice, with which he selected Russell. Although Russell received the highest salary paid to a National Basketball Association (NBA) rookie at that time (roughly $20,000), life as the only black player on the Celtics was not easy; Russell was excluded from virtually all team interactions except games and practices. He responded with a steely demeanor and a rugged individualism. He went public with his criticism of the NBA for its unacknowledged quota system that limited black players in the league. He defied convention by being the only player in the league to wear a beard, and even when he became popular, he made no effort to cooperate with the media or fans. "I owe the public nothing, and I'll pay them nothing," he insisted.

While basketball fans and even players and coaches of the time tended to focus mainly on offensive production, Russell demonstrated the value of defense. He was never a high scorer; during his career he averaged about 15 points per game with a season high of 18.9. Russell never developed an outside shot and his lifetime free throw percentage was a paltry 55 percent. But he was the first person to perfect the art of the blocked shot and the intimidating defense. He combined hair-trigger reflexes, a wide wingspan, and penetrating intelligence to turn the basket area into a no-man's-land. "Defense is a science and not a helter skelter thing you just luck into," he explained to those who wondered how he was so successful.

Blocked shots were so innovative that statistics on them were not kept in Russell's time, and so the extent of his dominance in this area cannot be quantified. But the effect on opponents was obvious. Opposing players found they could not drive to the basket and had to settle for outside shots. Those who challenged him often had their shots tipped away and grabbed by Russell, who then fed the Celtic guards streaking downcourt for uncontested layups.

Russell was such an intense player that he often became violently ill before games, especially important ones. Yet he always overcame it to play at a high level. It took Russell no time at all to show what an intimidating force in the middle meant to a basketball team. During his rookie season, while Russell averaged only 14.7 points per game, he led the league in rebounding with an average of 19.6, and the Celtics stormed into the NBA finals. There, in the deciding game seven of their contest against Saint Louis, Russell owned the backboards, grabbing 32 rebounds to go with his 19 points as the Celtics took their first championship.

He simply overwhelmed all opponents defensively during the next three seasons. He collected 22.7 rebounds per game in 1957–58, more than six better than his closest rival in this category. Most basketball experts point to his injury in game three of the championship series as the reason why Boston failed to defend its title that year. But they bounced back the following season, as Russell upped his rebounding average even higher to 23.0, and swept the Lakers in four straight games for the title.

The next year saw the arrival of WILT CHAMBERLAIN and the beginning of what is widely conceded to be the greatest individual rivalry in sport. Chamberlain, three inches taller and 50 pounds heavier than Russell, was an offensive machine who destroyed all NBA scoring records. His titanic battles against the game's greatest defensive player made for high drama. Chamberlain nearly always won the statistical duel. He even outdid his rival in Russell's specialty of rebounds, beating him out for the league title in that category in all but two seasons of their 10-year rivalry. Russell's team, however, nearly always won the game. Their rivalry came to be viewed as a moral lesson, as Russell was depicted as the hardworking team player and Chamberlain was viewed as a selfish individual.

The dichotomy was largely exaggerated; Russell usually played with better teammates than did Chamberlain. On the other hand, Russell's will to win—his ability to work with and inspire teammates and his ability to control a game at the crucial time—is unparalleled in sports. No other player in sports can match his record of winning 11 championships in 13 seasons, including eight in a row from 1959 to 1966.

Russell's value to the team was such that the Celtics made him player-coach in 1966, the first African-American coach in modern professional sports history. When the Celtics lost to Chamberlain's Philadelphia 76ers that season and their talent pool was drying up, it appeared that the great dynasty was finally dead. But Russell revived the Celtics, and, although they were not the most talented team, they prevailed again in 1968 and 1969. Not until Russell retired after that season did the Celtics era finally end.

Russell remained outspoken and independent throughout his career, with an attitude that earned him his share of enemies. "Because I've been uniquely successful and not very humble about it, people got tired of my success," he noted. Yet his value as a player has never been questioned. No other player with such modest offensive numbers has ever won the NBA's Most Valuable Player Award. Russell won it five times, including three straight seasons from 1961 to 1963 when Chamberlain was scoring baskets in droves. He won four rebounding titles, maintained an average of more than 20 rebounds per game for 11 seasons, and holds the NBA playoff record of 40 rebounds in a game.

There was never any question that Russell deserved to be in basketball's Hall of Fame, but he nearly did not get there. True to his defiant nature, Russell insisted he wanted no part of the Hall of Fame and fought against being inducted, but he was voted in against his will in 1974. He has held many administrative basketball positions since, including head coach at Sacramento, and has been recognized as one of the sport's most engaging television analysts.

Further Reading

Russell, Bill, and David Falkner. *Russell Rules: 11 Lessons on Leadership from the Twentieth Century's Greatest Winner.* New York: Penguin, 2001.

Russell, Bill, with William McSweeny. *Go Up for Glory.* New York: Coward, McCann, 1968.

Russell, Bill, with Taylor Branch. *Second Wind: The Memoirs of an Opinionated Man.* New York: Random House, 1979.

S

Sanders, Barry David
(1968–) *football running back*

The National Football League (NFL) has never seen another running back as exciting as Barry Sanders; nor has it ever known a more reluctant star. Sanders turned every handoff into an adventure and a high-stakes gamble. He lost more yards yet made more exciting long runs than any other back in pro history.

Barry David Sanders was born on July 16, 1968, in Wichita, Kansas. He was the seventh of 11 children of William Sanders, a carpenter and roofer, and his wife, Shirley, a strongly religious homemaker. Barry began playing football in fourth grade but was hampered in sports throughout his childhood by his unusually small size. On entering high school, he was only five feet tall and weighed barely 100 pounds. Although he grew to five feet, seven inches and 155 pounds as a junior, he was relegated to the bench at Wichita North High School in favor of his older brother Byron, who was the team's star running back.

Barry, in fact, was not given a chance to start at running back until the last five games of his senior year. Despite his late start, he finished second in the city in rushing. That success was too little, too late, to interest many college coaches, particularly given his size. Sanders put together a highlight tape of his runs to promote himself, but only two schools, Oklahoma State and Wichita State, expressed any interest.

In 1986, Sanders ended up at Oklahoma State, where he took his accustomed position on the bench as a freshman behind future All-Pro running back Thurman Thomas. As a sophomore, Sanders made good use of his few opportunities, beginning with a touchdown on the first kick-off return of the season. With Thomas gone to the pros in 1988, Sanders finally was able to win the running back position for himself. He started the season auspiciously by returning the season's first kick-off for a touchdown. Then, suddenly, college football fans began reading about a previously unknown running back gulping yardage and scoring touchdowns at a seemingly impossible rate. Sanders ripped off 310 yards against Tulsa, 320 yards against Kansas State, 312 yards and five touchdowns against Kansas. Even the perennial champion of the Big Eight Conference, Nebraska, had no answer for this explosive little back, who gained 189 yards and scored four touchdowns against the Cornhuskers. Whereas no one in National Collegiate Athletic Association (NCAA) history had gained 300 yards in a game more than once, Sanders did so four times. Sanders finished the season owning or sharing 30 NCAA rushing records, including most touchdowns in a season (37) and most yards in a season (2,628). One year after serving as a reserve back,

The enigmatic and elusive Barry Sanders walked away from a chance to become pro football's leading career rusher. *(Jed Jacobsohn/Getty Images)*

Sanders was the runaway winner of the Heisman Trophy as college football's top player.

When Oklahoma State was slapped with severe sanctions for recruiting violations, Sanders decided to skip his senior season and turn pro. Again Sanders faced doubts about his size, but when the Detroit Lions discovered he had a 42-inch vertical leap to go with his size, they realized he was a special athlete. As for his size, one NFL coach later commented that, given his powerful 31-inch thighs, his stature was misleading. "He's a 280-pound man who was cut off at the knees and had his shoes put back on," said Floyd Peters.

"People who hit him around those thunder thighs just bounce off." The Lions made Sanders the third selection in the first round of the 1989 draft.

Being drafted by the Lions was not a particularly fortunate occurrence for Sanders. The Lions had been a woeful team for many years, and their run blocking had been so poor that no Lion back had gained 100 yards in any game over the past two seasons. Throughout his career, Sanders played on mediocre teams that had trouble making use of his vast talent.

Sanders proved to be an exceptionally principled and unselfish individual. On signing his contract, he immediately tithed 10 percent to his hometown Paradise Baptist Church in Wichita. At a time when elaborately choreographed end zone dances were routine after touchdowns, Sanders simply handed the ball to the officials after he scored. In the final game of his rookie season, when Sanders needed only 10 yards to claim the NFL rushing title with the game already in hand, he declined to go for the yards: he simply was not interested in statistics and awards. Nonetheless, he gained 1,470 yards, scored 14 touchdowns, and was named NFL Rookie of the Year.

Opposing defensive players dreaded playing against a runner who had the quickness of a waterbug yet packed immense power in his legs. As MIKE SINGLETARY, one of the game's surest tacklers, explained, "If you try to blast him, chances are he'll spin out of it and you'll end up looking silly." Since no other runner in the game could change directions and accelerate as Sanders did, there was no way for opponents to prepare for his runs.

In 1990 Sanders earned his first rushing title with 1,304 yards and scored a career-high 16 touchdowns. The following year, it was like old college times when he played against the Minnesota Vikings as he galloped for 220 yards in only 23 carries. He finished that season with 1,548 yards, just behind EMMITT SMITH.

Sanders maintained his string of 1,000-yard seasons in 1992 and 1993, and he then broke loose for his second rushing title in 1994, with

1,884 yards. He repeated as rushing champion in 1996 with 1,553 and then ran wild in 1997, with 2,053 yards, the third best single-season total in pro history. Even when the Lions stumbled to a 5–11 mark in 1998, Sanders continued on his record-setting string of rushing for 1,000 yards or more every year of his career.

The Lions' perpetual mediocrity prevented Sanders from ever playing in a Super Bowl. But by the 1999 season he had closed to within 1,500 yards of WALTER PAYTON's all-time rushing record. Having shown no signs of slowing down, Sanders was a good bet to break the mark in 1999 and, if not then, the next season for sure. But, unconcerned as usual with records, he decided he had played enough football and, without warning, announced his retirement. With that, the enigmatic Detroit back turned his back on glory and mysteriously disappeared from public life.

Further Reading

Dieffenback, Dan. "One on One . . . Barry Sanders," *Sport*, November 1994, p. 24.

Graham, Judith, ed. *Current Biography 1993*. New York: H. W. Wilson, 1993.

King, Peter. "Out Like a Lamb," *Sports Illustrated*, August 9, 1999, pp. 38–43.

Zimmerman, Paul. "Lion King," *Sports Illustrated*, December 8, 1997, pp. 62–3.

Sanders, Deion Luwynn

("Prime Time")
(1967–) *football defensive back, baseball outfielder*

Deion Sanders enjoyed greater success as a two-sport professional athlete than any U.S. athlete in history, including BO JACKSON and the legendary Jim Thorpe. Building on his tremendous foot speed and lightning reactions on the athletic field, he transformed himself into one of the most outrageous, highly visible, and profitable entertainment personalities around.

Deion Luwynn Sanders was born on August 9, 1967, in Fort Myers, Florida. His father, Mims Sanders, was addicted to drugs and walked out on the family when Deion was two. That left his mother, Constance, to raise him, working two jobs to do so until she remarried five years later. Although they lived in a poverty-ridden housing project in a tough, drug-ridden neighborhood, she tolerated no misbehavior by her son. When he got into trouble throwing bricks at windows, she made him stay all night in the police station rather than go there to collect him.

Deion loved sports at an early age, beginning with T-ball at age five. In 1977 the 10-year-old starred on a Pop Warner football team that won a national championship. At first a shy, courteous youngster, he grew enchanted with the boastful MUHAMMAD ALI and later patterned some of his behavior after Ali's.

Despite his obvious talent and speed, Sanders was relegated to the bench on his North Fort Myers High School football team as a sophomore; at only 130 pounds, he was considered too small to play. A tireless worker in practice, he eventually grew enough to allow his talent to take over. Sanders played both quarterback and safety on the football team, averaged 24 points per game in basketball, and was named All-State as a baseball player.

Sanders turned down an offer to play baseball in the Kansas City Royals' organization and chose to attend Florida State University on a football scholarship. While in school, he also played baseball and ran track, sometimes participating in both sports on the same day. As a sprinter, he even qualified to run in the U.S. Olympic trials in 1988, although he declined the chance. He was most interested in playing football. As a freshman, he cracked the starting lineup as a cornerback who also returned punts and kicks. By his junior year, Sanders was regarded as one of the top pass coverage men in college, and the New York Yankees liked his baseball ability well enough to sign him to a two-year contract.

Sanders stayed in college and was rewarded with a spectacular senior season in which he led the nation in punt return yardage and grabbed the Jim Thorpe Award as the best college defensive back. Although he played some baseball in the Yankees' organization, the Atlanta Falcons made him the fifth selection in the first round of the 1989 draft. Sanders entered his pro career with considerable fanfare, much of it self-generated. He sported the nickname "Prime Time" as a declaration of his ability to perform under pressure, and he boasted openly of his ability. He explained his showy attitude by saying, "I'm a business man and my product is Deion Sanders. Prime Time is the way I market that product."

Although he participated in no preseason training camp because of baseball commitments, Sanders backed up his bravado by scoring on a 68-yard punt return in his first National Football League (NFL) action. He was named to the All-Rookie team and voted the league's top kick returner that year. His defensive work earned him All-Pro honors in 1991.

Sanders's already high media visibility jumped another notch in 1992, when he enjoyed a stellar season with the Atlanta Braves baseball club. Sanders led the major leagues in triples with 14, batted .304, and stole 26 bases. He worked out a deal with football and baseball for two weeks in October, shuttling between the Falcons and the Braves, who were making a postseason run. Sanders became the only person ever to score a touchdown and hit a home run in a professional game in the same week. He tied a World Series record with six stolen bases and batted a robust .533 for the series. That same season, he again led the NFL in kickoff return yardage.

In 1993, Sanders topped the National League in pinch hitting with a .429 average. Then followed a season of transition during which he moved to the Cincinnati Reds in baseball and the San Francisco 49ers in football. He was named the NFL Defensive Player of the Year in 1994 for making six interceptions and running them back for a league-leading 303 yards and three touchdowns despite the fact that opponents rarely challenged his side of the field. He played a key role in San Francisco's Super Bowl championship that year.

While his baseball career began fading, Sanders signed a lucrative free agent deal with the NFL's Dallas Cowboys. At first, he merely provided stellar pass coverage as a cornerback in the Cowboys' championship season of 1995. But as injuries decimated the team's pass-receiving core in 1996, Sanders again displayed his versatility by taking on double duty as a wide receiver. He caught 36 passes for 475 yards that season in addition to being an All-Pro cornerback, and he provided a key score for Dallas in its Super Bowl win with a 47-yard touchdown catch. Sanders then returned to punt-returning duty and in 1998 led the league with a 15.6 average and two touchdowns.

Although primarily a defender who ranked as the top pass coverage man of his era, Sanders was a threat to score any time he was on the field. During his career, he scored eight touchdowns on interception returns, six on punts, and three on kickoffs. Veteran NFL coach Sam Wyche said of Sanders, "There's always the constant threat of what he's capable of doing that you must account for. I can't respect the guy any more than I do."

Sanders considerably modified his strutting image in his later career after suffering depression and then experiencing a religious reawakening. He completed his baseball career in Cincinnati in 2001 and retired from football the same year.

Further Reading

Bradley, J. E. "Lord of the Realm," *Sports Illustrated,* October 9, 1995, pp. 34–36.

Graham, Judith, ed. *Current Biography 1993.* New York: H. W. Wilson, 1993.

Sanders, Deion. *Power, Money and Sex: It's a Man's Thing.* Nashville, Tenn.: Thomas Nelson, 1998.

Sayers, Gale Eugene
(1943–   ) *football running back*

Gale Sayers enjoyed a short but scintillating career with the Chicago Bears. JIM BROWN, widely considered the best running back in football history, once commented, "Every runner I know, deep down, would like to run the way Gale Sayers did. No one has ever run prettier."

He was born Gale Eugene Sayers on May 30, 1943, in Wichita, Kansas, the middle of three boys born to Roger and Bernice Sayers. The couple was hoping for a girl and had the name Gale picked out, so they bestowed it upon their son instead. Roger's income as a mechanic and car polisher provided a meager living for the family. When Gale was young, the family spent a year caring for his grandfather in the tiny community of Speed, Kansas, where they were the only African Americans. They then moved to a poor section of Omaha, Nebraska, where his parents often fought and drank, and Bernice often left the family for weeks at a time.

Gale showed exceptional athletic potential at an early age and played with a highly skilled group of friends. Beginning with flag football in the fifth grade, Sayers's youth football teams never lost a game. At Central High School, one of two Omaha high schools open to blacks, he followed the example of his older brother Roger, who became one of the nation's top high school sprinters. Sayers also starred in track; as a senior he long jumped 24 feet, 11 ¾ inches, best among high schoolers in the country, and also won the state title in the low hurdles. Football, however, was his main passion. He led the city in scoring in both his junior and senior years, tallying 108 points as his team was undefeated in his senior year.

Widely recruited for both sports, Sayers enrolled at the University of Kansas in 1961. Before this time, he had been so focused on sports that he had paid little attention to academics. Sayers confesses that he had to cheat in order to stay academically eligible. During his sophomore year, however, he married Linda, his high school sweetheart who provided the motivation and stability for him to get through college.

As a sophomore, he set a Big Eight Conference mark by gaining 283 yards against Oklahoma State. His season total of 1,125 yards, at a gaudy average of 7.2 yards per carry, led the conference and earned Sayers mention on many All-America teams. As teams focused on stopping him, his totals actually regressed during the next two seasons, yet he retained his All-America status and finished his career with 2,675 yards.

Sayers entered pro football during the bidding wars between two rival leagues. He was drafted in the first round by both the Chicago Bears of the National Football League (NFL) and the Kansas City Chiefs of the American Football League (AFL) in 1965, and he chose to sign with the more established Bears. The Bears waited until the third game of the season to see what Sayers could do, and he responded with the most incredible rookie season the league had ever seen. The six-foot, one-inch, 200-pound Sayers had so many moves and the ability to employ them without slowing down in the least that he was virtually unstoppable in the open field. Comedian and football fan Bill Cosby explained what defenders experienced in trying to tackle him by saying, "He would throw the right side of his body on one side of the field and the left side of his body kept going down the left side." Chicago made use of this talent by using him as a kick returner and pass receiver as well as a runner.

In his rookie season, Sayers scored an NFL record 22 touchdowns in a variety of ways: 14 by rushing, six on pass catches, one on a punt return, and one on a kickoff return. Included in this total were six touchdowns, another league record, scored in a single game against the San Francisco 49ers. A unanimous choice as Rookie of the Year, Sayers finished the season with 867 rushing yards in only 166 carries for a 5.2-yard average and another 507 yards gained in pass receptions. With Sayers providing the fireworks, the Bears won nine of their last 10 games. Had they started Sayers from game one, they likely would have made the playoffs. Incredibly, despite boasting the game's top offensive player, Sayers, and the top defensive player, Dick Butkus, Chicago never reached the playoffs during Sayers's career.

Sayers's open-field magic was on display for the full season in 1968. He led the league in rushing with 1,231 yards and also topped the league in a kickoff return average at 31.2 yards. The following season his total rushing yards slipped to 880 as he was called upon to carry the ball only 186 times.

In 1968, Sayers shot off to the best start of his career. Early into the ninth game of the season, he had already gained 856 yards on only 134 carries for an eye-popping average of 6.2 yards per carry. However, in that game, San Francisco's Kermit Alexander rolled into Sayers's knee on a legal tackle, causing serious injury. Sayers worked hard to rehabilitate the knee and returned to action the following season. Tragedy of another sort struck that fall, however, when his backfield running mate and road roommate, Brian Piccolo, was diagnosed with terminal cancer. The story of the unique bond between Sayers and Piccolo, who was white, inspired the nation at a time of severe racial unrest, and it was documented in the popular motion picture *Brian's Song*. Sayers, playing in pain for a team that won only one game all season, led the NFL in both rushing attempts (236) and yards (1,032). For his efforts, he was voted the league's Comeback Player of the Year, an award that he gave to Piccolo's wife.

In the third game of 1970, Sayers injured his other knee. Although this injury forced his retirement after only seven seasons, he was inducted into the NFL Hall of Fame in 1977 and continues to be regarded as the best all-purpose open-field runner in NFL history.

Further Reading

Blinn, William. *Brian's Song: Screenplay*. Toronto: Bantam, 1972.
"Football's Rambling Rookie," *Ebony*, January 1966, pp. 70–71.
Henderson, Ashyia, ed. *Contemporary Black Biography*. Detroit, Mich.: Gale Research, 2001.
Sayers, Gale, with Al Silverman. *I Am Third*. New York: Viking, 1970.

Scurry, Briana Collette
(1971–   ) *soccer goalie*

When the United States women's soccer team made history by winning both the Olympics and the World Cup in the 1990s, it was Briana Scurry who provided that crucial last line of defense.

Briana Collette Scurry was born on September 7, 1971, in Minneapolis, Minnesota, to Ernest and Robbie Scurry. As a youngster, she enjoyed sports and while in the fourth grade was intrigued by a school flier that announced the formation of a soccer league. She was the only girl who signed up, and the coaches placed her at the goal, where they said she would be safer. The following season, enough girls signed up for her to play on a girls' team. There, she tried all positions but eventually returned to goalie.

During her senior year at Anoka High School in 1989, Scurry led her team to the Minnesota State High School girls soccer championship. Her efforts in that tournament, along with her performance as a basketball player, earned her an award as the state's top female athlete that year.

Although she enjoyed basketball and wished to play it in college, she grew to accept that her greater talent was as a goalie. On that basis, she accepted a soccer scholarship from the University of Massachusetts. She became the team's starting goalie during her sophomore season and allowed only nine goals in 19 games. The following year she split the goalie duties with another player and even played three games at forward. But she returned to full-time duty in the nets for her senior year and was nearly unbeatable. Only eight of her 23 opponents were able to score at all on her as she led Massachusetts to a 17–3–3 record and the semifinals of the National College Athletic Association (NCAA) tournament.

The U.S. national soccer team invited her to try out, and she wasted little time in earning the starting job at goalie. In March 1994, she made her international debut with a shutout against Portugal. Scurry finished the season with six more shutouts in 11 appearances.

Scurry provided the solid anchor for a U.S. team that improved steadily throughout the 1990s. In 1995, she posted two shutouts and a goals-allowed average of 0.81 as the team notched a respectable 3–1–1 record in World Cup play. The following year she was in goal every minute of Team USA's Olympic competition in Athens, Georgia. A gold medal had seemed so out of the question that Scurry had vowed to run naked through the streets if the team won. The words echoed back to haunt her as the team rolled to a 4–0–1 mark to claim the gold.

Scurry continued to be the mainstay of Team USA's defense throughout the 1990s. She recorded 7 shutouts and a 10–1 mark in 1997, 12 shutouts and a 15–1–2 record in 1998, and 11 shutouts and a 17–2–1 record in 1999. The highlight of her career occurred in the prestigious World Cup championship in 1999. Scurry's reflexes thwarted the Brazilians on several scoring opportunities in the semifinals. Then, when the United States and China finished the championship game deadlocked, the title went down to a series of one-on-one penalty kicks against the goalies. It was Scurry's stop of China's third penalty kick that opened the door for the U.S. players to shoot their way to victory. With four shutouts in six games, and a goals-allowed average of only 0.47, Scurry easily won recognition as the World Cup All-Star goalie. Scurry then played on the 2004 U.S. Olympic team that earned a gold medal.

Further Reading

Wahl, G. "She's a Keeper," *Sports Illustrated*, July 12, 1999, pp. 36–38.

Farber, M. "Score One for Women," *Sports Illustrated*, August 12, 1996, pp. 34–36.

Sifford, Charles Luther
(1922–) *golfer*

Probably no athlete in modern times suffered so cruelly from racial prejudice as Charles Sifford. His battle to become the first man to crack into the elite professional golf circuit was so draining that he observed, "There's not a man on this tour who could have gone through what I went through to be a golfer."

He was born Charles Luther Sifford on June 2, 1922, in a racially mixed neighborhood of Charlotte, North Carolina. At age 10, he became a caddy at the Carolina Country Club, and he learned to play on the days when the course was closed and caddies were allowed to play. He became so good that in 1939 the members asked him to leave rather than allow him to show up white players. Sifford then moved to Philadelphia, where he caddied, taught golf, and honed his game on public courses.

In the 1940s, he began playing in segregated tournaments. From 1948 to 1960, he won the Negro National Open six times. The Professional Golf Association (PGA), however, maintained its "Caucasians only" rules until the 1960s. It was Sifford who first challenged that rule, beginning in 1953, by playing in the few open tournaments that allowed blacks. In 1957 he won the Long Beach Open, which put pressure on the PGA to allow him on tour. "They had rules," remembers Sifford. "Every time I won, they changed the rules. I kept fighting them."

Only after a series of lawsuits in 1960 did the PGA relent. Well past his prime at the age of 37, Sifford finally was admitted to PGA events. Even then he had to deal with death threats and constant heckling, had to change clothes in his car, and was even turned away from some private courses where tournaments were held. While playing at the Greensboro Open in 1961, Sifford was harassed by two dozen hecklers who screamed at him for 16 holes before the authorities finally stepped in.

Throughout the 1960s, Sifford persevered. He was among the top 60 money winners on the tour each year, and his winnings allowed him to maintain his presence on the tour. In 1967, he shot a sizzling 64 on the final round of the Greater Hartford Open to become the first African American to win a major PGA tournament. Even then, Sifford could not overcome the deep-seated prejudice in the sport. Although his Hartford victory made him clearly eligible to play in the prestigious Masters Tournament, course officials rejected his application every year.

Despite all the obstacles, Sifford earned more than $350,000 in his years on the PGA tour. He did even better on the Senior Tour, which began in 1980, boosting his career earnings to more than $1.2 million. All the time, he could not help but think what he could have done if he been allowed to play when he was in his prime. For a while, he remained deeply frustrated by his failure to open up the game to blacks, only a few of whom followed him to the pro level. But the world of golf changed radically in the 1990s when TIGER WOODS arrived on the scene and became not only the best golfer but the most popular. As the man who opened the door for Woods and others, Sifford felt vindicated. "It's not important, I guess, that I didn't make it big," he said. "It's important that I made it."

Further Reading

Bigelow, Barbara Carlisle, ed. *Contemporary Black Biography*. Vol. 4. Detroit: Gale Research, 1993.

Henderson, Edwin B. *The Black Athlete: Emergence and Arrival*. New York: Publishers Company, 1968.

Simpson, O. J.
(Orenthal James Simpson, "The Juice")
(1947–) *football running back*

O. J. Simpson was a durable, yet electrifying running back who set many National Collegiate Athletic Association (NCAA) and National Football League (NFL) yardage records as a running back.

His engaging personality gave him media celebrity, which guaranteed that his subsequent trial for murder would be one of the most highly publicized criminal cases of all time and would leave an indelible stain on his once glorious career.

He was born Orenthal James Simpson on July 9, 1947, in San Francisco, California, where he was one of four children raised by a single mother employed as a social worker. A calcium deficiency left him with weak legs as a small child, and he had to wear braces for many years. Eventually, though, those legs developed into the fastest pair in the neighborhood. While at Everett Junior High School, Simpson broke the school record for the 60-yard dash.

His speed helped Simpson stay clear of trouble during his days as a leader of a gang known as the "Superiors." Simpson admitted that he "could easily have come to a bad end if I hadn't gotten a break." The break was excelling at sports at Galileo High School, both as a baseball catcher and as a football player. O. J., as he called himself because he disliked his unusual first name, played as a lineman for a brief time before coaches noticed his exceptional speed and placed him at running back.

He made All-City as a running back, but his grades were not good enough to get him into a major university. Instead, he enrolled in 1965 at City College of San Francisco, where he improved his academic credentials while running roughshod over the opposition. Simpson gained 2,445 yards for a staggering average of 9.9 yards a carry, and he scored 54 touchdowns during his two junior college seasons. He then moved on to the University of Southern California (USC), a school with a powerhouse football program and a reputation for running the football. According to the USC coach, John McKay, "We never had to drive O. J." The self-motivated Simpson became a workhorse for the Trojans, leading them to a number-one ranking in the nation and a Rose Bowl victory in 1967. He then set NCAA records for rushing attempts in a season with 355 (an average of more than 35 per game) and yards gained with 1,709. One of the fastest running backs ever to play the game, Simpson ran the 100-yard dash in 9.4 seconds during the track season and was a member of USC's world-record-setting 440 relay team. *Sport* magazine named him its Man of the Year that season, the first time a college player had ever won the award.

The Buffalo Bills then claimed Simpson with the first pick of the 1968 college draft. However, they inexplicably failed to make use of his talent. He carried the ball only 181 times for 697 yards in his rookie season, a tremendous disappointment. Matters grew even worse the following year when he gained only 488 yards on 120 carries. After a third season of underuse, the Bills hired a new coach, Lou Saban, who recognized Simpson's value. He began collecting large, mobile offensive linemen and then turned Simpson loose behind them. The line became known as "The Electric Company" because they were the ones who turned on "The Juice," as Simpson was nicknamed. Running with a rare combination of speed and timing, Simpson rushed 292 times for a league-leading 1,251 yards.

The following year he entered camp with a goal of gaining 1,700 yards, but his linemen had more grandiose ambitions—the NFL's first 2,000-yard rushing season, well beyond JIM BROWN's NFL record of 1,863 yards. With his excited linemen keeping close tabs on his yardage progress, Simpson closed in on the record. He not only passed Brown, but on December 16, 1973, in a game against the New York Jets he pushed his season total over the magic 2,000 mark. He took 332 carries to set the mark, giving him a robust average of 6.0 yards per carry.

Simpson's production fell off the next year, although he notched his third straight 1,000-yard season. But he bounced back in 1975 to enjoy a year that some regard as superior to his record-setting 1973 season. O. J. carried the ball 329 times for 1,817 yards to win his third rushing title. He added 426 yards on 28 catches and set an NFL

record with 23 touchdowns (16 rushing and seven on pass receptions). He enjoyed one final stellar year in 1976, with 1,503 yards in 290 carries, before his production declined rapidly. The Bills traded him to his hometown San Francisco team in 1978, but running behind poor blocking, he rarely found any daylight. After two seasons with the 49ers, he retired.

During his career, Simpson amassed 11,236 yards and 76 touchdowns. He was named All-Pro five consecutive seasons (1972–76), American Football Conference (AFC) Player of the Year three times (1972, 1973, 1975), and NFL Player of the Year in 1975. Despite his gaudy statistics, however, Simpson never had the luxury of playing on a championship team in the pros. The Bills never won even a divisional title during his tenure, and he played in only one playoff game.

Simpson's good looks and gregarious nature propelled him to a career as a media celebrity in commercials, as a network football commentator, and as a movie actor. But that world came crashing down in June 1994, with the murder of his ex-wife, Nicole Brown Simpson, and her friend Ronald Goldman. When Simpson was charged with the crime, that event triggered a sensational trial that consumed the U.S. media. The case dragged on for more than a year before Simpson was found not guilty. The public, however, was largely convinced of his culpability, an opinion reinforced when Simpson lost a civil trial in which he was held responsible for the murders and ordered to pay millions of dollars in damages. Simpson was forced to sell most of his belongings, including the Heisman Trophy he won as the nation's top college player in 1968, and has become a pariah on the American sports scene.

Further Reading

Cerasini, Marc A. *O. J. Simpson: An American Hero, American Tragedy.* New York: Windsor Publishing Company, 1994.

Darden, Christopher. *In Contempt.* New York: Harper-Collins, 1996.

Schiller, Lawrence. *American Tragedy: The Uncensored Story of the Simpson Defense.* New York: Random House, 1996.

Simpson, O. J. *I Want to Tell You: My Response to Your Letters, Your Messages, and Your Questions.* Boston: Little, Brown, 1995.

Toobin, Jeffrey. *The Run of His Life.* New York: Random House, 1996.

Singletary, Mike

(Michael Singletary, "Samurai")
(1958–   ) *football linebacker*

The Chicago Bears' defense of the mid-1980s did not simply stop opposing offenses; they dismantled them. The leader of this rampaging defense was Mike Singletary, a man with the brains to direct the complex Bears scheme yet so fierce a hitter that he became famous for broken helmets.

Michael Singletary was born on October 9, 1958, in Houston, Texas, the youngest of Charles and Rudell Singletary's 10 children. Living in their bleak ghetto on Houston's southeast side, Mike was a sickly child who constantly battled pneumonia. Although he loved to watch sports, there appeared to be little chance that he would ever play them. His father, a stern Pentecostal preacher, believed that play was a sin. The children were not allowed to participate in sports and even failed physical education classes because their father would not let them wear the required shorts.

When Singletary was 12, however, his father left the ministry and divorced his wife. Mike was allowed to play football, and he did, even though he was small and uncoordinated—often the last to be chosen. But a junior high growth spurt put him up to average size, and his older brother's death in an automobile accident forged a serious determination in him to succeed.

Singletary never wanted to play anything but linebacker, and he did that so well at Worthing High School that he attracted attention from college scouts. He enrolled at Baylor University in 1977 and broke into the starting lineup as a freshman. Playing with maniacal intensity and a unique, head-first tackling style, Singletary recorded 30 or more tackles in a game three times during his college career, and he cracked 16 helmets. In both 1979 and 1980, he was named Southwest Conference Player of the Year.

Despite his achievements, all National Football League (NFL) teams passed on him in the first round of the 1981 draft, but Chicago selected him in the second round. He worked his way into the starting lineup as a rookie but was irritated when the Bears substituted for him on passing downs. Said Coach Mike Ditka, "He asked me what he had to do to be on the field, and then he did it." By 1983 Singletary was on the field for every down, and for the rest of his career he ranked either first or second on the team in tackles. Also in 1983 he earned the first of his 10 straight Pro Bowl appearances.

Singletary was valued as much for his leadership as for his tackling skills. He called the defensive sets for the Bears' famed defense, which allowed a league-low 198 points in 1985. Chicago then recorded two playoff shutouts before crushing New England in the Super Bowl. The following season, they allowed only 187 points en route to a 14–2 mark. Led by Singletary's defense, Chicago posted a 52–11 record from 1985 to 1988, the best four-year mark in NFL history.

Nicknamed "Samurai" for his wild-eyed intensity on the field, Singletary was mild-mannered and studious off the field. He twice won honors as the NFL's Defensive Player of the Year (1985, 1988) and missed only two games in 12 years before retiring after the 1992 season.

Further Reading

Graham, Judith, ed. *Current Biography 1993.* New York: H. W. Wilson, 1993.

Singletary, Mike, with Russ Pate, *Daddy's Home at Last: What It Takes for Dads to Put Families First.* Grand Rapids, Mich.: Zondervan, 1999.

Smith, Bruce Bernard
(1963–   ) *football defensive end*

Bruce Smith anchored the defensive line for a Buffalo Bills team that won four consecutive American Football Conference (AFC) titles in the 1990s. He was most noted for his ferocious pass rush from his defensive right end position.

Bruce Bernard Smith was born on June 8, 1963, in Norfolk, Virginia. His parents, Annie and George Smith, both worked long hours at minimum-wage jobs to provide a living for the family. Although Annie had played center in basketball and George had been a boxer, Bruce was anything but an athlete in his younger years. His main interest was eating, and as he ballooned to a flabby 270 pounds as a high school sophomore, he became the butt of much teasing.

Nurtured by a supportive family, Smith began to develop some self-confidence and some muscle to go with his bulk. To his surprise, he found he was good at sports. At Booker T. Washington High School, he played center on a basketball team that qualified for the state tournament, and he was named an All-American as a football lineman.

Smith went on to attend Virginia Tech University in 1981. Showing exceptional agility to go with his size, Smith became a disruptive force as defensive end. During his career he recorded 46 sacks, plus 25 tackles of running backs behind the line. Twice he was named the team's most valuable player.

Smith's ability to wreak havoc on a backfield made him the first selection in the entire 1985 college draft, being tapped by the Buffalo Bills. During his first years as a pro, Smith tended to coast on his natural talent rather than working on technique and conditioning. He had a unique ability to get so low to the ground while rushing at full speed that linemen could not block him. That ability was good enough to get him 6.5 sacks and win the AFC's Rookie of the Year Award. It was good enough to let him accumulate a team-record 15 sacks in 1986. It was even good enough for him

to be named the AFC's Defensive Player of the Year in 1987.

But problems began to surface. His self-centered attitude grated on teammates. His lack of discipline led to a four-game suspension for a drug violation in 1988. Smith fought through these problems to record 13 sacks in 1989. In 1990, after slimming from nearly 300 pounds to 265, a quicker Bruce Smith recorded 19 sacks as the Bills romped to their first of four consecutive AFC championships, and he was named the NFL's Defensive Player of the Year.

But a knee injury that destroyed his 1991 season helped him understand that he had to take more responsibility for his conditioning and for his role as a team player. Smith emerged as the Bill's defensive leader, and he was a key factor in the team's record of four straight Super Bowl appearances. In 1993, he was again named the AFC Defensive Player of the Year. After 15 seasons with the Bills, Smith signed with Washington in 2000 and showed he still had some fight left in him by recording 10 sacks. That gave him a total of 181 career sacks, second in NFL history only to REGGIE WHITE. As of the 2002 season, Smith continued to start at right defensive end for Washington.

Further Reading
Graham, Judith, ed. *Current Biography 1995*. New York: H. W. Wilson, 1995.
Telander, Rick. "Lean, Mean Sack Machine," *Sports Illustrated*, October 2, 1991, pp. 28–32.

Smith, Emmitt
(Emmit J. Smith III)
(1969–   ) *football running back*

He may not be big enough or fast enough according to National Football League (NFL) running back standards, but Emmitt Smith has been a yardage-gulping, touchdown-scoring machine at every level of the game. The linchpin of the Dallas Cowboys' Super Bowl championships of the

1990s, Smith will likely finish his career as pro football's all-time leading ground gainer.

Emmit J. Smith III was born on May 15, 1969, in Pensacola, Florida, to Emmitt, Jr., and Mary Smith. His interest in football stemmed from his father, who played semipro football along with working at the bus depot. According to Emmitt's mother, she could calm him even as an infant by setting him in front of a televised football game. The Smith household was a warm, nurturing environment, and Smith matured far ahead of other boys his age, both emotionally and physically. He spent many hours caring for his disabled grandmother, who lived next door to him.

After joining his first organized football league at age seven, he was moved up to play with 10-year-olds the following year. When he entered Escambia High School in 1983, the school's football team had not achieved a winning season in 21 years. Even though he was only a 14-year-old ninth-grader, Smith took it upon himself to change that. He gained 115 yards in his first game and finished the season with 1,525, playing against defenders three years older than he. In 1984, he completed the Escambia miracle, gaining 2,424 yards in leading the formerly hapless Gators to the state title. Smith followed this with an incredible 2,918 yards in powering Escambia to a second title the following season. Playing in only 11 games in 1986, he finished with 1,937 yards. He completed his high school career with 107 touchdowns and the unheard of total of 8,804 career yards and was named *Parade* magazine's National High School Player of the Year.

College was more of the same. Smith enrolled at the University of Florida to stay close to home and enjoyed instant success. In his first start as a freshman, against a formidable Alabama team, Smith carried the ball 39 yards for a school-record 224 yards. He reached 1,000 yards faster than any college back in history. Smith was voted All-Conference in his freshman, sophomore, and junior years. In a game against New Mexico State as a college junior, he tore apart the defense for 316

Durable Emmitt Smith proved he need not be fast or large to carry a Super Bowl offense on his shoulders. *(Brian Bahr/Getty Images)*

yards on 31 carries. He finished the season with 1,599 yards and fumbled only once in 316 carries. Having broken 58 school records, Smith bypassed his senior year and declared for the draft in the spring of 1990.

There was much debate among pro scouts regarding Smith's potential as a pro. Standing only five feet, nine inches, and weighing 210 pounds, he had neither the size of a pro power back nor the speed of a game breaker. Yet the Dallas Cowboys recognized that there were good reasons for his astounding production. Smith had a knack of finding and darting through small openings in the line. Although he was not large, his large thighs and low center of gravity made him difficult to tackle. Most important of all, Smith had a burning determination not to be stopped.

Dallas chose Smith with the 17th selection in the first round of the 1990 draft. For the first time in his life, he started slowly. After missing all of training camp as he held out for a better contract, he was relegated to the bench for the start of his first game and then managed only two yards in two carries. But he shook that off to crack the starting lineup in game two, and he finished the season with 937 yards and 11 touchdowns to win the NFL's Offensive Rookie of the Year honors.

Smith jumped into high gear in 1991, carrying the ball 365 times for a league-leading 1,563 yards and 12 touchdowns. He topped that the following season as he enjoyed his finest statistical year as a pro. Smith again led the NFL in rushing with 1,713 yards, added 335 more yards on 59 pass receptions, and scored 18 touchdowns. He then gained more than 100 yards in each of the Cowboys' playoff victories, including the Super Bowl.

According to Dallas offensive coach Norv Turner, Smith's value was not in making long, impressive runs. "His great games," said Turner, "are games where he just wears you down, play after play, over and over." Unlike many top running backs, Smith also provided stalwart pass blocking for his quarterback, Troy Aikman.

Smith's value to the Cowboys was clearly demonstrated in 1993. When he held out for a better contract at the start of the year, the Super Bowl champs promptly lost their first two games. The quickly signed Smith made up for lost time by winning his third straight rushing title with 1,486 yards, including 237 yards against the Philadelphia Eagles. Most impressive was his final regular season performance against the New York Giants. Dallas needed a win to gain crucial home-field advantage in the playoffs. Despite separating a shoulder during the game, Smith refused to go out. Playing on sheer courage, he gained 168 yards on 32 carries and caught 10 passes to boost Dal-

las to victory in overtime. Smith was rewarded for his efforts with the league's Most Valuable Player (MVP) trophy. He then gained 132 yards in the Super Bowl against Buffalo to rally the Cowboys from a halftime deficit, and he won the MVP Award for that game as well.

Running smartly behind a huge offensive line, Smith showed an instinct for finding the end zone. He scored 21 touchdowns in 1994 and then 25 in the following season, by far the best two-year total for any NFL running back. Avoiding the crippling hits that could cause injury, he ground out 1,000 or more yards year after year.

By the end of the 2001 season, although the Cowboys were no longer contenders, Smith recorded his 11th consecutive 1,000-yard season—a feat never before accomplished in the NFL. Already the leading touchdown scorer in NFL history, he finished the season within striking distance of WALTER PAYTON's career yardage record as well.

Further Reading

Graham, Judith, ed. *Current Biography 1993.* New York: H. W. Wilson, 1993.

Montville, Leigh. "A Man of Vision," *Sports Illustrated,* February 4, 1994, pp. 142–48.

Smith, Emmitt, III, with Steve Delsohn. *The Emmitt Zone.* Dallas, Tex.: Taylor Publishing, 2002.

Smith, Ozzie
(Osborne Earl Smith, "The Wizard of Oz")
(1954–   ) *baseball shortstop*

Ozzie Smith is one of the few baseball players to make it into the Hall of Fame on the basis of his fielding ability. The magic that one of baseball's smallest players performed with his glove as shortstop made him at one time the most popular player in the game.

Osborne Earl Smith was born on December 26, 1954, in Mobile, Alabama, the second of six children of Marvella Smith, a nurse, and her husband, Clovis, a laborer. When Ozzie was in elementary school, the family moved to the Watts section of Los Angeles. Clovis, who was not overly involved with the children anyway, left when Ozzie was in junior high school.

Although Smith loved to play sports, his small stature prevented others from accepting that he was a decent player. He was determined to overcome this handicap, and he spent hours at a time throwing a ball against the back step to develop his reflexes. After playing Little League ball, Smith developed into one of the more productive basketball and baseball players at Locke High School.

Major league and college scouts expressed no interest, however, in someone who stood barely five feet, seven inches, and weighed no more than 140 pounds. Fortunately, Smith was a good student and on the basis of his grades alone made it into California Polytechnic State University at San Luis Obispo. He continued to play baseball, and during his freshman year, his coach decided Smith's arm was strong enough to make the move from second base to shortstop. Smith showed remarkable instinct for the position. Before his senior year, he was named to a college all-star team that played in Taiwan and was named the team's most valuable player. While at school, Smith also learned to hit from both sides of the plate.

Smith rejected an offer to sign with Detroit in 1976, stayed in school, and signed with the San Diego Padres on graduation the following year. By 1978, he had advanced to the major leagues and finished second in the voting for Rookie of the Year. In 1980 he set a major league record for assists by a shortstop, led the league in turning double plays, and won his first Gold Glove. But for the most part, he labored in obscurity as a good-fielding, no-hit shortstop.

His break occurred when he was traded to Saint Louis in 1982. Delighting fans with his trademark cartwheel and backflip to open games, Smith anchored the Cardinals' infield. He led the league in assists for the fourth straight year as the

Cardinals won the National League pennant and the World Series that year.

Smith worked hard to improve his batting and in 1985 stunned his teammates by hitting .435 to win the Most Valuable Player (MVP) honors in the National League championship series that advanced Saint Louis to another World Series. He reached his zenith in 1987, when he batted .303, stole 43 bases, and led the league in shortstop assists, fielding percentage, and double plays in another pennant-winning season. His wide range, acrobatic dives, and vacuumlike glove earned him the nickname the Wizard of Oz and a reputation as the best fielder in baseball. Fans appreciated his efforts so much that in 1987 and 1988 he won more fan votes for the All-Star Game than any other player.

Smith set a major league record of winning the National League's Golden Glove award 13 consecutive years, and he also became the second person to record more than 20 steals in 16 straight seasons. He retired in 1996 and was selected for the Hall of Fame in 2002.

Further Reading

Boswell, Thomas. "The Wizardry of Oz," *Gentlemen's Quarterly*, April 1988, pp. 246–48.

Porter, David L. *Biographical Dictionary of American Sports*. Westport, Conn.: Greenwood Press, 2000.

Smith, Ozzie, with Rob Rains. *Wizard*. Chicago: Contemporary Books, 1988.

Smith, Tommie C.

(1944–) *track-and-field sprinter*

Tommie Smith will be seared forever in the memory of sports fans for his daring black power salute at the 1968 Olympics. The notoriety he achieved from that moment overshadowed a spectacular career as a sprinter.

Smith was born on June 4, 1944, in Clarksville, Texas. He grew up in California, where he became a track star at Lemore High School.

Smith went on to run world-class times at San Jose State in distances from 100 to 400 meters, and he long jumped nearly 26 feet. Running with the longest stride in the track world, the lean six-foot, three-inch, 185-pounder claimed a world record in the 200 meters in 1966 with a time of 20.0. The following year, he posted a world record of 44.5 in the 400 meters. Focusing on the 200 meters, he won both the National Collegiate Athletic Association (NCAA) and Amateur Athletic Union (AAU) championships in that event in 1967 to establish himself as the favorite for the 1968 Olympics. At the 1968 U.S. Olympic trials, however, his San Jose State teammate John Carlos, wearing controversial brush spikes, cast doubt on the issue by defeating Smith.

At the Mexico City Olympics that year, Smith breezed to a semifinal victory in an Olympic record time of 20.1, but he pulled a groin muscle in the process. "I was 80 percent certain I was out [of the finals]," Smith said. But with the leg heavily taped, he went out to give it his best shot.

In the finals, Smith's tender muscle held together as he took control of the race from the start. He began pulling away from Carlos 60 meters from the finish and raised his hands in triumph while still 10 meters from the line. Had he not done so, his world record mark of 19.83 would have been even more impressive.

Both Smith and Carlos, who finished third, were members of the Olympic Project for Human Rights, a group concerned with using athletics as a platform for advocating social justice. They had debated ways to make a political statement at the Olympics, without reaching any agreement. Before the medal ceremony for the event, the two met under the stands. There Smith pulled out a pair of black gloves that he had planned to wear in case the crusty, ultraconservative International Olympic Committee (IOC) chief, Avery Brundage, whom many African-American athletes despised, insisted on shaking his hand. On the spur of the moment, the two agreed to make a symbolic statement with the gloves in solidarity

with blacks in the United States who were objects of discrimination. "White America will only give us credit for an Olympic victory," Smith explained later. "They'll say I'm an American but if I did something bad, they'd say I'm a Negro."

When the national anthem began, Smith and Carlos, wearing black socks, each bowed their heads and raised a black-fisted glove in the air. In the words of ARTHUR ASHE, the gesture "forever changed the image of the black American athlete." Whereas today this is widely viewed as an elegant, nonviolent protest, outraged Olympic officials banned the two from the games. Smith, the holder of 11 world records, was shunned back in his home country, and he struggled to make a living until 1972, when Oberlin College in Ohio hired him as a track coach. He eventually settled into a long career as a social studies teacher and track coach.

Further Reading

Axthelm, Pete. "Boos and a Beating for Tommie," *Sports Illustrated*, January 29, 1968, p. 56.

Deford, Frank. "He Is Built for Chasing Beyondness," *Sports Illustrated*, May 22, 1967, pp. 34–36.

Wiggins, David K. *Glory Bound: Black Athletes in White America*. Syracuse, N.Y.: Syracuse University Press, 1997.

Stargell, Willie
(Wilver Dornel Stargell, "Pops")
(1941–2001) *baseball first baseman*

Affectionately known to his teammates as "Pops," the slugger Willie Stargell was the architect of one of baseball's most inspirational World Series triumphs.

Wilver Dornel Stargell was born on March 6, 1941, outside Earlsboro, Oklahoma. He and his mother, Gladys, were abandoned by his father before Willie was born. The struggling family moved to a public housing project in Alameda, California, when Stargell was four. There he got involved with a group of outstanding young base-ball players. Two of them eventually drew attention from pro scouts when they played for Encinal High School. Stargell was overlooked, and his coach had to plead with a Pirates scout to consider him. The scout was not impressed but agreed to take a chance. Stargell was then sent to Class C ball, the lowest rung on the professional ladder, in 1959. There he experienced terrifying racism: a man in Texas held a shotgun to Stargell's head and threatened to shoot him if he played.

By 1963 Stargell had filled out and developed into a power hitter who was good enough to make the Pittsburgh team as a reserve outfielder. He pushed his way into the starting lineup the following season, leading the Pirates in home runs with 21 and being voted to the All-Star game. In 1966 he blossomed into a star with a .315 batting average and 33 home runs. After two subpar seasons, he returned to the .300 ranks in 1969 with a .307 average and 29 home runs.

It was not until the 1970s, however, that Stargell and the Pirates began striking fear into opponents' hearts. Stargell led the National League with 48 home runs in 1971, many of them such monstrous blasts that Los Angeles Dodgers pitcher Don Sutton said, "Stargell doesn't just hit pitchers. He takes away their dignity." Stargell was a key cog in the Pirates' World Series win that year.

After the tragic death of star outfielder Roberto Clemente in a plane crash before the 1973 season, Stargell took over as the Pirates' team leader. Forced to move from the outfield to first base by knee surgery, he again led the league in home runs that year with 44 and runs-batted-in (RBIs) with 119. Injuries curtailed his production severely the following seasons, leading many to think Stargell was washed up. But he returned to win the National League Comeback Player of the Year Award in 1978 with a .295 average and 28 homers.

In 1979 Stargell forged the Pirates into a close-knit group, adopting the hit song, "We Are Family," as the team's theme. Old Pops Stargell, then 36, led the Pirates into the World Series with 32 homers and a .281 average. Facing Baltimore in the World Series, Stargell helped Pittsburgh erase a three-games-to-one deficit with one dramatic hit after another. He blasted 12 hits, including three home runs and a World Series record seven extra base hits, becoming the first man to sweep the Most Valuable Player (MVP) honors in the regular season, playoffs, and World Series. Said his teammate Dave Parker, "The man is a legend. Right now, to me, he's like a god."

Stargell retired after the 1980 season. His huge swing helped him rack up a Pittsburgh team record of 475 career home runs, as well as a National League record of 1,936 strikeouts. The best-loved Pirate of them all was voted into the Hall of Fame in 1988. He died of a stroke on April 9, 2001.

Further Reading

Blount, Roy, Jr. "This Big Man Is the Cool Man," *Sports Illustrated,* October 5, 1970, pp. 16–18.

Moritz, Charles, ed. *Current Biography 1980.* New York: H. W. Wilson, 1980.

Swoopes, Sheryl Denise
(1971–   ) *basketball player*

Sheryl Swoopes performed so spectacularly as a college and Olympic basketball player that she became the first woman to have a sports shoe named after her. She continued her success in the pros as a Women's National Basketball Association (WNBA) Most Valuable Player (MVP) and in winning the team championship in the league's first three seasons.

Sheryl Denise Swoopes was born on March 25, 1971, in Brownfield, Texas. Her father left the family when she was three months old, leaving her mother, Louise, to provide for her children. As a young girl, Sheryl dreamed of being a cheerleader but was unable to fulfill the dream because she had no money for cheerleading outfits.

She focused her energy instead on basketball, which she began playing at the age of seven with her older brothers. The brothers' rough play forced her to work hard to develop her talent. At the age of nine, she played on a team that finished second in a national tournament.

Nicknamed "Legs" because of her height, Swoopes began playing varsity basketball at Brownfield High School in her freshman season. A quick six-footer, she was nearly unstoppable around the offensive basket. In her junior season, she almost single-handedly carried Brownfield to the state title. Excelling in all phases of the game, she averaged 26 points, 14 rebounds, five assists, and five steals over her high school career. As a measure of her athletic ability, she also set a school record on the long jump.

Swoopes enrolled at the University of Texas but lasted only a weekend before homesickness overwhelmed her. She then attended nearby South Plains Junior College, where in 1991 she was named National Junior College Player of the Year. Staying in West Texas, she moved on to Texas Tech for her final two college seasons. As a junior, she led the team to their first conference title and the National Collegiate Athletic Association (NCAA) semifinals, but she suffered disappointment when she twisted her ankle and was cut from the 1992 U.S. Olympic squad. She took out her frustration on opponents the following season, averaging 28 points a game and leading her team to the NCAA finals. There she stunned Ohio State by scoring an NCAA championship record 47 points as Texas Tech squeaked out the win.

Unfortunately, there were few options available even for a superstar woman as a postcollege basketball player in the United States. Swoopes attempted to play in Italy but stayed only three months and returned home to Brownfield. She was working as a bank teller when she tried out for the 1996 U.S. Olympic team. This time she was successful and became a starter on a team that won all 52 of their games. As well as being a reliable scorer, Swoopes guarded Brazil's top scorer in the U.S. gold medal victory.

Swoopes then signed with the Houston Comets of the WNBA. Her career was delayed only slightly by time off for the birth of her first child. She joined CYNTHIA COOPER in creating a WNBA dynasty, and she played a key role in three consecutive Comets championships. She was named to the All-WNBA first team in 1998, 1999, and 2000, and she collected the league's Best Defensive Player and Most Valuable Player Awards in 2000. She is still playing and was the leading vote-getter in All-Star ballot 2002.

Further Reading

Corbett, Sara. *Venus to the Hoop*. New York: Doubleday, 1997.

Lessa, Christina. *Stories of Triumph: Women Who Won in Sport and Life*. New York: Universe, 1998.

T

Taylor, Lawrence Julius
(L. T.)
(1959–   ) *football linebacker*

Lawrence Taylor was one of the few defensive players who could dominate a pro football game. Virtually unstoppable on the blitz, he redefined the position of outside linebacker in the 1980s and moved the New York Giants back to the top of the league after a long decline.

Taylor was born on February 4, 1959, in Williamsburg, Virginia, the middle of three boys. He grew up on the edge of town in a middle-class environment provided by his father, Clarence, Sr., who worked in the shipyards and his mother, Iris, who taught school.

Lawrence's favorite sport as a boy was baseball, in which his stocky build suited him for catching duties. Football did not particularly interest him; he played it only on a Williamsburg Jaycees team rather than at Lafayette High School. Not until his junior year did friends persuade him to go out for the high school team. The inexperienced Taylor started out as a bench-warming lineman until the fifth game of the season, when his block of a punt won the game for his team. Taylor began to grow in confidence as well as in size. When he reported for practice his senior year he had added three inches, 25 pounds, and an aggressive attitude.

Sackmaster Lawrence Taylor was so dominant a linebacker that he altered the way National Football League (NFL) teams played football. *(Stephen Dunn/ Getty Images)*

Although Taylor vastly improved his play, college scouts still were not impressed with him. With help from his coach, Melvin Jones, he was able to attract a few scholarship offers, including one from the University of North Carolina. When Taylor arrived there in 1981, he earned a reputation as an undisciplined bully who treated classes as a joke. He nearly partied away his career until after his sophomore season when he settled down and focused on improving his play.

Meanwhile, he made a crucial switch of position from lineman and inside linebacker to outside linebacker. On the outside, Taylor could make better use of his speed. The numbers he racked up from that position astounded pro scouts: 16 sacks and 22 tackles behind the line in his senior season alone. Taylor was such a disruptive force that the chronically mediocre Tarheels posted a 10–1 mark that year.

Although the New York Giants were well stocked at linebacker and had glaring needs at other positions, they considered Taylor's mix of six-foot, three-inch, 245-pound size, 4.6-second speed at 40 yards, and catlike quickness to be too good to pass up, and they made him their first selection in the 1981 draft. In the opinion of Coach Bill Parcells, who took over the team a couple of years later, getting Taylor was the key to establishing a winning team in New York.

The rookie had a good deal to learn about playing linebacker, especially the techniques of pass defense, but had excellent teachers in All-Pro linebackers Harry Carson and Brad Van Pelt. While he was learning those skills, he relied on his pass-rushing ability to establish his presence among his peers. In his first season, "L. T.," as he became known, made 94 unassisted tackles and 9.5 sacks. Not only was he named the league Rookie of the Year, but he was also named All-Pro. His play helped the Giants to earn their first playoff berth in more than a decade.

Taylor confronted opposing offensive coaches with a problem they had never seen before. Previously, pass rushing was the domain primarily of linemen, but Taylor came at the quarterback from his linebacker position. He was too quick for the tackles to block and too strong for tight ends and backs; that meant that offenses had to come up with a special strategy just for Taylor. As the Philadelphia Eagles coach Dick Vermeil explained, "He has the ability to transfer to his feet what his eyes see quicker than anybody." Taylor's ability to wreak havoc made him the prototype for a new brand of linebacker, and soon all teams were searching for top athletes to place at the outside linebacker position.

Unfortunately, the Giants' weak offense was unable to take advantage of the team's superior defense in the early 1980s. While Taylor continued to make All-Pro, the Giants lost. Then, as the Giants began to improve in 1985, something seemed to be wrong with L. T. Although he showed flashes of brilliance and recorded 13 sacks that season, his intensity appeared to wane. The problem turned out to be cocaine addiction; in February 1986, he checked into a drug rehabilitation center.

Taylor emerged from treatment with new-found zeal for his work. Turned loose from his pass defense duties so that he could rush the passer more, he terrorized opposing quarterbacks with 20.5 sacks and numerous knockdowns, plus 105 individual tackles. Taylor was the unanimous choice as the National Football League's (NFL's) Most Valuable Player, becoming only the second defensive player to win the award. Stoked by Taylor's barely controlled rage ("I'm a wild man in a wild game," he declared), the Giants flattened all opposition that year. In the playoffs, they pounded San Francisco 49–3, blanked Washington 17–0, and then defeated Denver 39–20 to win New York's first football title since the 1950s. Taylor reigned as the NFL's sack king for the decade, posting 110 from his rookie season to 1989.

His up-and-down career took another turn for the worse in 1988, when he failed a drug test. As a repeat offender, he was suspended for four games and threatened with life expulsion for any more offenses. Taylor stayed clean and finished his career with another Super Bowl win in 1988. Unfortunately substance abuse problems and brushes with the law continued to dog him when his playing career ended in 1993 and cast a shadow over his induction into the Pro Football Hall of Fame in 1999.

Further Reading

Lieber, Jill. "Blitzer by Himself," *Sports Illustrated,* September 19, 1988, p. 53.

Moritz, Charles, ed. *Current Biography 1990.* New York: H. W. Wilson, 1990.

Zimmerman, Paul. "LT on LT," *Sports Illustrated,* September 16, 1991, pp. 40–42.

Taylor, Marshall Walker
(Major Taylor)
(1878–1932) *bicycle racer*

Marshall Taylor, also known as Major Taylor, was one of the first African-American world champions in any sport. In the words of sports historian Edwin Henderson, Taylor's career as a bicycle racer "was as brilliant around the turn of the century as was the meteoric glory of JESSE OWENS or JOE LOUIS in the annals of sport two generations later."

He was born Marshall Walker Taylor on November 26, 1878, outside Indianapolis, Indiana. His father found employment as a coachman at the home of a wealthy white Indianapolis family who offered housing for the Taylors and provided an education for Marshall. At one point, this family presented Marshall the gift of a bicycle. He showed such a knack for controlling his bike that in 1892 a local bike shop hired him to demonstrate bicycle stunts outside the shop to attract customers. That year Taylor began entering amateur bicycle races, which had grown into one of the more popular forms of entertainment in the area. According to some reports, he was goaded into his first race by hecklers at a cycling race.

Unfortunately, Taylor was so good at racing that he infuriated white cyclists. After unofficially breaking the world cycling record for one mile in August 1896, he was banned from Indianapolis's Capital City racetrack, and the whites-only League of American Wheel Men banned bicyclists of "inferior race" the same year. Frustrated by discrimination, Taylor moved to Worcester, Massachusetts, where his employer planned to set up a bicycle factory.

Taylor entered the professional racing circuit in December 1896, and he finished eighth in his first race. Within two years, he stood at the top of his sport with seven world records to his credit. In 1899 he slashed his own world record in the mile from 1:41 to 1:19. That same year, he captured the world bicycle championship at the one-mile distance.

Taylor was equally adept at sprinting and long-distance racing. He set a world mark of 23 $\frac{2}{5}$ seconds for the $\frac{1}{5}$-mile distance and yet was once able to win a 75-mile road race in a driving rainstorm by a margin of nearly an hour. In 1900, he finally was able to circumvent racial roadblocks to complete his first U.S. sprint championship series, which he won. Frustrated by battling officials and fans because of his race, he traveled in 1901 to Europe, where cycling was enormously popular. There he challenged and defeated the reigning bicycling racing champions of the Continent. He continued touring worldwide until 1904, after which he took a two-year break from competition.

Taylor returned to racing in 1907 and remained a championship competitor until he retired from the sport in 1910. A man of quiet dignity who was known for clean living, he refused to violate the Sabbath by racing on Sunday. After his racing career, Taylor suffered a series of business calamities. He died penniless in a Chicago charity hospital on June 21, 1932.

Further Reading

Great Athletes of the Twentieth Century. Vol. 17. Pasadena, Calif.: Salem Press, 1994.

Henderson, Edwin B. *The Black Athlete: Emergence and Arrival.* New York: Publishers Company, 1968.

Young, A. S. *Negro Firsts in Sports.* Chicago: Johnson Publishing Company, 1963.

Thomas, Debi
(1967–   ) *figure skater*

Debi Thomas not only became the first African-American world figure skating champion, but she did it the hard way. Even though she eschewed the obsessive full-time training life-style of most of her competitors, she bested East Germany's superstar Katarina Witt in her prime. Although Witt regained the edge in subsequent competition, Thomas thrilled spectators with her daring athleticism.

Thomas was born on March 15, 1967, in Poughkeepsie, New York, to Janice and McKinley Thomas. Both were computer specialists and they moved to San Jose, California, when both were offered computer jobs in Silicon Valley. Debi grew up in one of the few black families in her upscale neighborhood. She became interested in skating at the age of four after attending an Ice Follies show. Her parents bought her ice skates at age five but did not begin her figure skating lessons until she was nine, the year that she won her first competition. At 10, she hired Scottish coach Alex McGown as her personal instructor and began competing at a club near their home.

By this time, her parents were divorced, and Debi lived with her mother. The cost of lessons and other training necessities was sometimes beyond her budget and Debi sometimes had to back off for periods of time. At first, Coach McGown did not detect much potential in Debi. But her athleticism and quick mastery of skills soon set her apart from the rest. At age 12 she could accomplish a triple jump, a move so difficult that some of the best skaters in the world were loath to attempt it. Her training efforts paid off that year as she finished second at the national

Debi Thomas was the first African American to win a medal in the Winter Olympics. *(Pascal Rondeau/Getty Images)*

novice finals. Encouraged by her progress, Janice allowed her daughter to devote full-time to her training while keeping up on her schoolwork through correspondence courses. However, when Debi finished a disappointing fourth in a subsequent regional competition, the Thomases had a change of heart and vowed never again to let skating come before her education.

Thomas returned to school and for a time put skating on the back burner. But she was an excellent student and discovered she could handle both the demands of San Mateo High School and the demands of competitive training. She began training six hours a day, six days a week. For four years, Janice Thomas drove 150 miles a day, getting herself and her daughter where they needed to be for work, school, and practice.

Debi Thomas gradually began moving into the highest echelons of U.S. figure skating. Between 1983 and 1985, she advanced from 13th place at the U.S. Nationals to second and achieved a number-five ranking in the world. She became especially known for her sensational jumps and her aggressive routines. Yet at the same time she handled her studies well enough to gain entrance into prestigious Stanford University in 1985.

Figure skating on the international level demanded so much time and energy that it was unheard of for a top skater to attempt to be a full-time student. Thomas not only took on college but tackled a difficult premed curriculum with a major in medical microbiology. The experts insisted the overload was hurting her development as a skater. Her coach once complained, "When Debi arrives at the rink for training, she's exhausted."

Somehow, though, Thomas was able to manage, taking short breaks from skating when she needed to. Introducing a risky free-skating program that included an unprecedented five triple jumps, Thomas captured first place at the U.S. nationals in 1986. She then traveled to Geneva, Switzerland, for the world championships. At that time, the undisputed queen of international figure skating was East Germany's sultry Katarina Witt. Dazzling the judges with her style and powerful spinning leaps, however, Thomas stunned Witt by beating her out for the title. The event was the beginning of an intense rivalry between the two fierce competitors.

The demands of her schedule began taking their toll on Thomas during her sophomore year. She was unable to maintain her high level of performance and lost both her world title and her U.S. title. As the 1988 Olympics approached, she realized that something would have to give. She decided to take a year off from school to focus on the Olympics, training at a facility in Boulder, Colorado. Not only did Thomas train harder, but she sought out advice from experts such as ballet dancer Mikhail Baryshnikov to help her improve her presentation.

As the 1988 Olympics approached, the pressure again built up to a crushing level, fueled by the intense media focus on the cold war aspect of her rivalry with Witt. Coincidentally, both skaters chose to skate to the same music from the opera *Carmen.* At the Calgary Olympics, Witt took a slim lead going into the final freestyle program. Her performance was not quite up to her usual standards, however, and left the door open for Thomas. Attempting to make an immediate impact on the judges, Thomas planned to begin her program with two triples. Unfortunately, she landed on two feet on her first jump and never recovered from her shaky start. Thomas was so disappointed at having let down the American public that she cried every day for three weeks. Although her bronze medal was the first Winter Olympic medal won by an African American, she tended to downplay descriptions of her as a pioneer role model. "I didn't think I had to see a black woman do this to believe it's possible."

Both Thomas and Witt actually provided a much better demonstration of their talent in the 1988 world championships that followed the Olympics. Fighting off painful tendinitis, Thomas whipped the Cincinnati, Ohio, crowd into a frenzy with her most dynamic performance yet. This inspired Witt to skate what many experts believed was her best program ever to capture the championship by a slim margin.

Drained by the pressure and grueling schedule, Thomas retired from competition that year. She skated professionally for a while and then threw her energy into medical school, completing her studies at Northwestern University in 1997. Reflecting on her stellar career, she once commented, "I had ridiculously large dreams, and half the time they came true."

Further Reading

Brennan, Christine. *Inside Game.* New York: Scribner, 1996.

Oblender, David G., ed. *Contemporary Black Biography.* Vol. 26. Detroit, Mich.: Gale Research, 2001.

Thomas, Frank Edward

("The Big Hurt")

(1968–) *baseball first baseman*

One of the largest men ever to play professional baseball, Frank Thomas has patience and discipline at the plate that have made him one of the best combined power-average hitters in the game.

Frank Edward Thomas was born on May 27, 1968, in Columbus, Georgia, the youngest of five brothers. His parents, Frank, Sr., and Charlie Mae Thomas, worked as a bail bondsman and textile worker, respectively. When Frank, Jr., was nine, he was devastated when his younger sister died, and it was at about that time that he began dedicating himself to becoming a pro athlete.

Thomas starred as a basketball power forward and a football tight end at Columbus High School, in addition to playing his favorite sport, baseball. He hoped to be drafted by a major league team after graduation. However, convinced that the six-foot, five-inch, 250-pound Thomas was headed for a football career, no baseball team drafted him. Thomas ultimately enrolled at Auburn University.

Thomas saw limited action as a tight end on the football team as a freshman but went on to set a school record in baseball that spring with 21 home runs. After suffering a knee injury that knocked him out of the entire football season, he abandoned that sport and focused solely on baseball.

In 1988, Thomas tried out for the U.S. Olympic baseball team but was cut. The rejection provided a powerful motivator to work on his game. That year he batted .403 with 19 home runs and was named College Player of the Year by *Baseball America*. The Chicago White Sox made him a first-round draft selection that year and assigned him to their minor leagues. He was called up to the major league club in August and showed that he belonged at the top level of competition by batting .330 in 60 games.

In 1991, he maintained his high level of play by batting .318, with 32 home runs, and leading the American League in walks with 138. Although he finished third in the balloting for Most Valuable Player (MVP), he guarded against overconfidence by taping the letters *DBTH* above his locker to remind him "Don't Believe the Hype." Thomas worked hard on his defense as well as on his batting. Thomas was determined to hit for high average as well as power. He realized that with the large strike zone he presented, he would have to be extremely selective in his swings. In being selective, he not only eliminated swinging at bad pitches but began drawing walks in record numbers. The batting coach Walt Hriniak remarked, "I've seen power hitters before, but never anyone who understood hitting like him."

In 1993, Thomas set Chicago White Sox club records by hitting 41 home runs and batting in 128 runs, to go along with a .317 average. That performance was so far above that of anyone else in the league that Thomas was the unanimous choice as Most Valuable Player. "The Big Hurt," as he was nicknamed, repeated as MVP in 1994 with a .353 average and 38 home runs. In 1997, he led the American League in batting with .347, and in 1999 he broke his own club power records with 43 home runs and 143 runs-batted-in (RBIs). In the 2002 season Thomas battled back from his injuries to hit .252, with 28 home runs.

Further Reading

Callahan, G. "Hurt So Good," *Sports Illustrated*, April 19, 1999, pp. 60–62.

Graham, Judith, ed. *Current Biography 1993*. New York: H. W. Wilson, 1993.

Thomas, Isiah

(Isiah Lord Thomas III)

(1961–) *basketball guard*

Isiah Thomas is regarded as one of the quickest men to step on a basketball court. His speed and tenacity more than made up for his small size as he became the leader of the Detroit Pistons.

He was born Isiah Lord Thomas III on April 30, 1961, in Chicago, Illinois, the ninth and youngest child of Mary and Isiah Thomas II. Shortly after Isiah's birth, his father lost his factory job. Grinding poverty led to a separation and Thomas lived on Chicago's tough West Side with his mother, a determined woman who once faced down neighborhood gang leaders with a shotgun. When Isiah was 12, she moved her family five miles to the west to get away from the violence; the trade-off was that they lived in a house with no working heat or plumbing.

Throughout his life Isiah played basketball constantly with his older brothers. His skill led to a scholarship at Saint Joseph High School in the western suburb of Westchester. Thomas arose at 5:30 every schoolday to ride city buses for an hour and a half to school. The superquick guard drew more than 300 college recruiters before settling on Indiana University. As a freshman, Thomas led the Hoosiers to the Big Ten championship and paced the team in scoring, assists, and steals. The following year, Indiana again won their conference title and advanced to the finals of the 1981 National Collegiate Athletic Association (NCAA) tournament against North Carolina. There, Thomas and the Hoosiers charged back from a half-time deficit to win the national title. Thomas led all scorers with 23 points and earned the tournament Most Valuable Player (MVP) honors.

With nothing left to accomplish in collegiate basketball, Thomas entered the National Basketball Association (NBA) draft after his sophomore year. The Detroit Pistons selected him with the second choice of the draft. Proving he could thrive among the giants of the NBA, Thomas averaged 17 points per game in helping Detroit improve by 18 wins over the previous season. In 1981–82, he boosted his scoring average to a career-best 22.9 points. By 1983–84, the Pistons under Thomas's direction became consistent winners. The following season, Thomas etched his name in the NBA record book with 1,123 assists.

In the mid-1980s, Detroit advanced further each year in the playoffs. In 1988, they made it to the finals and pushed the Los Angeles Lakers to a seventh game in the championship. Playing on a severely sprained ankle, Thomas scored 25 points in the third quarter of the game, but it was not enough to gain the victory. The following year, stressing defense over offense, the Pistons finally earned their title with a sweep of the hobbled Lakers, with Thomas leading the scoring. The Pistons then repeated the victory in 1990 over the Portland Trailblazers.

Thomas played his entire career with Detroit before retiring in 1994. He finished his career with a 19.2 scoring average and ranked fourth in career assists. Playing at his best when the competition was the greatest, Thomas earned the MVP award twice in the 11 years he was voted to the All-Star team. A natural leader, Thomas served as president of the NBA Players Association and president of the Continental Basketball League and in 2001 took over as coach of the Indiana Pacers.

Further Reading

Kindred, David. *Heroes, Fools, and Other Dreamers: A Sportswriter's Gallery of Extraordinary People.* Atlanta: Longstreet Press, 1989.

Thomas, Isiah. *The Fundamentals: 8 Plays for Winning the Game of Business and Life.* New York: Harper-Collins, 2001.

Thomas, Isiah, with Matt Dolbeck. *Bad Boys: An Inside Look at the Detroit Pistons' 1988–1989 Championship Season.* Culver City, Calif.: Hightop Sports, 1992.

Tolan, Eddie

(Thomas Edward Tolan, "The Midnight Express")
(1908–1967) *track-and-field sprinter*

The United States tradition of excellent African-American sprinters actually predates the famed JESSE OWENS. It was, in fact, Eddie Tolan who laid the foundation for the black American dominance of the short sprints a few years before Owens's achievements.

Thomas Edward Tolan was born on September 29, 1908, in Detroit, Michigan. After winning the city high school championship and Michigan state high school title in both the 100- and 220-yard dashes, he attended the University of Michigan. He dominated in the shorter sprints throughout his college years, earning a national reputation as "The Midnight Express." At the same time, he was an excellent student who hoped to study medicine but became a schoolteacher when medical school avenues were closed to him.

Tolan did not appear to be the stereotypical track athlete. He stood only five feet, seven inches, tall; wore glasses when he ran; and had a habit of chewing gum even during races. Yet throughout his college years, he reigned as the nation's top sprinter. In 1929, he set a world record of 9.5 seconds in the 100-yard dash and 10.4 in the 100 meters. A year later, he lowered his 100-meter time to 10.2. Despite his success, however, Tolan's career nearly ended after an incident of racial discrimination. Angered at being denied lodging with the rest of his team while at an Amateur Athletic Union (AAU) meet in Chicago, Tolan threatened to leave. Even when a meet official warned that his career would be over if he left, Tolan stayed only after his mother persuaded him to do so.

After winning a fistful of National Collegiate Athletic Association (NCAA) and AAU championships in the sprints, Tolan ran into serious opposition at the 1932 U.S. Olympic trials, in which Marquette University's Ralph Metcalfe defeated him in both the 100 and the 200 meters.

At the Olympics in Los Angeles, Tolan and Metcalfe staged a furious duel in the 100 meters. Metcalfe false-started and so had to use caution in the starting blocks to prevent a second false start and disqualification. Tolan took advantage of this to surge into the lead at 40 meters, only to be caught by the hard-charging Metcalfe 20 meters

from the tape. The two appeared to hit the tape dead even. Several hours later, after reviewing film of the finish, officials determined that Metcalfe reached the line first. However, rules stated that the winner was the first runner to cross the finish, and the tape showed that Tolan got across the line first. He won the gold, although both were timed in an Olympic record 10.3.

In the 200 meters, Tolan's conserving efforts nearly cost him a medal. At the end of the second semifinal heat, believing he was assured of qualifying for the next round, he coasted to the finish. He miscalculated, and a fast-closing Canadian runner missed eliminating him by a foot. In the finals, however, Tolan pulled away from the field with 50 meters to go. He survived a stumble near the finish line to hold off a fellow American, George Simpson, as well as Metcalfe, who finished third. Thus, Tolan became the first African-American Olympic sprint champion, creating a legacy that continues to this day. He died on January 31, 1967, of a heart attack.

Further Reading

Great Athletes of the Twentieth Century. Vol. 18. Pasadena, Calif.: Salem Press, 1994.

Henderson, Edwin B. *The Black Athlete: Emergence and Arrival.* New York: Publishers Company, 1968.

Tunnell, Emlen Lewis
(1925–1975) *football defensive back*

Emlen Tunnell was the first pro football player to gain recognition as a defensive back. He set a record for career interceptions that lasted for more than two decades and now stands in second place for that statistic, despite the league's vastly increased passing emphasis in recent years, which has provided greater opportunity for interceptions.

He was born Emlen Lewis Tunnell on March 29, 1925, in Bryn Mawr, Pennsylvania, and grew up in Radnor, Pennsylvania. He made the varsity football team at Radnor High School as a freshman, and he attracted the attention of college scouts through his running and passing prowess. But as a freshman at Toledo University, he landed awkwardly on his neck, suffering a fracture that doctors told him would end his playing days. After a period of recovery, Tunnell then switched from football to basketball, and he performed well enough to lead Toledo to the prestigious National Invitational Tournament (NIT) in 1943.

Later that year, Tunnell heeded the call for volunteers to help with the military effort in World War II. His injuries disqualified him from service with the army, but he was able to go on active duty with the United States Coast Guard. While on shore leave, he often ignored the medical warnings and played in a Connecticut football league with the Fleet City Bluejackets. This went so well that, on leaving the service, he landed a football scholarship at the University of Iowa. Tunnell starred for the Hawkeyes as both a running back and a defensive back until an eye injury forced him to miss his entire senior year. The pros, who had only recently begun accepting African-American players, forgot all about him and he was not drafted.

Nevertheless, Tunnell would not give up on his dream of playing football. In 1948 he went to the training camp of his favorite team, the New York Giants, and asked for a tryout. The Giants agreed and were impressed by his combination of size (six feet, one inch, 200 pounds) and quickness. Although he was the size of many pro linebackers at the time, the Giants decided to give him a try at defensive back. Tunnell proceeded to intercept four passes in one game to gain a permanent starting position.

Tunnell continued to pilfer passes at a record rate, and, even more valuable to the Giants, he returned them a great distance. In 1951, he intercepted nine passes and returned four of them for touchdowns. The following year he ran back seven interceptions for a total of 149 yards. His elusiveness in the open field made him an equally dangerous punt returner and kickoff returner. He led the National Football League (NFL) in punt return yards in 1951 and 1952. During his career he set the record for punt return yardage (2,209) and punts returned for touchdowns (five). A solid tackler as well as a feared pass defender, he was named All-NFL four times with the Giants. In the words of New York coach Jim Lee Howell, "Emlen changed the theories on defensive safeties."

Defying the predictions of doctors, Tunnell avoided injury throughout his career and played in 158 games in a row. After eight years with the Giants, he finished his career with the Green Bay Packers in 1962, winning NFL titles with both teams. He went on to become the first black position coach in the NFL in 1966 and the following year was the first African American voted into the Pro Football Hall of Fame. He died in 1975 of a heart attack.

Further Reading

Allen, George. *Pro Football's 100 Greatest Players.* Indianapolis: Bobbs-Merrill, 1982.

Great Athletes of the Twentieth Century. Vol. 18. Pasadena, Calif.: Salem Press, 1994.

Tyson, Mike
(Michael Gerard Tyson)
(1966–) *boxer*

Boxing experts agree that Mike Tyson had the physical gifts to be perhaps the greatest heavyweight boxer in history before his career disintegrated in the late 1990s amid controversy and scandal.

Michael Gerard Tyson was born on June 30, 1966, in Brooklyn, New York, and grew up under grim circumstances. His father, Jimmy Kirkpatrick, ran off before Mike was born, and his mother, Lorna Tyson, was a heavy drinker who struggled to raise her four kids in one of the toughest neighborhoods of New York. Tyson grew up as wild and vicious as his surroundings. At the age of 10, he already had the size and strength to take part in muggings and other crimes that frequently landed him in juvenile detention facilities.

One such facility was the Tryon School for Boys, where an instructor recognized Tyson's potential as a boxer and put him in contact with the veteran trainer Cus D'Amato. D'Amato became a much-needed father figure to Tyson, likely saving him from a short and violent life of crime. At 14, Tyson was released from detention into the trainer's care.

Although fans later dismissed him as an overpowering brute, Tyson was actually a student of the sport, spending countless hours studying films of boxing matches to learn techniques. Realizing that he had a potential champion on his hands, D'Amato kept Tyson under wraps as he trained and sparred. Word of Tyson's incredible talents leaked out, however, and by the time he turned pro in May 1985, the media were intrigued by this mysterious 18-year-old. Showing surprising hand speed and savvy to go with a lethal arsenal of punches, Tyson dispatched one hapless opponent after another. In his 15 victorious fights in his first pro year, only four opponents lasted past the first round. The following year, Tyson racked up 13 more wins without a loss and, in fact, was never seriously challenged.

On November 22, 1986, Tyson knocked out Trevor Burbick to become, at 20 years, 145 days, the youngest world heavyweight champion in history. From 1987 to 1989 the bull-necked, 5-foot, 11-inch, 225-pound Tyson consolidated the disputed heavyweight championship with wins over his rival claimants, Bonecrusher Smith and Tony Tucker. After knocking out former heavyweight champion Larry Holmes in four rounds, he finally gained recognition as undisputed champion with a savage beating of Michael Spinks. Although Spinks had won an Olympic gold medal and was undefeated as a pro, he lasted only 91 seconds against Tyson.

Just when Tyson seemed invincible, he lost his focus after the death of D'Amato. Believing he could easily dispose of journeyman fighter Buster Douglas, he neglected to train for the fight, and on February 10, 1990, Douglas knocked him out in the 10th round of their match. That started a spiral of erratic behavior that included a conviction and three-year imprisonment for the rape of a beauty pageant contestant in 1993. Just when it seemed he had a chance of rehabilitating his career, he disgraced himself again by biting off a piece of Evander Holyfield's ear during their championship fight, resulting in his disqualification and suspension from the sport. Rather than reigning as the best fighter in history, he became a pariah and his remarkable gift for boxing was wasted, as evidenced by the beating he suffered at the hands of Lennox Lewis in their 2002 title fight.

Further Reading

Berger, Phil. Blood Season: Tyson and the World of Boxing. New York: Morrow, 1989.

Heller, Peter Niels. Bad Intentions: The Mike Tyson Story. New York: DeCapo Press, 1995.

Hoffer, Richard. A Savage Business: The Comeback and Comedown of Mike Tyson. New York: Simon & Schuster, 1998.

O'Connor, Daniel. Iron Mike: A Mike Tyson Reader. New York: Thunder's Mouth Press, 2001.

Torres, Jose. Fear and Fire: The Inside Story of Mike Tyson. New York: Warner, 1989.

Tyus, Wyomia
(1945–) track-and-field sprinter

Wyomia Tyus was the first Olympic athlete, male or female, to defend her title in the 100-meter dash.

She was born on August 29, 1945, in Griffin, Georgia, to Willie and Maria Tyus, who worked at a dairy and a laundry, respectively. Growing up in the segregated South, Tyus had to ride a bus for an hour to a black school although better schools were much closer. She became active in running by chasing after her three older brothers, who were constantly trying to lose her. Fortunately for Wyomia, her father was unusual for his time in that he encouraged his daughter to participate in sports. As Tyus once explained, "To be African-American in Georgia at that time meant there was nothing to do, and if you were poor, you could do even less." Sports gave her an opportunity to achieve success.

At Fairmont High School, she concentrated mainly on basketball, with track as a side interest. But after winning a state sprint title, she received an invitation to attend Tennessee State coach Ed Temple's summer track clinic. Thinking it would provide a fun vacation, she attended the prestigious camp. She liked it so much that she attended Tennessee State on a track scholarship in 1963.

Although she ran well in college, she had difficulty keeping up with her teammate Edith McGuire. At the 1964 U.S. Olympic trials, Tyus was pleased to earn a spot on the team with her third-place finish in the 100 meters behind McGuire and Marilyn White. During the preliminary heats at the Tokyo Olympics, however, she seemed to find a fresh reservoir of speed, equaling WILMA GOLDEAN RUDOLPH's world record in the second round. In the final, she burst into the lead at the start of the gun and braced herself for McGuire to overtake her as usual. But it did not happen. Tyus captured the gold medal, and from that point on, neither McGuire nor anyone else had much success catching her. In 1965, she ran a world record time in the 100 meters at a meet featuring the United States and the Soviet Union, and she continued as the top woman sprinter into 1967.

After suffering burnout and a mediocre season in 1967, Tyus rededicated herself to the sport in 1968. The powerful five-foot, seven-inch, Tyus needed every bit of her training in the Mexico City Olympics that year, as all five women who shared the world record of 11.1 seconds were competing in the 100 meters. In the final, three of those rivals—Barbara Ferrell, Irna Szewinska of Poland, and Raelene Boyle of Australia—all equaled the world record. But overcoming a false start, Tyus sped past them all to defend her Olympic title in a new world record of 11.0 seconds, a mark that stood for 16 years. Tyus then anchored the U.S. 4 × 100 meter relay team to a gold medal in a world-record time, and she finished eighth in the 200 meters.

She retired after the Games, but with the establishment of the International Track Association in 1972, she reentered competition. Tyus was the leading money-winner among women, and in 1974 won all 22 of her races. When the professional track circuit was dissolved that year, she retired again and went on to work as a teacher and naturalist at an outdoor camp in the Los Angeles school district.

Further Reading

Carlson, Lewis H., and John J. Fogerty. *Tales of Gold.* Chicago: Contemporary Books, 1987.

Condon, Robert J. *Great Women Athletes of the 20th Century.* Jefferson, N.C.: McFarland & Company, 1999.

Great Athletes of the Twentieth Century. Vol. 18. Pasadena, Calif.: Salem Press, 1994.

U

Upshaw, Gene
(Eugene Thurman Upshaw, Jr.)
(1945–) *football offensive guard*

As a powerful, mobile offensive guard for the Oakland Raiders, Gene Upshaw was the only person to play in Super Bowls in the 1960s, 1970s, and 1980s. He has since become one of the most influential figures in all of sports.

Eugene Thurman Upshaw, Jr., was born on August 15, 1945, in Robstown, Texas, the oldest of three boys. His father, Eugene, Sr., worked in the oil fields of south Texas, while his mother, Cora, worked as a domestic. Gene and his brothers attended a four-room schoolhouse and toiled many hours picking cotton.

Gene's favorite sport was baseball, and he pitched his team to within one game of the Little League World Series in 1958. After starring on the mound in high school, he was on the verge of signing a professional baseball contract when his father told Gene that if he did not go to college, he would be booted out of the house. Reluctantly, Upshaw enrolled at nearby Texas A & I University in 1963.

Having suddenly grown to nearly the size of his younger brother, Marvin, a football star, Gene decided to try football at Texas A & I to see whether he could earn a scholarship and ease his money problems. It took the coaches only three days to see Upshaw's potential and award that scholarship, although finding the right position for the late starter was tough. He finally settled in to playing center and guard.

By his senior year, Upshaw improved enough to earn honorable mention as a Little (small school) All-American and was projected to be a third-round draft choice of the pros. But in postseason All-Star games, he so manhandled his opposition that he moved up to the first round, in which he was selected by the Oakland Raiders. The Raiders had a specific purpose in mind for the six-foot, four-inch, 265-pound Upshaw. He was placed at left guard to neutralize Buck Buchanan, the giant defensive tackle of their archrival, the Kansas City Chiefs, who had disrupted Oakland's attack.

Upshaw neutralized not only Buchanan, but everyone else as well. His blend of strength, speed, and intelligence helped him go to six Pro Bowls and win American Football Conference (AFC) Lineman of the Year honors in 1973 and 1974. His blocking helped his team reach the playoffs 11 times in his 16-year career, including two Super Bowl wins. Although he excelled at pass blocking, Upshaw's trademark was his open-field block on the cornerback on end sweeps. He was never better than in the 1977 Super Bowl, when he and the massive left tackle, Art Shell, obliterated the Minnesota Vikings' right side, allowing Clarence Davis to run at will to an easy victory.

Few linemen have exhibited the leadership qualities of Upshaw. He served 10 years as a Raiders captain and began moving up the ranks of the National Football League (NFL) players in 1970. After his retirement in 1982, he became executive director of the union. He brushes off criticism that he takes a combative stance in his job, saying, "If you're black and you take a strong stand, you're militant." He has been largely responsible for football's relatively calm labor situation at the turn of the century, and he was named by *The Sporting News* as the 13th most powerful man in sports.

Further Reading

Great Athletes of the Twentieth Century. Vol. 18. Pasadena, Calif.: Salem Press, 1994.

Phelps, Shirelle, ed. *Contemporary Black Biography.* Vol. 18. Detroit, Mich.: Gale Research, 1998.

Washington, Ora

(1898–1971) *tennis and basketball player*

Long before ALTHEA GIBSON achieved fame for breaking racial barriers in tennis in the 1950s, Ora Washington gained a reputation as a magician with a tennis racquet. Although she may have been the most dominating women's tennis player ever, she was never allowed to test her skill in the major white-sponsored tournaments.

Washington was born in 1898 in Germantown, Pennsylvania. Her life was shattered when she was a teen when her sister died. Trying to help her deal with her grief, a Young Women's Christian Association (YWCA) instructor in Germantown introduced her to the sport of tennis as a distraction. Washington threw her energy into the sport and quickly developed into a champion. In 1924, she won her first African-American National Tennis Tournament in Baltimore over Dorothy Radliffe. Over the next 12 years, Washington did not lose a match. In the words of the *Chicago Defender,* "Her superiority is so evident that her competitors are frequently beaten before the first ball crosses the net." Washington was so limber and confident that she never even bothered to warm up before a match. Although she was taller and stronger than most opponents, she did not try to overpower them. Rather, according to ARTHUR ASHE, "She held the racquet halfway up

the handle and seldom took a full swing. But no woman had her foot speed. . . . She was clearly the first woman to dominate her sport."

After breezing through competition in the African-American National Tennis Organization, Washington moved to the American Tennis Association in 1929, playing the top ranks of black tennis players. There she won the singles title seven consecutive years, took a year off, and then won again in 1937.

Washington's career closely overlapped that of white U.S. women's star Helen Wills Moody, who won seven Wimbledon singles titles from 1923 to 1931 and eight U.S. Open singles titles from 1927 to 1938, including four consecutive seasons in which she won both prestigious championships. As each woman was virtually unchallenged during much of this time by her respective peers, competition between the two would have generated great interest. Moody, however, refused to consider the idea, and neither the Wimbledon nor the U.S. tournaments organizers had any intention of opening up their competitions.

Ironically, Washington's skill ruined her tennis career. She so seldom encountered any serious opposition that competition began to bore her. Instead, she began to take up the new challenge of basketball. In 1931, she began playing for a traveling squad sponsored by the *Philadelphia Tribune.* As the star center and captain for the squad and also for the Germantown Hornets, Washington enjoyed success similar to that in her tennis experience. In one nine-year span, during which she traveled thousands of miles, her teams lost only six games.

For a number of years, Washington did double duty in basketball and tennis. But in the late 1930s, she retired from tennis in response to complaints that she was so dominant that she was discouraging younger players and driving them out of the sport. She continued to play basketball into the late 1940s, when she retired with more than 200 basketball and tennis trophies on her mantel. Washington died in 1971.

Further Reading

Ashe, Arthur, Jr. *A Hard Road to Glory: A History of the African-American Athlete, 1919–45.* New York: Warner, 1988.

White, Reggie

(Reginald Howard White, "Minister of Defense")
(1961–2004) *football defensive end*

For most of his career, the Reverend Reggie White was equally at home pounding on offensive tackles and preaching the gospel. White won fame as the most devastating pass rusher of his era and one of the most colorful, outspoken evangelical figures in all of sports.

Reginald Howard White was born on December 19, 1961, in Chattanooga, Tennessee, to Thelma White, a single parent, and grew up in a multiracial neighborhood in the city. When he was seven, his mother married Leonard Collier and moved to live with him in Kansas for a year while Reggie stayed with his grandmother. Reggie was always far bigger than other kids, and his size gave him a big advantage at sports. Baseball was his passion until he saw O. J. SIMPSON play in a game on television, and then he switched his allegiance to football.

At age 13, White experienced a profound religious experience that grabbed hold of him for the rest of his life. From that point, he carried his Bible with him wherever he went. He declared that he wanted to be a football player and a minister, and he set about fulfilling that dream. He began playing school football and basketball in ninth grade and soon ran into a coach who made him rethink his commitment to football. Robert Pullian saw enormous potential in White, whom he considered "a nice, big Sunday school boy who didn't want to hurt anybody." With Reggie's mother's secret permission, he drove Reggie unmercifully in practice to help him build the toughness he would need to succeed at pro sports. White stuck it out, and by his senior year, he developed into an All-American football lineman, an All-State basketball center, and a third-place finisher in the shot put at the state meet.

He enrolled on a football scholarship at the University of Tennessee, where he got lazy, thinking his six-foot, five-inch, 300-pound size would overwhelm opponents. But after repeated injuries, he understood the value of conditioning, and he developed a fierce work ethic in the weight room. As a senior, White played like a man among boys for Tennessee. He recorded 15 sacks and more than 100 tackles to earn Southeastern Conference Player of the Year honors.

Instead of going on to the National Football League (NFL), however, White signed a lucrative contract with the home-state Memphis Showboats of the fledgling United States Football League (USFL). He played two seasons at Memphis before he bailed out of the floundering league and signed with the Philadelphia Eagles in 1985. Since the USFL had played in the spring, White entered his first NFL campaign four games into the season with no time to rest from the grueling season. Yet, in his first game as an Eagle, he recorded 10 tackles and 2.5 sacks. Despite missing four games, he finished the season among the league leaders in sacks with 13, and he played the run equally well. As a result, he earned the NFL's Defensive Rookie of the Year Award.

For the next several years, White was as terrifying a defensive lineman as the league had seen. With White playing alongside a trio of strong, fast, and aggressive line mates, the Eagles collapsed opposing offensive lines and ransacked the backfield. In 1986, White recorded 18 sacks, and he increased that to 21 the following year. Meanwhile, he became so vocal both on and off the field about his Christianity that he was given the nickname "Minister of Defense."

As he gained experience, White developed pass-rushing techniques that, when combined with his strength and speed, astonished his opponents. Dallas Cowboy lineman Larry Allen was one of many who found himself tossed about as if he were a rag doll. Recalling his introduction to White's famous bull rush, Allen said, "One second I was blocking him, the next second I was flying through the air thinking, 'What is this?'" The scary aspect was that White threw the 327-pound Allen aside with one hand.

White's final years in Philadelphia were marred by team controversies and contract disputes, as well as the off-season death of his line mate Jerome Brown. Year after year, the Eagles failed to advance in the playoffs, and White became so frustrated by the overall situation that he played out his option and became a free agent in 1992. NFL teams wooed White so lavishly that his "Reggie Tour" of NFL cities became national news. White ended up shocking even himself by choosing small-city Green Bay in the end, but he was convinced that God was calling him to play for the Packers. White proved to be the marquee player the Packers needed to attract other free agents to the small town. With the veteran defensive end serving as inspirational leader of the defense, the Packers improved each year. During the off-season, White founded and worked for an inner-city church in Knoxville.

In December 1995, White suffered a hamstring tear that ended his streak of 166 consecutive

Reggie White, the outspoken "Minister of Defense," combined a passion for defense with a passion for preaching. *(University of Tennessee Athletic Department)*

games. Such a severe injury typically takes months to heal, but White miraculously returned to the Packer lineup two weeks later and helped the team defeat the San Francisco 49ers in the playoffs. Even his presence, however, was not enough to get Green Bay past the Dallas Cowboys in the National Football Conference (NFC) championship game.

In 1996, White's long goal of a championship finally came to fruition. He anchored a defense that allowed the fewest points in the NFL, sparking Green Bay to a 13–3 record. The Packers then swept through the playoffs and into the Super

Bowl, where White recorded three sacks in the team's 35–21 victory over New England.

In 1998, he notched 16 sacks and was named the NFL's Defensive Player of the Year. He retired on this high note, only to yield to the urge to get back on the field in 2000 with the Carolina Panthers. In this final season, White sacked quarterbacks five times to raise his NFL-record sack total to 198. Green Bay general manager Ron Wolf labeled White "as good a player as ever to play the position in the history of the game." White died on December 26, 2004.

Further Reading

White, Reggie. *In the Trenches*. Nashville, Tenn.: Thomas Nelson, 1996.

White, Reggie, with Steve Hubbard. *God's Playbook: The Bible's Game Plan for Life*. Nashville, Tenn.: Thomas Nelson, 1988.

Whitfield, Mal

(Malvin Greston Whitfield)
(1924–　) *track-and-field middle-distance runner*

Mal Whitfield was one of the most versatile runners in U.S. track-and-field history and the only U.S. runner to win consecutive Olympic gold medals at 800 meters.

He was born Malvin Greston Whitfield on October 11, 1924, in Bay City, Texas. He joined the military after high school and was an air force sergeant when he attended Ohio State University in the late 1940s. It was there that he built a solid record as a middle-distance runner. After finishing second in the 880-yard run in the Amateur Athletic Union (AAU) meet in both 1946 and 1947, he became nearly unbeatable in the event.

In the 1948 U.S. Olympic trials, Whitfield survived an exhausting day, winning the 800 meters in 1:50.6, running a qualifying heat of the 400, and then winning the 400 final in 46.6, all in one after-

noon. At the 1948 London Olympics, he was pegged as an underdog to his friend Jamaican Royal Air Force pilot Arthur Wint. Yet Whitfield felt supremely confident, because of his knowledge that Wint was a chain smoker, who would thus lack the stamina to outkick him in a close race. Before the race, he joked about Wint, "If he ever dreamt that he was going to beat me in the 800 meters, he better wake up in the morning and apologize to himself." Sure enough, in the Olympic final, Whitfield surged into the lead at the end of the first lap and withstood Wint's late charge to win the gold medal in an Olympic record time of 1:49.2. Wint, however, took the gold medal in the 400, with Whitfield getting third.

Although his running career was interrupted by the Korean War, in which he flew 27 bombing missions, from 1948 to 1954 Whitfield won every championship race he ran at 800 meters or 880 yards. Included in this streak was the 1952 Olympic 800, which proved to be a carbon copy of 1948. Not only did Whitfield sprint out to a lead and barely fight off Wint at the tape, but his time was exactly the same as his winning time four years earlier.

During his career, Whitfield won more middle-distance Olympic medals than any other U.S. athlete in history. In addition to his two golds in the 800 and his bronze in the 400 in 1948, he won a gold medal in the 1948 4 × 400 relay and a silver in the same event in 1952. Between Olympics, he dominated the event in U.S. competition, winning AAU national titles in 1949, 1950, 1951, 1953, and 1954. He added a 440 AAU national crown in 1952.

Whitfield had such a tremendous range of ability that he could have competed well at any distance. Among his impressive times were a 10.7 in the 100 meters and 4:12.6 in the mile. Although he ran for a win rather than for time, he recorded six world records, including 1:48.6 in the 880, which he achieved in 1954. That accomplishment helped him become the first African American to win the Sullivan Award, annually bestowed on the United States's best amateur athlete. After retiring, he became a track coach.

Further Reading

Henderson, Edwin B. *The Black Athlete: Emergence and Arrival.* New York: Publishers Company, 1968.

Wallechinsky, David. *The Complete Book of the Olympics.* Boston: Little, Brown, 1991.

Wilkens, Lennie
(Leonard Randolph Wilkens)
(1937–) *basketball guard*

Lennie Wilkens quietly enjoyed a Hall of Fame National Basketball Association (NBA) career, then, just as quietly, became the winningest coach in pro basketball history.

He was born Leonard Randolph Wilkens in Brooklyn, New York, on October 28, 1937, a child of a mixed marriage. He had to grow up fast when his father, a chauffeur, died suddenly, leaving five-year-old Lennie as the oldest of Henrietta Wilkens's four children. Lennie began working at age seven delivering groceries and later worked as a roofer, clerk, and painter. "When you grow up without a dad in a tough neighborhood, you have to prove yourself all the time," Wilkens recalled. "I didn't mind doing that because it was a way of life."

In his precious spare time, he learned to play basketball on the playgrounds. Because of his family obligations, he was able to play only a half-year of high school basketball. That was not enough to gain any exposure, but a local priest, Father Manion, saw potential in him and wrote a letter of recommendation for him to Providence University in Rhode Island. The university coach investigated and, after seeing Wilkens perform in a summer league game, offered him a scholarship.

Wilkens worked hard in school, majoring in economics with the intention of becoming a teacher. On the basketball team, he became the starting point guard and developed a reputation for solid defense. He led the Friars to the National Invitational Tournament (NIT) finals in 1960, in which he was named the tournament's Most Valuable Player (MVP). After being disappointed by rejection by the U.S. Olympic team that year, he was pleasantly surprised when the Saint Louis Hawks made him the sixth player chosen in the NBA draft. Showing exceptional poise and leadership for a young player, Wilkens immediately cracked into the Hawks' starting lineup. Although his individual statistics were never gaudy, Wilkens's defense and team play won the appreciation of the experts, who named him to the All-Star Team every year from 1963 to 1973. His finest year was 1968, when he finished second to WILT CHAMBERLAIN in balloting for league MVP. The following year, he was traded to Seattle, where he led the NBA in assists with an average of 9.1 per game in a dual role as player-coach. Wilkens finished his career with brief stops in Cleveland and Portland. When he retired in 1976, he ranked second in career assists to OSCAR PALMER ROBERTSON.

Wilkens returned to coaching at Seattle in 1977. He took over a 5–17 team and led them all the way to the NBA championship series. The following year, his Supersonics won the title, four games to one, over the Washington Bullets. Wilkens went on to coach for Cleveland, Atlanta, and Toronto. On January 6, 1995, he surpassed Boston's Red Auerbach as the winningest coach in NBA history, with 939, a total to which he has added since. He was voted into the Hall of Fame as a player in 1990, and he was the only person the NBA named as both one of the top 50 players and top 10 coaches of all time.

Further Reading/Viewing

Mabunda, Mpho, and Shirelle Phelps, eds. *Contemporary Black Biography.* Vol. 11. Detroit: Gale Research, 1996.

Wilkens, Lenny. *The Basics.* Lenny Wilkens Legacy, VHS, 1998.

Williams, Doug

(Douglas Lee Williams)
(1955–) *football quarterback*

Doug Williams established once and for all that African Americans could succeed at the quarterback position. He was the first black quarterback to lead his team to a Super Bowl win.

He was born Douglas Lee Williams on August 9, 1955, in Zachary, Louisiana, to Robert and Laura Williams, a construction worker and cook, respectively. While growing up in a house with no indoor plumbing, he idolized his older brother, Robert, who encouraged him to follow his lead into sports. Doug began playing quarterback in seventh grade. Although he passed for 1,180 yards and 22 touchdowns in his senior year at Chaneyville High School, the primarily black schools Grambling and Southern were the only colleges to recruit him.

His college career at Grambling started poorly as he was red-shirted in football and neglected his grades. In his second year, however, he moved up from third-string to starter, a position he maintained for his college career. Williams, known as "The Grambling Rifle" for his strong arm, led Grambling to a 35–5 mark and four straight conference championships. He threw 93 career touchdown passes, was named All-American by the Associated Press, and finished fourth in the Heisman Trophy balloting.

At that time, black pro quarterbacks were a rarity. The only African-American quarterback taken in the first round of a National Football League (NFL) draft was Eldridge Dickey in 1968, whom the Oakland Raiders immediately switched to wide receiver. Only two blacks, James Harris and Joe Gilliam, had briefly won starting positions as NFL quarterbacks. The six-foot, four-inch, 220-pound Williams showed such obvious ability, however, that the Tampa Bay Buccaneers selected him as their first choice of the 1978 draft and installed him as their starter.

Before Williams's arrival, Tampa Bay had won only two games in its two years of existence. Williams led the team to respectability, throwing 18 touchdown passes and being named to the All-Rookie team while guiding the team to five victories. In 1979, he quarterbacked the Bucs, who had developed a powerful defense, to a 10–6 record and their first Central Division title. Under his direction, Tampa Bay made the play-offs twice more in the next three seasons.

In 1983 Williams was devastated by his wife's death of a brain tumor and his father's leg amputations. Tampa Bay added to his misery by offering him less money than most teams' backup quarterbacks were making. Williams then signed with the Oklahoma Outlaws of the fledgling United States Football League (USFL), for whom he played three injury-riddled seasons. When the league folded in 1986, the Washington Redskins were the only team interested in Williams—and as a backup.

He threw only one pass for Washington in 1986, but by the end of 1987 he had won the starting job in time for the play-offs. Williams led the team into the Super Bowl, in which he played the best game of his career. He won the game's Most Valuable Player (MVP) Award for setting a Super Bowl record with 340 yards passing and four touchdown passes in one quarter in the Redskins' easy win over Denver.

Appendicitis in 1988 and a back injury the following year took his NFL career to an abrupt end. He turned to coaching, and in 1998 he was named head coach at his alma mater, Grambling.

For years, the continuing dearth of black NFL quarterbacks caused Williams to scoff that his achievements were an anomaly. "What did I change?" he asked. "Nothing . . . the NFL would still rather draft a white guy from Slippery Rock than give a black quarterback a chance." But his efforts bore results in 1999, when African-American quarterbacks Donovan McNabb, Daunte Culpepper, and Akili Smith were all drafted in the first round.

Further Reading

Leavy, W. "The Triumphs and Tragedies of Doug Williams," *Ebony*, October 1988, pp. 51–52.

Phelps, Shirelle, ed. *Contemporary Black Biography.* Vol. 22. Detroit, Mich.: Gale Research, 1999.

Thompson, Clifford, ed. *Current Biography 1999.* New York: H. W. Wilson, 1999.

Williams, Doug, with Bruce Hunter. *Quarterback: Shattering the NFL Myth.* Chicago: Bonus Books, 1990.

Williams, Serena (1981–) and Venus Ebone Starr Williams (1980–)
tennis players

Nearly a quarter-century passed without any African American duplicating ARTHUR ASHE's success in Grand Slam tennis. At the end of the 1990s, however, Venus and Serena Williams each claimed Grand Slam titles and between them totally dominated the women's game in 2001–02.

Venus Ebone Starr Williams was born on June 17, 1980, in Lynwood, California, and Serena Williams was born on September 26, 1981, in Saginaw, Michigan. They were the last of five girls born to Richard and Oracene Williams. The girls grew up in Compton, California, where Richard owned a security company and Oracene worked as a nurse.

Outspoken and unorthodox, Richard has created controversy that has often overshadowed their careers. He is a self-taught tennis buff who, in his own words, "went to my wife and said, 'Let's have kids and make them tennis players.'" Their first three daughters did not take to the sport, but Venus and Serena did. They learned their game, not in private camps and lessons but on the public courts of their crime-ridden neighborhood. "We've been shot at on the tennis court," says Richard Williams. "But now gang members know us and protect us when the shooting starts."

Venus was a prodigy who began attracting widespread attention at age seven, and she was the top-ranked girl in Southern California's 12-and-under division at the age of 10. When she moved up to the next level, Serena took over as number one.

So determined was Richard to allow the girls a normal life that he took drastic measures. First, he had them switch elementary schools three times in an effort to escape reporters, and then he pulled them out of junior competition altogether. In 1991 the family moved to Florida so the girls could enroll at Rick Macci's tennis academy. At first, they were placed in private schools, but by 1993 they were being home-schooled. Tennis experts declared they were sabotaging their careers by avoiding the junior tennis circuit, but Macci declared of Venus, "Putting her in a traditional developmental system would be like putting her in jail." Venus and Serena had plenty of competition against each other as they practiced six hours a day, six days a week, for four years.

Richard allowed them to turn pro at the earliest possible moment, at age 14, but then entered them in very few tournaments. Again, he was concerned with giving them a normal teenage experience. It was not until 1997 that Venus emerged in the French Open and began regular Women's Tennis Association competition, with Serena following shortly behind. The two presented intimidating figures to their opposition. Venus towered over most competitions at six feet, one inch; moved well; and owned a blistering serve that was measured at more than 120 miles per hour. Serena, although shorter at 5 feet, 10 inches was more muscular and equally athletic. They also drew attention for the intricate arrangement of beads in their hair—Venus once put 1,800 red, white, and blue beads in her hair for a Wimbledon tournament.

In 1998, the Williams sisters began realizing their potential. Playing with Justin Gimelstab, Venus won the mixed-doubles division of the Australian Open. In quick succession, she went on to claim singles titles at the IGA Classic and the Lipton International, and she cracked into the top

Sisters Venus (left) and Serena Williams show off their tennis gold medals from the 2000 Sydney Olympics. *(Gary M. Prior/Getty Images)*

10 rankings. Serena, who had struggled with a 304th ranking in 1997, moved up to number 21 in 1998. She fired a warning shot to her competitors that year by defeating number-two-ranked Lindsay Davenport.

In 1999, both Venus and Serena advanced to the semifinals of the U.S. Open. Venus lost to number-one-seed Martina Hingis, but Serena advanced to the finals, in which, only her third year as a pro, she upset Hingis 6–3, 6–2. Hingis later commented that she felt as though the sisters worked together to beat her, one softening her up while the other finished her off. The sisters then joined together to win the women's doubles championship the next day.

Serena's surprising victory at the U.S. Open seemed to inspire Venus to take her game to the next level. In 2000, she went on a 36-match winning streak during which she won titles at the prestigious Wimbledon tournament in London and the U.S. Open, and she then took the gold medal at the Sydney Olympics, all within a span of less than three months.

Venus continued her domination in 2001, repeating her Wimbledon title with a convincing 6–1, 3–6, 6–0, victory over Justine Henin of Belgium. The ultimate satisfaction for the Williams family then occurred at the 2001 U.S. Open. There, Serena, ranked number 10 in the world, dispatched number-one-rated Hingis 6–3, 6–2, in one semifinal, while Venus, seeded number four, took care of number-two-ranked Jennifer Capriati, 6–4, 6–2. That set up an all-Williams final match, the first time two African Americans had ever competed in a Grand Slam final.

It was a difficult situation for these two sisters, who are so close that they share a house in Florida, are rarely seen apart when traveling, and share dreams of running a fashion design school together. The first time they met in a pro match, their father could not bring himself to watch. But this was a historic moment, and there emerged an edge of rivalry between them. Venus hinted at her advantage when she noted of Serena, "She's too competitive. That could be her weakness. She takes it to an extreme." Sure enough, Serena came out overly aggressive in their match. Venus took control in the fifth game and went on to a decisive 6–2, 6–4, win, her third Grand Slam title in two years. Serena, however, easily defeated Venus in the finals of the 2002 French Open, then beat her in a closely fought match for the Wimbledon title, and pulled off a third triumph in an all-Williams Grand Slam final that year during the U.S. Open. The sisters continued their dominance by creating all-Williams finals in five major events in 2002 and 2003, with Serena coming out on top all five times.

The Williams sisters have already earned millions of dollars in prize money to go along with their multimillion-dollar endorsement deals. Partially because of the strident nature of their father, the tennis community has been polarized in their attitudes toward the sisters. The sisters' tendency to ignore the media and their failure to congratulate or compliment opponents have left them open to charges of arrogance. On the other hand, they have won praise as exceptionally well-rounded, well-spoken young women, who have increased the popularity of tennis, particularly among minority groups who have not previously been part of the sport's fan base.

Further Reading

McNulty, M. "The Venus and Serena Effect," *Tennis,* December 2000, pp. 50–53.
Price, S. L. "American Revolution," *Sports Illustrated,* September 17, 2001, pp. 40–45.
Rineburg, Dave. *My Seven Years as Hitting Coach for the Williams's.* Hollywood, Fla.: Fell Publishers, 2002.
Stein, Joel. "The Power Game," *Time,* September 3, 2001, pp. 54–63.

Wills, Maury
(Maurice Morning Wills)
(1932–) *baseball shortstop*

Before Maury Wills, no one in the National League had stolen more than 40 bases in a season in more than 20 years. Running wild on the base paths in 1962, Wills was the man most responsible for putting speed back into baseball in the 1960s.

Maurice Morning Wills was born on October 20, 1932, in Washington, D.C. His father, the Reverend Guy Wills, worked as a machinist in the Washington Navy Yard and as pastor of a Baptist church. In a neighborhood with few sports facilities, Wills learned baseball playing with tennis balls and broomsticks on an asphalt playground.

When JACKIE ROBINSON electrified sports fans in 1947, Wills was inspired to take up the game more seriously. He developed into a top pitcher at Cordoza High School and attracted brief interest among major league scouts. One look at the five-foot, eight-inch hurler's frame, however, convinced most scouts that he could never be a big league pitcher. But the Brooklyn Dodgers noticed his speed and thought he might use it to become a fine position player.

Wills signed with the Dodgers in 1951, beginning a long and discouraging trek through all levels of the minor leagues. Not until 1959 did the Dodgers, desperately in need of a good infielder, call him up to the parent club in midseason. Wills immediately solidified the team's infield defense, and the Dodgers won the pennant. He then started all six games of the team's World Series win over the Chicago White Sox.

Having earned the starting position for 1960, Wills nearly blew it when he started off the season in a horrendous batting slump. But after working hard on new stances, he recovered to bat .295 for the season. In addition, he used his speed as an offensive weapon, leading the league in stolen bases with 50, nearly double the total of the previous year's winner. He then kept a stranglehold on the stolen base title, winning it six consecutive years.

Wills is primarily known for his spectacular season in 1962. Although he was only the fourth-fastest runner on the Dodgers team, Wills's instant acceleration and knowledge of pitchers' delivery patterns made him almost unstoppable on the base paths. "I don't think I might steal a base," he said that year. "I know I can." After swiping his 72nd base on August 26, he set his sights on a record long thought to be unbreakable, Ty Cobb's mark of 96 stolen bases in a season set back in 1915. He surpassed the National League record of 82 on September 9 and, despite nursing a tender hamstring, surpassed Cobb's mark by eight bases. Remarkably, he was thrown out only 13 times in 117 attempts. Along with his .299 average and Gold Glove performance at shortstop, his baserunning earned him the league's Most Valuable Player Award.

Wills made an exciting run at his own record in 1965 but fell just short with 94 stolen bases as the trigger man in the Dodgers' 1965 world championship season. He was traded to the Pittsburgh Pirates in 1966 and finished his career with Montreal in 1972. A five-time All-Star, the slick-fielding Wills posted a fine .281 career average to go with his 586 stolen bases. His example spawned a flock of fleet-footed base runners such as LOU BROCK and RICKEY HENDERSON, who learned how to win ball games with their speed on the base paths.

Further Reading

Moritz, Charles, ed. *Current Biography 1966*. New York: H. W. Wilson, 1966.

Wills, Maury, and Mike Celizic. *On the Run: The Never Dull and Often Shocking Life of Maury Wills*. Westport, Conn.: Meckler, 1991.

Winfield, Dave
(David Mark Winfield)
(1951–   ) *baseball outfielder*

Dave Winfield is the only person ever to have been drafted by four different professional teams in three sports. He chose baseball and enjoyed a long career as one of the most consistent hitters and fielders in the game.

He was born David Mark Winfield on October 3, 1951, in Saint Paul, Minnesota, the younger of two sons of Frank and Arline Winfield. He grew up with his mother after his parents separated when he was three.

Dave began playing youth baseball at age 10 and moved into other sports as well. He starred in both baseball and basketball in high school, and he turned down an offer by the Baltimore Orioles in favor of attending the University of Minnesota. Winfield made good use of his college years, earning a double major in black studies and politics while being one of the few athletes in recent years to play two sports at a major university. The six-foot, six-inch, Winfield played forward for the Golden Gopher's Big Ten champion basketball team, then doubled as a pitcher and outfielder on the school's baseball team. In 1972, his pitching and hitting carried the team to the College World Series, in which he was voted the Most Valuable Player of the series.

That set off a wild scramble among pro teams for Winfield's services. He was drafted by the San Diego Padres of baseball, the Atlanta Hawks of the National Basketball Association (NBA), the Utah Stars of the American Basketball Association (ABA), and, even though he had never played football, as a tight end by the Minnesota Vikings, who were intrigued with his multiple talents. Winfield signed with the Padres and became one of the rare players to jump straight into the major leagues without any minor league training.

Winfield spent eight years with the San Diego Padres, during which he demonstrated consistency both at the plate and in left field. His best season with them was 1979, when he hit .308 with 34 home runs and 118 runs batted in. Then followed eight tumultuous seasons with the New York Yankees, during which he drove in more than 100 runs five seasons in a row. Winfield missed an entire season as a result of back surgery in 1989, then returned to win the American League's Comeback Player of the Year Award with the California Angels. After being disparaged by New York owner George Steinbrenner for a dismal World Series performance in 1981, Winfield gained redemption with the Toronto Blue Jays in 1992 by scorching a game-winning double in the 11th inning of their World Series–clinching win in game six. He then played two seasons in Minnesota and finished his 22-year career with Cleveland in 1995.

A model of consistency during his career, he maintained a .283 lifetime average while blasting 465 home runs and winning seven Gold Gloves. He was selected 12 times for the All-Star game, in which he fashioned a .361 average against the league's top pitchers. Winfield is also nationally known for his charity work and scholarship awards for minorities.

Further Reading

Moritz, Charles, ed. *Current Biography 1984.* New York: H. W. Wilson, 1984.

Winfield, Dave, with Eric Swenson. *The Complete Baseball Player.* New York: Avon, 1990.

Woodard, Lynette
(1959–) *basketball player*

Lynette Woodard holds the distinction of being the first woman basketball player recruited to play for the legendary Harlem Globetrotters.

Woodard was born on August 12, 1959, in Wichita, Kansas, the youngest of five children of Eugene and Dorothy Woodard. One of her older cousins was Geese Ausbie, who played for the popular barnstorming Harlem Globetrotters. From age five, Lynette tried to imitate some of the basketball skills and tricks of Ausbie and his teammates. But there were no opportunities for girls in her town to play in any league, and so she had to content herself with pickup games with her older brother, Darrell.

In her sophomore year at Wichita North High School, Woodard finally got a chance to play against other girls. Having grown to almost six feet, with better dribbling, passing, and shooting skills than the other players, she was virtually unstoppable and she led her team to two state high school championships.

Coaches at the University of Kansas persuaded her to stay close to home after her graduation from high school in 1977. As a freshman guard at Kansas, she led the nation in rebounding with a 14.8 average and finished second in scoring at 25.2. The following season she moved up to number one in scoring and led the nation in steals. During her senior year of 1981, she won the Wade Trophy as the best female college player. By the time she graduated, Woodard held National Collegiate Athletic Association (NCAA) women's records for points in a season (1,177), points in a career (3,199), and rebounds in a single game (33) and led the country in steals three times. She was the first person to be named a Kodak All-American all four years of college as she led her team to a 108–32 mark in her career. Furthermore, she demonstrated her academic skill when she was twice named an Academic All-American.

During her college years, Woodard also played on several U.S. women's teams. She suffered a crushing disappointment, however, when the United States declared a boycott of the 1980 Olympics, depriving her of one of the few venues for national recognition. Because there was no professional women's league available in the United States, after her graduation from Kansas Woodard went to Italy to play professional ball. But she returned after a year to take an assistant coaching job at Kansas.

Her opportunity to shine in public finally occurred in the 1984 Olympics when she was named captain of the U.S. women's team. She joined CHERYL DEANNE MILLER as the stars of a team that won all of their games by 28 or more points in claiming the gold medal. Woodard then competed against 18 other top players for a spot on the Harlem Globetrotters, and she won the job. Her presence sparked increased attendance at Globetrotter events as she spent two years playing more than 200 games a year. "I hope the publicity from my play on the Globetrotters helps a woman's professional basketball league become viable and stable," she said.

Her goal was finally realized a decade later as the Women's National Basketball Association (WNBA) came into existence. Although well past her prime, she left retirement to join the league, and she played with Cleveland for three seasons. In the meantime, she was the first woman voted into Kansas University's Athletic Hall of Fame.

Further Reading

Great Athletes of the Twentieth Century. Vol. 20. Pasadena, Calif.: Salem Press, 1994.

Johnson, R. S. "Far Above the Crowd," Sports Illustrated, January 26, 1981, pp. 41–42.

Woodruff, John Youie
(1915–   ) track-and-field middle-distance runner

JESSE OWENS was not the only African American to embarrass the Nazis in the 1936 Olympics. At those games, John Woodruff quietly established himself as the world's top middle-distance runner.

John Youie Woodruff was born July 15, 1915, in the small town of Connellsville, Pennsylvania, just south of Pittsburgh. His father, the son of Virginia slaves, worked in the steel mills and stone quarries to support his family of 12 children. John tried to quit school at 16 to follow him into factory work, but with the country still in a depression, he was unable to land a job. That proved a blessing in disguise. After Woodruff returned to school, his football line coach noticed he was able to stay with the team's star sprinter in conditioning drills. He persuaded Woodruff to go out for track, and he posted a 4:44 time in his first mile. Unchallenged in high school, Woodruff ran an outstanding 4:23 as a senior without ever pushing himself.

Woodruff went on to the University of Pittsburgh, the only member of his family to attend college. During his freshman year, he made the finals of the Amateur Athletic Union (AAU) 880-yard competition only to get boxed in and lose the race by a foot. In only his third year of competitive running, he beat out the world-record holder Ben Eastman for a spot on the 1936 U.S. Olympic team in the 800 meters.

At the Berlin Games, Woodruff tried to avoid traffic problems by getting out to an early lead in the preliminaries. But in the finals, he grew timid. The result was one of the strangest races in Olympic history. Content to let others set the pace, Woodruff found himself boxed in halfway through the race. A tall man who ran with an unusually long stride, Woodruff found the slow pace frustrating. He slowed to a fast walk to let the pack pass so that he could work himself free and then ran several extra yards passing the pack on the outside. Somehow he caught veteran Phil Edwards of Canada. The two seesawed positions down the home stretch, and Woodruff claimed the gold medal.

Woodruff returned to college and turned in a consistent career as the nation's top middle-distance runner. In 1937, he met his closest rival, Elroy Robinson, in an 800-meter race in Dallas, Texas. Robinson set a brutal pace, but Woodruff stayed with him and outlasted him to the tape in 1:47.8, well under the world record. Track officials, however, later announced the track was six feet short of a quarter-mile and so Woodruff's record was not certified. He remained convinced to the end of his life that track officials had lied merely to deprive a black man of a world record.

Woodruff would likely have added to his Olympic résumé but World War II forced cancellation of the games in 1940 and 1944. He had to settle for a world indoor record of 1:47.6 run in 1940 and an overall best of 1:47.0 the same year. Woodruff was widely recognized as a classy individual. According to Archie Williams, "There was no award for most respected athlete on that (1936 Olympic) team, but if there had been, it might well have gone to Woodruff."

Woodruff graduated from the University of Pittsburgh in 1939 and earned a master's degree in sociology from New York University in 1941. In his later years, he taught school and worked as a special investigator for the New York Department of Welfare.

Further Reading

Carlson, Lewis H., and John J. Fogerty. *Tales of Gold.* Chicago: Contemporary Books, 1987.

Wallechinsky, David. *The Complete Book of the Olympics.* Boston: Little, Brown, 1991.

Woods, Tiger
(Eldrick Woods)
(1975–) *golfer*

Tiger Woods emerged at the beginning of the 21st century as perhaps the most influential athlete in the world. Playing at a sport that has been controlled by the most formidable bastions of white exclusivity, he elevated his game far above that of his peers. Woods became, far and away, the greatest drawing card in golf, and his enormous popularity aroused interest in the game in legions of minority youth.

He was born Eldrick Woods on December 30, 1975, in Orange County, California, the only child of Earl and Kultida Woods. Lieutenant Colonel Earl Woods had raised a previous family before his divorce and remarriage to Kultida, a Thai woman whom he met overseas. He had since retired from military service and become a contracts administrator for the county, and he had purchased a modest two-bedroom home in Cypress. Although his son was named Eldrick, his father called him "Tiger" in honor of a Vietnamese colleague who had saved his life twice in one day.

Earl Woods claimed that he knew before Tiger reached his first birthday that his son would be a golf star. The infant seemed fascinated watching his dad, who had taken up the game only a year earlier, practice swinging in the garage. At nine months of age, copying his dad, Tiger teed up a ball, swung perfectly, and hit it into the center of the practice net. According to Earl, "I almost fell off my chair. It was the most frightening thing I've ever seen."

Recognizing that he had a golf prodigy on his hands, he fashioned a cut-down iron for Tiger to swing. At the age of 18 months, Tiger began joining his father at the driving range. When he was two, he was filmed by a television news crew and he played his first hole of golf, scoring an 11. By the time he was five, he was playing with a full set of clubs.

Off the golf course, life did not progress so smoothly. On Woods's first day of kindergarten, older boys tied him to a tree and threw stones at him while shouting racial insults. As the years went by, he learned to keep calm when slighted and took his father's advice to "retaliate with your golf clubs." Yet for much of his life he remained largely unaware of his status as a minority player in a white person's sport.

At age eight Woods won the Junior World Championship for ages 10 and under, and he repeated the following year. Although his parents went into debt to support their son's hobby, later accusations that they were stage parents were unfounded. At no point did they put pressure on him either to play or to win. It was Tiger himself who became obsessed with the sport. He dropped Little League baseball when it began to interfere with his golf time. At age 10, he declared he would study accounting in college so that he would be able to stay on top of the people who managed his golf winnings. Any time Kultida Woods needed to discipline him she had only to take away his golf clubs.

As he moved up in age brackets, Woods continued to monopolize Junior World Competition. He won the championship six times, including the 15–17 age division at age 15. His growing reputation made it difficult for him to blend in at Western High School, particularly when he won the 1993 Dial Award as the nation's top high school athlete.

Woods became increasingly aware of his importance as a minority figure in golf. The Professional Golf Association (PGA) had restricted membership to "Caucasians only" until the early 1960s. In 1990, while Woods was in high school, a heated controversy flared up over the playing of that year's PGA Tournament at an Alabama site that continued to refuse admission to African Americans. For Woods, it was a difficult issue. When sportswriters began promoting him as his sport's great black hope, he had difficulty thinking of himself as black; his mother was Thai with some Chinese and white heritage and his father was African American with American Indian and Chinese mixed in. When asked about his heritage, Woods often responded, "The bottom line is I'm an American and proud of it." Yet the pioneer black golfer CHARLES LUTHER SIFFORD had been a hero of his, and his own father had undergone the uncomfortable experience of being the first black baseball player in the Big Eight Conference. Woods gradually came to accept his role as a role model to minorities and frequently gave free golf clinics to inner-city youth.

In 1994, Woods enrolled at Stanford University, where he was a good student and again tried to fit in with the rest of the students. As a freshman, he won his first college tournament, and he came from six holes down that year to win the U.S. Amateur, making him the youngest player to win the tournament in its 94-year history. Woods won nine of the 13 National Collegiate Athletic Association (NCAA) tournaments in which he participated, and he continued to dominate national amateur golf tournaments. Occasionally, he would be invited to tee off with the pros. Although he never contended for a title on these occasions, he had the game's top players shaking their heads at his potential. Woods had the most fundamentally sound swing anyone had ever seen, and the speed of his club head allowed him to drive the ball well over 300 yards. In addition, he had a masterful understanding of how to play each shot. Nearly all predicted a fantastic career was in store for him when he turned pro.

That time occurred sooner than Woods had originally anticipated. Frustrated by hassles from the NCAA regarding its bewildering eligibility rules and having long since run out of credible opposition at the amateur level, he left college after his sophomore year and turned pro during the summer of 1996 at the Greater Milwaukee Open. Although he finished in 60th place, he created a stir by managing a hole-in-one in his first pro appearance. As an indication of Woods's potential celebrity status, the 20-year-old signed endorsement contracts worth more than $60 million over five years at the onset of his career, a figure rivaled in the sports world only by MICHAEL JORDAN.

Woods adapted quickly to the pressure of professional golf. In only his fifth tournament, the Las Vegas Invitational, he tied Davis Love III and then won the playoff that followed. Woods then captured the Walt Disney Tournament and finished in the top five in five straight tournaments to earn status as the PGA's Rookie of the Year easily.

Woods's most sensational splash was at the Masters Tournament in April 1997. There, on one

Tiger Woods not only cracked into the most racially exclusive of the pro sports but quickly became the game's most popular player. *(Andy Lyons/Getty Images)*

of golf's most historic courses, the tour's youngest member annihilated the field to win by 12 strokes. Even golf legend Jack Nicklaus observed that Woods seemed to be playing a different game than all the rest of them.

However, just when experts were predicting that Woods would rewrite the golf record books, he went into a sophomore slump. Most glaring was his failure to win any of golf's four major championships (Masters, U.S. Open, PGA, and British Open) in 1998. In 1999, he won only the PGA. Some observers even began to say that Woods had been overrated.

The 2000 tour put an end to such talk once and for all. Woods began the season with a victory at the Mercedes Championship in January, then captured the Pebble Beach Pro-Am the following month. In June, he fired a 6-under-par 65 to start the U.S. Open and never let up. Woods raced to a 10-stroke lead after three rounds, spoiling all suspense for the tourney's final day. He completed play 15 strokes ahead of his nearest competitor, the largest margin of victory in U.S. Open history.

The following month, Woods continued his torrid pace, blistering the British Open course in

19-under-par for an eight-stroke win. This made him the youngest player ever to win all of golf's four major prizes. Woods finally ran into a challenge at the PGA in August. There Bob May tied him at the end of regulation play. But Woods, of whom his biographer John Strege wrote, "His approach to a match, particularly a match of historic significance, is that of a man who equates a loss with a mortal wound," maintained his unequaled concentration to win the playoff. That made Woods the first golfer to win three major championships in a year since Ben Hogan had in 1953. All told, Woods won nine tournaments that year, the most by any player on the tour in a half-century, and he won more than $9 million in prize money.

He then capped off his record run with a two-stroke victory at the Masters. This gave him an unprecedented four straight major tournament wins, a feat that prompted many sports commentators to label him the greatest athlete of his time. Woods continued his stranglehold on golf's major tournaments with easy victories at the Masters and at the U.S. Open in 2002. After struggling through a long slump that caused many to question whether he had already peaked as a player, Woods opened the 2005 season with three tour victories, including a dramatic playoff win to capture his fourth Masters title.

Further Reading

Owen, David. *The Chosen One: Tiger Woods and the Dilemma of Greatness.* New York: Simon & Schuster, 2001.

Rosaforte, Tim. *Tiger Woods: The Making of a Champion.* New York: St. Martin's Press, 1997.

Strege, John. *A Biography of Tiger Woods.* New York: Broadway Books, 1998.

Woods, Earl, with Pete McDaniel. *Training a Tiger: A Father's Guide to Raising a Winner in Both Golf and Life.* New York: HarperCollins, 1997.

Woods, Tiger. *How I Play Golf.* New York: Warner, 2001.

BIBLIOGRAPHY AND RECOMMENDED SOURCES

Allen, George. Pro Football's 100 Greatest Players. Indianapolis, Ind.: Bobbs-Merrill, 1982.

Ashe, Arthur, Jr. A Hard Road to Glory: A History of the African-American Athlete, 1919–45. New York: Warner, 1988.

Ballret, William. Writing by the Rebels Who Changed Sports. New York: Thunder's Mouth Press, 1999.

Carlson, Lewis H., and John J. Fogerty. Tales of Gold. Chicago: Contemporary Books, 1987.

Chadwick, Bruce. When the Game Was Black and White. New York: Abbeville, 1992.

Clark, Dick, and Lerry Lester, eds. The Negro League Book. Cleveland, Ohio: Society for American Baseball Research, 1994.

Corbett, Sara. Venus to the Hoop. New York: Doubleday, 1997.

Davis, Michael D. Black American Women in Track and Field. Jefferson, N.C.: McFarland, 1992.

Harrington, Denis J. The Pro Football Hall of Fame. Jefferson, N.C.: McFarland, 1991.

Henderson, Edwin B. The Black Athlete: Emergence and Arrival. New York: Publishers Company, 1968.

Lessa, Christina. Stories of Triumph: Women Who Won in Sport and Life. New York: Universe, 1998.

Mullan, Henry. The Ultimate Encyclopedia of Boxing. London: Carlton Books, 1996.

Nelson, Cordner. Track's Greatest Champions. Los Altos, Calif.: Tafnews Press, 1986.

Oglesby, Carole, et al., eds. Encyclopedia of Women and Sport. Phoenix: Oryx Press, 1998.

Page, James A. Black Olympic Medalists. Englewood, Colo.: Libraries Unlimited, 1991.

Pepe, Phil. Talkin' Baseball. New York: Ballantine, 1998.

Peterson, Robert. Only the Ball Was White. New York: Gramercy, 1970.

Riley, James. The Biographical Encyclopedia of the Negro Baseball Leagues. New York: Carroll & Graf, 1994.

Smith, Jessie Carney, ed. Notable Black American Women, Book II. Detroit: Gale Research, 1996.

Suster, Gerald. Champions of the Ring. London: Robson, 1994.

Wallechinsky, David. The Complete Book of the Olympics. Boston: Little, Brown, 1991.

Walsh, Peter. Men of Steel. London: Robson Books, 1993.

Wiggins, David K. Glory Bound: Black Athletes in White America. Syracuse, N.Y.: Syracuse University Press, 1997.

Woolum, Janet. Outstanding Women Athletes. Phoenix, Az.: Oryx Press, 1998.

Young, A. S. Negro Firsts in Sports. Chicago: Johnson Publishing, 1963.

ENTRIES BY
AREA OF ACTIVITY

AUTOMOBILE RACING
Ribbs, Willy

BASEBALL

Catcher
Campanella, Roy
Gibson, Josh

Centerfielder
Bell, Cool Papa
Charleston, Oscar
    McKinley
Flood, Curt
Griffey, Ken, Jr.
Mays, Willie
Puckett, Kirby

First Baseman
Leonard, Buck
McCovey, Willie Lee
Stargell, Willie
Thomas, Frank Edward

Infielder
Banks, Ernie
Carew, Rod
Doby, Larry
Jeter, Derek Sanderson
Morgan, Joe Leonard
Robinson, Jackie
Smith, Ozzie
Wills, Maury

Pitcher
Gibson, Bob
Newcombe, Donald
Paige, Satchel

Right/Left/Center Fielder
Aaron, Hank
Bonds, Barry Lamar
Brock, Lou
Doby, Larry
Gwynn, Tony
Henderson, Rickey
Jackson, Bo
Jackson, Reggie
Robinson, Frank, Jr.
Winfield, Dave

BASKETBALL (MEN)

Center
Abdul-Jabbar, Kareem
Chamberlain, Wilt
Ewing, Patrick Aloysius
Malone, Moses Eugene
Olajuwon, Hakeem Abdul
O'Neal, Shaquille Rashaun
Robinson, David Maurice
Russell, Bill

Point Guard
Archibald, Nate
Frazier, Walt
Haynes, Marques Oreole

Johnson, Magic
Robertson, Oscar Palmer
Thomas, Isiah
Wilkens, Lennie

Power Forward
Barkley, Charles Wade
Duncan, Tim
Hayes, Elvin Ernest
Malone, Karl

Small Forward
Baylor, Elgin Gay
Carter, Vince
Erving, Julius
Hawkins, Connie
Hill, Grant Henry

Shooting Guard
Bryant, Kobe
Drexler, Clyde Austin
Gervin, George
Iverson, Allen
Jordan, Michael Jeffrey

BASKETBALL (WOMEN)

Center
Leslie, Lisa Deshawn

Guard
Cooper, Cynthia
Edwards, Teresa
Woodard, Lynette

Forward
Holdsclaw, Chamique
Miller, Cheryl Deanne
Swoopes, Sheryl Denise

BICYCLING
Taylor, Marshall Walker

BOXING

Heavyweight
Ali, Muhammad
Foreman, George
Frazier, Joe
Jackson, Peter
Johnson, Jack
Louis, Joe
Tyson, Mike

Lighter Weights
Ali, Laila
Armstrong, Henry
Hagler, Marvin
Hearns, Thomas
Leonard, Sugar Ray
Robinson, Sugar Ray

FIGURE SKATING
Thomas, Debi

FOOTBALL

Defensive Back
Lane, Night Train
Lott, Ronnie
Sanders, Deion Luwynn
Tunnell, Emlen Lewis

Defensive Lineman
Greene, Joe
Jones, Deacon
Page, Alan Cedric
Smith, Bruce Bernard
White, Reggie

Linebacker
Motley, Marion

Singletary, Mike
Taylor, Lawrence Julius

Offensive Lineman
Brown, Roosevelt, Jr.
Parker, Jim
Upshaw, Gene

Quarterback
Williams, Doug

Running Back
Allen, Marcus Lemarr
Brown, Jim
Campbell, Earl Christian
Davis, Ernie
Dickerson, Eric Demetric
Dorsett, Tony
Faulk, Marshall
Jackson, Bo
Motley, Marion
Payton, Walter Jerry
Pollard, Fritz
Sanders, Barry David
Sayers, Gale Eugene
Simpson, O. J.
Smith, Emmitt

Receiver
Carter, Cris
Hayes, Bob
Rice, Jerry Lee

GOLF
Elder, Lee
Sifford, Charles Luther
Woods, Tiger

GYMNASTICS
Dawes, Dominique

HOCKEY
Fuhr, Grant Scott

HORSE RACING
Murphy, Isaac

SOCCER
Scurry, Briana Collette

TENNIS
Ashe, Arthur, Jr.
Gibson, Althea
Washington, Ora
Williams, Serena
Williams, Venus Ebone Starr

TRACK (MEN)

Decathlon
Campbell, Milt
Johnson, Rafer Lewis

Hurdles
Calhoun, Lee Quency
Dillard, Harrison
Moses, Edwin Corley

Jumps
Beamon, Bob
Boston, Ralph Harold
Lewis, Carl
Owens, Jesse

Middle Distance
Whitfield, Mal
Woodruff, John Youie

Sprints
Evans, Lee Edward
Greene, Maurice
Hayes, Bob
Johnson, Michael
Lewis, Carl
Owens, Jesse
Smith, Tommie C.
Tolan, Eddie

TRACK (WOMEN)

Heptathlon
Joyner-Kersee, Jackie

Hurdles
Devers, Gail

Jumps
Coachman, Alice
Joyner-Kersee, Jackie

Middle Distance
Jackson, Madeline
    Manning

Shot Put
Brown, Earlene
    Dennis

Sprints
Ashford, Evelyn
Brisco-Hooks, Valeri
Coachman, Alice
Devers, Gail
Faggs, Mae
Griffith Joyner, Florence
Jones, Marion
Rudolph, Wilma Goldean
Tyus, Wyomia

VOLLEYBALL
Hyman, Flo

WEIGHTLIFTING
Davis, John

WRESTLING
Kemp, Lee

ENTRIES BY YEAR OF BIRTH

PRE-1900
Charleston, Oscar McKinley
Jackson, Peter
Johnson, Jack
Murphy, Isaac
Pollard, Fritz
Taylor, Marshall Walker
Washington, Ora

1900–1910
Bell, Cool Papa
Leonard, Buck
Paige, Satchel
Tolan, Eddie

1911–1920
Armstrong, Henry
Gibson, Josh
Louis, Joe
Motley, Marion
Owens, Jesse
Robinson, Jackie
Woodruff, John Youie

1921–25
Campanella, Roy
Coachman, Alice
Davis, John
Dillard, Harrison
Doby, Larry
Gibson, Althea

Newcombe, Donald
Robinson, Sugar Ray
Sifford, Charles
Tunnell, Emlen Lewis
Whitfield, Mal

1926–1930
Haynes, Marques Oreole
Lane, Night Train

1931–1935
Aaron, Hank
Banks, Ernie
Baylor, Elgin Gay
Brown, Earlene Dennis
Brown, Roosevelt, Jr.
Calhoun, Lee Quency
Campbell, Milt
Elder, Lee
Faggs, Mae
Gibson, Bob
Johnson, Rafer Lewis
Mays, Willie
Parker, Jim
Robinson, Frank, Jr.
Russell, Bill
Wills, Maury

1936–1940
Boston, Ralph Harold
Brock, Lou

Brown, Jim
Chamberlain, Wilt
Davis, Ernie
Flood, Curt
Jones, Deacon
Robertson, Oscar Palmer
Rudolph, Wilma Goldean
Wilkens, Lennie

1941–1945
Ali, Muhammad
Ashe, Arthur
Carew, Rod
Frazier, Joe
Frazier, Walt
Hawkins, Connie
Hayes, Bob
Hayes, Elvin Ernest
McCovey, Willie Lee
Morgan, Joe Leonard
Page, Alan Cedric
Sayers, Gale Eugene
Smith, Tommie C.
Stargell, Willie
Tyus, Wyomia
Upshaw, Gene

1946–1950
Abdul-Jabbar, Kareem
Archibald, Nate
Beamon, Bob

Erving, Julius
Evans, Lee Edward
Foreman, George
Greene, Joe
Jackson, Madeline Manning
Jackson, Reggie
Simpson, O. J.

1951–1955
Campbell, Earl Christian
Dorsett, Tony
Gervin, George
Hagler, Marvin
Hyman, Flo
Malone, Moses Eugene
Moses, Edwin Corley
Payton, Walter Jerry
Smith, Ozzie
Williams, Doug
Winfield, Dave

1956–1960
Allen, Marcus Lemarr
Ashford, Evelyn
Brusco-Hooks, Valeri
Dickerson, Eric Demetric
Griffith Joyner, Florence
Gwynn, Tony
Hearns, Thomas
Henderson, Rickey
Johnson, Magic
Kemp, Lee
Leonard, Sugar Ray

Lott, Ronnie
Ribbs, Willie
Singletary, Mike
Taylor, Lawrence Julius
Woodard, Lynette

1961–1965
Barkley, Charles
Bonds, Barry Lamar
Carter, Cris
Cooper, Cynthia
Drexler, Clyde Austin
Edwards, Teresa
Ewing, Patrick Aloysius
Fuhr, Grant Scott
Jackson, Bo
Jordan, Michael Jeffrey
Joyner-Kersee, Jackie
Lewis, Carl
Malone, Karl
Miller, Cheryl Deanne
Olajuwon, Hakeem
    Abdul
Puckett, Kirby
Rice, Jerry Lee
Robinson, David Maurice
Smith, Bruce Bernard
Thomas, Isiah
White, Reggie

1966–1970
Devers, Gail
Griffey, Ken, Jr.

Johnson, Michael
Sanders, Barry David
Sanders, Deion Luwynn
Smith, Emmitt
Thomas, Debi
Thomas, Frank Edward
Tyson, Mike

1970–1975
Faulk, Marshall
Greene, Maurice
Hill, Grant Henry
Iverson, Allen
Jeter, Derek Sanderson
Leslie, Lisa Deshawn
O'Neal, Shaquille
    Rashaun
Scurry, Briana Collette
Swoopes, Sheryl Denise
Woods, Tiger

1976–1980
Ali, Laila
Bryant, Kobe
Carter, Vince
Dawes, Dominique
Duncan, Tim
Holdsclaw, Chamique
Jones, Marion
Williams, Venus Ebone Starr

POST-1980
Williams, Serena

INDEX

Boldface locators indicate main entries. *Italic* locators indicate photographs.